SERVICE CHAF
LAW AND PRACTICE

SERVICE CHARGES – LAW AND PRACTICE

THIRD EDITION

PHILIP FREEDMAN
Partner, Mishcon de Reya

and

ERIC SHAPIRO
Consultant, Moss Kaye Pembertons Ltd

with tax notes by
BRIAN SLATER, ATII
Tax Specialist, Finers Stephens Innocent

JORDANS
2002

Published by
Jordan Publishing Limited
21 St Thomas Street
Bristol BS1 6JS

British Cataloguing-in-Publication Data

A catalogue record for this book is available
from the British Library.

ISBN 0 85308 710 5

Typeset by Mendip Communications Ltd, Frome, Somerset
Printed by Henry Ling Limited, The Dorset Press, Dorchester, DT1 1HD, UK

PREFACE

Service charges are almost invariably the subject of conflict between those who arrange the expenditure and those who are ultimately called upon to pay for it. The *Report of the Committee of Inquiry on the Management of Privately Owned Blocks of Flats* (DoE, 1985) ('the Nugee Report') revealed, as one might have expected, an almost universal holding of grievances by tenants of flats about the conduct of the management of their blocks of flats and the amount of service charges. Mutual mistrust, lack of proper consultation by landlords and managing agents, and failure to take proper account of the tenants' views seem rife in both the residential and the commercial spheres. While bad management is all too common, in many cases problems arise simply because the parties fail to recognise each other's legitimate requirements. A guide to good practice called 'Service Charges in Commercial Properties' published by seven property industry bodies states that its purposes are to encourage a good working relationship and to secure co-operation between owners and occupiers through consultation and communication.

A distinction can be drawn between those multi-occupied properties which are let at market rents and those which are sold on long leases (or, as in the case of some class B1 or warehouse units, sold freehold). In the former cases, the landlord's rental income growth and capital value will usually depend upon the continuing quality of the buildings (in addition to their location and other market factors), whereas in the latter cases the ground rents (if any) are either fixed for many years or escalate on a basis usually unrelated to the state of the buildings. Landlords in the former cases have a financial stake in the maintenance and improvement of their buildings, while the interest of landlords in the latter cases may wane once all the flats or units comprised in the development have been sold, except perhaps where they hope to make a profit from the provision of services – a usually unattainable desire, and undesirable (except for a fair management fee).

Tenants, on the other hand, might be expected to have an interest in the proper maintenance of their buildings, irrespective of whether they are paying market rents under short- or medium-term leases, or ground rents under long leases. B1 and warehousing tenants require their premises and accessways to be kept in repair in order not to endanger or disrupt their processes or the flow of their goods, and office tenants expect their buildings to be maintained both for the proper functioning of their businesses or professions and to present a quality appearance to their customers or clients; but neither want the premises improved at their expense. Flat-owners are normally keen to have their blocks well maintained and, where appropriate, improved to preserve the asset value of their flats.

These factors appear to indicate a good deal of common ground between the interests of landlords and tenants. However, the cost of repairing and servicing buildings is a major independent consideration for both landlords and tenants and it can impact on potential rent levels. Institutional landlords usually insist that lettings of commercial properties should be on clear leases, under which the tenants not only pay a full market rent, but also meet the entire costs involved in maintaining, servicing and renewing the properties. Until recently, these clear leases were the norm rather than the exception, and inclusive rents were rare save in the case of short residential lettings or very short commercial lettings. Tenants who used to be asked to pay relatively low contributions towards a limited range of services are now usually required to pay for roof renewals, the replacement of plant and equipment and other heads of expenditure which were at one time traditionally met by their landlords. The situation today is not so clear-cut since tenants now frequently ask for capped service charges or for limitations to be placed on the costs which can be included.

Commercial tenants justifiably view their rents, service charges, general rates and water charges as a package of costs for the occupation of their premises, and take the total into account when viewing their overheads or production costs. Flat-owners have found that flats which are liable to constant, high service charges are not only expensive to run, but also suffer a reduction in their resale value, except in the most prestigious locations. It is, therefore, understandable that tenants of both commercial and residential properties are generally keen to minimise their service charge liabilities by opposing expenditure which they consider is unnecessary or premature and, in many cases, they fail to take account of their own longer-term interests as well as the interests of their landlords.

This book sets out both to summarise the current state of the law on service charges as at 15 April 2002, and to give guidance on the management process and on related accountancy matters. Brian Slater, ATII, tax principal at Finers Stephens Innocent, has contributed detailed notes on VAT and on the taxation problems of service charges. Suggestions for drafting service charge clauses are also included.

The scheme of this book is to deal first with matters which are common to both residential and commercial property (**Chapter 1**) and then to deal specifically with matters which only affect residential property (**Chapter 2**), before going back to common matters of a special nature, such as VAT and sinking funds. It will be seen that almost all of the relevant case-law comes from disputes relating to residential property because that is the area most litigated, but the principles laid down in the cases apply generally to all property. The statute law on service charges, however, is confined to residential property and does not apply to commercial premises.

PHILIP FREEDMAN   ERIC SHAPIRO
Mishcon de Reya   Moss Kaye Pembertons Ltd
London WC1   London NW3

15 April 2002

CONTENTS

TABLE OF CASES

References in the right-hand column are to paragraph numbers.

TABLE OF STATUTES

References in the right-hand column are to paragraph numbers and to Appendix 3 where extracts from statutory materials are set out.

TABLE OF STATUTORY INSTRUMENTS

References in the right-hand column are to paragraph numbers and Appendix 3.

TABLE OF ABBREVIATIONS

BRE   Building Research Establishment

CLRA 2002   Commonhold and Leasehold Reform Act 2002

EPA 1990   Environmental Protection Act 1990

GIA   Gross Internal Area

HA 1996   Housing Act 1996

LTA 1985   -   Landlord and Tenant Act 1985
LTA 1987   Landlord and Tenant Act 1987
LVT   Leasehold Valuation Tribunal

NIA   Net Internal Area

RTM   right to manage

VAT Act 1994   Value Added Tax Act 1994
VAT Regulations 1995   Value Added Tax Regulations 1995, SI 1995/2518

1993 Act   Leasehold Reform, Housing and Urban
                             Development Act 1993
1995 Act   Landlord and Tenant (Covenants) Act 1995
1996 Act   Housing Act 1996

1 MATTERS APPLICABLE TO COMMERCIAL AND RESIDENTIAL LEASES

For the reason given in the Preface, most of the court cases cited in this chapter are related to disputes under residential lettings but, nevertheless, the principles applied in them are (unless otherwise stated) to be taken as applying to commercial as well as residential property.

1.1 Landlords, management companies and maintenance trustees

1.1.1 The supplier of the services

Services to a tenant may be provided by the landlord, a management company, or a maintenance trustee, depending upon the express or implied terms of the tenant's lease or tenancy agreement. In the case of short residential lettings and lettings of parts of commercial buildings, service obligations are usually undertaken by the landlord. Under long leases of residential flats, the obligations may be imposed either on the landlord, or (quite frequently) on a management company controlled by the tenants, or occasionally on a maintenance trustee. Those maintenance obligations which are imposed by statute (eg under ss 11 to 16 of the Landlord and Tenant Act 1985, which replaced ss 32 to 33 of the Housing Act 1961) are almost invariably placed upon the landlord.

As to whether a particular service has to be provided as a matter of contractual obligation, as distinct from being at the landlord's discretion, see **1.3.2**.

1.1.2 The landlord

It is often advantageous to tenants if it is the landlord who is responsible for the services. In the case of larger commercial buildings the landlord will frequently be a substantial property company which, particularly where the building is let at full market rents, will be keen to preserve the value of its reversionary interest in the property. Such a landlord may be likely to ensure prompt attention to any necessary repairs to the building. However, it is unlikely to be as cost-conscious as a tenants' management company.

1.1.3 Management company

The management company is a device frequently adopted by landlords who wish to avoid taking on management and maintenance responsibilities. The landlord incorporates a company which joins in the leases in order to covenant to carry out the service obligations, usually including all main repairs and sometimes including insurance. In such cases the courts will *not* normally imply into the tenants' leases any obligation on the landlord to deal with such matters even if the management company defaults.

Example

Hafton Properties Ltd v Camp; Camp v Silchester Court (Croydon) Management Co Ltd [1993] EGCS 101, Official Referee: A management company joined in a 99-year lease of a flat and covenanted with the tenant that the company would provide services and manage and maintain the block. The landlord gave the tenant only a covenant for quiet enjoyment of the flat. Could the tenant claim damages from the landlord when the company failed to perform its covenants? **Held**: No.

Normally the tenants are made members or shareholders in the company. At first glance, it may seem desirable for tenants to have full control over the management and maintenance of their properties in this way, and in the case of leasehold flats a scheme involving a management company which will not be under the control of the flat-owners may be unaccceptable to flat purchasers and their mortgagees.

However, in practice the efficiency of such companies depends on the time and enthusiasm of the tenants and problems can arise if some tenants, for their own personal reasons, wish to delay the incurring of heavy expenditure on repairs or renewals. Too often one finds blocks of flats controlled by tenants' management companies, where major repairs have been postponed indefinitely due to a majority of the tenants not wishing to fund the expenditure. On the other hand, the Nugee Committee found that 80 per cent of those landlords in their survey, whose blocks were maintained by residents' companies or associations, found this arrangement satisfactory.

The risk of incurring costs which might not fall within the service charge, and thus might not be recovered from the tenants, has, perhaps, more serious consequences for a management company than for a commercial landlord. Since management companies normally have no assets other than the service charge monies, the inability to recover part of its expenditure could lead to the company being put into liquidation because of unpaid creditors (see *Re Cranley Mansions Ltd* [1994] 1 WLR 1610). This would be to the detriment of the tenants (at least, in the absence of a covenant by the landlord in the leases that he would perform the services if the company defaulted). Where this risk is perceived to arise, and the tenants will not unanimously agree to the expenditure, the directors of the company should consider making an application to the court in the name of the company for a declaration that the expenditure will fall within the service charges and be recoverable from the tenants (see **1.6.5**).

1.1.4 Maintenance trustee

This is another device enabling the landlord to avoid having to undertake management and maintenance, but without passing control of such matters to the tenants. An outside company is employed to act as trustee of the maintenance fund and joins in the leases (or sometimes in a supplemental document) in order to covenant to use the fund for the provision of the specified services. If the maintenance trustee fulfils his function properly, this type of management can work well.

1.1.5 Terminology in this book

Except where it is necessary to distinguish between landlords, management companies and maintenance trustees, the expression 'landlord' is used in this book to mean the party (whether or not actually the landlord) responsible for providing the services under the terms of the letting. Those terms may be set out in a document called a 'lease' or a 'tenancy agreement', and in this book the word 'lease' will be used to cover both.

1.1.6 Documents ancillary to the lease

Since arrangements between the parties to a lease may be binding on their successors even if contained in separate deeds or even 'side letters' rather than in the lease itself, all documents supplemental to the lease need to be taken into account when determining the true terms of the letting (see *System Floors Ltd v Ruralpride Ltd* [1995] 1 EGLR 48, CA).

1.2 The contractual basis of the service charge

1.2.1 Basic contractual position

The fact that the tenant has the benefit of service does not, of itself, mean that he is required to pay for those services. Generally, no tenant is obliged to pay a service charge except so far as the terms of his lease may provide for one. The tenant's lease is a contract between the landlord and the tenant and (subject to the intervention of Parliament or the courts – as mentioned later) the precise wording of the clauses of the lease creating the landlord's obligation to provide services to his tenant and creating his entitlement to a service charge from his tenant must be considered carefully in order to ascertain the extent of the tenant's liability.

Example

Riverlate Properties Ltd v Paul [1975] Ch 133, CA: Clause 6 of the 99-year lease of a maisonette set out the landlord's obligations in a number of subclauses; subclause (a) dealt with external and structural repairs; (b) with insurance; (c) with external redecoration; and (d) with payment of water rates. The tenant's covenant for contribution only mentioned the costs incurred by the landlord under clause 6(b) to (d). Was the tenant liable to contribute to the costs of external and structural repairs mentioned in clause 6(a)? **Held**: No; the landlord had to provide those works at his own cost for the entire duration of the term of the lease.

In the case of management companies of which the tenants are members, provisions imposing service cost liabilities on tenants are occasionally contained in the articles of association of the company in addition to, or instead of, in the leases. Provisions in the articles are sometimes also used in an attempt to find an indirect route to make the tenants responsible for contributing to a shortfall arising due to the irrecoverability of an item of cost through the service charge (see **1.1.3**) but this has not been tested in the courts.

As to the possible inclusion of service charge arrangements in documents other than the lease itself, see **1.1.6**.

1.2.2   No presumption of full recoupment

Where a service charge clause is unclear or ambiguous, the courts will generally interpret it narrowly and determine ambiguities or uncertainties in the tenant's favour. Even under a lease which contains a detailed service charge clause, there may be landlord's expenditure which falls outside the wording of the clause and, thus, cannot be charged to the tenant. When construing a service charge clause, there is usually no presumption that it will have been intended to recoup all the landlord's expenditure.

Example

Rapid Results College v Angell (1986) 277 EG 856, CA: The lease obliged the landlord to maintain the external walls, structure and roof of the building. The lease of the offices on the second floor required the tenant to pay 50 per cent of the cost of maintenance of the 'exterior . . . in respect of the premises being the offices on the First and Second floors'. Did the tenant have to pay towards maintenance of the roof immediately above the second floor? **Held**: No; the roof was not part of 'the exterior' of 'the first and second floor offices'. Dillon LJ said: 'It does not follow automatically ... that the services rent must necessarily cover everything the landlords are to do ...' (See also *Riverlate Properties Ltd v Paul* noted at **1.2.1**.)

A possible exception to this approach may be where the lease provides for the services to be supplied by a management company which is controlled by the tenants. Such a company ordinarily has no assets other than the management fund and, in such cases, it will not be in a position to perform its task without full funding from the tenants. In those circumstances the courts may attempt to interpret the service charge provisions, *so far as possible*, on the basis of full recoupment of the cost of those services which the company is obliged to provide.

Example

Embassy Court Residents' Association Ltd v Lipman (1984) 271 EG 545, CA: The lease of a flat required the tenant to pay towards the costs of performance of the landlord's covenants (mainly for external and structural repair of the block), required the tenant to become a member of the company, and provided for the company to become the landlord by the grant to it of an overriding lease. The landlord's covenants did not mention employing managing agents, but the company, which was a company limited by guarantee of which the tenant and the other flat-owners were members, did so when the flat-owners who had been running it got fed up. Was the tenant liable to pay towards the managing agents' proper fees? **Held**: Yes; when the tenant's lease was granted the parties must have contemplated that the company should take such steps as were reasonably necessary and conducive to the performance of its administrative functions and that the flat-owners accepted an obligation to contribute, pro rata, such sums as were necessary for the discharge by the company of its necessary administrative expenditure.

However, this approach will not assist the management company to recover costs which are undeniably outside a precise and unambiguous list of recoverable costs set out in the lease or in the memorandum and articles of association of the company or where a tenants' management company was not envisaged by the terms of the lease.

Examples

Broadwater Court Management Company v Jackson-Mann (1997) EGCS 145, CA: A company established by the tenants of a block of flats acquired the freehold. The service charge provisions in their leases did not expressly include costs relating to annual auditing and the filing of statutory returns under the Companies Acts. Could such costs be included in the service charges? **Held**: No; this was not intended at the time when the leases were granted.

Mullaney v Maybourne Grange (Croydon) Management Co Ltd (1986) 277 EG 1350: The wooden window-frames in a tower bock of flats gave constant trouble. The management company had them replaced by maintenance-free double glazing. Was the tenant liable to pay towards the cost of this under service charge provisions covering (a) the 'repair' of the block, or (b) the cost of providing 'additional services or amenities'? **Held**: No; installing new-type windows was neither a repair nor a service or amenity. (Note: In *Sutton (Hastoe) Housing Association v Williams* [1988] 1 EGLR 56 the Court of Appeal did not disagree with the above decision but, nevertheless, held that in the case before them the replacement of old wooden windows with double-glazed units could be chargeable as a 'repair'.)

Bratton Seymour Service Co Ltd v Oxborough [1992] EGCS 28, CA: The company was formed to maintain the common parts of a residential estate. The plots were sold and the conveyances imposed a covenant on each purchaser to contribute towards the costs of maintaining the drive, water supply and drainage system. Was a plot purchaser, as a member of the company, liable to contribute to the costs of the company maintaining amenity areas not mentioned in the covenant? **Held**: No; additional burdens on members cannot be added by implication into the articles of association of the company.

Note that lack of funds does not usually absolve a landlord from his liability to provide the services (see **1.11**).

Occasionally, a lease may contain a specific declaration that the intention of the service charge clause is to achieve full recoupment of all expenditure (as in paragraph 1 of the specimen service charge schedule set out at **B.2** in **Appendix 1**), and the court would have to give weight to such a declaration when interpreting the operative provisions, but this is quite rare.

1.2.3   Sweeping-up clauses

When a lease is drafted, the landlord and his solicitor cannot be expected to foresee every conceivable item of future expenditure which should be covered by the service charge. To avoid the risk of the landlord incurring costs which might fall outside the services or works listed in the landlord's covenants or in the list of chargeable expenditure, many service charge clauses contain a 'sweeping-up' provision entitling the landlord to charge not only for the services specifically listed but also for other services which he may decide to provide.

Sweeping-up clauses are discussed in more detail at **1.3.3**.

1.2.4   Overriding leases

Sometimes, after a lease has been granted to a tenant (T), an overriding lease is granted by the landlord (L1) so as to interpose an intermediate landlord (L2) between L1 and T. An overriding lease might be of an entire building or of one or more individual flats or other parts of a building. One particular situation in which an overriding lease of an individual part might arise would be under s 19 of the Landlord and Tenant (Covenants) Act 1995 (see **1.20.9**).

The interposition of an overriding lease can create a problem in relation to service charges which are payable to the landlord (as distinct from being payable to a third party such as a management company). Imagine that T's lease requires T to pay a service charge calculated at 10 per cent of the total service costs of the building incurred by 'the Landlord', who up to the grant of the overriding lease will be L1. This would have been drafted to reflect the fact that L1 was the landlord of the whole building and would be supplying all the services in it. As from the grant of the overriding lease, L2 becomes 'the Landlord' in place of L1, who is now L2's landlord. The overriding lease will almost certainly impose on L2 an obligation to pay to L1 the same amount of service charge as was formerly payable by T, that is 10 per cent of the service costs incurred by L1. Accordingly, L2 will expect to recover the same amount from T, who is now his tenant. However, T's lease requires him to pay only 10 per cent of the service costs incurred by 'the Landlord', who is now L2. Does this mean that T need only pay to L2 a sum equal to 10 per cent of the amount of service charge that L2 has to pay to L1, leaving L2 to meet the difference? It is hoped that this would not be the case, but finding T liable to pay 100 per cent of the service charge payable by L2 to L1 may depend on whether the text of the particular lease leaves room for the court to interpret the references to service costs incurred by 'the Landlord' as meaning those incurred by L1 rather than by L2 (see *Adelphi v Christi* (1983) 269 EG 221). (If the premises are a residential flat, L2 might be able to solve this problem by obtaining a court order varying T's lease, under s 35 of the Landlord and Tenant Act 1987 – see **2.15**.)

A related problem would arise concerning the effect of the landlord's covenants to provide the services. If T's lease imposes covenants on 'the Landlord' to maintain the structure and common parts of the entire building and to provide other services, T can now require L2 to comply with those covenants. However, L2 will not normally be in a position to perform them himself, nor wish to do so, since his overriding lease will comprise only the part of the building which is let to T; all L2 can do in this respect is to require L1 to perform those covenants, under the terms of the overriding lease.

1.3   Identifying the chargeable costs

1.3.1   Old-fashioned contribution clauses

Older forms of lease frequently contain quite brief and restricted contribution clauses, such as:

> 'to pay a fair proportion of the cost of maintaining and repairing party walls and structures, shared pipes and wires, and other things used in common'.

In such cases there is a strong chance that many items normally included in a modern service charge clause, particularly true services (such as porterage, heating, etc) as distinct from repairs and maintenance works, may not be covered by the wording and, thus, will not be chargeable to the tenant (under the principles set out at **1.2**).

However, the scope of this type of clause may not be quite as narrow as the first impression gives.

Examples

Twyman v Charrington [1994] 1 EGLR 243, CA: The tenant, in his lease of the ground floor and basement of a building, covenanted to pay a proportion of the landlord's expenditure in repairing 'mutual or party structures and other items which may belong to or be used for the demised premises in common with other premises'. Was the tenant liable to contribute towards the cost of repairs to the roof located above the second floor? **Held**: Yes; although the roof was not a party structure so far as the demised premises were concerned, it benefited every part of the building and was therefore a 'mutual' structure or, alternatively, something 'used in common'.

Daejan Properties v Bloom (2000) EGCS 85, CA: The lease of a commercial garage in the basement of a block of flats imposed on the tenant a covenant to contribute to the cost of 'repairing . . . all walls, fence walls, fences, drains and other conveniences . . . used in common with the owners or occupiers of adjoining or contiguous premises'. Did this include the paving, asphalt membrane and concrete slab over the garage, forming the entrance driveway of the flats? **Held**: Yes.

1.3.2 Modern service charge clauses

Modern service charge clauses can be drafted in many ways but generally fall into three categories:

(1) those which directly link the service charge to the costs incurred by the landlord in performing his service covenants contained elsewhere in the lease, eg by providing that the service charge is a percentage of:

> 'the costs and expenses incurred by the Lessor in carrying out his obligations under Clause 3 of this Lease';

(2) those which list the chargeable items (usually under the title of 'Heads of Charge' or similar) quite independently of the landlord's covenants, eg by providing that the service charge is a percentage of:

> 'the costs and expenses of such works services facilities and amenities listed in Part 2 of this Schedule as may from time to time be provided by the Lessor';

(3) a combination of (1) and (2), of which the specimen provisions in para 9.1 of the specimen service charge schedule set out at **B.2** in **Appendix 1** are an example, extending both to the cost of performing the landlord's covenants and the cost of other, discretionary, classes of expenditure.

Type (2) and (3) provisions can be misleading as they may give the tenant the impression that the landlord is obliged to provide all the listed services, but this may not be so. The fact that the landlord is entitled to charge if he provides a particular service does not, of itself, imply that he is contractually obliged to provide that service – the provision of the service may be at his discretion.

Examples

Duke of Westminster v Guild (1983) 267 EG 762, CA: The tenant of a mews building covenanted to 'pay and contribute to the landlords a fair proportion with other lessees interested therein of the expenses of . . . repairing . . . drains . . . belonging . . . to the demised premises or . . . used jointly'. The drain serving the premises was blocked with earth. Part of the drain was situated within the demised premises (and fell within the tenant's repairing covenant) and the remainder ran beneath the landlord's private mews. The tenant constructed a new drain between the premises and the private sewer serving the mews.

Could the tenant recover any of the cost from the landlord on the basis that the landlord was obliged, by implication, to repair the drain in the mews and had failed to do so? **Held**: No; such an implication was not to be inferred. The landlord had a discretion whether or not to carry out the works mentioned in the contribution covenant.

Russell v Laimond Properties Ltd (1984) 269 EG 947, QBD: Resident porters were employed by the landlord of a block of flats for several years. The landlord covenanted 'to provide ... the services of such maintenance staff as [he] shall consider necessary for the performance of the matters specified ...'. The possible service charge costs were separately listed in a schedule and included the cost of porterage and of providing, maintaining and repairing a flat for staff. The landlord decided to sell the porter's flat and use outside maintenance staff. Could the flat-owners obtain an injunction to stop him? **Held**: No; a covenant by the landlord to provide a resident porter could not be inferred from the schedule of chargeable items. The covenant required a maintenance man to be available at certain times in connection with expressly mentioned matters such as the central heating system, but this did not necessarily involve him residing in the block.

Accordingly, in order to check whether a service is obligatory, the landlord's covenants must be examined.

It is of critical importance to interpret correctly the wording of the service charge clause and, if that clause refers in turn to the landlord's covenants, the wording of those covenants. If it is found that certain types of work do not fall within any of the descriptions of work set out in the detailed clauses, the sweeping-up provision (if any) will have to be considered (see **1.2.3** and **1.3.3**) in order to see whether it covers them. If it does not, the expense in question cannot be included in the service charge. Sweeping-up provisions can be found in both types of clause and the existence of a well-drawn sweeper provision will reduce the risk of the landlord incurring irrecoverable expenditure.

A number of typical items found listed in landlord's service covenants or heads of charge are discussed at **1.4** to **1.8**.

1.3.3 Sweeping-up clauses and variation rights

For the reasons mentioned at **1.2.3** and **1.3.2**, many service charge clauses contain provisions intended to sweep up into the service charge the cost of services or works not otherwise specifically mentioned. This may appear in the lease:

(a) in a definition of the chargeable costs, for example:

> '"Total expenditure" means the expenditure incurred by the Lessor in any accounting period in carrying out its obligations under Clause 3 of this Lease *and any other costs and expenses reasonably incurred in connection with the Building*';

(b) by a separate head of charge in the list of chargeable costs, for example:

'the cost of providing such other services and performing such other works as the landlord shall deem appropriate or desirable';

(c) by a landlord's covenant in a similar form to (b), such as:

'to provide such other services and perform such other acts as the landlord may deem appropriate or desirable';

(d) by a provision giving the landlord the right to vary or add to the listed services (see **1.9**).

In the example quoted in (a) above, the words in italics will catch the cost of any works or services which the landlord '*reasonably*' decides to carry out (see, for example, *Fluor Daniel Properties Ltd v Shortlands Investment Ltd* [2001] EGCS 8 and **1.10.2**), but which are not covered by his express obligations under clause 3 of that lease. Some sweeping-up clauses do not contain this reasonableness qualification, but give the landlord wider discretion (subject to any statutory or common law implication of reasonableness – see **1.10** and **2.3**). Other sweeper clauses may be drafted so as to narrow down the scope of unspecified services by confining them to matters carried out '*for the benefit of the tenants in the Building as a whole*', '*in the interests of good estate management*', or by similar limiting phrases.

The effectiveness of these clauses in sweeping up unspecified costs depends entirely on their wording taken in the context of the lease as a whole. In most cases, but not invariably, these sweeper clauses are just as narrowly construed as the main charging provisions. The use of the word 'services' in some sweeper clauses may itself have a limiting effect.

Examples

Mullaney v Maybourne Grange (Croydon) Management Co Ltd (1986) 277 EG 1350: The service charge clause entitled the management company to recover the cost of 'providing and maintaining additional services or amenities'. Did this cover the costs incurred by the company in replacing wooden window frames with different maintenance-free frames? **Held**: No; since window frames were neither 'services' nor 'amenities'.

Jacob Isbicki & Co Ltd v Goulding & Bird Ltd [1989] 1 EGLR 236: Wall cleaning was not on the list of chargeable items in the lease, but the landlord had power at his discretion to 'add to, extend, vary or make any alteration in the rendering of the said services or any of them', and proposed to clean the external walls by sand-blasting. Could he charge for this? **Held**: No; the power quoted above gave the landlord a limited right to vary the services whilst remaining within the types of service listed, and did not give the landlord the right to embark upon a kind of service not contemplated by the main provisions. Furthermore, the proposal was not a 'service' in the normal sense.

Sun Alliance and London Assurance Co Ltd v British Railways Board [1989] 2 EGLR 237: The specified service costs included the cost of operating and maintaining equipment, and the sweeping-up clause covered 'the cost of providing other services'. Could the landlord include in the service charge the capital cost of installing a window-cleaner's cradle system at a cost of £70,000? **Held**: Yes; the provisions quoted were wide enough; the fact that it was capital expenditure was irrelevant (see **1.4.7**).

Lloyds Bank plc v Bowker Orford (1992) 31 EG 67, ChD: The service charge extended to 'any other beneficial services'. Did this include the repair of the exterior of the building and the repair and decoration of the internal common parts? **Held**: No; they were not 'services' in the sense used in the clause; the quoted words were only apt to cover matters such as lift operation, caretaking, security, cleaning and lighting the common parts and the provision of constant hot water.

Whether such clauses are likely to encompass legal and other professional costs, particularly in connection with service charge disputes, is discussed at **1.6.3** and **1.6.4**, and the inclusion of the costs of environmentally friendly measures is considered in **Chapter 6**.

Where the scope of the sweeper clause is unclear, a landlord who wishes to rely on the clause in order to be able to recover the cost of proposal expenditure should seek the tenants' agreement, failing which the landlord could apply to the court for a declaration on the point (see, for example, *Reston Ltd v Hudson* (1990) 2 EGLR 51, ChD).

Whether sweeper clauses may be subject to an implied test of reasonableness is discussed at **1.10.3**.

1.3.4   A presumption against profit-making

It is likely that the courts will assume that, in the absence of clear wording to the contrary, the service charge provisions are not intended to give the landlord a profit on the provision of services but merely to provide reimbursement of cost.

Example

Jollybird Ltd v Fairzone Ltd [1990] 2 EGLR 55, CA: The lease contained an ambiguously worded heating charge clause which, on one reading, would have entitled the landlord to charge more than actual cost. **Held**: That interpretation must be rejected in favour of the clause being interpreted to give reimbursement only.

However, this in itself will not prevent the landlord from recovering more than 100 per cent of total costs if the percentage contributions payable under each lease total more than 100 per cent.

1.3.5   Costs expended or costs contracted

Many service charge clauses are expressed to cover costs and expenses which the landlord 'expends' or 'incurs' or which 'become payable' by him. In some circumstances, it will be important to know whether the wording allows the charging of costs which have not yet been paid out or have not yet even fallen due, but which will become payable at a later date when work which has already been contracted between the landlord and his builders or suppliers is completed. The landlord may be keen to charge the cost to his tenants at the time or even before he contracts for the work to be done, particularly in cases where the leases will have expired by the time payment falls due or as a way of financing the work if the lease does not provide expressly for payments on account.

Example

> *Capital & Counties Freehold Equity Trust Ltd v BL plc* [1987] 2 EGLR 49: The service charge covered costs which may 'be expended or incurred or become payable' in respect of the listed services. Some work was ordered by the landlord shortly before the end of the lease, to be carried out afterwards. Did costs 'incurred', in contradistinction to costs 'expended', mean costs for which a contractual commitment was entered into by the landlord even though payment might be made at a later date, so that those costs were 'incurred' before the lease expired and could be included in the service charge payable by the tenant? **Held**: No; in the context, the words 'become payable', 'expended' and 'incurred' were synonymous, and meant that payment was made or fell due during the service charge accounting period in question. The intent of the landlord's covenants and service charge provisions, read as a whole, was that the service obligations and the service charge were to be coterminous and that only services performed during the term of the lease were chargeable.

For a different distinction between 'cost' and 'sums expended', see *Gilje and Others v Chalgrove Securities Ltd* [2001] EWCA Civ 1777 (unreported) at **1.8.3**.

1.4 Repairs, renewals, replacements, improvements and services

1.4.1 Basic principles

Many service charges cover the cost of 'repair' of the exterior, main structure, common parts and shared plant machinery and service media (pipes, wires, etc) of the building. The word 'repair' commonly features in both landlord's service covenants and heads of charge (see **1.3.2**).

Ascertaining the scope of the word 'repair', and any other words used to describe the nature of works for which the landlord can charge, is extremely important, particularly because tenants usually resent paying for works other than straightforward maintenance or redecoration. Tenants of new buildings frequently object to being potentially liable to pay for the repair of inherent structural defects, whilst tenants in older buildings may object when the landlord seeks to include in the service charge the cost of refurbishing and modernising the entrance and common parts of the building or even renewing an old roof.

The meaning of the word 'repair' has been considered in numerous cases and is a large complex topic; the following is only a brief summary of the position.

For the position where the landlord fails to carry out necessary repairs at the appropriate time, see **1.4.11**.

1.4.2 Repair

The word 'repair' has been defined as the rectifying of damage or deterioration, that is 'the putting back into good condition of something that, having been in good condition, has fallen into bad condition' (per Lord Evershed MR in *Day v Harland and Wolff Ltd* [1953] 2 All ER 387), or 'making good damage so as to leave the subject so far as possible as though it had not been damaged' (per Atkin LJ in *Anstruther-Gough-Calthorpe v McOscar* [1924] 1 KB 716). These definitions of repair have more recently been cited with approval by the Court of Appeal in *Quick v Taff-Ely District Council* [1985] 3 All ER 321 and *The Post Office v Aquarius Properties Ltd* (1987) 54 P&CR 61.

Words similar to 'repair', such as 'amend', 'maintain', 'uphold', etc, will generally be interpreted as the same as 'repair': *Halliard Property Co Ltd v Nicholas Clarke Investments Ltd* (1984) 269 EG 1257, per French J, and *Fluor Daniel Properties Ltd v Shortlands Investment Ltd* [2001] EGCS 8 (see **1.10.2**).

Even if an item is plainly out of repair by virtue of having been damaged or having deteriorated compared with its previous condition, nevertheless there are limits to the remedial work falling within the scope of 'repair':

(1) the nature and standard of repair is to be determined by reference to the class and character of the property at the date on which the lease was granted, so that upgrading (unless an unavoidable result of remedying the disrepair – eg the replacement of broken Victorian sanitary fittings with currently available modern fittings) falls outside repair; thus, the 'repair' of heating and air conditioning plant means keeping it in working order so that it performs as it did when it was installed, not to the standard now expected of new plant (*Ultraworth v General Accident* (2000) EGCS 19, Tech & Constr Court);

(2) the word 'repair' may not be apt to cover work which would be effectively an alteration to the whole or substantially the whole of the structure of the building, or which would produce a building of a wholly different character to that which had been let, or which would cost an amount which is out of proportion to the previous value of the building and would substantialy enhance the value and life span of the building: *McDougall v Easington District Council* (1989) 58 P&CR 201, CA (summarising the effect of a number of earlier authorities including the landmark decision in *Ravenseft Properties Ltd v Davstone (Holdings) Ltd* [1979] 1 All ER 929).

Often the distinction between 'repair' and 'improvement' is very fine and hard to draw (see **1.4.8**). In some cases the issue of 'reasonableness' is invoked in determining whether proposed work is or goes beyond repair (see **1.10.2**).

If the landlord's duty is to 'keep' in repair, this requires him to prevent disrepair from occurring and would therefore appear to encompass preventive work where disrepair is imminent (see **1.4.11**).

Occasionally, it is unclear whether a certain element of the building is repairable by the tenant or by the landlord. This may occur where the definition of the extent of the tenant's demise is imprecise. It may, alternatively, be unclear whether certain proposed work is within the meaning of 'repair' or other such expression used in the service charge clause, as discussed at **1.4.3** to **1.4.8**. In such cases, it may be prudent for the landlord to apply to the court for a declaration on the issue, as in *Reston Ltd v Hudson* [1990] 2 EGLR 51 (see **1.4.3**). As to the costs of such an application, see **1.6.5**.

1.4.3 Patching or long-term remedy

Repair work can involve either patching up or replacing the damaged or deteriorated parts: *Inglis v Buttery* (1878) 3 App Cas 552, per Lord Blackburn; *Anstruther-Gough-Calthorpe v McOscar* [1924] 1 KB 716, per Scrutton LJ; *Greg v Planque* [1936] 1 KB 669, per Slesser LJ. Generally, the party responsible for carrying out the repair has the choice whether to execute the long-term repair/replacement or a 'patching-up', as long as the immediate result of either course of action will be to put the dilapidated or damaged item back into proper repair.

Examples

Manor House Drive Ltd v Shahbazian (1965) 195 EG 283, CA: In the lease of a maisonette, the landlord covenanted to 'maintain repair and redecorate the main structure and roof of the building', and the tenant was liable to pay towards the costs incurred. On surveyor's advice, the landlord installed a new zinc roof. The tenant argued that the roof could have been patched up for less cost. Could the landlord recover the cost of the new roof? **Held**: Yes.

Murray v Birmingham City Council [1987] 2 EGLR 53, CA: The landlord was liable for external repairs to the tenant's house, and chose periodically to patch up the roof on a piecemeal basis whenever parts of it leaked, rather than replacing the entire roof. Had the landlord properly fulfilled his obligation? **Held**: Yes.

Reston Ltd v Hudson [1990] 2 EGLR 51, ChD: The landlord, liable at the tenants' cost to 'repair' the window-frames of a block of flats, proposed to replace all the window-frames in circumstances in which a piecemeal replacement of individual timbers in many rotted frames would be impractical and more expensive. Was he entitled to do so? **Held**: Yes.

However, where an item is beyond sensible patching up, it must be replaced.

Example

Stent v Monmouth District Council (1987) 54 P&CR 193, CA: The wooden front door of a council house rotted, previous wooden doors having also rotted due to the exposed location of the house. Was the council, under its obligation for external repairs, liable to replace the rotten wooden door with a new aluminium door of better design? **Held**: Yes; since that was what a reasonable landlord would do.

Furthermore, it may be implied in some cases that the landlord is under a general duty to act *reasonably* when deciding the type of repair work (see **1.10** and **2.3**).

1.4.4   Structural and external repair

An obligation to repair, or a right to charge for the cost of repairing, the 'structure', 'exterior' or other specified part of a building must be interpreted in the context of the lease as a whole. In some cases it will be plain, even if not clearly expressed, that it is intended that the landlord's works shall include repair of all parts of the building that are not demised to the tenants.

'Structural repair', a phrase sometimes met in the context of covenants to repair the structure of a building, has been held to mean the repair of structural parts only, thus excluding repair of the finishes: *Granada Theatres Ltd v Freehold Investment (Leytonstone) Ltd* [1959] Ch 952, CA.

Sometimes, the service costs will cover repair of the 'main structure'. In *Samuels v Abbints Investments* (1963) 188 EG 689, Ungoed-Thomas J held that a landlord's covenant to repair the 'main structure' of a block of flats required him to repair the outside bricks of the external walls (although this may have been influenced by the fact that the lease defined the plaintiff's flat as including 'the internal and external walls ... but excluding the outside brick, steel or concrete work').

The word 'structure' has also been judicially considered in the different context of the Landlord and Tenant Act 1954. In *Romulus Trading Co Ltd v Trustees of Henry Smith's Charity* [1989] EGCS 165, CA, it was held that the statutory expression 'work of construction' meant interference 'with the structure of the building', and it was observed that 'structure' was not necessarily confined to external and load-bearing walls, but further guidance on the meaning of the word was not given. The precise extent of 'structure' is, therefore, unclear at the present time.

Where the repair of structural parts necessarily entails further works, the obligation to carry out structural repair may include those further works: *Smedley v Chumley & Hawkes Ltd* (1982) 44 P&CR 50 (see **1.4.5**).

What if the service costs include the repair of the 'exterior' of the building? Again, in a different context, 'exterior' has been given a wide meaning by the courts. In cases under the Housing Act 1961 (now the Landlord and Tenant Act 1985) the 'exterior' has been held to include accessways and staircases: *Brown v Liverpool Corporation* [1969] 3 All ER 1345.

The expression 'external wall' was held in *Pembury v Lamdin* [1940] 2 All ER 434, CA, to mean a wall forming part of the enclosure of the premises, not necessarily a wall exposed to the atmosphere.

Whether windows and window-frames are part of the 'exterior' or 'outside walls' of a building will depend upon the overall intent of the various clauses and the physical nature of the building. In buildings with glass curtain-walling, for example, it will often be apparent that the windows are merely sections of that curtain-walling. 'It would appear that windows in the outer wall of a building may, in certain contexts and for certain purposes, be regarded as part of the walls': Lord Evershed MR in *Hoiday Fellowship Ltd v Hereford* [1959] 1 All ER 433; see also *Boswell v Crucible Steel Co* [1925] 1 KB 119; *Ball v Plummer* (1879) 23 Sol Jo 656, CA.

Often the courts adopt a flexible, common-sense approach to these references to parts of the building, as in *Plough Investments Ltd v Manchester City Council* [1989] 1 EGLR 244, where Scott J treated the phrase 'main timbers', in a landlord's repairing covenant, as referring to the steel frame of the building – there were no 'timbers' in the strict sense of wooden members.

1.4.5   Whether repair includes rectifying inherent defects

Generally speaking, the remedying of a defect found to be inherent in the construction of a building will not of itself fall within an obligation to 'repair', since the defectively constructed part will not have been previously in any better condition.

Examples

Halliard Property Co Ltd v Nicholas Clarke Investments Ltd (1984) 269 EG 1257: Did the tenant's covenant to 'repair' the premises make him liable to rebuild an unsupported wall, described by the judge as a 'jerry-built structure', when it collapsed during the term of the lease? **Held**: No.

Post Office v Aquarius Properties Ltd (1985) 276 EG 923, CA: Did the tenant's covenant to 'repair' an office building oblige the tenant to alter the construction of the basement walls so as to render the basement watertight? **Held**: No.

Quick v Taff-Ely Borough Council (1985) 276 EG 452, CA: The windows of a council house were badly designed and were prone to cause condensation, which damaged the tenant's contents and decorations but did not damage the walls or other parts of the house itself. Did the landlord, under his covenant to 'repair' a house, have to replace them with different windows? **Held**: No.

Eyre v McCracken (2000) 80 P&CR 220, CA: Water ingress, facilitated by the absence of any damp-proof course, caused damage to parts of a building. Did the necessary works of 'repair' include installing a damp-proof course? **Held**: No.

Holding & Barnes plc v Hill House Hammond Ltd (2000) WL 877816, ChD: The landlord covenanted to keep in repair the structure and exterior of the building. Did 'repair' include installing a damp-proof course? **Held**: No.

However, if an inherent defect in one element of a building causes damage to occur to another, previously sound, part of the building, the part so damaged will require to be rectified in a modern competent manner under the obligation to 'repair' and that may extend to remedying the underlying inherent defect if the damaged part cannot sensibly be repaired without it. However, this is a matter of fact and degree in each case, so it is difficult to derive precise rules which would apply in every case (compare, for example, *McCracken* and *Holding & Barnes*, above, with *Elmcroft* and *Welsh*, below).

Examples

Ravenseft Properties Ltd v Davstone (Holdings) Ltd [1979] 1 All ER 929, QBD: The tenant of a building covenanted 'when where and so often as occasion shall require well and sufficiently to repair renew rebuild uphold support . . .' the premises. The external stone cladding had not been installed with expansion joints and there were no metal ties between the stone slabs and the concrete frame. The cladding was bowing dangerously due to its expansion being greater than that of the frame. Did the tenant's covenant require him to remedy the problem in accordance with current building methods by cutting the cladding and installing ties and plastic expansion-absorbing material at a cost of about £155,000? **Held**: Yes; the fact that the building was built without expansion joints or ties did not exonerate the tenant. However, if the cost of the remedial work would have been a substantially higher proportion of the cost of rebuilding the entire building, it would have gone beyond repair.

Elmcroft Developments Ltd v Tankersley-Sawyer (1984) 270 EG 140, CA: The landlord covenanted to 'maintain and keep the exterior of the building and the roof, the main walls, timbers and drains thereof in good and tenantable repair and condition'. Was the landlord liable to remedy deterioration caused by rising damp, the damp-proof course having been positioned below ground level? **Held**: Yes.

Smedley v Chumley & Hawke Ltd (1982) 44 P&CR 50: The landlord covenanted 'to keep the main walls and roof in good structural repair'. A main wall cracked because the building had been built on a partly unsupported concrete raft, one end of which had subsided. Was the landlord liable to carry out remedial work including major underpinning, since the wall could not be properly repaired otherwise? **Held**: Yes.

Welsh v Greenwich London Borough Council (2000) EGCS 84, CA: The landlord covenanted 'to maintain the dwelling in good condition and repair'. The property was not properly insulated and suffered from damp and condensation, which damaged the walls as well as the tenant's fittings. Was the landlord liable to provide thermal insulation? **Held**: Yes.

Where the express terms of the lease go beyond 'repair' and include obligations such as to 'rebuild', 'renew' or 'rectify inherent defects', the limitations on the scope of 'repair' will not be decisive and the additional wording must be closely examined. The covenant may, in fact, be divisible so as to provide a covenant to repair and a separate covenant to rectify inherent defects.

In *Credit Suisse v Beegas Nominees Ltd* [1994] 4 All ER 803, it was held that an obligation to 'keep the building in good and tenantable condition' required leaking cladding which had a design defect to be replaced by a totally new cladding system.

1.4.6 Replacements and renewals

Where the lease expressly includes the words 'rebuilding' or 'renewal', this is likely to widen the scope of work covered by the clause, but even a simple covenant to 'repair' will usually, by implication, include a certain amount of rebuilding and replacement of elements of the building which have deteriorated, as mentioned in **1.4.2**.

Example

> *Minja Properties v Cussins* (1998) 30 EG 114, ChD: A landlord had the right to enter a building in order 'to effect repairs to the building'. Did 'repair' include replacing rusted windows with new double-glazed sealed window units? **Held**: Yes; since the windows needed replacing and renewal of parts of a building is within 'repair'.

As for plant and equipment, an obligation to 'repair' or 'maintain' such items usually carries with it an obligation to replace the plant and equipment when necessary. This will also apply where the obligation is expressed simply as a covenant to provide the particular service (eg hot water or central heating) without even mentioning the plant and equipment. The fact that the expenditure is of a capital nature, rather than revenue, is generally irrelevant. However, this implied obligation will not necessarily be taken to require or authorise the upgrading of plant and machinery which is in working order.

Examples

> *Yorkbrook Investments Ltd v Batten* (1985) 276 EG 545: The landlord covenanted to provide hot water. Was he liable to replace the boiler system when necessary, even though the lease did not expressly mention the boiler system? **Held**: Yes.

> *Lloyds Bank plc v Bowker Orford* (1992) 31 EG 67, ChD: The service charge covered the provision of hot water and lighting of the common parts. Did this encompass not only the operation of the existing hot water and lighting systems but also the replacement of the plant and equipment when necessary and even the provision of necessary additional equipment? **Held**: Yes.

Where the obligation is to 'repair' and it is possible (even if exceptionally expensive) to repair the item rather than replace it with something totally different, the obligation may require the expensive repair rather than the cheaper replacement.

Example

Creska v Hammersmith London Borough Council (1998) 37 EG 165, CA: The lease of an office building required the tenant to keep it in repair. The underfloor heating system broke down and would be very expensive to repair. Could the tenant satisfy its repairing obligation by leaving the underfloor system and installing storage heaters? **Held**: No; the existing system had to be repaired.

Also see **1.10** (as to reasonableness tests) and **4.2** (as to sinking funds, reserve funds and depreciation).

1.4.7   Capital expenditure

If a particular item of expenditure is to be chargeable to the tenants through the service charge, the wording of the service charge clause must be apt to cover the item in question; if it is, the cost is prima facie chargeable, *whether or not* the work is an improvement, a replacement or renewal, the remedying of an inherent defect, or other non-standard type of expenditure. The fact that, for some purposes, the expenditure may be considered as a capital item is normally irrelevant.

Examples

Sun Alliance and London Assurance Co Ltd v British Railways Board [1989] 2 EGLR 237: The specified service costs included the cost of operating and maintaining equipment, and the sweeping-up clause covered 'the cost of providing other services'. Could the landlord include in the service charge the capital cost of installing a new window-cleaner's cradle system at a cost of £70,000? **Held**: Yes.

Yorkbrook Investments Ltd v Batten (1985) 276 EG 545, CA: The lease contained a landlord's covenant 'to provide and maintain ... an adequate supply of heating in the hot water radiators ... and to remedy any mechanical breakdown in the hot water and central heating systems'. Did this require the landlord to incur the capital cost of replacing antiquated and unserviceable equipment? **Held**: Yes.

Lloyds Bank plc v Bowker Orford (1992) 31 EG 67, ChD: The service charge was to cover the 'total cost' of providing the listed services, which included provision of constant hot water in the lavatories, and keeping the common parts lighted. Did this encompass capital expenditure on installing, when necessary, new hot water plant and equipment and new lighting? **Held**: Yes.

1.4.8 Improvements

Where the service costs are restricted to the cost of 'repair' or 'maintenance', the question may often arise as to the extent to which the landlord is entitled to charge for work involving improvement. This question might arise not only where the landlord wishes to carry out works which are obviously improvements (such as refurbishing common parts to a higher standard), but also where it is proposed to replace worn or damaged fittings with upgraded or environmentally friendly items (eg gas boilers for an oil-fired system, or energy-efficient light fittings for traditional lighting).

There are four elements of the meaning of 'repair' that must be considered when approaching this question.

(1) According to the meaning of the word 'repair' (discussed at **1.4.2**), 'repair' only becomes necessary if the premises concerned are 'out of repair', since the word 'repair' has been defined as the rectifying of damage or deterioration. Premises are not 'out of repair' unless they have been damaged or have deteriorated from an earlier better physical condition. Thus, the treatment or replacement of the fabric of a building or its plant and machinery cannot be within the meaning of 'repair' if the item concerned is not out of repair (within the above meaning) at that time. Carrying out work to premises which have not deteriorated or been damaged is not 'repair' but improvement, and if the service charge covers only 'repair', the cost of that work would fall outside the scope of the charge. If the recoverable cost is that expended under a covenant to 'keep in repair', the cost of such work can be charged if deterioration has occurred or is clearly imminent (eg a roof at the end of its life even if not yet leaking). An example might be the replacement of old, but perfectly functioning, sanitary fittings with new fittings; since the old fittings were not out of repair, their replacement is not repair but improvement.

(2) Whilst 'repair' can include patching where to do so is reasonable practice, it is for the party liable to do the repairs to choose, in those circumstances, whether to patch or to carry out longer lasting repairs. As Mustill LJ said in *McDougall v Easington District Council* (1989) 58 P&CR 201: 'Often there will be a choice of methods for solving the problem . . . it must be a matter of judgment for the paying party which method to adopt.' The reference to 'the paying party' means the party responsible for carrying out the work, whether or not he can obtain reimbursement from another party. Therefore the landlord will be the paying party even if he can recover the cost of the work through a service charge. An example is *Manor House Drive Ltd v Shahbazian* (1965) 195 EG 283 (summarised at **1.4.3**) where a landlord successfully claimed the cost of replacing the roof of a block of flats instead of patching it up. However, if the landlord unreasonably selects a more costly or long-term remedy, the tenant might have an argument against the charge, by virtue of an express or implied 'reasonableness test' (see **1.10**).

(3) The standard of work for 'repairs' is that which is necessary to bring the premises back into the condition in which, having regard to the age, character and locality of the property at the date on which the lease was granted, the premises would be reasonably fit for occupation by a reasonably minded, incoming tenant of the class who would be likely to take it and ignoring any change, during the term of the lease, in the class of persons likely to require the property. As Lord Esher MR said of a tenant's repairing covenant in *Lister v Lane and Nesham* [1893] 2 QB 212, CA, 'He has to repair that thing which he took; he is not obliged to make a new and different thing.' Carrying out work which goes beyond this standard would fall outside 'repair'; an example might be the replacement of a deteriorated linoleum floor with marble. An exception to this rule is where the work must inevitably be carried out in a way which exceeds the original standard because of current building practice (as in (4) below) or by virtue of the limited choice of materials available. A further exception is where it is reasonable to install an improved version of a particular item as the replacement for the item in disrepair – such as an aluminium, sealed door unit for a rotten wooden door (*Stent v Monmouth District Council* (1987) 54 P&CR 193, CA) or double-glazed maintenance-free windows for rusted or rotten frames (*Sutton (Hastoe) Housing Association v Williams* [1988] 1 EGLR 56, CA; *Minja Properties v Cussins* (1998) 30 EG 114, ChD).

(4) If work of 'repair' is necessary because of damage or deterioration, it must be done in accordance with the principles of good building practice at the time the work is done and, if this involves a degree of updating, will nevertheless be considered to be within the repair. There is no notion of 'betterment' where the work can only properly be done with a degree of improvement. On this basis, in *Ravenseft Properties Ltd v Davstone (Holdings) Ltd* [1980] QB 12, a tenant under a covenant to 'repair' was held to be required to insert new expansion joints as an integral part of the repair of stone cladding, notwithstanding that such joints had not been incorporated in the original construction; and in *Halliard Property Co Ltd v Nicholas Clarke Investments Ltd* (1984) 269 EG 1257, French J said that if the tenant was liable to reinstate a collapsed 'jerry-built' structure, the reinstatement would have had to be carried out properly and lawfully, in accordance with building regulations, codes of practice and byelaws.

The difficulty of applying these rules in individual cases is illustrated by the differing conclusions of the courts in the cases summarised at **1.4.5**. In many cases, it will be a close judgment as to whether the rectification of a defect such as the absence of a damp-proof course or proper insulation or ventilation is required under a covenant to 'repair'.

There is, of course, no rule preventing a service charge clause from expressly requiring the tenant to pay towards improvements.

See also **1.4.6** in relation to the replacement of plant and machinery.

1.4.9   Services

Where the provision in the lease uses the word 'services', eg in a clause covering the cost of other 'services' which the landlord decides to provide, the interpretation of that word will depend upon the context.

Examples

Mullaney v Maybourne Grange (Croydon) Management Co Ltd (1986) 277 EG 1350: The wooden window-frames in a tower block of flats gave constant trouble. The management company had them replaced by maintenance-free double glazing. Was the tenant liable to pay towards the cost of this, under service charge provisions covering the cost of providing 'additional services or amenities'? **Held**: No; installing new-type windows was neither a service nor an amenity.

Jacob Isbicki & Co Ltd v Goulding & Bird Ltd [1989] 1 EGLR 236: Wall cleaning was not on the list of chargeable items in the lease but the landlord had power, at his discretion, to 'add to, extend, vary or make any alteration in the rendering of the said services or any of them', and proposed to clean the external walls by sand-blasting. Could he charge for this? **Held**: No; the proposed work was not a 'service' in the normal sense.

Lloyds Bank plc v Bowker Orford (1992) 31 EG 68, ChD: The service charge extended to 'any other beneficial services'. Did this include the repair of the exterior of the building and the repair and decoration of the internal common parts? **Held**: No, these works were not 'services' in the sense used in the clause; the quoted words were only apt to cover matters such as lift operation, caretaking, security, cleaning and lighting the common parts and the provision of constant hot water.

1.4.10   Overriding limitations

Even if certain items of expenditure appear to fall within the wording of the service charge provisions of a lease, the effect of statute law or common law may be to exclude such items of expenditure from the service charge if they fail to meet certain 'reasonableness' and other tests.

This is dealt with in more detail in **1.10**, with the special rules applicable to residential lettings described in **2.3**.

1.4.11   Landlord's delays

If the landlord fails to carry out his repairing or redecorating obligations at the appropriate time, the effect may be to allow disrepair to worsen to a state at which costly remedial work, which otherwise would have been avoided, becomes necessary.

In some such cases, the tenants may be able to contend that these extra costs should be excluded from the service charge since they arise out of the landlord's breach of obligation, but even if this is proved it appears that the landlord can set against this the cost saving of having omitted the earlier work.

Example

Postel Properties Ltd v Boots The Chemist (1996) 41 EG 164, QBD: The tenants argued that the need for major work to glazing was the result of lack of maintenance; moisture ingress should have been avoided by regular painting. The tenants failed to satisfy the judge, Ian Kennedy J, on the detailed facts, but in any event he said: 'The removal of the more extensive rust which time has allowed to develop does not add significantly to the overall cost . . . so far as [the landlords] may have been guilty of delay and so increase the final cost in terms of the extent of the corrosion, that is more than balanced by the saved costs of repainting in 1990 . . .'.

In order for a tenant to maintain a claim against the landlord in this way, the tenant would have to be able to establish that the landlord had been obliged contractually to carry out the appropriate remedial work when it first became necessary. The scope of obligations such as 'to repair' has been discussed at **1.4.1** to **1.4.8**, and the question of whether the landlord is actually obliged to carry out particular works or is merely entitled to do them at his discretion has been discussed at **1.3.2**.

In the case of 'repair', the time when the landlord is obliged to carry out the remedial work depends upon whether the part which is out of repair is or is not included in the tenant's demise. Where it is not demised to any tenant (eg the common parts or main structure of a multi-let building, where each tenant is demised only the interior of his flat or office suite), the landlord will be expected to know the condition of the parts which he has retained and therefore he will be required to carry out repairs as soon as they become necessary. Indeed, the usual covenant to 'keep in repair' such retained parts of a building may be breached by the landlord as soon as disrepair occurs, thus effectively requiring the landlord to carry out preventive work in order to prevent disrepair from arising.

Example

British Telecommunications plc v Sun Life Assurance Society plc [1995] 2 EGLR 44, CA: A landlord covenanted to keep the external walls of a commercial building in repair. Repairs became necessary, which the landlord carried out within a reasonable time from the disrepair occurring. Was the landlord nevertheless liable to pay damages to the tenant for the period from the moment of disrepair until the repairs were completed? **Held:** Yes; since the breach of covenant to 'keep in repair' occurred immediately upon the occurrence of disrepair.

On the other hand, where the landlord's repairing obligation relates to parts which are included in a tenant's demise, the landlord's obligation to carry out repairs does not arise until the landlord has been given notice (however informally) of the state of disrepair.

Example

O'Brien v Robinson [1973] AC 912, HL: The landlord of a house, the whole of which was let to the tenant, was under a covenant (imposed by statute) to keep the structure of the house in repair. The bedroom ceiling fell in, due to structural defect. Was the landlord liable to pay for the damage caused to the tenant's furniture and effects? **Held**: No; he was only liable to repair the ceiling. Where the disrepair is of something included in the tenant's lease, the landlord's covenant to repair requires the landlord to take action only when the landlord has information that the disrepair has occurred, and the landlord then has a reasonable opportunity to carry out the repair. The collapse of the ceiling therefore was not due to any breach of covenant by the landlord, so the landlord was not liable for the damage it caused.

However, where the landlord is required, either by the terms of the lease itself or by statute, to consult with the tenants before carrying out particular works, it will presumably be the case that the landlord's obligation to start that work will not arise until the prescribed period for consultation (or, if no period is prescribed, a reasonable period for consultation) has elapsed.

If the landlord fails to carry out necessary repairs at their due time (that time being ascertained under the above rules), he can be sued for damages for breach of covenant. The tenant's claim can extend to damages for distress and inconvenience caused to him as well as for any costs of remedying physical damage caused to his belongings.

Example

Wallis v Manchester City Council [1998] 41 EG 223, CA: The landlord of a house, the whole of which was let to the tenant, was under a covenant (imposed by statute) to keep the structure of the house in repair. The landlord was in breach of covenant by failing to repair a collapsed wall, rotten windows, a failed damp-proof course, loose plaster, leaking rainwater pipes, etc. Could the tenant recover damages for distress and inconvenience? **Held**: Yes; the damages for distress and inconvenience should be of an amount sufficient to reflect the reduced rental value that the premises in their actual condition would have commanded compared with the rent actually payable.

A similar principle was applied in *Electricity Supply Nominees v National Magazine Co* [1998] EGCS 162, Official Referee, where the tenant of offices obtained damages for loss of amenity due to the landlord failing to comply with his covenant to use reasonable endeavours to maintain the lifts and air conditioning equipment, which broke down excessively often.

In *Broadwater Court Management Company v Jackson-Mann* [1997] EGCS 145, CA, the landlord was guilty of serious delay in carrying out some necessary repairs in a block of flats and the tenant of one flat was awarded damages of £25 per month for loss of amenity.

1.5 Insurance costs and rectifying damage by insured risks

1.5.1 Insurance premiums and valuation fees

Leases of parts of buildings almost always contain a covenant by the landlord to insure the building and the landlord's plant, machinery, service media, etc against fire, storm, impact, and various other perils. Third party or public liability is also usually included in the matters to be insured. It is becoming increasingly common for insurers to be asked to provide insurance cover for certain types of environmental liabilities, such as accidental pollution and clean-up costs in the case of industrial buildings, and for terrorism cover.

Whether the cost of insuring against all these risks can be recharged to the tenants depends, as in the case of other service costs, on the wording of the lease; many leases give the landlord the right to select the insured risks at his discretion – whether this is subject to an implied limitation that he must act reasonably, and not extravagantly, and whether a landlord is obliged to 'shop around' for competitive insurance rates, is discussed at **1.10**.

Leases generally provide for the tenant to pay towards the landlord's insurance by way of 'additional rent', separately from the service charge, but occasionally the cost of insurance will, instead, be included within the scope of the service charge. The same principles should determine the ability to charge for the insurance, whichever of these formulae is adopted.

Some leases expressly allow the landlord to include, in the service charge, the cost of obtaining, usually at unspecified intervals, professional valuations for insurance purposes. Even in the absence of such a provision, it is strongly arguable that the cost of an insurance valuation can be charged where the landlord is entitled to charge the *cost* of insuring, rather than just the insurance *premiums*; the insurance valuation fee can be said to be a cost incurred in arranging the insurance (see the 'cost' argument, discussed at **1.6.2**).

It seems to be generally accepted that a landlord who arranges insurance through his own agency with the insurers may keep the commission paid by those insurers (see *Castlebeg Investments (Jersey) Ltd v Lynch* (1989) 57 P&CR 493; *63 Perham Road Ltd v Mayfield* (1995) 2 EGLR 206), but, arguably, he must give the tenants the benefit of any discount he receives.

As to the ability of tenants to challenge the landlord's choice of insurer, see **1.10.2**.

1.5.2 Duty to apply insurance monies

The landlord's insuring covenant will normally provide for the landlord either:

(a) to make good any damage caused by insurance risks; or

(b) to apply insurance monies in making good such damage.

The former provision would oblige the landlord to commence the repairs without waiting for the insurance monies to be paid to him by the insurers. As such, many landlords prefer the latter type of provision, which implies an obligation to pursue the insurance claim against the insurers with reasonable speed if it is not expressly set out in the lease.

Example

> *Vural v Security Archives Ltd* (1990) 60 P&CR 258, ChD: The landlord covenanted to insure the building and to lay out insurance money, once received, in reinstating the premises, but the covenant did not expressly require him to submit or pursue a claim under the insurance. Was it implied that, if damage occurred, the landlord would make and prosecute his claim under the policy with all reasonable speed? **Held**: Yes.

This may apply even where the lease requires the tenant to insure the property but in practice the landlord insures and the tenant contributes to the premiums (*Adami v Lincoln Grange Management Company* (1998) 17 EG 148, CA).

1.5.3   Cost of rectifying damage by insured risks

Although few service charge clauses specifically deal with the point, it is probably to be inferred that service costs referable to remedying damage by risks covered by the landlord's insurance policies are to be first met out of the insurance monies, with only any unrecovered shortfall being charged within the service charge. Most service charge clauses are designed to afford the landlord reimbursement of actual cost and, plainly, the cost to the landlord of carrying out the work will be just the shortfall, if any, between the actual cost of the remedial work and the amount received under the insurance policy. However, there may be an issue over meeting the shortfall, discussed at **1.5.4**.

1.5.4   Shortfalls from excesses and exclusions

Many leases require the landlord to insure for the full rebuilding cost of the property. However, even if there is no under-insurance, a shortfall might arise where the terms of the insurance policy provide, as they commonly do, for excesses or exclusions. These may be imposed in respect of risks which have materialised more frequently than originally envisaged by insurers (eg subsidence), or in relation to new perils (such as terrorist action), or threatened liabilities (such as third party liability for the effects of gradual pollution, which has commonly been excluded from policies since mid-1990).

If his insuring covenant obliges the landlord to insure for the *full reinstatement cost* (plus professional fees etc) and does not expressly allow for excesses and exclusions to be contained in the insurance policy, the landlord may arguably be in breach of his covenant if the policy does not effectively cover the full amount because of an excess or exclusion. In such a case, it might be possible for the tenants to recover the amount of the shortfall from the landlord as damages for his breach of covenant although the landlord may seek to set off the increase in premiums that would have been payable insurers had agreed to remove the excess. It was established in *Enlayde Ltd v Roberts* [1917] 1 Ch 109 (summarised below) that an inability to obtain insurance cover for certain perils free of exclusions does not exonerate a landlord who gives an unqualified covenant to insure against those perils, and a similar result obtained in a mortgage case in 1940 on the same point (*Moorgate Estates Ltd v Trower* [1940] 1 All ER 195, ChD).

Example

Enlayde Ltd v Roberts [1917] 1 Ch 109: The landlord covenanted to insure a building against fire. It transpired that damage by enemy action, which caused a fire, was excluded from the policy. Was the landlord in breach of his insuring covenant, even though insurance without that exclusion was unavailable? **Held**: Yes.

However, it is not clear whether those decisions still stand. Since almost every insurance policy is subject to some exclusion or excess it could be argued that it should be an implied term of the lease that the insurance can be subject to normal or usual provisions of that type. This problem is particularly relevant where insurers are refusing to grant or are imposing limits on cover for certain risks, eg subsidence, acts of terrorism, etc.

1.6 Managing agents' and other professional fees

1.6.1 Management fees

Whether managing agents' fees can be included in a service charge depends on the wording of the service charge clause. It seems that the courts will be reluctant to interpret the lease as entitling the landlord to recoup such fees, unless the wording of the service charge clause clearly provide for this. (See also **1.2.2**.)

A possible exception to this restrictive approach may be where, under the terms of the lease, the services are being provided by a company controlled by the tenants who cannot be expected to have the time or expertise to manage the property themselves; the company may be held, impliedly, to have power to appoint managing agents to administer its functions. However, this depends upon the individual wording used and the circumstances at the date of the lease.

Examples

Embassy Court Residents' Association Ltd v Lipman (1984) 271 EG 545, CA: The landlord's covenants did not mention employing managing agents, but the landlord was a company limited by guarantee of which the tenant and the other flat-owners were members, and it appointed managing agents when the flat-owners, who had been running it, got fed up. Was the tenant liable to pay towards the managing agents' proper fees? **Held**: On the facts, yes; but (per Cumming-Bruce LJ) 'If an individual [ie as distinct from a residents' company] 'wants to [employ managing agents] and to recover the costs from the lessee, he must include explicit provisions in his lease.'

Lloyds Bank plc v Bowker Orford [1992] 31 EG 67, ChD: The service charge schedule in the lease did not expressly provide for the service charge to include managing agents' fees, but it did contain a declaration that the tenant could not object to 'the employment of managing agents to carry out and provide on the lessors' behalf services under this Part of this Schedule'. Did this imply that managing agents' fees for general management could be included in the service charges? **Held**: No; it simply meant that the tenant could not refuse to pay for a service merely because it had been decided by the agents and not by the landlord. (However, see **1.6.2**.)

A clearer provision enabling managing agents' fees to be included in the service charge would be the express inclusion of managing agents' fees in any list of chargeable items in the service charge clause, or (where the service charge clause is expressed to cover the cost to the landlord of performing his covenants) the express inclusion of a landlord's covenant to employ managing agents.

Where a management fee *is* chargeable, it is likely to be interpreted (in the absence of express wording to the contrary) as meaning an appropriate fee for managing the building and administering the services, but *not* for collecting the rent on behalf of the landlord. However, this does not necessarily mean that the management fee cannot be calculated by reference to the rent, provided that it is a proper fee for administering the chargeable services and not for rent collection; however, it is unlikely to be best practice to charge this way. A fee comparable with that which other agents might properly charge for management, excluding rent collection, will often be a guide to what is reasonable.

Example

Parkside Knightsbridge Ltd v Horwitz (1983) 268 EG 49, CA: Expenditure incurred by the landlord in respect of management was chargeable. The landlord company engaged its parent company to manage the block, and by 'normal accounting processes' (ie book entries) paid the parent company a management fee based on a rough, notional allocation of its overheads. The fee was low by comparison with quotations received from four well-known firms of surveyors and managing agents. Those quotations were for the management work excluding rent collection; one firm quoted 5 per cent of the gross rents, the second 4 per cent of the gross rents, the third 15 per cent of the service costs and the fourth 14 per cent of the service costs. Could the fee be included in the service charge? **Held**: Yes; (1) it was a reasonable charge, since the quotations indicated the market cost of management; (2) it had been expended – the parent company was a separate legal entity from its subsidiary the landlord company, and the book entries counted as payment.

Some leases specify the amount of management fee that can be charged, for example as a percentage of total service costs. In one case, the lease referred to the RICS scale; this was abolished during the term of the lease, and the court held that a reasonable fee could be charged instead (*Thames Side Properties Ltd v Brixton Estate plc* [1997] NPC 5, ChD).

In some cases, it may be implied that professional fees are only to be included in the service charge if they are 'reasonably' or 'properly' incurred (see **1.10.3**).

1.6.2 Professional fees relating to particular chargeable items

Irrespective of whether or not general management fees are recoverable through the service charge, it may be possible for a landlord to recoup fees paid to agents or other professionals (eg building surveyors) for arranging and supervising *particular* works or services, which themselves fall within the service charge. This, however, would not entitle the landlord to recoup fees paid to the agents for *general* management of the building, unless management was mentioned as a chargeable service in its own right.

The justification for including in the service charge the professional fees for arranging particular works is that where (as is usually the case) the service charge is expressed to cover the 'cost' or 'expense' of a specified item, it can be argued that the 'cost' or 'expense' includes the cost of engaging a professional person for specifically arranging and supervising the provision of that item.

Examples

Concorde Graphics Ltd v Andromeda Investments SA (1983) 265 EG 386, ChD: Vinelott J said: 'while the costs, charges and expenses recoverable under clause 2(3) clearly do not extend to the whole fee paid to managing agents for managing the estate and collecting rents, a fee may be justifiable in so far as the managing agents are called on to arrange and supervise works and services the costs of which do fall within clause 2(3)'.

Lloyds Bank plc v Bowker Orford [1992] 31 EG 67, ChD: The service charge covered the 'total cost to the lessors ... of providing the services'. Did this entitle the landlord to include in the service charges the managing agent's fees for organising and supervising the provision of those particular services? **Held**: Yes.

For fees to be chargeable in this way, they must relate properly to services or works which are themselves chargeable within the service charge. If the fees relate to investigation into problems which prima facie are likely to be chargeable, those fees can be charged up to the moment, if any, when the investigating professional proposes a remedy which will fall outside the chargeable categories; thereafter the fees may not be chargeable within the service charges. The lesson here is that such consultants should be instructed in stages, with their advice being considered at each stage, having regard to the scope of the service charge.

Examples

Holding & Management Ltd v Property Holding & Investment Trust plc [1989] 1 WLR 1313, CA: Consulting engineers were engaged to investigate defects in the external walls of the building. The engineers prepared a report recommending a scheme of rebuilding which was so extensive that it went beyond the meaning of 'repair' and fell outside the scope of the services for which the plaintiffs, as maintenance trustees, were responsible. Nevertheless, the engineers assisted the maintenance trustees in promoting that scheme, but it was eventually withdrawn in favour of more modest remedial work. How much of the engineers' fees could be included in the service charge? **Held**: Only the fees for work done up to the time they made their report.

Plough Investments Ltd v Manchester City Council [1989] 1 EGLR 244, ChD: The landlord covenanted to repair and maintain the external walls and main timbers of the building, and the service charge covered the costs so incurred. Some cladding came away from a part of the steel frame which had rusted. Consulting engineers engaged by the landlord carried out a structural survey of not only that part but also the entirety of the building and proposed that all the cladding be removed and the whole frame shot-blasted and encased in concrete to stop future rusting. Since 'repair' means dealing with parts which have actually deteriorated, but not parts which are presently unaffected, this proposal was rejected by the court in favour of remedying only the parts which had deteriorated. How much of the engineers' fees could be included in the service charge? **Held**: Not the engineers' fees for reporting on the entire steel frame, but only fees in connection with work which was properly a repair, ie relating to the parts which had actually rusted. (Note: more recently it has been decided that a covenant to 'keep in repair' requires work to be done when necessary to prevent imminent disrepair occurring, see **1.4.2** and **1.4.11**.)

1.6.3 Costs of environmental assessments

The landlord might consider arranging an environmental assessment of the building. The Building Research Establishment (BRE) has devised a series of systems for assessing the environmental merits of different types of building. Distinct systems apply to new office buildings, existing office buildings, new homes and superstores and supermarkets. Research is currently under way which will lead to a fifth system, for industrial buildings. Buildings or developments are offered a number of credits for a given list of features, which are normally assessed by a BRE-appointed independent assessor. The systems tackle matters such as CO_2 emissions, noise, lighting, water economy and ventilation.

BREEAM 4/93, the scheme relating to existing office buildings, is particularly relevant. The assessment is in two parts. The first relates to the building fabric and services and the second to operation and management. Opportunities for participating in the scheme might arise when refurbishment is being contemplated or, more generally, as part of a management initiative to improve environmental conditions. Charges for BREEAM 4/93 typically range from between £4,000 and £5,000.

The landlord might have difficulty in recovering the cost of environmental assessment through the service charge unless the sweeping-up or management provisions are sufficiently widely drawn, since, in many cases, there may not be, prior to the exercise, any indication that the fabric or services of the building are out of repair (see **1.4.2**), fail to comply with statutory requirements, or are otherwise in a condition requiring something to be done which would fall within the scope of the service charge. Just as many modern service charge clauses allow for periodic insurance valuations and surveys to be carried out at the tenants' expense through the service charge, an express provision entitling the landlord to carry out, and charge for, environmental assessments would now seem appropriate.

1.6.4 Costs of collecting arrears of service charge

When the landlord sues a tenant for arrears of service charge and obtains judgment successfully, the landlord will usually be awarded costs, but not necessarily on a full indemnity basis (see **1.20**). Often the costs recovered from the defaulting tenant will be less than the actual legal and other costs, and the question arises whether the shortfall and other unrecovered costs (eg where a tenant is insolvent), can be recouped by the landlord from the tenant generally, through the service charge.

In the absence of specific wording, a right expressed in the lease in general terms for the landlord to charge legal or other professional fees within the service charge will, generally, be construed as limited to those fees incurred in connection with management. This might cover the cost of enforcing, on defaulting tenants, those lease covenants which benefit the tenants generally. However, this would not, without express provision, cover the cost of suing or forfeiting for arrears of service charges.

Examples

Sella House Ltd v Mears [1989] 1 EGLR 65, CA: The service charge covered the fees of managing agents and 'other professional persons as may be necessary or desirable ...'. Could the service charge include legal costs incurred by the landlord in seeking to recover arrears of service charges from tenants? **Held**: No.

Iperion Investments Corporation v Broadwalk House Residents Ltd [1995] 2 EGLR 47, CA: The tenant of a flat embarked on unauthorised structural alterations. The landlord obtained an injunction and also, but unsuccessfully, sought forfeiture of the tenant's lease. Could the costs of the landlord's proceedings be included in the service charges under the head of the 'costs properly incurred by the landlord ... in the proper and reasonable management' of the block? **Held**: Yes; both the injunction and forfeiture applications were incurred in 'managing' the property.

Morgan v Stainer [1993] EGCS 162, ChD: A group of tenants sued the landlord for breaches of covenant and the case was settled, the tenants agreeing to pay certain maintenance charges and the landlord agreeing to pay the tenants' taxed legal costs which exceeded £80,000. The tenants' leases expressly required the tenants to pay towards the landlord's costs in obtaining the maintenance contributions from any tenant in the building. Could the landlord, under this clause, recover back from the tenants the costs he had paid them? **Held**: No; the costs had not been incurred for the purpose of recovering the maintenance charges but in resisting the tenants' proceedings; the agreement by the landlord to pay the costs included an implied agreement not to seek to recover them through the back door. By implication, the costs mentioned in the lease were limited to those reasonably and properly incurred, which these were not; the lease clause was not intended to apply to the type of costs involved here.

It is possible (but not certain) that the *Sella House* decision might have been different if the landlord had been a tenants' management company with no other source of funds, see **1.2.2**.

1.6.5   Costs of court applications for declarations

In some cases, particularly where the wording of the lease is unclear or the proposed works are non-routine, it may be sensible for the landlord to apply to the court for a declaration as to whether proposed works can properly be carried out and be charged within the service charge. In such a case, it may be that the costs of the court application can be included in the service charge if the service charge clause entitles the landlord to charge for the costs of management or to charge for costs which he reasonably incurred in the discharge of his obligations.

Example

Reston Ltd v Hudson [1990] 2 EGLR 51: The landlord made an originating application to the court for a declaration as to whether certain proposed works could properly be carried out and be charged within the service charges under the leases, which were imprecisely drafted. Could the costs of the court application be included in the service charges under provisions in the leases permitting the charging of 'the costs of management' and 'all outgoings, costs and expenses whatsoever, which the lessor may reasonably incur in the discharge of its obligations'? **Held**: Yes. (Note: the tenants did not appear before the court and the point was decided without argument.)

1.7   In-house management charges

1.7.1   Basic rule

Many substantial landlords have their own, in-house, property management departments. Just as in the case of separate managing agents, the court is unlikely to interpret the service charge clauses (in the absence of a clear provision) as entitling the landlord to include a fee for in-house management, particularly where the landlord does not employ persons especially to carry out that function for the particular property. Most service charge clauses will be interpreted as being intended to give the landlord reimbursement of sums actually expended, and the landlords' in-house overheads will not normally be covered by general wording.

Example

Cleve House Properties v Schildof (1980) CLY 1641, Deputy Judge Gray, Bloomsbury and Marylebone County Court: The landlord was a company which did not employ managing agents but carried out management in-house by its directors, and sought to charge a management fee calculated at 15 per cent of the service costs. The service charge, under the then current housing legislation, covered any 'liability incurred or amount defrayed' in respect of the services. Was the management fee chargeable? **Held**: No; the service charge was limited to sums paid out or liable to be paid out by the landlord, and this did not include overheads such as the directors' remuneration.

1.7.2   Circumventing the difficulty

Where a lease plainly allows the landlord to charge outside managing agent's fees in the service charge, but does not mention in-house management charges, and the landlord would prefer to carry out the management in-house, it seems that the landlord may be able to circumvent this problem by setting up a separate, subsidiary company, appointing it as the managing agent, and paying that company a proper fee for carrying out the management. It appears that fees can then be included in the service charge.

Example

Parkside Knightsbridge Ltd v Horwitz (1983) 268 EG 49, CA: Expenditure incurred by the landlord in respect of management was chargeable. The landlord company engaged its parent company to manage the block and, by book entires, paid the parent company a reasonable management fee. Could the fee be included in the service charge? **Held**: Yes; the parent company was a separate legal entity from its subsidiary, the landlord company, and the book entries counted as payment.

In *Parkside*, the Court of Appeal applied the time-honoured, company law rule that a subsidiary company is a separate legal entity from its holding company, so that the parent was treated as a separate agent. The application of that rule in the context of service charges is, however, perhaps surprising, since the courts have been known to 'lift the veil' or 'pierce the veil' of corporate identity in some other property cases (eg *DHN Food Distributors Ltd v London Borough of Tower Hamlets* [1976] 1 WLR 852; *Hillbank Properties Ltd v Hackney London Borough Council* (1978) 37 P&CR 218), although the non-piercing principle has been followed by the London Rent Assessment Committee in *Eaton Square Properties v Ogilvie* (2000) 16 EG 143 (see **2.7.1.2**).

1.8   Caretakers and their accommodation

1.8.1   Provision of caretaker or porter

An obligation on the landlord to provide the tenants with the services of a porter or caretaker may be set out expressly in the lease, or the lease may give the landlord the discretion to provide such services, if he thinks fit.

Examples

Hupfield v Bourne (1974) 28 P&CR 77: The landlord of a block of luxury flats covenanted to 'employ such persons as shall be reasonably necessary for the due performance of [his] covenants . . . and for the proper management of the block'. He provided a resident caretaker at the time the lease was granted. Was he obliged to continue to provide a resident caretaker? **Held**: Yes; it was 'reasonably necessary' within the covenant mentioned.

Russell v Laimond Properties Ltd (1984) 269 EG 947, QBD: Resident porters were employed by the landlord of a block of flats for several years, including when the leases were granted. The landlord covenanted 'to provide . . . the services of such maintenance staff as [he] shall consider necessary for the performance of the matters specified . . .'. The possible service charge costs were separately listed in a schedule and included the cost of porterage and of providing, maintaining and repairing a flat for staff. Was the landlord obliged to provide a resident porter? **Held**: No; the necessary maintenance tasks could be performed by outside contractors.

(See also **1.3.2**.)

Where the lease contains an express covenant by the landlord to provide a resident porter, that obligation will not be fulfilled by the provision of non-resident staff, even if they perform similar specific tasks.

Example

Posner v Scott-Lewis [1986] 3 WLR 531: The landlord covenanted to provide a resident porter. The porter went to live elsewhere but remained employed by the landlord on terms that he would return daily to perform his duties. Was that sufficient compliance with the landlord's obligation? **Held**: No; the presence of a resident porter gave the tenants a feeling of enhanced security; a mandatory injunction was granted ordering the resumption of resident porterage.

1.8.2 Charging caretakers' employment costs

Even if there is no implied or express obligation on, or power for, the landlord to employ a caretaker, a right to charge the whole or part of the cost of employing one might be implied to the extent that the caretaker attends to the particular services which are expressly chargeable on the basis that the 'cost' of providing the services includes the cost of engaging someone to perform them.

Example

Concorde Graphics Ltd v Andromeda Investments SA (1983) 265 EG 386, ChD: Vinelott J said: 'while the costs, charges and expenses recoverable under clause 2(3) clearly do not extend to the whole fee paid to managing agents for managing the estate and collecting rents, a fee may be justifiable in so far as the managing agents are called on to arrange and supervise works and services the costs of which do fall within clause 2(3). Similarly, part of the expense of providing a full-time caretaker may be attributable to work done by the caretaker in attending to matters within clause 2(3)'.

1.8.3 Charging the cost of staff accommodation

Many leases which require or permit the landlord to engage porters or caretakers also contain express provisions enabling the landlord to charge, within the service charge, a rent for any accommodation he might provide for the porter or caretaker (eg a caretaker's flat), in addition to the actual paid outgoings of that accommodation.

Even where the service charge clause does not expressly entitle the landlord to charge such rent, a right for the landlord to do so may be inferred if the lease contains a landlord's covenant to provide a resident or non-resident porter or caretaker and the service charge is expressed to cover all the costs and expenses of the landlord in performing his covenants. However, this is less likely to apply where the service charge clause expressly mentions certain costs relating to staff accommodation but does not mention the rental cost of providing it.

Where the landlord provides accommodation for a porter or caretaker within the property or in another building owned by the landlord, the landlord may be able to include a *notional* rent in the service charge. This is especially so where the lease allows the porter to reside away from the building; it can be reasoned that if the landlord had to arrange accommodation for the employee in a building not owned by the landlord, the landlord would have to pay rent for it and, thus, rent would be an expected cost of the service. Even where the porter is required, under the landlord's covenants, to reside in the same building, notional rent may still be treated as a 'cost', albeit in the sense of rental income forgone as opposed to money spent.

Examples

Agavil Investments Ltd v Corner (1975) 13 October (unreported): The landlord covenanted to provide a resident caretaker, who was to be housed in the block or elsewhere. The service charge covered the 'costs and expenses' of providing this and other services. The caretaker lived in a flat in the block. Could the landlord include, in the service charge, a sum equal to the rent he would otherwise have obtained for that flat? **Held**: Yes.

Lloyds Bank plc v Bowker Orford [1992] 31 EG 67, ChD: The landlord covenanted to use best endeavours to provide the listed services, which included the employment and housing of a resident caretaker. The service charge covered 'the total cost to the landlord ... of providing the services ... and defraying the costs and expenses relating and incidental to such services'. The caretaker lived in a flat in the block. Could the landlord include, in the service charge, a sum equal to the rent he would otherwise have obtained for that flat? **Held**: Yes.

Gilje and Others v Chalgrove Securities Ltd [2001] EWCA Civ 1777 (unreported), CA: The leases of flats in a block which included a caretaker's flat provided for the service charge to cover 'monies expended by the lessor in ... providing the services and management and administration called for under clause 5 ...'. The lessor's obligations under that clause included providing a resident caretaker. The list of service charge items included the cost of gas, electricity and rates of the caretaker's flat. Could the landlord include a notional rent for the flat in the service charge, either directly or by notionally paying the caretaker a higher salary to include rent? **Held**: No; so far as the clause was unclear, it was to be interpreted against the landlord. Whilst listing certain items of cost, such as gas, did not exclude all other items (contrary to Neuberger J in *Bowker Orford* – see **1.3.3** etc), the phrase 'monies expended' meant monies actually paid out and a reasonable prospective tenant reading the lease would not have expected the service charge to include notional rent. This was different from the position in *Agavil* (above).

An alternative basis to market rent forgone, for assessing the 'cost' of providing such accommodation, according to the deputy judge in *Russell v Laimond Properties Ltd* (1984) 269 EG 947 (see **1.8.1**), might be a fair return for the landlord on the capital cost or value of the accommodation, but this has not been followed in the other decisions.

Where a notional rent is charged, it seems appropriate for the rent to be assessed as if the tenants were renting the flat for 'the business of providing the services to the block/estate' and thus the same basis should be used as if there was a tenancy under the Landlord and Tenant Act 1954 with rent valued in accordance with s 34 of that Act.

1.9   Varying the services

1.9.1   Basic principles

As has been seen, the lease or tenancy agreement constitutes a contract between the landlord and the tenant. Like most other contracts, it cannot be varied (subject to exceptions mentioned in **1.9.2** and **1.9.3**) otherwise than by agreement between the parties. In the absence of specific provisions in the lease allowing changes in the services, the landlord is not entitled to change or discontinue any services which the terms of the lease expressly oblige him to provide. However, landlords frequently desire to depart from the strict requirements of leases, often for perfectly valid reasons. A lease might, for example, oblige the landlord to provide hot water through an existing system; if that is an oil-fired system, a change to gas boilers would be a sensible departure.

Naturally, there is no reason why the landlord should not seek the consent of each tenant in a building to the discontinuance or substitution of a particular service. Any agreement with tenants should make it clear whether the variation is intended to endure for any substantial period (whether or not it is the full residue of the term of the lease) and should, ideally, be set out in a formal deed executed by the landlord and the tenant and expressed to bind their successors (with any mortgage of the tenant joining to give his consent). In this way, there will be an effective variation of the lease, which will continue to apply even if the present tenant assigns the lease. However, if this is impracticable, a variation by agreement in correspondence will usually suffice in the short term, although it must be remembered that it will not bind the tenant's mortgagees nor, in some cases, an assignee.

The landlord must bear in mind, however, that if he discontinues or substitutes a service notwithstanding that one or more tenants withhold their agreement, he may be in breach of covenant towards those tenants, who could seek damages or, in appropriate cases, obtain a mandatory injunction ordering the landlord to restore the service (see *Posner v Scott-Lewis* [1987] Ch 25 at **1.8.1**).

If a former tenant or guarantor has continuing liability for the tenant's obligations (see **1.20.8**), the amount of those liabilities cannot be increased as a result of a lease variation made on or after 1 January 1996 by the landlord and the present tenant (Landlord and Tenant (Covenants) Act 1995, s 18). Furthermore, major lease variations made without the consent of a guarantor may under common law rules have the effect of wholly releasing the guarantor from all his liabilities in respect of the lease, although minor variations will not release him (see *Metropolitan Properties Company v Bartholomew* [1995] NPC 172).

1.9.2   Variation clauses

Some leases contain provisions entitling the landlord to vary the services or to discontinue services which he considers obsolete, sometimes entirely at his discretion or after balloting the tenants, and in such cases a landlord who wishes to vary the services should follow the procedure laid down by the lease. However, it appears that such provisions, unless worded very carefully to give the landlord wide discretion, may be narrowly interpreted so as to limit the landlord to keep within the types of services which are specifically mentioned in the lease (see **1.3.3**). Where such powers are contained in non-negotiable standard clauses in leases to consumers, see **1.10.6**.

1.9.3   Varying the lease

Variation by agreement is discussed at **1.9.1**. Where the lease of a residential flat fails to contain satisfactory provisions as to (amongst other things) services and service charges, an application might be made to the court to order the lease to be varied. This procedure is governed by Part IV of the Landlord and Tenant Act 1987, discussed at **2.15**. It does not apply to business premises or, except as to insurance provisions, to houses.

1.10   Express or implied tests of reasonableness

1.10.1   Express terms as to reasonableness

In those cases where the lease sets out a reasonableness test which qualifies the service charge, the fact that a particular type of expenditure falls within the wording of the service charge clause will not result in the sum spent on that item being chargeable to the tenant, if the tenant can successfully challenge that expenditure on the ground that it was not reasonably incurred.

Some leases make express provision for service costs to be limited to those which the landlord 'reasonably' incurs; others simply refer to the 'reasonable cost' of providing the listed services. In some instances, there might be a difference in meaning between these. Incurring costs 'reasonably' may mean that both the decision to do the work and the actual cost of it must be reasonable, whilst 'reasonable cost' may mean merely that the amount of the cost must be reasonable for the work done but that the decision to do the work did not have to be taken reasonably.

Some leases contain an obligation on the landlord to minimise the costs so far as possible, for example:

> 'the landlord will use its reasonable endeavours to maintain the service charges reserved hereunder at the lowest figure reasonably consistent with the due performance of its obligations hereunder'.

Such provisions are sometimes found coupled with a provision excluding the tenant from objecting to the cost of individual items, such as:

'provided that the Tenant shall not be entitled to object to any item comprised in the service costs by reason only that the materials, works or services in question might have been obtained or performed at a lower cost'.

However, this may appear to contradict earlier references to reasonableness or a covenant to keep the charges to the minimum, and will need cautious interpretation.

1.10.2 Effect of reasonableness tests

Where there is a test of reasonableness, this might be applied in different ways, but one principle followed in a number of cases is that the test requires a consideration whether the tenant, having regard to the duration of his lease, ought fairly to contribute to the costs of the particular work or service.

Examples

Postel Properties Ltd v Boots The Chemist (1996) 41 EG 164, QB: The lease reserved as a service charge a proportion of 'the expenses and outgoings reasonably and properly incurred' by the landlord on certain works and services, including keeping the roofs in good and substantial repair, and the landlord convenanted to carry out the work 'economically and efficiently'. The tenants disputed various costs including the cost of replacing, to an improved specification, flat roofs which were constantly leaking and had a short life expectancy. **Held**: The majority of the cost was chargeable. 'Sensible work of repair to preserve the fabric in a realistic way is entirely consistent with the duty to perform the landlord's obligations efficiently and economically.' It was 'reasonable' for the landlord to select a more durable grade of top sheeting than a basic standard and at a modest increase in cost. However, priming large areas of steel while they were accessible was a separate piece of work which was unnecessary and the cost not chargeable.

Scottish Mutual Insurance Company v Jardine (1999) EGCS 43, QBD, Tech & Constr Ct: The landlord carried out long-term expensive repairs to the roof of a block, ostensibly in performing its repairing obligations towards an existing tenant whose lease had only a few months left before it expired. In reality, the work was done to assist the landlord in letting a vacant part of the building. Was the short-term tenant liable to pay a full contribution towards the cost under his obligation to pay 'a fair proportion' of repair costs 'reasonably and properly incurred'? **Held**: No; these repairs had not been carried out in pursuance of the landlord's repairing covenant in his lease, under which lesser works would have been reasonable and proper having regard to the short unexpired term. A reduced contribution was payable.

Fluor Daniel Properties Ltd v Shortlands Investment Ltd [2001] EGCS 8, ChD: The landlord of an office building covenanted to 'maintain repair amend renew ... the air conditioning system' and to provide conditioned air at a reasonable temperature. The service charge covered the cost of performing those covenants and also had a sweeper clause covering 'the reasonable cost of carrying out other work or services of any kind whatsoever which the landlords may reasonably consider desirable for the purpose of maintaining or improving services in the Building'. The landlord also covenanted to use its best endeavours to maintain the service charge at the lowest reasonable figure, subject to no objection being made solely on the ground that a service could have been provided at lower cost. The landlord decided to replace all the air conditioning plant at the end of its normally expected lifespan, even though most of it was still working satisfactorily and rarely broke down. The tenant refused to pay towards the cost. **Held**: To replace plant which was working satisfactorily went beyond the covenant to 'maintain repair amend renew ...' all of which presupposed some malfunctioning which would prevent the provision of a reasonably acceptable service; for the same reason, it was also outside the scope of the covenant to provide conditioned air. As for the sweeper clause, it was not 'reasonable' to do these works since they were not reasonably required in order to maintain the service (it might have been different if the service, even if supplied to the standard applicable at the date of the lease, had ceased to conform to the reasonable current requirements of the tenants of the building). The express test of reasonableness in the sweeper clause limited the work and services to the standard such as the tenants, given the lengths of their leases, could fairly be expected to pay for – the landlord could not reasonably overlook the relatively limited interest of the paying tenants.

The question here is not whether a reasonable landlord would have decided to carry out the particular work, but rather whether the individual tenant ought reasonably to be required to pay towards its cost. In both the *Scottish Mutual* and *Fluor Daniel* cases noted above, the relative shortness of the individual tenant's lease compared with the landlord's long-term interest was a factor taken into account in deciding that the landlord's scheme of works was excessive and fell outside the recoverable service charge. The *Fluor Daniel* decision took this approach from the Court of Appeal judgment in *Holding & Management Ltd v Property Holding & Investment Trust plc* [1989] 1 WLR 1313 (noted at **1.10.3**). The issue was considered from the tenant's viewpoint even though the leases referred to costs reasonably incurred by the landlord and works which the landlord reasonably considered desirable. The reasonableness of the landlords' conduct was assessed by how far the landlords had considered the question as to what works should the particular tenants fairly be expected to pay towards.

One possible consequence of directing attention to the individual tenant's position appears to be that, even if the service charge clauses are in fact identical in all the leases in a building, particular works might fall outside the service charge under one tenant's lease but might fall within another's, simply because the leases have different unexpired terms. This would be consistent with the general rule that every lease is interpreted individually, but would undoubtedly create management problems for landlords. It remains to be seen whether the position would be different if the lease stated (as some leases do) that all the leases in the building were in the same form and that it was intended that every tenant would be liable to pay his due proportion of the service costs in order to give the landlord full recovery.

If the service charge clause does not expressly impose a reasonableness qualification, will such a qualification be implied by the courts? This question is discussed at **1.10.3**.

1.10.3 Is there an implied test of reasonableness?

Where the lease does not expressly place a limitation of reasonableness on the service charges or service expenditure, the implication has been drawn by the Court of Appeal, in respect of *residential* leases, that the terms of the lease will not have been intended to give the landlord an unfettered right to be extravagant at the cost of the tenant and that it is to be implied that the landlord can only include, in the service charge, those costs which are fair and reasonable. This may be implied either in relation to the entire service charge or in respect of individual elements or heads of charge.

Examples

Finchbourne v Rodrigues [1976] 3 All ER 581, CA: The service charge was expressed to cover the costs incurred by the landlord in performing his services. The tenants challenged certain items on the grounds that the landlord had spent more than was reasonable. **Held**: There must be an implied term that the service costs claimed were to be fair and reasonable, since it cannot have been intended to give the landlord unfettered discretion to be extravagant or adopt the highest conceivable standard at the tenants' cost.

Holding & Management Ltd v Property Holding & Investment Trust plc [1989] 1 WLR 1313, CA: Parts of the external walls of a block of flats needed repair. The maintenance trustees intended to carry out a major scheme of rebuilding recommended by their engineers. The tenants proposed a much less expensive scheme of repair recommended by their engineers. The leases provided for the service charge fund to be used for the 'repair' of external walls but also contained a sweeper clause that covered 'such other repairs and such improvement works and additions ... as the Maintenance Trustee shall consider necessary to maintain the Building as a block of first class residential flats or otherwise desirable in the general interests of the tenants'. It also included 'all legal costs incurred ... in the enforcement of the covenants ... contained in the leases'. Could the major scheme be charged under the repair clause or the sweeper clause and could the trustees include in the service charge the legal costs of these proceedings even if they lost? **Held**: (1) The major scheme fell outside the repair clause. 'A prudent building owner bearing the costs himself might well have decided to adopt such a scheme, despite its expense. But what is in question is whether owners of 75-year leases in the building could fairly be expected to pay for such a scheme under an obligation to "repair" '. (2) The sweeper clause was not intended to overlap the 'repair' clause and did not include work to the external walls; but in any event the sweeper clause did not give the trustees a free hand to require the residents to pay for all works, whatever they might be, which the trustees might consider necessary: 'It is necessarily implicit in this paragraph that the [trustees] will act reasonably'. (3) The costs clause, read fairly, embraced only those legal costs which were *reasonably* or *properly* incurred, and the costs of pursuing an excessive scheme were not reasonably or properly incurred and so were not chargeable.

This gives rise to two questions: (1) is this reasonableness test to be implied invariably into every service charge clause; and (2) does it apply equally to business leases as to residential leases?

As to the first question, it was said in *Firstcross Ltd v Teasdale* (1983) 265 EG 305 that the imposition of the reasonableness test amounted to a rule of law applicable to *every* lease reserving a variable service charge. However, the House of Lords has, in the past, rejected the creation, by the courts, of rigid rules of law for implying terms into formal documents (see *Suisse Atlantique Société d'Armement Maritime SA v NV Rotterdamsche Kohlen Centrale* [1966] 2 All ER 61) and has also rejected the suggestion that the court has power to introduce terms into leases merely because they think them reasonable (see *Liverpool City Council v Irwin* [1977] AC 239). The preferred view is the approach taken by the judge in *Wigglesworth v Property Holdings & Investment Trust Ltd* (1984) 270 EG 555, to the effect that *Finchbourne v Rodrigues* creates only a *rebuttable* presumption of a reasonableness test to be used when interpreting the wording of a lease, and that this presumption could be displaced if the implication of a reasonableness test would be inconsistent with the context. This view is supported by the decision in *Havenridge v Boston Dyers Ltd* [1994] 2 EGLR 73, CA, in which it was held that an express provision in a lease that the landlord could charge for 'properly' expended insurance premiums left no room for the court to infer any other qualifying words such as 'reasonably'. The sole test under that lease was whether the landlord acted 'properly', ie in the normal course of business, when arranging the insurance. This line of reasoning has recently been followed in another Court of Appeal decision and is now well established.

Example

Berrycroft Management Co Ltd v Sinclair Gardens Investments (Kensington) Ltd [1997] 1 EGLR 47, CA: Leases of flats in a block allowed the landlord to nominate 'insurers of repute' to be used by the management company for insuring the block. The freehold changed hands and the new landlord nominated new insurers whose premiums were higher than the current insurers. Should further limitations on the landlord's choice of insurer be implied? **Held**: No; the limit on the landlord's discretion had been specified in the leases as 'insurers of repute' and no further limitation should be inferred. Provided that the new insurance was arranged in the normal course with reputable insurers, it could not be challenged. (The tenant's challenge under the legislation applicable to residential leases gave the same result – see **2.3.3**.)

The second question is whether the implied reasonableness test, rebuttable or not, also applies to commercial leases. In 1968, the court in *Bandar Property Holdings Ltd v JS Darwen (Successors)* [1968] 2 All ER 305 had held that no reasonableness test should affect the amount of insurance premium which a landlord was entitled to be reimbursed by his tenant under the terms of a commercial lease. After the decision in *Finchbourne Ltd v Rodrigues*, this approach was challenged in *Gleniffer Finance Corporation Ltd v Bamar Wood & Products Ltd* (1979) 37 P&CR 208, but the point was left undecided. Furthermore, the statement in *Firstcross v Teasdale*, to the effect that the *Finchbourne* rule applies automatically to every variable service charge clause, did not distinguish between residential and commercial lettings, although both cases related to leases of residential flats. Most recently, in the *Berrycroft* case (above), the Court of Appeal has expressed the view that the *Bandar* decision was correct and that no reasonableness test should be implied into provisions for the payment of insurance premiums.

It can be argued that in respect of commercial lettings, more than in the case of residential lettings, the tenant is normally in a good position to negotiate amendments to the offered form of lease. The Court of Appeal has refused to imply, into a commercial lease, a landlord's covenant to repair a private drain serving the demised premises, stating: 'the tenant ... will ordinarily be well advised to demand an express covenant to this effect': *Duke of Westminster v Guild* (1983) 267 EG 762. Similar observations were made in the *Havenridge* case (above). A similar cautious approach to the circumstances in which terms are to be implied into negotiated documents was taken in the leading case of *Philips Electronique Grand Public SA v British Sky Broadcasting Ltd* [1995] EMLR 472 (CA).

1.10.4   The Supply of Goods and Services Act 1982

It appears that Part II of the Supply of Goods and Services Act 1982 may have the effect of implying obligations on the landlord and his managing agents as to the *quality of services* to be provided. Section 13 of the Act provides that, where a supplier is supplying a service in the course of a business, there is an implied term that the supplier will carry out the service with reasonable care and skill. Furthermore, s 15 of the Act stipulates that, where the contract for the supply of a service does not specify the amount to be charged, *the charge must be reasonable*. It could be argued that most service charge clauses *do* specify the amount to be charged, not as a sum of money but by a formula, ie it is to be equal to the amount spend by the landlord (see dicta of Evans LJ in the *Havenridge v Boston Dyers Ltd* [1994] 2 EGLR 73). However, the correctness of this argument is uncertain.

Under s 16 of the Supply of Goods and Services Act 1982, these implied terms may be varied by agreement between the parties, subject to any limitations imposed by the Unfair Contract Terms Act 1977. Accordingly, where it is part of the landlord's business to supply services to its tenants (which is likely to be the case with respect to most multi-occupied buildings), it will be implied into the lease that the services will be carried out with reasonable care and skill and that the charges will be reasonable, unless there is anything in the lease to the contrary.

If the lease does contain provisions to the contrary (for example a stipulation that the tenant cannot challenge the cost of any service on the grounds that it might have been obtained more cheaply), the question arises whether such provisions might be rendered ineffective by the Unfair Contract Terms Act 1977. If that Act does apply, the provisions purporting to exclude the challenging of cost must pass the test of reasonableness, and it is unlikely that a total ban on challenging the level of costs would be considered reasonable. The application of the Unfair Contract Terms Act 1977 to service charges is, however, doubtful: Schedule 1 of the Act provides that the Act does not apply to any contract so far as it relates to 'the creation or transfer of an interest in land'. Whilst on a narrow interpretation this merely excludes from the Act an agreement for lease or the parts of a lease creating the demise, but would not prevent the Act from applying to the rest of the lease, the Court of Appeal has now held that the exclusion applies to every integral part of the lease, including the provisions as to rents and service charges (see *Unchained Growth plc v Granby Village (Manchester) Management Co Ltd* (1999) EGCS 116, CA). However, see also **1.10.6**.

In the *Havenridge* case (above), it was held that the arrangement of insurance by the landlord was not a 'service' caught by the 1982 Act.

1.10.5 The Restrictive Trade Practices Act 1956

Service charge provisions in leases will not ordinarily fall within the ambit of the Restrictive Trade Practices Act 1956 (*Ravenseft Properties Ltd v Director General of Fair Trading* [1978] QB 12).

1.10.6 The Unfair Terms in Consumer Contracts Regulations 1999

In July 1999, the Secretary of State for Trade and Industry made these regulations under the European Communities Act 1972. They apply to terms which have not been individually negotiated contained in contracts between a seller or supplier and a consumer (being a person, not a firm or company). Certain categories of transactions are excluded, but land transactions are not mentioned as being either included or excluded. The Department of Trade and Industry has indicated that it considers that land transactions such as short residential lettings are caught by these regulations.

In general terms, the regulations encompass non-negotiable standard clauses relating to the supply of goods or services where the supplier is acting in the course of business and the consumer is an individual who is not entering into the agreement for the purpose of his business or profession. The regulations are therefore more likely to apply to service clauses in standard form residential leases than to leases of commercial property.

The effect of the regulations, broadly, is to invalidate unfair terms, defined as terms which, contrary to the requirement of good faith, cause a significant imbalance in the parties' rights and obligations under the agreement, to the detriment of the consumer. Examples of unfair terms are set out in Sch 2 to the regulations and include terms purporting to exclude liability on the part of the seller for injury, terms allowing the supplier to alter the services without a valid reason which is set out in the agreement, terms allowing the supplier to determine whether the services conform to the agreement, and terms which require any dispute to be referred to arbitration rather than court proceedings. However, terms which define the main subject-matter of the agreement, or concern the adequacy of the price or remuneration as against the services supplied, are not subject to the fairness test if they are set out in plain, intelligible language.

1.11 Funding expenditure and charging interest on borrowed funds

1.11.1 Landlord's obligation irrespective of funding

Unless the leases state unequivocally otherwise, the landlord is contractually obliged to provide the services which he convenants to carry out, even if he has no funds to cover the cost.

Examples

Marenco v Jacramel Co Ltd (1964) 191 EG 433, CA: The tenant of a flat sued the landlord for breach of his covenant for external repairs. Could the landlord defend this claim on the ground that the tenants had not paid past service charges and were unwilling to give security for the cost of these further works? **Held**: No.

Francis v Cowcliffe (1977) 33 P&CR 368: The tenant of a third-floor flat sought an order for specific performance of the landlord's covenant to maintain the lift. The landlord had bought a new lift but could not afford to install it. Did the landlord's lack of funds absolve him from his obligation to repair or renew the lift? **Held**: No.

If the leases do not provide for interim service charge payments, or if the interim charges are inadequate, the landlord will normally have to fund the expenditure from its own resources or by borrowings, until the service charges are ultimately collected from the tenants in accordance with the provisions of the leases.

Can the landlord withhold services from a tenant who fails to pay his service charges? Generally the answer is that he cannot. Even if the landlord's service covenant is prefaced by words such as 'subject to the tenant paying the service charge', this will *not* normally be treated (without more explicit wording) as making payment by the tenant a precondition of the landlord being obliged to continue providing the services.

Example

> *Yorkbrook Investments Ltd v Batten* (1985) 276 EG 545, CA: The landlord's covenant to provide the services began: 'Subject to the Lessee paying the Maintenance Contribution pursuant to the obligations under Clause 4 hereof ...'. The tenant had withheld payment, alleging that the landlord was in breach of some of his obligations. Did this absolve the landlord of his obligation to continue to provide the services? **Held**: No; taking the scheme of the lease as a whole and noting that the tenant could challenge individual items of service cost under the housing legislation, these words were not intended to create a condition precedent to the landlord's service covenants.

Even if the clause was expressly worded to make payment of the service charge a precondition of the tenant's entitlement to have the benefit of the services, the withdrawal of services from a *residential* occupier might, in some cases, constitute a criminal offence under s 1(3A) of the Protection from Eviction Act 1977.

Furthermore, the tenant's liability to make payments on account will often be dependent upon the landlord complying with procedures under the service charge clause which require the landlord to make proper estimates of the annual costs.

Example

> *Gordon v Selico Co Ltd* (1986) 278 EG 53, CA: The maintenance trustee's covenant to provide the services began 'Subject to the payment by the Lessee of the Maintenance Contribution in accordance with the provisions of Clause 4 hereof ...'. The lease required the maintenance trustee to make a computation of the estimated maintenance provision for the year, on which the interim demands were to be based. The maintenance trustee demanded payment of a sum not supported by any proper computation. The tenant withheld payment for various reasons, including alleging that the maintenance trustee was in breach of numerous obligations. Did this failure to pay absolve the maintenance trustee of the obligation to continue providing the services? **Held**: No; the proper computation of the annual provision under the lease was a necessary preliminary to any demand for maintenance contributions, so no proper demand had been made.

1.11.2 Interest on borrowed funds

As stated at **1.11.1**, where leases do not provide for interim payments on account of the service charge, or where they stipulate inadequately low interim payments, the landlord will normally be obliged to fund the service costs himself until such time as the service charges or excess can be demanded. Some leases expressly provide for the service charge to include interest paid by the landlord on funds borrowed to meet service expenditure, or notional interest where the landlord has paid for the services out of his own resources.

If the service charge clause is silent on this point, it was, for several years, thought to be established firmly that the courts will infer that such interest *cannot be* included in the service charge (*Boldmark Ltd v Cohen* (1986) 277 EG 745; *Frobisher (Second Investments) Ltd v Kiloran Trust Co Ltd* [1980] 1 All ER 488).

However, doubt has been cast on that rule by the case of *Skilleter v Charles* (1992) 13 EG 113, in which the Court of Appeal expressed the view that '. . . a term that interest should be so chargeable . . . could . . . be implied either on the basis that it is necessary to give business efficacy to the terms of the lease or, alternatively, on the basis of the officious bystander test'. The report of that case does not indicate any detailed argument on the point or any reference to the earlier cases cited above, and the decision can be argued to be confined to the particular facts, since it involved a badly drafted clause which appeared to have been intended to enable the landlord to charge his interest costs but the wording used failed to achieve that result. It is, therefore, likely that the *Boldmark* and *Frobisher* decisions remain correct indications of how this issue will be decided in other cases where the service charge clause is totally silent on the matter. The position might however be different where the landlord is a tenants' management company with no other source of funds, see **1.2.2**.

Where interest cannot be charged, the landlord might find it possible to arrange for the contractor engaged to carry out the works to price his work so as to include a finance cost and agree to be paid after the time when, once the work is done, service charge invoices can be sent to the tenants.

1.12 Consultation with tenants

1.12.1 Good practice

Most leases lay down no procedure for tenants to be consulted before service expenditure is incurred. However, forms of lease vary so widely that it is advisable, in each case, to check whether the lease contains any specific provisions in this respect. The fact that many landlords fail to consult their tenants before incurring service costs is an unfortunate indication of the lack of thought and consideration which is prevalent in these matters.

It seems sensible (irrespective of the strict legal obligations) that landlords and their managing agents should keep their tenants informed of any changes in service arrangements which involve alterations in the practical administration of the building or in the amount of service charges, and should consult with the tenants before embarking upon any major new expenditure or substantial reorganisation of the services or administration. In addition, competitive estimates or quotations should be obtained for any items of substance to avoid allegations of extravagance (see **1.10**).

Consultation is encouraged by guidance notes and codes of practice for commercial property (see **7.1** and **7.2**). Consultation could be particularly important where voluntary (as opposed to compliance-driven) environmental initiatives are concerned. An example is the integration of environmental considerations into purchasing or tendering processes. This could arise where works are carried out or services are provided in pursuance of the landlord's obligations. Even where tenants agree, or the lease requires, that environmental considerations shall be given a place in purchasing and tendering decisions, there could be a wide range of views about how those obligations ought to be met in practice. A requirement or decision to use only environmentally benign products, or contractors with a sound environmental policy, could be interpreted in a number of ways. Environmental product information can be very difficult to interpret and claims about the 'greenness' of particular products can be misleading. Whilst industry groupings are still in the early stages of developing environmental management policies and systems, and until professional bodies and others have developed widely accepted codes of practice and guidelines, references in leases to environmental requirements are likely to be couched in broad terms. Even if a provision in a lease requires adherence to a particular guideline or code, these are unlikely to contain detailed and specific requirements. In these circumstances, landlords would be well advised to consult with their tenants on matters falling within this area.

1.12.2   Express consultation requirements

Where the service charge clause does lay down a consultation procedure, it might be interpreted as an absolute precondition to the tenant's liability, ie disqualifying the landlord from claiming the service charge unless he has followed the specified procedure. It is, therefore, most important for the landlord to follow strictly any consultation procedure laid down in the lease.

Examples

CIN Properties Ltd v Barclays Bank plc [1986] 1 EGLR 59, CA: The clause governing contributions towards external and structural repairs required the landlord to obtain estimates or tenders in the open market and precluded him from accepting any tender or estimate or contracting for or ordering the work without the approval of the tenant, which was not to be unreasonably withheld. The landlord embarked on works in that category without observing this procedure. Did this preclude him from charging for these works? **Held**: Yes.

Northway Flats Management Co Ltd v Wimpey Pension Trustees Ltd (1992) 31 EG 65, CA: The service charge clause contained a proviso that 'in respect of major or substantial repairs the Landlord shall, before carrying out such works submit a copy of the specification of works and estimates obtained upon such specification to the Tenant for consideration and if the Tenant shall not have raised any objection thereto within 21 days ... the Tenant shall be deemed to have accepted the specification and estimates as reasonable ...'. The landlord omitted to follow that procedure for major external repairs. Did this preclude him from charging for these works? **Held**: Yes.

1.12.3　Statutory rules for residential leases

The statutory provisions for compulsory consultation with tenants of residential flats are described in **Chapter 2**.

1.13　Apportionment between tenants

1.13.1　Common methods of apportionment

Leases vary in the method by which they define or provide for the ascertainment of each individual tenant's proportion of the total service costs of the building. The most common formulae are:

(1)　a fixed percentage set out in each lease;

(2)　a statement in each lease that the proportion is to be determined by the ratio of rateable values of the various lettable parts of the building;

(3)　a statement in each lease that the proportion is to be determined by the ratio of floor areas of the various lettable parts of the building;

(4)　a statement in each lease that the proportion is to be a 'fair', 'proper', 'due' or 'reasonable' proposition, perhaps determined by the landlord's surveyor.

The first method (a stated, fixed percentage) is sometimes coupled with an indication of the basis on which the stated percentages have been calculated. It may also be accompanied by a provision enabling the proportions to be varied from time to time if circumstances require (see **1.13.5**) although this is by no means universal. Neither the rateable value basis nor the floor space basis will be appropriate in every case. For example, in a centrally heated building certain parts may consume more central heating than others due to higher ceilings, larger windows, or other design causes, and may justify bearing a higher proportion of the heating costs. In those cases, detailed consideration should be given to an equitable basis of apportioning any such unevenly incurred costs (see **1.13.4**).

1.13.2　Proportion by reference to rateable values

A lease may provide that the tenant's proportion of the service costs is to be in the proportion which the rateable value of his demise bears to the total of the rateable values of all parts of the building *from time to time*. This may mean that the proportion must be recalculated each time the rateable value of any part of the building changes and that (unless the wording provides otherwise) the new proportion takes effect as from the date when the change in rateable value takes effect under rating law (*Moorcroft v Doxford* (1980) 254 EG 871). This can present problems when that date does not coincide with the start of the service charge accounting year, since the service charge accounts must then be split at the date of change of the rateable value, and the service charges must be separately calculated for the parts of the accounting year before and after that date. However, it may be necessary to recalculate accounts for a completed accounting period when a rateable value change is back-dated as a result of a rating appeal (*Universities Superannuation Fund v Marks & Spencer plc* [1991] 11 Ch 370, at first instance). In the case of residential property, rateable values ceased to be reassessed as from 1 April 1990, and so should not be incorporated into new residential leases.

1.13.3   Proportion by reference to floor areas

Where a lease stipulates that the service costs are to be borne between the tenants in the ratio of the floor areas of their respective parts of the building *from time to time*, a recalculation will usually have to be carried out whenever any lettable part of the building is altered in a way which changes the floorspace (as in the case of the rateable value basis mentioned above). The method of measurement (net usable, gross external, etc) must be consistent throughout the building and should ideally be specified in the leases. To avoid each tenant disputing the measurement of his demise, there should be provision for one person, such as the landlord's surveyor, to determine the measurements conclusively (except, perhaps, in the case of manifest and substantial error).

In the case of complexes such as major shopping centres which contain units of widely varying sizes, landlords are often faced with an argument from large space users that a large unit, compared with a small unit, will not generate an amount of usage of common parts and services in direct proportion to its size. This would be particularly so, it is argued, in the case of large retail units in which significant areas are used for storage rather than sales. Such tenants would want a diminishing calculation to be applied either to the entire service charge or to selected items of charge. However, it is becoming less common for retail units to contain large storage areas; the ability to take daily deliveries of stock results in a greater proportion of the unit being used as sales area than was previously common. Indeed, traders in smaller units may justifiably contend that the larger units, invariably occupied by well-known multiple occupiers, attract more customers per square foot than they do themselves and that any weighting should be against the large user. If that competing argument is well founded, it may be best to abandon any fine-tuning and base the service charge apportionment on plain unadjusted floor areas. It would be risky for a landlord to grant fairly long leases with a fixed formula which might be discredited during the term of the lease at a time when the landlord has to grant new leases of other units to tenants who will not agree to the same formula; a shortfall in service charge recovery might then arise.

If a weighted service charge has to be adopted, one method is a points system; the relevant service costs are apportioned between the units in proportion to the service charge points allocated to them, and points are allocated to each unit according to floor areas on a reducing scale set out in the leases, for example:

- the first 1,000 sq ft of the unit: 5 points per 1,000 sq ft;

- the next 3,000 sq ft of the unit: 4 points per 1,000 sq ft;

- the next 3,000 sq ft of the unit: 3 points per 1,000 sq ft, and so on.

Another method would be to use a notional floor area arrived at by discounting the actual measured area, for example:

- the first 1,000 sq ft multiplied by 1;

- the next 3,000 sq ft multiplied by 0.8;

- the next 3,000 sq ft multiplied by 0.6, and so on.

1.13.4   Fair or reasonable proportion

Where the lease provides that the service charge is to be a 'fair', or 'proper', or 'due', or 'reasonable' proportion of the total service costs, it will often state that this proportion is to be determined by the landlord's surveyor.

It is likely that, in making such a determination, the surveyor will be acting as an expert. Care must be taken to make a professionally competent and sustainable decision. Legal advice might need to be taken as to matters which should properly be taken into account, including whether such matters should be viewed at the date of the lease or having regard to subsequent events.

In one case, a judge held that in assessing a 'fair proportion' one should take into account not only the relative areas of the premises demised by each tenancy but also other factors which were relevant to fairness. This included, in that case, the short length of the unexpired term of the lease and the limited benefits which the tenant would obtain from the landlord's expenditure.

Example

Scottish Mutual Insurance Company v Jardine (1999) EGCS 43, QBD, Tech & Constr Ct: The lease required the tenant to pay, as a service charge, a 'fair proportion' of the costs 'reasonably and properly incurred' by the landlord in carrying out his obligations, which included repairing the exterior and structure of the building. The lease had only a few months left before it expired. The landlord carried out expensive long-term repairs to the roof of the building, instead of patching it up. The landlord's main motive in doing so was to facilitate the letting of a vacant part of the building to a new tenant. **Held**: The 'fair proportion' should not be calculated by relative floor areas, but this tenant should pay a reduced proportion reflecting the limited benefit to him due to the shortness of the unexpired term of his lease and the fact that it was not 'reasonable' for the landlord to carry out long-term repairs in order to fulfil the landlord's repairing obligations under this particular lease.

1.13.5   Unevenly shared services

In many cases, particularly in mixed-user buildings (such as blocks containing lock-up shops with separate offices or flats above), not all the tenants in the building will enjoy the benefit of the landlord's services to the same extent. For example, parts of a building may not be served by the central heating system which serves other parts, or may consume, disproportionately, more central heating energy due to higher ceilings or more windows. Certain tenants in a building may not require use of the lifts. Equally, some tenants in a building (such as those leasing lock-up shops) may have a degree of direct responsibility for the external repair of their part of the building, while tenants of other parts of the same building (eg upper-floor offices) may contribute through the service charge to the landlord's expenditure on external repairs. For these reasons, it may be necessary to divide the service charges into separate parts, with each part being individually apportioned between tenants according to usage.

Example

A two-storey building comprises a ground floor containing two lock-up shops, and an upper floor comprising four office suites of equal size. The offices are centrally heated and access is through a shared entrance hall and staircase. The shops are unheated and do not use the office entrance. All the leases impose internal repairing obligations on the tenants, with the landlord carrying out external repairs. The leases of the offices additionally require the landlord to provide central heating and to maintain the shared entrance hall and staircase. The service charge provisions of the leases should stipulate the following contributions towards the landlord's expenditure.

Demise	Contribution for central heating and shared access	Contribution for external repairs
	%	%
Shop 1	—	25
Shop 2	—	25
Office 1	25	12.5
Office 2	25	12.5
Office 3	25	12.5
Office 4	25	12.5
	100	100

Where the lease provides for the service charge to be calculated by applying a single percentage to the total service costs, rather than separate percentages for individual items of cost, it will be difficult for the tenant to argue that his service charge should be calculated by excluding from those total costs the cost of a particular chargeable item, merely because he does not directly benefit from it.

Examples

Broomleigh Housing Association v Hughes (1999) EGCS 134, ChD: The lease required the tenant to pay a stated percentage of the service costs incurred by the landlord. The landlord replaced all the windows in the block apart from those of the tenant's flat, since the tenant had already replaced them, albeit without the landlord's consent. The tenant refused to pay that part of his service charge which related to the cost of installing new windows in the rest of the block. An arbitrator appointed under the Independent Housing Ombudsman Scheme found that the present landlord had permitted the tenant to retain his new windows and that the previous landlord had relieved other tenants in similar situations from contributing to such costs and held that this tenant was entitled to the same treatment. The landlord appealed to the court. **Held**: The tenant was liable to pay his specified proportion of all the service costs, as provided in his lease, even though he did not directly benefit from the new windows. The present landlord's waiver of the tenant's breach of covenant in installing his own new windows did not affect the tenant's service charge obligations, nor did the tenant have any legitimate expectation that he would be relieved from part of the contractual service charge.

Billson v Tristrem [2000] L&TR 220, CA: The tenant of a basement flat was liable to pay 20 per cent of the costs incurred by the landlord on various repairs, including repairs to certain common parts. Some of the common parts were used only by the tenants of the upper part of the building. The lease contained contradictory provisions as to whether the basement tenant had to pay towards costs relating to parts he did not use. **Held**: The overall intention of the lease was that the tenant would pay 20 per cent of the landlord's entire costs relating to the building, even though this included parts which did not directly benefit this tenant.

1.13.6 Varying fixed proportions

Changes in circumstances may result in a need to change the proportions in which the total service costs are split between the tenants in a building. Some forms of lease give the landlord or his surveyor express power to vary these proportions in appropriate circumstances. If, however, the leases specify fixed proportions applicable to each flat and contain no provision for them to be varied, there are only two ways in which variation can be brought about. The first way is with the consent of each tenant whose proportion the landlord desires to alter. The problems which may arise, and the method of recording agreement on variations, are discussed at **1.9**. The second way, which is applicable if any tenant refuses to agree a variation, but only appropriate if the landlord can show that the variation is reasonable and has been brought about by lawful changes in circumstances, is to apply to the court. It appears that the court may be willing to order a variation of a lease in some circumstances, but the scope of this power is uncertain.

Examples

Pole Properties Ltd v Feinberg (1981) 259 EG 417, CA: Alterations to the hot water system shared between two blocks of flats rendered inappropriate the proportion of the costs of running the system specified in the tenant's lease as his liability. Did the court have power to order the proportion set out in the tenant's lease to be changed to the new proper figure? **Held**: Yes.

Mylles v Hall, 14 January 1980, unreported: A former caretaker's flat was sold off on a long lease. Were the tenants of the other flats in the building entitled to require a reduction of the service charge percentages in their leases (which added up to 100 per cent without the caretaker's flat)? **Held**: No. (Note: It appears that the court did not have the benefit of full argument on the point, and the decision may, therefore, be doubted.)

1.13.7   Specially requested services

Problems frequently arise where some tenants in a building require the landlord to provide services which other tenants in the same building consider unnecessary. For example, an international company occupying part of an office block may ask the landlord to provide 24-hours-a-day access, with security guards or commissionaires in attendance at all times. Other tenants in the building may be satisfied with access or security only during limited hours and may object to having to contribute towards the additional costs of night access. Whether these additional costs can be included in the total service charge payable by all the tenants depends on the wording of the service charge clauses in their leases.

If it is unclear whether the additional costs are covered, it will be relevant to consider the tenants' rights under the leases. For example, if the leases give the tenants right of access over the common parts during specified hours only, it may be implied that porterage costs can only be charged so far as they relate to those specified hours of access. Whether the extra costs of late working might then be covered by a sweeping-up provision depends upon the wording of that provision. If, therefore, some tenants ask the landlord to provide extended or additional services for their own benefit and it is not absolutely plain that the costs of these additional services will fall within the service charges payable by the tenants as a whole, the landlord should ask those tenants who are making the request to agree that they alone will pay the entire additional costs.

1.14   Indexed service charges

1.14.1   When appropriate

Occasionally, a service charge may be of an initial specified sum of money, with increases index-linked in some way, perhaps to a published index, such as the Index of Retail Prices, or linked to the cost of a particular component, such as oil or gas.

Indexing to the cost of fuel is probably most appropriate only in special cases, eg where the service charge is limited to cover hot water or heating and the amount of the charge is designed to include sums for maintenance or depreciation of plant, which would otherwise be difficult or cumbersome to compute on an annual cost basis.

1.14.2 Problems with indices

The draftsman must take care to ensure that the indexation provisions are properly drawn and do not create an unintended cumulative effect that results in the increase exceeding a true reflection of the indexation.

The greatest problems with published indices are that they may cease to be produced or that the basis of computation may be changed by the body which produces them. It is traditional for indexation clauses to contain provisions designed to meet these possibilities. However, such provisions must be carefully drawn, although sometimes the courts will come to the rescue.

Examples

Cumshaw Ltd v Bowen [1987] 1 EGLR 30, ChD: The leases of flats in a house required the landlord to repair the roof and main structure of the building, and reserved a service charge of an initial specified sum, to be increased annually in proportion to the increases in the Index of Retail Prices above the figure prevailing in August 1960, namely 110.4. The clause expressly provided that if the Index of Retail Prices ceased to be published by HM Government, or was no longer available to the public, the service charge should be computed, instead, by reference to the actual cost of the services. In the mid-1970s, the government rebased the Index to a new base figure of 100, and over the years the 'basket' of commodities which made up the figure changed from that used in 1960. Could the landlord invoke the change-over clause and compute the charge by reference to actual cost, which would produce a higher service charge figure? **Held**: No; the rebasing and alteration in the basket of commodities did not mean that the Index had 'ceased', and so the change-over clause could not be invoked. Instead, the Index increase had to be mathematically adjusted, before being used to calculate the new service charge, so as to adjust for the rebasing but not for the new basket of commodities.

Jollybird v Fairzone Ltd [1990] 2 EGLR 55, CA: The charges for central heating reserved by the leases in a building were expressed to be a fair proportion of the costs incurred, with two provisos; the first imposing a minimum charge of 1.3 pence per square foot; the second being a provision that 'the sum payable may be increased proportionately at any time by the lessor if the cost of fuel for supplying such heating shall at any time exceed the cost thereof at the date of the lease'. Was this second proviso to be applied? **Held**: No; since the basic computation was to be based on the cost in any event, the second proviso was to be disregarded because it was either inappropriate or would result in the landlord making a profit on the heating charge.

The *Fairzone* case is a clear example of a badly drafted set of clauses and extreme care must be taken in the drafting of indexed service charge provisions.

In the absence of any clear wording giving only one party the right to invoke the provision, either the landlord or the tenant can exercise a provision for a service charge to be adjusted in line with the specified index (see *IVS Enterprises Ltd v Chelsea Cloisters Management Ltd* (1994) EGCS 14, CA).

1.15   Interim charges

1.15.1   Interim payments or reimbursement on demand

Some service charge clauses provide for regular payments (usually called 'interim payments') on account of the eventual charge, with the balance becoming payable when accounts of the annual costs have been prepared. Others simply provide for payment of the tenant's contribution towards the actual expenditure whenever the landlord demands payment, but without advance payments. The former category is generally found in modern leases under which substantial services are provided, whereas the latter is commonly found in older leases or those where services are minimal.

1.15.2   Right to interim payments

Some older leases make no provision for interim contributions, but simply provide for the tenant to pay his proportion of the landlord's actual expenditure. Depending on the precise wording, this may prevent the landlord from demanding any contributions until he has actually disbursed the expenditure. It seems that a landlord will only be entitled to demand advance payments on account of the service charge if the lease or tenancy agreement expressly makes provision for this. This point was left open in *Daiches v Bluelake Investments Ltd* (1985) 275 EG 462, but there appears little likelihood of a landlord successfully arguing for an implied term that interim payments will be made.

Where the lease fails to provide for interim payments in advance of the costs being expended, it is clearly in the landlord's interest to demand the contributions from the tenant at the earliest possible moment. In some cases the contribution clause will enable demands to be issued at any time and, in such cases, a prudent landlord or managing agent will issue a demand as soon as any significant item of expenditure has been incurred so as to recoup his costs with the minimum of delay. Whether he is entitled to charge interest for funding the expenditure may be uncertain (see **1.11**).

As to cases where interim contributions are to be based on estimated provisions, see **1.15.3**.

1.15.3   Amount of interim contribution

Where a lease provides for the payment of interim charges, the amount which the landlord or his agent is entitled to demand by way of interim charge is governed by the terms of the lease. Many forms of lease purport to give the landlord or his agent an unfettered discretion to dictate the amount of the interim contribution but, plainly, the preparation of proper estimates of the service costs and their circulation among the tenants is highly desirable to foster good landlord and tenant relations.

Some leases expressly require the landlord to prepare and furnish the tenant with a proper estimate of the current year's anticipated expenditure, on which the interim contribution is to be based. In those cases, no interim payment will (unless the lease states otherwise) be due until that procedure has been followed.

Example

Gordon v Selico Co Ltd (1986) 278 EG 53, CA: The lease required the maintenance trustee to make a computation of the estimated maintenance provision for the year, on which the interim demands were to be based. The maintenance trustee demanded payment of a sum not supported by any proper computation. Was that sum payable? **Held**: No; the proper computation of the annual provision under the lease was a necessary preliminary to any demand for maintenance contributions, so no proper demand had been made.

Occasionally, leases provide that the amount of the interim contributions can only be varied at specified times by the landlord or his agent giving a formal notice to the tenants and, in some cases, the increase is limited to reflecting the actual service charge of the previous accounting year. Whatever the provisions of the lease may be with regard to interim contributions, as a matter of contract the procedures laid down by such provisions must be followed closely if the tenant is to be legally obliged to pay any interim contributions.

Once an interim charge has been properly specified and demanded under the terms of the lease, it will be recoverable from the tenant, even if the preparation of the final service charge accounts of the actual expenditure is delayed, and it seems that a 'reasonable' estimate need not be based on past certified accounts.

Example

Peachey Property Corporation Ltd v Henry (1963) 188 EG 875, QBD: The lease provided for service charge accounts to be served by 6 April each year or as soon thereafter as possible, and required the tenant to pay interim charges of 'whatever ... the Lessor's managing agents shall certify as being a reasonable interim sum to be paid on account of the annual contribution'. The managing agents had certified a figure for interim payments in November 1959. Was that figure still binding on the tenant in 1963, the agents not having prepared any accounts in the meantime? **Held**: Yes.

1.15.4   Implied limits on interim contributions

So far, there has been no reported court decision indicating any common law implied term that, where the lease appears to give the landlord a discretion as to the amount he can charge on account of the service charge, such interim charges can only be demanded if they are of a reasonable amount, but a court decision to that effect might not be entirely unexpected having regard to the reasoning in *Finchbourne v Rodrigues* [1976] 3 All ER 581 (see **1.10.2**).

1.15.5   Effect of non-payment on landlord's duties

Failure by a tenant to pay interim service charges will not normally absolve the landlord from his obligation to provide the services (see **1.11**).

1.16   Preparation and certification of accounts

1.16.1   Annual costs

As has been seen at **1.2** and **1.3**, the items which can be included in the total costs for service charge purposes are confined to those specified in the lease. The following paragraphs relate to those service charge clauses which deal with the expenditure on an annual basis. They usually make it clear that the chargeable costs in any year are to be those costs expended or incurred during the accounting period in question.

However, the wording of some service charge clauses has the effect that the cost of work contracted for by the landlord in one accounting year, but payable by him in a later accounting year, can only be included in the service charges for the period in which payment falls due (see the discussion on the meaning of 'expended' or 'incurred' at **1.3.5**).

1.16.2   Apportionment of periodic costs

Some service charge clauses provide that expenditure which relates to a period which overlaps two accounting periods is to be apportioned between those periods, eg:

> 'including such reasonable part of all such expenses costs outgoings and expenditure as aforesaid which are of a periodically recurring nature (whether recurring by regular or irregular intervals) whenever disbursed incurred or made and whether prior to the commencement of the term hereof or otherwise . . .'

Such a provision would apply, for example, to annual maintenance contracts which run from a date during an accounting period; the maintenance fees payable under the contract must then be apportioned between the two accounting periods.

Example

A lease contains a service charge clause with the above provision. The accounting period specified by the lease is from 1 January to 31 December in each year. On 1 October 2000 the landlord entered into a boiler maintenance contract for one year from 1 October 2000, at a maintenance fee of £3,000 for the year. The service charge accounts for the year 2000 should include the following proportion of that fee:

$$£3,000 \times \frac{92 \text{ days (1 Oct to 31 Dec)}}{365 \text{ days}} = £756.20$$

The accounts for the year 2001 would include the balance of £2,243.80, plus the duly apportioned part of the next maintenance fee, and so forth.

However, many managing agents take the view that this is an unnecessarily complicated approach to service charge costs and that it is simpler and equally appropriate to include the whole maintenance fee in the accounts of the year in which the fee is paid, since this is reasonable taking one year with another. They therefore prefer service charge clauses not to include any provision for apportioning periodic items across overlapping periods.

Another frequent provision is for the service costs to include provision for a reserve or sinking fund. This is discussed in detail in **Chapter 4**.

1.16.3   Form of certificate

Many modern forms of service charge clause require the landlord or his agent to prepare annual accounts of the service charge expenditure. The lease may require the accounts to be 'certified' by an accountant or surveyor, or simply be signed by the landlord, his agent, or his surveyor.

It is essential that the accounts should be prepared and certified strictly in accordance with the contractual provisions of the lease in order that any sums which become payable upon the issue of the accounts (such as excess service charges) will be legally recoverable from the tenants. This usually requires the wording of the certificate to follow the wording contained in the service charge clause referring to the certificate. Examples are given in **Appendix 2**.

1.16.4   Time-limits

Most leases provide for the accounts or certificate to be issued 'as soon as practicable' (or similar) after the end of each accounting period. However, occasionally a more specific time-limit is imposed.

Time-limits laid down by a service charge clause for the preparation or service of the accounts or certificate will not normally be deemed to be 'of the essence' and, thus, delays by the landlord will not normally prevent him from eventually recovering the service charges from the tenants.

Example

West Central Investments Ltd v Borovik (1977) 241 EG 609, QBD: The lease required the landlord to have accounts prepared at the end of each accounting year and served on the tenant within two months. Accounts for 1970, 1971, 1972 and 1973 were not prepared until 1974. Was the landlord nevertheless entitled to the charges shown on them? **Held**: Yes; time was not of the essence under the two-month stipulation.

In the case of residential leases, the Landlord and Tenant Act 1987 imposes certain time-limits (see **2.8.3**).

1.16.5   Conclusiveness of the certificate

Leases often state that a certificate of the expenditure is binding and conclusive. In 1969, it was held that such a stipulation was invalid since it attempted to oust the jurisdiction of the court on a question of law, the question whether a particular item of expenditure fell within the service charge being a 'question of law' as it turned on the proper legal interpretation of the lease (*Re Davstone Estates Ltd's Leases* [1969] 2 Ch 378). However, some years later the Court of Appeal held that questions of law *can* validly be referred to the conclusive determination of an expert to whom a dispute is referred and will *not* be invalid as ousting the court's jurisdiction (*Jones v Sherwood Computer Services Ltd* [1992] 1 WLR 277; followed in *Nikko Hotels (UK) Ltd v MEPC Ltd* [1991] NPC 41, ChD). The exact wording of the certification clause will determine whether, and to what extent, the expert's determination is to be conclusive and unchallengeable (*Mercury Communications Ltd v Director General of Telecommunications* [1996] 1 All ER 575; *British Shipbuilders v VSEL Consortium plc* [1997] 1 Lloyd's Rep 106).

However, it is unclear how far those decisions will undermine *Davstone* in relation to service charge certificates, since all those cases involved the referral of disputes to *independent* experts and few leases provide for the service charge certificate to be given by an independent expert; it is unlikely that the courts would readily interpret the provisions of a lease as vesting the power to determine such questions of law in the landlord himself or in the managing agents who themselves arranged the expenditure they now seek to certify. However, there is some authority for the courts upholding an agreed provision that the claimant's certificate of the amount due is to be conclusive. In an unreported decision of Ognall J, a clause in a guarantee, which provided that a certificate signed by an officer of the lender would be conclusive evidence of the amount of the guaranteed debt then owing, was held to prevent the guarantors from being heard to dispute the amount claimed (*DQ Henriques Ltd v Ismail* (1992) 6 February (unreported)).

Where the lease provides for the certificate to be given by an accountant, he may be taken to be more independent than the managing agent but, if he is generally employed by the landlord, he may be viewed as not totally independent – and there have been cases in which the courts have refused to recognise conclusive certification by anyone not wholly independent of the landlord.

Example

Finchbourne v Rodrigues [1976] 3 All ER 581, CA: The service charge was expressed to cover the costs incurred by the landlord in performing his services and the annual amount was to be ascertained and certified by the managing agents acting as experts. The 'managing agents' who issued the service charge certificate were, in reality, the same persons as the landlord. Was the certificate binding on the tenant? **Held**: No; the 'managing agents' were not independent agents as envisaged by the lease.

The safer view is, therefore, to assume that a certificate issued by anyone other than a wholly independent person cannot be conclusive. Furthermore, the possibility of the supporting invoices, etc, having to be produced to the tenant may need consideration (see **1.16.6**).

Where the lease does not state that a certificate is to be conclusive, the courts will not readily infer conclusive status for the certificate. If a certificate is not conclusive, either the landlord or the tenant can seek to have it reopened if there was a mistake in the calculation.

In those cases where the certificate is stated to be conclusive and the law recognises this (see earlier), the certificate will normally be binding on the landlord as well as on the tenant. If there has been a miscalculation which has resulted in under-recovery of the service costs, the landlord himself may wish to reopen the calculation. Whether he can do so will depend therefore upon the wording of the clause. Service charge clauses commonly provide that the certificate of total service costs is to be conclusive, but they do not usually provide that the statements showing the liability of individual tenants are also to be conclusive. If the miscalculation lies in those individual statements rather than in the certificate of total service costs, the landlord may be able to issue revised individual statements even if the costs certificate is conclusive, so long as the total service costs remain undisturbed.

Example

Universities Superannuation Scheme v Marks & Spencer plc (1999) 04 EG 158, CA: The lease provided for the service costs to be certified and to be contributed between the tenants based on rateable values. After the certificate was issued and the contributions had been demanded from the tenants, the landlord realised that the apportionment had been miscalculated and had led to under-recovery of the service costs. The landlord sought to reopen the matter. **Held**: The service charge provisions had the clear purpose of reimbursing the landlord for all the service costs. The primary obligation on the tenant was to pay his proper share. The certification provisions did not state that the certificate was to be conclusive; furthermore, the certificate only covered the total costs and not the apportionments, which were in a separate statement. The landlord was entitled to reopen the apportionment and demand the balance from the tenant.

The statutory provisions dealing with the certification of accounts in relation to residential flats are described in **2.10**.

As to recovery by a tenant of amounts overpaid, see **1.21**.

1.16.6   Tenant's inspection of invoices, etc

Some leases expressly give the tenant the right to inspect the service cost records, books, invoices and vouchers. Even if the lease does not give the tenant an express right of inspection, it is normally considered good management practice for the landlord or his agents to allow inspection in order to foster a good landlord and tenant relationship and to avoid distrust.

In addition, in many cases the landlord would be obliged to produce these items on disclosure in the course of any legal proceedings for recovery of the service charge. An exception may be where the lease provides that the certified accounts will be conclusive as to the amount spent on individual items of cost – see **1.16.5**.

1.17   Determination of disputes

1.17.1   Express provisions in the lease

Some leases make express provision as to the means of determining disputes about the service charge. They may, for example, provide for the dispute to be referred to arbitration.

However, if the lease provides that a dispute is to be decided by the landlord's surveyor, the court will normally infer this to mean an *independent* surveyor who is not connected with the landlord or his managing agents, since the inference is drawn that the surveyor must be in a position to consider the dispute in a quasi-arbitral capacity and must, therefore, be sufficiently independent of the parties connected with the dispute.

Example

Concorde Graphics Ltd v Andromeda Investments SA (1983) 265 EG 386, ChD: The service charge clause provided that any 'difference' as to the service charge was to be settled by 'the landlord's surveyor', whose decision was to be final and binding. The tenant disputed the service charge. A firm of agents were both the managing agents and the landlord's surveyors. Was their certificate of the service charge final and binding? **Held**: No; the managing agents clearly cannot perform the duty of deciding the difference which has arisen – as managing agents they, on behalf of the landlord, had made the claim that the tenant disputed; the landlord must appoint other surveyors to determine the dispute.

(See also *Finchbourne v Rodrigues* at **1.16.5**.)

1.17.2   Where the lease is silent

If the terms of the lease do not specify any means of determining a dispute in relation to the service charge, there are three alternative procedures which might be adopted:

(1) the landlord and the tenant might agree in writing to refer the matter to the determination of a third party acting as either an expert or an arbitrator; or

(2) one party or the other might apply to the court for a declaration on the true interpretation of the lease or on the correctness of the service charge certificate and calculation; or

(3) the landlord might sue the tenant for payment of the service charge, with the tenant defending the action on the ground that the amount claimed is wrong.

Applying to the court in advance of the expenditure for a declaration as to whether intended expenditure will be recoverable through the service charge has been encouraged by the courts in a number of cases (see **1.3.3**).

Prior to embarking on these formal procedures, the parties could try to resolve their dispute by mediation if they both agree.

Where the landlord successfully sues a tenant for disputed service charges, the landlord can expect to be awarded his costs, but (at least if the dispute appears to be made in good faith) normally on the standard basis (under which less than the full costs are recovered) and not on an indemnity basis (see *Church Commissioners for England v Metroland Ltd* [1996] EGCS 44, ChD, where the tenant unsuccessfully argued against the landlord's interpretation of the lease and also unsuccessfully sought rectification of the lease).

The procedure for determining disputes under the statutory provisions applicable to residential flats is set out in **2.12**.

1.18   Assignment of lease

1.18.1   Investigation prior to assignment of lease

Before a prospective assignee agrees to take an assignment of a lease under which a service charge is payable, he (or his solicitor or surveyor) should make enquiries on the following matters with the present tenant and, if possible, the landlord or managing agent:

(a) the level of service charges over the preceding three years, including the current estimated level;

(b) any likely increase in that level over the next few years;

(c) any major renewals, repairs or improvements likely to cause a severe increase in the service charge at a future time;

(d) the extent to which such future costs are covered by sinking or reserve funds;

(e) whether all service charges have been paid, in full, for past completed accounting years;

(f) whether there are or have been disputes concerning the service charges.

However, even truthful replies to these will be no substitute for a proper survey of the building or estate, and enquiries of other existing tenants.

1.18.2   Effect of assignment of lease

Some, but not all, leases granted for 21 years or more are registered at the Land Registry. In the near future, many shorter leases will be registered at the Land Registry when the minimum term for registration is reduced under the Land Registration Act 2002. The date on which an assignment of a lease takes effect depends on whether or not the lease has been registered.

If a lease is not registered at the Land Registry, it becomes vested in the assignee immediately on the completion of a deed of assignment. Consequently, once the landlord or managing agent becomes aware of an assignment having taken place, all notices under the lease and all demands for sums thereafter becoming due should be addressed to the assignee.

However, in the case of a lease which is registered at the Land Registry, the lease does not vest in the assignee until the assignment deed (in this case, called a 'transfer') has been registered at the Land Registry. During the gap between the completion of the transfer deed and its registration, the lease remains vested in the assigning tenant although the assignee owns it beneficially (or 'in equity' as the law puts it). Accordingly, during that period, notices and demands from the landlord should be served on both the assigning tenant and the assignee. Where the landlord serves a notice to forfeit under s 146 of the Law of Property Act 1925 in that situation, the assignee will be entitled to the usual rights to seek relief from forfeiture (*Brown & Root Technology Ltd v Sun Alliance & London Assurance Co Ltd* [1997] 18 EG 123, CA; *High Street Investments v Bellshore Property Investments* [1996] 35 EG 87, CA).

Once the assignment or transfer takes effect under the above rules, the assignee becomes liable, at common law and (in respect of leases which are not 'new tenancies' – mentioned below) by the Law of Property Act 1925, from that date onwards to pay the rents reserved by the lease and to perform all those covenants in the lease which 'touch and concern the land'. These covenants are usually taken to include all obligations relating to the state of the property, including covenants to pay service charges. However, it is generally considered that this is confined to covenants between the tenant and the actual landlord, so that a third party (such as a separate management company) cannot hold an assignee liable on covenants made by the tenant with the third party unless the assignee delivers to the third party a deed in which he covenants to observe those covenanted obligations (or, where a licence to assign is needed, includes such a direct covenant in the licence deed).

The Landlord and Tenant (Covenants) Act 1995 (the '1995 Act') introduced new, rather clearer, provisions on this subject in respect of 'new tenancies'. These are leases granted on or after 1 January 1996, but excluding those granted pursuant to legally binding agreements for lease, options, pre-emption agreements or court orders made before that date (1995 Act, s 1(3), (6), (7)). When a 'new tenancy' is assigned, s 3 of the 1995 Act provides that the assignee becomes liable, as from the assignment, to comply with all the tenant's subsisting obligations other than any of a purely personal nature. This covers obligations not only towards the landlord but also to a third party such as a separate management company (1995 Act, s 12). However, it is not completely clear whether the benefits of the management company's obligations pass automatically to the assignee, so mutual deeds of covenant between an assignee and a management company may still be desirable.

An assignment or transfer of a lease is valid to vest the lease in the assignee, even if the lease stipulates that the landlord's consent was required for an assignment and that consent was not obtained.

Example

Old Grovebury Manor Farm Ltd v Seymour Plant Sales (1979) 252 EG 1103, CA: The original tenant assigned his lease in breach of his covenant not to assign it without the landlord's consent. The landlord served a forfeiture notice under s 146 of the Law of Property Act 1925 on the original tenant. Was it a valid notice? **Held**: No; the unauthorised assignment was effective to vest the lease in the assignee, who was now the tenant, so the notice should have been served on the assignee.

If the assignment took place without the consent of the landlord where required by the lease, the landlord may wish to consider seeking forfeiture of the lease, in which event nothing should be done which is consistent with the lease still continuing (eg registering the notice of assignment, or demanding or accepting rent or service charges).

The provisions of the Law of Property Act 1925, s 196 apply to notices 'required to be served' by any instrument affecting property, unless the instrument evinces a contrary intention and will, therefore, normally apply to any notice which a lease requires the landlord to serve on the tenant. Furthermore, the provisions probably also apply to notices which the lease merely empowers, but does not 'require', the landlord to serve (in *Holwell Securities Ltd v Hughes* [1974] 1 All ER 161, CA, it was held that a notice exercising an option fell within s 196, which is plainly a notice which the grantee need not serve if he does not want to, but is required to serve if he wants to exercise the option). Where s 196 applies, notices can be addressed to the tenant merely as 'the Lessee' of the premises concerned, without his name (see s 196(2)), and this is useful where the landlord is uncertain of the assignee's correct name.

1.18.3   Is assignee liable for arrears of service charge?

In the absence of any specific provision in the lease (or in any licence for assignment or deed of covenant) is an assignee of the lease liable for unpaid service charges which became due and payable before the date of the assignment to him?

If the service charge is reserved as rent (usually as an additional rent to the basic rent for the premises) the answer (where the lease which was assigned is not a 'new tenancy', see **1.18.2**) is that the assignee is not liable for sums payable in respect of a period falling prior to the date of assignment, because rent is to be treated as accruing from day to day under the provisions of the Apportionment Act 1870 (*Parry v Robinson Wylie Ltd* (1987) 54 P&CR 187, in which an assignee was held not to be liable for a backlog of increased rent following a review where the review date preceded the assignment).

Where, instead of reserving the service charge as rent, there is simply a tenant's covenant to pay the service charge, the answer is similar: the assignee is not liable for sums which became payable on a date prior to the assignment. This is because under the common law an assignee is liable only for his own breaches of covenant and will not be liable for a predecessor's breaches unless they are 'continuing' breaches of covenant (such as a failure to repair the premises). Thus, the assignee will be free from liability for his predecessor's 'once-and-for-all' breaches, and it seems that failure to pay a sum of money (rent or service charge) on the date it becomes due is a 'once-and-for-all' breach (*London and County (A & D) Ltd v Wilfred Sportsman Ltd* [1970] 2 All ER 600, CA; *Re National Jazz Centre Ltd* [1988] 38 EG 142). The person who was the tenant when the sum fell due remains liable to the landlord to pay it and can be sued for payment, but the assignee cannot be sued unless he gave the landlord a direct covenant to pay future *and past* rents and service charges, which is unusual.

This, seemingly, does not preclude the landlord from seeking to forfeit the lease for non-payment of service charge, even after the defaulting tenant has assigned the lease. However, the landlord cannot claim payment of the arrears from the assignee.

Where the assigned lease is a 'new tenancy' (see **1.18.2**), the Landlord and Tenant (Covenants) Act 1995 provides that the assignee is not liable for defaults occurring before the assignment to him (1995 Act, s 23(1)).

It must also be noted that the right to forfeit a lease on the grounds of a once-and-for-all breach (as distinct from a continuing breach) can be lost or 'waived' by the landlord or his agent, after becoming aware of the breach, doing any act which indicates that the landlord is treating the lease as still subsisting (such as giving a licence to assign, registering a notice of assignment from the assignee, or demanding further rent or service charges). Thus, if the landlord wishes to bring forfeiture proceedings against the assignee, perhaps to pressurise him into paying the arrears, no act of waiver should be carried out before the writ of forfeiture is issued and served.

Where the lease requires the landlord's consent to be obtained for assignments, the landlord should consider withholding consent if there are substantial arrears of rent or service charges. However, the question of the reasonableness of withholding consent is a complicated topic outside the scope of this book (particularly with regard to the risk of the landlord being liable in damages under the Landlord and Tenant Act 1988 for delaying or refusing consent without good reason). Where consent for assignment is not required, the landlord might refuse to register notices of assignment until arrears are paid off. Whatever the legality of this device, it is often successful in practice.

1.19 Changes of landlord

1.19.1 Landlord's obligations

On a transfer of the landlord's interest in a property, the new landlord becomes liable to perform all those landlord's covenants in leases granted before 1 January 1996 which 'run with the land' (Law of Property Act 1925, s 142). This will normally include the covenant to provide the landlord's services. Similarly, in respect of the landlord's obligations under 'new tenancies' (see **1.18.2**), all those obligations become binding on the new landlord as from the transfer to him of the landlord's interest, except any landlord's obligations of a purely personal nature (1995 Act, s 3).

Where the change of landlord results from the landlord granting an overriding lease, particular issues can arise in relation to service charges (see **1.2.4**).

1.19.2 Benefit of tenant's obligations

The new landlord also becomes entitled to enforce the tenants' obligations under the leases. In relation to tenancies which are not 'new tenancies' under the 1995 Act, this includes the right to sue tenants for arrears of rent or service charges which fell due before he became their landlord (*London and County (A & D) Ltd v Wilfred Sportsman Ltd*) (see **1.18.3**). In relation to tenancies which are 'new tenancies' under the 1995 Act, the new landlord's rights against the tenant are confined to matters arising (or, in the case of continuing breaches, continuing) after he has acquired the reversion to the lease, unless rights in relation to prior defaults are assigned to him by the old landlord (1995 Act, s 23(1), (2)), although this would not prevent the new landlord from forfeiting the lease on the ground of past arrears of service charge (1995 Act, s 23(3)).

A new landlord should, therefore, ensure that he (and any new managing agent he may appoint) takes over all records, contracts and other papers relating to the management of the building and the service charge functions, and takes control of any unexpended service charge funds, including reserve or sinking funds. Where the new landlord will be dealing with the collection of service charges which include costs expended before he became the landlord, he should ensure that the contract under which he is buying the building entitles him to call upon the old landlord to comply with all relevant terms of the leases and all statutory requirements. These may include the supply of summaries of the costs, the provision of proper annual accounts and certificates, and the right of tenants to inspect invoices and other records.

1.19.3 Notice to tenants of change of landlord

When there is a change of landlord, each tenant should be notified in writing immediately. This is compulsory in the case of residential property (Landlord and Tenant Act 1985, s 3) and is desirable for every type of property to avoid tenants continuing to pay rent or service charges to the old landlord, which they are entitled to do until they receive the notice (Law of Property Act 1925, s 151).

1.20   Recovery of arrears and other remedies

1.20.1   Preconditions for claiming arrears

The service charge will fall contractually due only once all procedures laid down by the lease for fixing and demanding the service charge have been followed, including the observance of any procedure laid down for determining any dispute, should there be one.

Example

> *Concorde Graphics Ltd v Andromeda Investments SA* (1983) 265 EG 386, ChD: The service charge clause provided that any difference as to the service charge was to be settled by the landlord's surveyor, whose decision was to be final and binding. The landlord obtained payment of a disputed service charge demand by threatening distress. Was this lawful? **Held**: No; the dispute procedure laid down in the lease had to be observed before any enforcement could take place.

Accordingly, no action should be brought for recovery of alleged arrears of service charge unless all accounts and certificates specified in the lease have been properly prepared and delivered to the tenant and, if the lease specifies that a dispute must be settled by a particular procedure (eg by an independent surveyor) and there is a dispute on the matter, the specified procedure must be followed.

As for arrears of service charge which became payable on a date prior to a change of tenant upon an assignment of the lease, see **1.18**.

As for arrears due when the tenant or occupier is a foreign state or foreign diplomat, see **1.22**.

1.20.2   Set-off of damages for breaches of landlord's covenants

Where the landlord has been in breach of covenant and the tenant claims damages, the tenant can (subject to one proviso) set off that claim against the sums payable to the landlord under the lease, even if the damages claim is unliquidated (ie the monetary amount is not ascertained) at the time the sums fall payable (*British Anzani (Felixstowe) Ltd v International Marine Management (UK) Ltd* [1979] 2 All ER 1063; *Melville v Grapelodge Developments Ltd* (1979) 254 EG 1193; *Lee-Parker v Izzet* [1971] 1 WLR 1688). Therefore, in proceedings by the landlord for recovery of service charges, the tenant may be entitled to claim set-off for any damages to which he may be entitled due to breach of covenant by the landlord.

The proviso mentioned above is that the tenant does not have this right where the lease expressly prohibits any set-off from the service charge. It was previously questioned whether a provision excluding set-off is effective to prevent set-off being claimed in the course of legal proceedings, since set-off is governed by the rules of the court. However, there has recently been a line of cases in which the validity of a prohibition on set-off has been accepted (see *Hong Kong & Shanghai Banking Corp v Kloeckner & Co AG* [1990] 2 QB 514; *Stewart Gill Ltd v Horatio Myer & Co Ltd* [1992] 2 All ER 257; *Coca-Cola Financial Corporation v Finat International Ltd* [1996] 3 WLR 849). The prohibition in the lease must expressly refer to 'set off'; a requirement to pay without 'any deduction' is not to be construed as prohibiting set-off (*Connaught Restaurants Ltd v Indoor Leisure Ltd* [1993] 2 EGLR 108, CA). Where the tenant does have a right of set-off, this can be exercised even against the remedy of distress where the service charge is recoverable as rent (*Eller v Grovecrest Investments Ltd* [1994] 2 EGLR 45, CA).

Statute law may, in some cases, invalidate a prohibition against set-off. Where a party to an agreement contracts as a consumer on the other's written standard terms of business, s 3 of the Unfair Contract Terms Act 1977 provides that the other cannot, by a term of the contract, exclude liability for breach, except insofar as the term satisfies the requirement of reasonableness. Section 13 of that Act applies the rule also to terms restricting the consumer's remedies in respect of a breach. In *Stewart Gill Ltd v Horatio Myer & Co Ltd* [1992] 2 All ER 257 the Court of Appeal held that this applied to a clause prohibiting set-off contained in a commercial contract for the sale and installation of a conveyor system, and that the clause failed the reasonableness test and was void. However, it has now been held that the Unfair Terms Act 1977 does not apply to any of the integral provisions of a lease (see **1.10.3**) so a provision in a lease requiring service charges to be paid without any set-off or deduction (other than any deduction required by statute) will be valid and enforceable by the landlord.

1.20.3   Claiming interest for late payment

Leases often make express provision for the tenant to pay interest on rent and (sometimes) on other sums which are not paid within a certain time after their due date. In the event of non-payment of service charges by the tenant, the lease should be checked to see whether the tenant is contractually obliged to pay interest and, if so, for what period and at what rate.

If the lease does not expressly provide for interest to be paid on arrears, there will be no contractual obligation on the tenant to pay interest. However, if the landlord commences court proceedings against the tenant for recovery of the arrears, interest can be included in those proceedings by virtue of s 35A of the Supreme Court Act 1981 in relation to High Court proceedings and by virtue of s 69 of the County Courts Act 1984 in relation to actions in the county court. Although interest under s 35A is at the discretion of the court, it is a discretion which must be exercised judicially (*Allied London Investments Ltd v Hambro Life Assurance* (1985) 274 EG 148).

1.20.4   Recovery as if rent

If the service charges are reserved in the lease by way of additional rent, or if the lease provides that arrears of service charge are recoverable as if they were rent, the type of proceedings which can be brought for recovery of arrears include those designed for the recovery of arrears of rent (see *Escalus Properties Ltd v*

Robinson and Others [1995] 4 All ER 852, CA). It also appears that the remedy of distress is available. However, such a provision is equally capable of being invoked by the tenant as the landlord; thus in the *Escalus* case it resulted in the tenant's mortgagees being entitled to automatic relief from forfeiture (which is applicable to arrears of rent) on tendering the arrears of service charge.

A payment made under threat of distress or effected by distraining will be recoverable from the landlord if it is subsequently found that the sum was not properly due and, thus, the threatened distress would have been unlawful (*Concorde Graphics Ltd v Andromeda Investments SA* (1983) 265 EG 386, cited at **1.20.1**). In addition, where the landlord has wrongly distrained, he may be liable to a penalty. It is, therefore, important not to exercise the remedy of distress, unless the amount claimed has been properly certified due under the terms of the lease and is not in dispute.

Distress cannot be levied to recover a sum which the tenant simply fails to pay in breach of an arrangement under which the landlord and the tenant have been operating but which is outside the terms of the lease.

Example

D'Jan v Bond Street Estates plc [1993] EGCS 43, CA: Although the lease provided for regular, quarterly advance payments of the estimated service charge, recoverable as if rent, the landlord had a practice of demanding, at the end of each quarter, a payment in arrear based on his actual expenditure. The tenant stopped a cheque which he had given the landlord under this procedure, since he was dissatisfied with the work done. Could the landlord distrain for the amount involved? **Held**: No; in the absence of any specific agreement substituting, for enforcement purposes, the adopted procedure in place of the procedure laid down in the lease, distress could only be levied for a sum payable under the terms of the lease.

If the lease does not reserve the service charge as rent or provide for arrears to be recoverable as if rent, the proceedings for recovery of arrears will be as a debt, and distress will not be available.

1.20.5 Forfeiture

If the landlord wishes to seek forfeiture on the ground of non-payment of service charges, he must first serve on the tenant a notice, under s 146 of the Law of Property Act 1925, specifying the default and requiring the tenant to pay within a reasonable time. The reasonable time (which need not be specified in the notice) need not be very long; 14 days will probably suffice. However, if the service charge is reserved as additional rent, there will be no need to serve a s 146 notice, since forfeiture for non-payment of rent is excluded from s 146 (s 146(11)).

If no notice under s 146 is required, or if the requisite notice has been served and payment has not been received within a reasonable time from service of the notice, the landlord will be entitled to proceed to seek forfeiture of the lease.

Since non-payment of a sum when it falls due is a once-and-for-all breach of covenant (see **1.18.3**), the right to forfeit must be preserved by avoiding acts of waiver.

If the tenant seeks relief from forfeiture under s 146, the landlord may be able to persuade the court to impose serious terms designed to ensure that the arrears of service charge are paid speedily; in some cases, even more onerous terms may be imposed (see *Khar v Delbounty* [1996] NPC 163, CA).

As to the special rules relating to the forfeiture of residential leases, see **2.13.3**.

1.20.6 Withholding of services

The question of whether a landlord can withhold services from a tenant who has failed to pay his service charges is considered at **1.11.1**.

1.20.7 Costs of the proceedings

If the landlord obtains judgment against the tenant for arrears of service charge, he will normally be awarded his costs of the proceedings. The basis of awarded costs is at the discretion of the court but, usually, costs are awarded on the 'standard' basis of 'a reasonable amount in respect of all costs reasonably incurred', with any doubts being resolved in the payer's favour, and the costs being 'taxed' by the court, if they have not been agreed between the parties.

However, costs can be awarded on an 'indemnity' basis where it appears to the court to be appropriate and, on that basis, all costs are allowed, except insofar as they are of an unreasonable amount or have been unreasonably incurred, with any doubt being resolved in favour of the receiving party. Where the lease expressly provides for costs to be recovered on a full indemnity basis the court will give weight to this, although it is not conclusive, and it does not avoid the power of the court to tax costs (*Bank of Baroda v Panessar* [1986] 3 All ER 751; *Gomba Holdings (UK) Ltd v Minories Finance Ltd (No 2)* [1993] Ch 171, CA; *Church Commissioners for England v Ibrahim* [1997] 03 EG 136, CA).

The wording of the lease as to indemnity costs must be clear and unambiguous on this. In *Primeridge Ltd v Jean Muir Ltd* [1992] 1 EGLR 273, a clause entitling the landlord to 'all proper costs' when recovering arrears was held not to mean a full indemnity for costs, contrasting with the entitlement to 'all costs, charges and expenses which you may incur' in the *Baroda* case, which was interpreted as a full indemnity. The phrase 'indemnity basis' is not essential to achieve this; the expression 'all expenses incurred by the lessor' may have the same effects (see *Fairview Investments Ltd v Sharma* (1999) 14 October (unreported), CA).

1.20.8 Liability of previous lessees

A lease is a contract between the landlord and the tenant. One result of this is that, in respect of leases other than 'new tenancies' (see **1.18.2**), the original tenant (and any guarantor for him) remains bound by the obligations under the lease, including the obligation to pay service charges, throughout the entire term of the lease, notwithstanding that he may have assigned the lease. Consequently, the original tenant (and any guarantors) can usually be sued for service charges payable under the lease arising at any time during the contractual term of the lease.

Where the lease has changed hands a number of times, it may also be possible to sue the intervening assignees if they gave the landlord direct covenants that they would pay the rents and service charges throughout the residue of the term of the lease (see *Royton Industries Ltd v Lawrence* [1994] 1 EGLR 110). Such direct covenants may be contained in a licence for assignment (where the landlord's licence for assigning is required) or in a separate deed of covenant.

However, in respect of leases which are 'new tenancies' under the Landlord and Tenant (Covenants) Act 1995 (see **1.18.2**), a previous tenant will not have continuing liability for defaults occurring after he lawfully assigned the lease (1995 Act, s 5) and the same applies to a guarantor for that tenant (1995 Act, s 24), but they remain liable for defaults occurring prior to the assignment (1995 Act, s 24(1)). Further, the assignee might be required to give the landlord an authorised guarantee agreement under the 1995 Act, s 16, in cases where the landlord's consent for the assignment is required. Under an authorised guarantee agreement, the assignor agrees to be a guarantor for the assignee's liabilities under the lease, up to the time of the next lawful assignment.

In respect of business premises which an assignee, under the provisions of Part II of the Landlord and Tenant Act 1954, continues to occupy beyond the expiry of the term of the lease, original and intervening tenants who are liable under the above rules will not normally be liable for service charges in respect of a period after the term expiry date, since the Act operates by continuing the 'tenancy' between the then tenant and the then landlord, rather than by extending the contractual term. However, they might be liable if the lease expressly provides for this, eg where the 'term' is defined in the lease as including any period of statutory continuation.

Examples

Thames Manufacturing Co v Perrotts (Nichol & Peyton) Ltd and Others (1984) 271 EG 284, ChD: Perrotts were the original tenants under a 1972 lease, and the second, third and fourth defendants were the sureties for them. The lease was assigned, with the landlord's consent, in January 1980 to the fifth defendant, who lost the protection of the Landlord and Tenant Act 1954 but failed to vacate when the lease expired in June 1980 and failed to remedy dilapidations. Were Perrotts and their sureties liable to the landlord for damages for disrepair? **Held**: Yes; as original tenant and sureties their liability continued, even in respect of a period in which, having assigned the lease, they were not in a position to perform the repairs.

City of London Corporation v Fell [1993] 2 EGLR 131, HL: In 1979 the original tenant assigned his lease to a company. The company held over, under Part II of the Landlord and Tenant Act 1954 after the expiry of the lease in 1986, but then went into liquidation and did not pay rent for that period. The lease did not refer to a holding-over period in the definition of the term. Was the original tenant liable? **Held**: No.

Herbert Duncan Ltd v Cluttons [1993] 1 EGLR 93, CA: The original tenant assigned his lease to an assignee. The lease included a covenant for payment of rent throughout the term, which was defined as including any period of continuation under the Landlord and Tenant Act 1954. The assignee held over, under the Landlord and Tenant Act 1954, after the expiry of the lease in 1990. The landlord obtained a consent order for interim rent for that period, but the assignee did not pay it. Was the original tenant liable? **Held**: Yes (but only for rent at the level last payable contractually under the lease, and not for the additional amount bringing it to the level of the interim rent, since that extra amount was payable by reason of the Act rather than by reason of the lease).

1.20.9   Notice of claim for arrears

Since 1 January 1996, if the landlord wishes to claim payment of service charges from a former tenant or former guarantor who has continuing liability (see **1.20.8**), he must serve on that person a notice in a prescribed form within six months of the sum in question first becoming due under the lease (Landlord and Tenant (Covenants) Act 1995, s 17). Service of the notice is a precondition for liability. If the notice is not served within the six-month period, the former tenant or guarantor will not be liable for that particular payment. A specimen of the prescribed form appears in **Appendix 2**.

If a former tenant or guarantor pays arrears in response to a statutory notice, he may be entitled to require the landlord to grant him an overriding lease under s 19 of the 1995 Act.

1.21   Recovery of overpayments

It used to be that where an overpayment was made due to a mistake by the paying party as to the correct amount legally due from him, he could not recover the overpaid amount for the payee (see, eg, the *Concorde Graphics* case ((1983) 265 EG 386) at **1.20.1**) because of an ancient rule that payments made under a mistake of law were not recoverable.

However, the House of Lords decided in 1998 that this rule was no longer good law (*Kleinwort Benson v Lincoln City Council* [1998] 4 All ER 513, HL). This change in the law has enabled tenants to reclaim excess rent that they paid to the landlord by mistake (eg *Nurdin & Peacock plc v DB Ramsden & Co (No 2)* (1999) 09 EG 175) and the same will presumably apply to the recovery of an overpayment of service charge if it is found that a lesser sum should have been paid. Exactly what limitation rules will apply to claims relating to payments made several years earlier has yet to be determined.

1.22 Diplomatic and state immunity

1.22.1 State immunity

A tenant which is a foreign state will enjoy certain immunity from legal proceedings in the UK courts, under the State Immunity Act 1978, although the immunity can be waived (see **1.22.2**). The immunity is subject to a number of exceptions set out in the 1978 Act which (amongst other things) allow proceedings to be brought against the relevant state relating to its interest, possession or use of immoveable property in the UK or relating to its obligations arising out of such interest, possession or use (s 6(1)). However, this exception does not allow a UK court to issue injunctions, orders for specific performance or orders for recovery of possession against a foreign state in relation to land or other property, unless the state has expressly agreed to submit to those remedies (s 13(2)). Accordingly, these provisions normally allow a landlord to enforce covenants in leases only by claiming damages for breach.

An alternative basis under which a landlord could seek exception from the tenant's state immunity might be under s 3 of the 1978 Act, which allows proceedings to be brought against a foreign state for breaches of contract where the broken obligation was to be performed wholly or partly in the UK. Since a lease is a form of contract, s 3 appears (like s 6) to allow landlords to bring actions for breach of covenant under a lease, although the courts have indicated, without deciding the point, that it may be more appropriate to use the exception under s 6(1) mentioned above in such cases (per May LJ in *Intpro Properties (UK) Ltd v Sauvel* [1983] 2 All ER 495, CA).

The exceptions to immunity in ss 3 and 6 of the 1978 Act do not allow a landlord to seek possession of premises if they are being used for the purpose of a diplomatic mission (1978 Act, s 16(1)(b); *Intpro Properties (UK) Ltd v Sauvel* (above); Diplomatic Privileges Act 1964, Sch 1, art 22; *Westminster City Council v Government of the Islamic Republic of Iran* [1986] 3 All ER 284, ChD). As for the special protection enjoyed by such premises, see **1.22.4**.

1.22.2 Waiver of state immunity

State immunity from court proceedings will not apply if the state has agreed in writing to submit to the jurisdiction of the UK courts (1978 Act, s 2(1)). However, simply agreeing to submit to that jurisdiction is not sufficient to allow a UK court to issue injunctions, orders for specific performance or orders for recovery of possession against the foreign state in relation to land or other property, unless the state has expressly agreed to submit to those remedies (1978 Act, s 13(2)).

1.22.3 Diplomats

A tenant who is a foreign diplomatic officer will enjoy personal immunity from civil proceedings in the UK courts under Art 31 of Sch 1 to the Diplomatic Privileges Act 1964. This immunity is also given to members of his family forming part of his household, unless they are UK citizens (Art 37). Again there are exceptions to immunity set out in that Act, but the exceptions are more limited than in the case of state immunity. The relevant exceptions will allow a landlord to bring 'a real action relating to private immoveable property' (but not property held for use as a diplomatic mission for the foreign state – see below) and 'an action relating to a professional or commercial activity exercised by the diplomatic agent in the . . . [UK] . . . outside his official functions'. These would presumably allow a landlord, for example, to bring proceedings against a foreign diplomat in respect of a lease of premises which the diplomat used for the purpose of a business outside the scope of his diplomatic functions.

As for immunity in relation to leases of residential premises occupied by diplomats, see **2.19**.

1.22.4 Premises used as a mission

Where the premises, whoever is the tenant, are used as a professional mission for the purposes of the foreign state, further special rules apply. The premises are inviolable; officers of the UK government must not enter them; the UK government is under a duty to take all appropriate steps to protect the premises against any intrusion; and the premises are immune from search, requisition, attachment or execution (1964 Act, Sch 1, Art 22; *Westminster City Council v Government of the Islamic Republic of Iran* [1986] 3 All ER 284, ChD). This prevents the landlord from entering the premises or seeking forfeiture of the lease.

1.22.5 Waiver of diplomatic immunity

As in the case of state immunity, both a diplomat's personal immunity and the immunity of a mission can be waived. The waiver must be by the foreign state (1964 Act, Sch 1, Art 32, para 1) or by the head of the mission (1964 Act, s 2(3)). Merely submitting to the jurisdiction of the English courts is not sufficient to allow the execution of a judgment obtained under that jurisdiction; unless execution is also expressly mentioned in the waiver, there will be immunity from execution of a judgment even if the court has jurisdiction to issue the judgment itself (1964 Act, Sch 1, Art 34, para 4).

2 SPECIAL RULES FOR RESIDENTIAL LETTINGS

The Landlord and Tenant Act 1985 (as amended by certain subsequent Acts) sets out a statutory code for service charges and related matters in respect of residential dwellings. Its most important features are:

(a) service costs can only be recovered if they are reasonably incurred;

(b) only works or services performed to a reasonable standard can be charged;

(c) prior consultation is required in respect of certain costs; and

(d) tenants must be given written warnings in respect of any costs which will be included in a demand which will be served on them more than 18 months after the costs are incurred.

The legislation operates by adding a layer of conditions and requirements to those which are contained in the lease. Accordingly, when assessing the liability to service charges of the tenant of a residential property, one starts by determining the contractual scope of the service charge (see **Chapter 1**) and then one applies the statutory provisions.

The main changes in this legislation were effected by the Housing Act 1996 and the Commonhold and Leasehold Reform Act 2002; those changes are reflected in this book. Extracts from the legislation appear in **Appendix 3**.

In relation to statutory control over service charges payable under residential estate management schemes, see **5.5**.

2.1 Lettings to which the Landlord and Tenant Act 1985 applies

2.1.1 Relevance of legal rules of general application

The principles of general application, set out in **Chapter 1**, apply to residential lettings, except insofar as overridden by the statutory code mentioned in this chapter.

In general terms, the statutory code applies (subject to the exemptions set out in **2.1.3**) to cost-related, variable service charges levied by a landlord or management company in respect of residential dwellings. It does not apply to fixed (static) service charges or to premises occupied wholly or mainly for business purposes.

2.1.2 Scope

Subject to the exemptions mentioned at **2.1.3**, s 18 of the Landlord and Tenant Act 1985 ('LTA 1985') provides that the statutory code will apply to:

(1) a *service charge*;

(2) of which all or part will *vary according to the relevant costs*;

(3) which is *payable* as part of, or in addition to, rent *by the tenant*;

(4) of a *dwelling*.

The following definitions apply to the words and phrases italicised above.

> *Service charge* means payment for 'services, repairs, maintenance, improvements or insurance or the landlord's costs of management' (LTA 1985, s 18(1)).

> *Landlord* means 'any person who has the right to enforce payment of a service charge ...'.

> *Relevant costs* means 'costs or estimated costs incurred or to be incurred by or on behalf of the landlord or a superior landlord in connection with the matters for which the service charge is payable' and includes overheads (LTA 1985, s 18(2) and (3)).

> *Dwelling* means a building or part of a building occupied or intended to be occupied as a separate dwelling, together with any yard, garden, outhouses and appurtenances belonging to it or usually enjoyed with it (LTA 1985, s 38).

> *Tenant* includes a statutory tenant (within the Rent Act 1977 or the Rent (Agriculture) Act 1976); but where the rent is registered under Part IV of the Rent Act 1977, these provisions apply only if a variable service charge is registered under s 71(4) of the 1977 Act (LTA 1985, s 27). Where the dwelling or part of it is sublet, 'tenant' includes the subtenant (LTA 1985, s 30).

The reference in the LTA 1985 to service charges which *vary according to the relevant costs* is wide enough to encompass even a service charge of a fixed initial amount which increases mathematically in proportion to the cost of just one element (*Fountain Hoteliers Ltd v Legge-Bourke*, 30 November 1981, unreported).

The fact that the definition of 'service charge' refers only to 'services, repairs, maintenance, improvements or insurance or ... management' does not have the effect of limiting service charges to these matters; if the cost of anything else is covered by the service charge clause in the lease, that cost can be included in the service charge without the constraints of the LTA 1985 being applied to that particular cost (*Sutton (Hastoe) Housing Association v Williams* [1988] 1 EGLR 56, CA; *In the Matter of Bedfordshire Pilgrims Housing Association* (2000) 23 March (unreported), Lands Tribunal).

The inclusion of the cost of 'improvements' as an element of the service charges caught by the LTA 1985 was added by Sch 9 to the Commonhold and Leasehold Reform Act 2002, with effect from a date to be fixed. Prior to that, the cost of improvements was not subject to any of these statutory controls (see the *Sutton (Hastoe)* case, above).

The provision about sublettings (quoted above) is that, where a dwelling is sublet, '"tenant" includes the subtenant'. It does not state that '"tenant" *means* the subtenant' and leaves open the possibility that both the tenant and the subtenant can be tenants having the protection of the Act. If so, the tenant can claim protection against service charges demanded from him by the freeholder, and the subtenant can claim the protection of the Act when the tenant seeks to recover that service charge from him.

However, the question arises whether the control over service charges imposed by the LTA 1985 applies only to individual leases of single dwellings, or could equally apply to leases which demise more than just a single dwelling. This could be, say, where a lease demises a flat and a car-parking space or garage to be used with it; or demises two or more flats which the tenant either intends to combine into one large flat or intends to sublet individually; or even where a flat is let together with wholly non-residential premises such as a shop or office in the same building. Apart from the policy consideration whether a tenant of a multiple letting (as distinct from the tenant of a single flat) needs or deserves the protection of the LTA 1985, plainly hardship could arise if such a tenant sublets individual flats and then finds himself paying an uncontrolled service charge to his landlord whilst not being able to obtain full recovery from his subtenants whose individual contributions are subject to the controls imposed by the Act.

The only reported case on this question is *Heron Maple House Ltd v Central Estates Ltd* [2002] 13 EG 102, where Judge Roger Cooke in the Central London County Court, in a carefully reasoned judgment, concluded that the scope of the LTA 1985 was not confined to leases of single dwellings. The case involved a mixed commercial and residential block, managed by the freeholder. The residential section, which included a substantial number of flats, was let on a headlease. The headlessee sublet the whole of that section to a subtenant who subunderlet the individual flats. All the leases reserved service charges which included sums expended by the freeholder on major repairs. The freeholder incurred large expenditure which, if the LTA 1985 applied, fell within the requirements of the Act for consulting with tenants and obtaining competitive quotations (see **2.2**). However, the freeholder had not consulted the headlessee and the headlessee had not consulted his subtenant. This would make the expenditure irrecoverable if the LTA 1985 applied. The judge held that the LTA 1985 applied to both the headlease and the sublease, even though they both comprised more than just a single flat, so the freeholder could not recover the expenditure from the headlessee who could not (even if he paid it voluntarily) recover it from the subtenant.

However, county court decisions do not create binding legal precedent and need not be followed by other judges. Furthermore, Judge Cooke observed that this was a 'peculiar problem' on which leave to appeal to the High Court should be given if sought. Accordingly, the *Heron Maple House* decision cannot be taken to have settled the issue and the authoritative decision of a higher court is needed.

A separate regime has been introduced by the Commonhold and Leasehold Reform Act 2002 in relation to 'administration charges'. This could apply to charges made by landlords for supplying tenants with documents or inspection and copying facilities in relation to service charge expenditure, and the rules are described at **2.22**.

2.1.3   Particular landlords

Section 26 of the LTA 1985 exempts from the statutory code tenancies granted by:

(a)   a local authority;

(b)   a new town corporation; or

(c)   the Development Board for Rural Wales,

unless they are 'long tenancies'. A long tenancy granted by such a specified body will be subject to the provisions of LTA 1985, ss 18 to 24 but not s 25 which relates to offences.

The following are defined by s 26(2) as 'long tenancies' for this purpose:

(a)   a tenancy for a fixed term exceeding 21 years, whether or not terminable earlier by tenant's notice or by forfeiture;

(b)   a tenancy which is perpetually renewable (and, therefore, is deemed by s 145 and the Fifteenth Schedule to the Law of Property Act 1922 to be for a term of 2,000 years) unless it is a subtenancy granted out of a superior tenancy which is not a long tenancy; and

(c)   a tenancy granted under the 'right-to-buy' provisions of Part V of the Housing Act 1985.

A tenancy granted by one of the bodies mentioned, which is terminable by notice after death of the tenant, will not be treated as a long tenancy (and will, therefore, be outside the statutory code) unless granted by a grant-registered housing association at a discounted premium in accordance with a proper shared-ownership, lease scheme (LTA 1985, s 26(3)).

Where a right to manage (RTM) company takes over the management of the property (see **2.21**), most of the statutory provisions of the LTA 1985, and other related legislation, will continue to apply (see **2.21.6**).

The application of this regime to the Crown is currently set out in the Landlord and Tenant Act 1987 (LTA 1987), s 56, which is to be amended (from a date to be fixed) by Sch 14 to the Commonhold and Leasehold Reform Act 2002 and is to be supplemented by s 172 of that Act.

2.2 Consultation with tenants and obtaining estimates

2.2.1 Terms of the lease

Most leases do not lay down any procedure for tenants to be consulted before service expenditure is incurred. However, forms of lease vary so widely that it is advisable, in each case, to check whether the lease contains any specific provisions in this respect (see **1.12**).

Just as in the case of other types of letting, consultation prior to major expenditure is desirable in any event to foster the landlord and tenant relationship and smooth the way for the ultimate recovery of the costs through the service charge. Furthermore, in the case of flats sold on long leases, the ground landlord has little financial interest in the running of the block and is, in reality (although perhaps not in law), merely acting as agent for the tenants in administering the services. He should, therefore, act in their best interests and take account of their views, since it is their interests which are affected by his decision.

2.2.2 Scope of the statutory consultation procedure

Where the statutory code under the LTA 1985 applies (see **2.1**), the landlord must comply with the consultation requirements set out in s 20 of that Act. This section was amended by the Commonhold and Leasehold Reform Act 2002. Currently consultation is required only in relation to works (not services) and only where the cost of the work exceeded amounts specified from time to time by regulations made by the Secretary of State. Consultation will be required under the amended section (in force as from a date to be fixed) either:

(a) in relation to work (on a building or other premises) whose cost exceeds an amount to be specified in regulations, or

(b) in relation to entering into a 'long-term agreement' running for over 12 months under which costs may exceed an amount to be specified in regulations.

The subject-matter of these 'long-term agreements' within (b) above is not restricted and could relate to anything falling within the scope of service charges regulated by the LTA 1985 (see **2.1**). However, regulations may exclude certain categories of long-term agreement from the consultation requirements.

The regulations may prescribe the threshold cost figures either in respect of the costs to be charged for the work or under the agreement (as applicable) or in respect of the contributions to be made to them by one or more tenants through their service charges. No regulations bringing this new consultation regime into effect had been made at the publication date of this book.

In respect of (a), under the previous version of this section it was held that the total cost of separate items of work which were really a single project had to be aggregated for this purpose; this had the effect of requiring consultation in respect of additional work found to be necessary during the course of a project even though the cost of the additional work alone was below the prescribed level for consultation (*Martin v Maryland Estates* (1999) 26 EG 151, CA). It is envisaged that this will equally apply to the new section.

2.2.3 The consultation requirements

Under the old version of s 20, the consultation requirements were set out in the section (see **Appendix 3**). The amended section provides, instead, that the consultation requirements are to be prescribed by regulations to be made by the Secretary of State (s 20ZA(4), (5)). No such regulations had been made at the publication date of this book. It is expected that the old version of s 20 will be kept in force until the regulations have been made.

2.2.4 Dispensing with the requirements

Section 20(6) of the LTA 1985 enables a Leasehold Valuation Tribunal ('LVT') to dispense with all or any of the current consultation requirements laid down by s 20(4) or (5) (as applicable) if the LVT is satisfied that the landlord acted reasonably. In relation to the new consultation regime under the amendments being made by the Commonhold and Leasehold Reform Act 2002, the LVT may dispense with compliance where it is satisfied that it is reasonable to dispense with them (s 20ZA(1)). The application for dispensation from the consultation requirement may be made before or after the event and an application might be made in advance, say where there is only one potential supplier of the intended works or service. The mere fact that the works were reasonably necessary and that the costs were of a reasonable amount may not be a sufficient excuse for the landlord failing to follow the statutory procedure. A satisfactory justification for not following the procedure might be, for example, that there was an emergency where the tenants themselves would suffer hardship if there was a delay (eg repairing a leaking pipe or water tank).

Example

> *Wilson v Stone* (1998) 26 EG 153, LVT: The landlord entered into a contract with a builder to carry out urgent work to the building where there was a danger of collapse. A tenant challenged the recovery of the cost under s 20. **Held**: The consultation requirement should be waived in these circumstances.

However, the landlord or his agent should ensure that the steps taken without following the proper procedure should be confined to those which are necessary to deal with the emergency, and that the procedure should be followed closely in respect of less urgent work.

Where initial work, commenced after the correct procedure has been observed, shows the need for urgent additional work (eg dry rot in roof timbers is disclosed when the original roof is stripped), it is probably in order for the landlord to notify the tenants and proceed with the additional work on a day-rate basis with the same contractor, if it would be unreasonable to delay the work. However, care should be taken not to under-specify the basic works if there is a probability that a need for further major work will be revealed by opening up (in such cases, the building contract should be placed in two parts).

2.2.5 Effects of non-compliance

2.2.5.1 Criminal penalties

If any person (other than bodies excluded by LTA 1985, s 26(1) – see **2.1.3**) without reasonable excuse fails to perform any duty under ss 21 to 23, that person can be found guilty of an offence and liable on summary conviction to a fine not exceeding level 4 on the standard scale under the Criminal Justice Act 1982, s 37. If the offence is committed by a company with the consent or connivance of, or due to the neglect of, a director, manager, secretary or similar officer of the company or any person purporting to act in that capacity, he, as well as the company, will be guilty of the offence.

2.2.5.2 Non-recoverability of costs

If the landlord fails to follow the consultation procedure in cases where this is required due to the cost of the work being above the prescribed amount (see **2.2.2** para (a) above), the service costs on which the service charges are calculated must be limited to the prescribed amount, so the landlord has to bear himself the amount by which the cost of the works exceeds that level (LTA 1985, s 20(4)).

If the landlord's failure to consult is in relation to entering into a long-term agreement (see **2.2.2**, para (b) above), the service costs on which the service charges are calculated must wholly exclude all sums payable under the agreement, so that the landlord has to bear the entirety of those costs himself (LTA 1985, s 20(4)).

2.2.6 Recognition of tenants' associations

Recognition of tenants' associations for the purpose of the service charge provisions of the LTA 1985 is governed by s 29 of that Act. The rules are:

(1) the association must comprise 'qualifying tenants' with or without other tenants. 'Qualifying tenants' is defined in s 29(4) as tenants who may be required by the terms of their leases to contribute by service charges to the same service costs;

(2) the association must either be:

    (a) recognised by the landlord, who must give written notice to the secretary of the association that he recognises it for these purposes, or

    (b) recognised by a certificate of a member of the local Rent Assessment Committee panel;

(3) a landlord's notice can be withdrawn by six months' written notice and a certificate can be cancelled;

(4) the Secretary of State has power to make regulations in connection with Rent Assessment Committee Panel applications and certificates.

Thus, if the landlord refuses to recognise a tenants' association, the association can apply to the panel for a recognition certificate. An appeal from the panel's decision may be made to the High Court. In *R v London Rent Assessment Panel, ex parte Trustees of Henry Smith's Charity Estate* [1988] 1 EGLR 34, the High Court upheld a landlord's objection to the recognition of a tenants' association representing tenants in five blocks of flats, on the ground that each block should have its own association so as to represent one service charge regime.

2.2.7 Surveyors appointed by tenants' associations

A recognised tenants' association has power to appoint a surveyor for the purposes set out in Housing Act 1996 ('HA 1996'), s 84, namely, to advise on any matters relating to, or which may give rise to, service charges payable to a landlord by one or more members of that association. By s 84(2) of HA 1996, only a surveyor who is qualified to carry out a management audit can be appointed (see **2.16**).

The appointment is effected by the association giving written notice to the landlord setting out the name and address of the surveyor, the duration of his appointment and the matters in respect of which he is appointed. The appointment will cease for the purposes of s 84 if the association so notifies the landlord in writing or if the association ceases to exist.

The detailed powers of the surveyor are set out in Sch 4 to the HA 1996. This allows the surveyor to appoint assistants and gives the surveyor the right to require the landlord or any other relevant person to afford him reasonable facilities for inspecting those documents of which he reasonably requires sight for the purposes of his functions, and to afford him reasonable facilities for taking copies of or extracts from those documents. The 'other relevant person' will be anyone who is responsible for applying the proceeds of the service charge or is under an obligation to the tenant in respect of any of the works or services covered by the service charge. The surveyor is to give notice to the landlord or other person of the facilities that he requires, and the facilities are to be provided within one week or as soon as reasonably practical. A reasonable charge may be made by the landlord or other person for providing copying facilities. No direct charge can be made for allowing inspection of documents, but if the terms of the lease allow the service charge to include management costs which are defined widely enough to include the cost of providing any of these facilities to the surveyor, the landlord is entitled to include them in the costs on which the service charge is based.

The surveyor also has the right, under Sch 4, to inspect any common parts of the relevant building, or any other premises affected by the management functions reflected in the service charge. On being requested to do so, the landlord must afford the surveyor reasonable access to those premises for inspection. Again, the landlord cannot make a direct charge for giving this access, but this does not prevent him from including any costs of doing so as part of his management costs within the service charge, if the service charge clause permits.

The county court has jurisdiction to deal with disputes arising out of these provisions. The Schedule also contains provisions dealing with the situation where the landlord, after receiving a notice or request from the surveyor, disposes of his interest in the property. In addition, it deals with a situation where a superior landlord holds, or has control of, service charge documents.

2.3 Reasonableness tests

2.3.1 Overriding of contractual terms

As mentioned in **1.10**, the fact that a particular type of expenditure falls within the wording of the service charge clause may not necessarily result in the sum spent on that expenditure being recoverable from the tenant. Even careful adoption of the statutory consultation procedure described above does not guarantee that the cost will be chargeable. The reason for this is that there are two further ways in which the tenant can challenge individual items of expenditure in the courts. The first is under the common law and the second is under statute.

2.3.2 Common law rule

This has been considered (at **1.10**) in respect of the assumption drawn by the courts that the terms of a residential lease will not have been intended to give the landlord an unfettered right to be extravagant at the cost of the tenant. Consequently, variable service charge clauses in residential leases are prima facie subject to an implied term that expenditure can only be included if it was incurred reasonably.

2.3.3 Statutory tests of reasonableness

Where s 18 of the LTA 1985 applies (see **2.1**) the provisions of s 19 of the Act provide two statutory limitations (in addition to any common law implied test of reasonableness) on the costs which can be included in the service charge ('relevant costs'):

(1) costs can be taken into account only to the extent that they are reasonably incurred; and

(2) costs incurred on the provision of services or the carrying out of works are only to be taken into account if the services or works are of a reasonable standard.

As for the procedure for settling disputes concerning these limitations, see **2.12**.

The question arises whether limitations under s 19 apply to every element of the service charge or only to those falling within the definition of service charge in s 18, ie services, repairs, maintenance, insurance and management and (once the changes under the Commonhold and Leasehold Reform Act 2002 apply) improvements. This issue arose in relation to the cost of improvements in *Sutton (Hastoe) Housing Association v Williams* [1988] 1 EGLR 56, CA, in which one judge stated that the provisions of Sch 19 to the Housing Act 1980 (which were, on this point, substantially re-enacted in the LTA 1985) had 'no impact upon a service charge imposed in order to pay for some other item'. However, the other judge seemed to think (although his judgment is unclear) that the statutory reasonableness test did apply to the cost of the improvements. The point, therefore, is not beyond doubt, but in any event the cost of improvements is being brought within the scope of s 18 by the 2002 amendments (see **2.1.2**).

The effect of provision (1) above appears to be that if unnecessarily extensive work is carried out, the costs of such part of the work as is reasonably necessary can be included in the service charge, but the costs of the remainder cannot. Subject to the landlord acting reasonably, the usual rule (described at **1.4.3**) applies, namely that the landlord has the power to decide exactly how he will provide the repair or other service (see *Hi-Lift Elevator Services v Temple* (1994) 70 P&CR 620, CA).

Provision (2), at first glance, appears to mean that if the services or works are carried out to a reasonable standard the cost can be charged, but that if they are not to a reasonable standard no part of the cost can be charged. This strict, literal interpretation has been rejected by the courts and, where services or works are carried out to a less-than-reasonable standard, the court will allow the landlord to make a fair charge for the work done, on a *quantum meruit* basis.

Example

> *Yorkbrook Investment Ltd v Batten* (1985) 276 EG 545, CA: The services did not reach a reasonable standard. At that time the service charge was governed by s 91A of the Housing Finance Act 1972 which provided that 'a service charge shall only be recoverable ... in respect of the provision of chargeable items to a reasonable standard ...'. Did this mean that no charge could be made for the items which had been carried out below a reasonable standard? **Held**: No; such a Draconian result cannot have been intended; the county court judge was right to allow the landlord to charge a proportion of the costs expended on the substandard items.

The meaning of 'reasonably incurred' in s 19 of the Act is that the landlord did not act unreasonably in incurring the cost. This does not require the landlord to ensure that the cost is as low as possible, provided he acted reasonably and in the normal course.

Examples

Berrycroft Management Co Ltd v Sinclair Gardens Investments (Kensington) Ltd [1996] EGCS 143, CA: Leases of flats in a block allowed the landlord to nominate 'insurers of repute' to be used by the management company for insuring the block. The freehold changed hands and the new landlord nominated new insurers whose premiums were higher than the current insurers. This was challenged by the tenants. Would the higher premiums be recoverable as 'reasonably incurred'? **Held**: Yes; so long as the insurance was arranged in the normal course, it was not unreasonably incurred even though the premiums were higher than some alternative insurers would charge.

Wandsworth London Borough Council v Griffin [2000] 26 EG 147, Lands Tribunal: The landlord of a block of flats replaced leaking flat roofs with pitched roofs and replaced the defective metal-framed windows with uPVC double-glazed units. The tenant argued that the landlord should have simply replaced the roof coverings and overhauled the window-frames. **Held**: These costs were 'reasonably incurred' since they were better value for money over the terms of the leases, taking into account both initial and future costs, even though the initial cost alone was higher. Further, the landlord was entitled to take account of the work needed to the whole of its estate, which had been built as a single estate and was still being managed as such.

Gilje and Others v Charlegrove Securities Ltd [2000] 44 EG 148, Lands Tribunal, Judge Rich QC: The lease imposed an obligation on the landlord to provide a resident housekeeper, but the county court determined that, on the true interpretation of the lease, the landlord was not entitled to include in the service charge a notional rent for the housekeeper's flat. The landlord sought to overcome this by agreeing an increased salary for the housekeeper but paying her an amount after deducting the weekly rental value of the flat. Could the whole of that salary be included in the service charge? **Held**: No; since such an excessive salary would not be 'reasonably incurred'.

For further examples of reasonableness tests, see **1.10**.

As regards management fees, it appears that provision (1) allows the making of a 'reasonable charge', the reasonableness of which can be evidenced by a comparison with fees charged by other managing agents: *Parkside Knightsbridge Ltd v Horwitz* (1983) 268 EG 49, CA (see **1.7.2**). Recent decisions by Leasehold Valuation Tribunals as to reasonable management fees have varied. Some were fixed at between 12 per cent and 15 per cent of the total service costs, whilst others were fixed at a rate per flat, eg £200 per flat. The selection of managing agents is itself covered separately by s 30B of the LTA 1985 (see **2.14**).

The procedure for a tenant to challenge the service charge under s 19 of the LTA 1985 is set out at **2.12.2**. The charging of unreasonable service charges is also a ground on which tenants may apply to the court to appoint a manager to run the building in place of the landlord (LTA 1987, s 24, as amended by HA 1996, s 85).

2.3.4   Other statutes

As discussed more fully in **1.10.4**, it seems that Part II of the Supply of Goods and Services Act 1982 may also have the effect of implying obligations on the landlord and his managing agents to carry out services with reasonable care and skill, and implying a term that the charge must be reasonable. It may also be necessary to consider the regulations discussed at **1.10.6**, although service charges are rarely levied in the case of short residential lettings which are most likely to be caught by the regulations. Further, the provisions of the LTA 1985 will in most cases have the effect of turning even unreasonable service charge clauses into a fair and reasonable regime.

2.4   Grant-aided works

2.4.1   Application of these rules

The rules in s 20A of the LTA 1985 apply to service charges covered by s 18 of that Act (see **2.1**).

2.4.2   Credit for grants

By s 20A of the LTA 1985, where otherwise chargeable costs are incurred for which a grant has been or is to be paid under Part XV of the Housing Act 1985 or Part VIII of the Local Government and Housing Act 1989, the amount of the grant is to be deducted from the costs so as to reduce the service charge by that amount.

This also applies to the outstanding balance relating to external works determined for the landlord under s 130(3) and (4) of the Local Government and Housing Act 1989 where the landlord participates as an assisted participant in a group repair scheme under Part VIII of that Act.

2.5   Management and professional fees

2.5.1   Fees for management

In respect of service charges caught by s 18 of the LTA 1985 (see **2.1**), s 18(1) expressly applies the statutory rules under that Act to 'the landlord's costs of management'. Hence, the reasonableness tests under s 19 will apply to management charges (see the discussion at **2.3.3**). Many residential tenants will be able to seek a 'management audit' to assess whether the service charge functions are being discharged in an efficient and effective manner (see **2.16**).

If the service charge clause expressly permits the landlord to charge for in-house management, such a charge may be caught by s 18 and thus subject to the reasonableness tests mentioned, since s 18(3)(a) defines 'costs' as including overheads.

2.5.2 Costs of proceedings

The common law position concerning the inclusion in management fees of legal and other costs relating to court and tribunal proceedings between the landlord and a tenant has been discussed at **1.6.5**.

In the case of the service charge coming within s 18 of the LTA 1985 (see **2.2**), s 20C of the LTA 1985 allows a tenant to make an application to the LVT for an order that all or any of the costs incurred or to be incurred by the landlord in connection with proceedings under the LTA 1985 are to be excluded from the service charge payable by that tenant or by any other person or persons specified in the application (eg the other tenants contributing to the same service charge). The application is to be made to the court or tribunal in which the proceedings are taking place and the current rules governing such applications are in the Leasehold Valuation Tribunals (Service Charges, Insurance or Appointment of Managers Applications) Order 1997, SI 1997/1853. If the proceedings have been concluded, the application may be made afterwards. The court or tribunal may make such order as it considers just and equitable in the circumstances.

An appeal from the LVT's decision under s 20C can be made to the Lands Tribunal with the leave of the LVT or, if the LVT refuses leave, with the leave of the Lands Tribunal (LTA 1985, s 31A(6)). The Lands Tribunal has expressed the view that such an appeal should not be a rehearing, but should be handled as a true appeal in which the LVT's discretion, if properly exercised, should not ordinarily be interfered with (*Barrington Court Developments Ltd v Barrington Court Residents Association* [2001] 29 EG 128, Lands Tribunal).

Whilst the LVT has no power to make an award of costs in relation to such proceedings before it, the Lands Tribunal has such power in respect of proceedings before it, including applications for leave, but may order a party to pay a fixed sum of reasonable amount towards the other party's costs where the costs he is claiming are disproportionate (*Barrington Court Developments Ltd v Barrington Court Residents Association* (above)).

Examples

Iperion Investments Corporation v Broadwalk House Residents Ltd [1995] 2 EGLR 47, CA: The landlord of a block of flats invalidly purported to forfeit the lease of a tenant who had embarked on unauthorised alterations. The tenant obtained a court order against the landlord to regain possession of the flat and the landlord obtained an injunction to stop the alterations. The landlord was ordered to pay half the tenant's costs of the proceedings. The service charge provisions of the tenant's lease allowed the landlord to include the costs he incurred in those proceedings. Was the judge right to make an order under s 20C that this tenant's service charge was not to include any costs relating to the proceedings? **Held**: Yes; the obvious circumstance which Parliament must be taken to have had in mind in enacting s 20C is a case where a tenant has been successful in litigation against the landlord and yet the costs of the proceedings are within the service charge that would otherwise be recoverable from the tenant.

Tenants of Langford Court v Doren Ltd (2001) 5 March (unreported), Lands Tribunal: The LVT appointed a manager under the LTA 1987 on the application of the tenants, but refused to make a s 20C order excluding from the service charges the costs incurred by the landlord in opposing that application, because over half of the various grounds put forward by the tenants in support of their application were unfounded and the tenants' aggressive and unco-operative attitude towards the landlord's manager had contributed to the problems. Was the LVT justified in exercising its discretion under s 20C in that way? **Held**: Yes; the Lands Tribunal would not interfere with the LVT's exercise of its discretion under s 20C in these circumstances.

The rules governing costs incurred in connection with appeals to the Lands Tribunal are amended, as from a date to be fixed, by s 175 of and Sch 12 to the Commonhold and Leasehold Reform Act 2002 (see **Appendix 3**).

2.6   Irrecoverable costs under short lettings

2.6.1   Tenancies for under seven years (ss 11 to 13 of the LTA 1985)

A short tenancy of a dwelling may be affected by the provisions of ss 11 to 12 of the LTA 1985 (formerly ss 32 to 33 of the Housing Act 1961) or ss 8 to 10 of the LTA 1985 (formerly ss 6 to 7 of the Housing Act 1957). Where these provisions apply, they impose repairing obligations on the landlord *and* prohibit or restrict the recovery of the costs from the tenant.

The type of tenancy to which ss 11 to 12 of the LTA 1985 apply is defined in s 13 of the Act to cover:

(1) any tenancy of a dwelling;

(2) granted on or after 24 October 1961;

(3) for a term of *less* than seven years (or granted for a term exceeding seven years but with a landlord's option to terminate it within the first seven years) without a tenant's option for renewal which, if exercised, would result in a total term of seven years or more.

The length of the term under (3) above is measured from the date from which the lease or agreement expresses the term to run, or the date when the tenancy was actually granted, whichever is later. For example, if a lease granting a term of seven years from 25 March 1992 was not actually granted until 27 March 1992, the term will be treated under the LTA 1985 as being *less* than seven years (ie from 27 March 1992 to 25 March 1999, a term of seven years, less two days) and would be caught by s 13.

However, these provisions do not apply to:

(1) tenancies which are comprised in an agricultural holding (LTA 1985, s 14(3));

(2) leases granted after 3 October 1980 to the Crown, a government department, a local authority, a registered housing association or certain other
bodies (LTA 1985, s 14(4) and (5));

(3) business tenancies to which Part II of the Landlord and Tenant Act 1954
applies (LTA 1985, s 32(2));

(4) short tenancies granted on a renewal where the previous tenancy fell outside
the s 11 rules (LTA 1985, s 14(3)).

2.6.2 Landlord's obligations under s 11 of the LTA 1985

Tenancies caught by s 13 of the LTA 1985 are subject to the provisions of s 11(1)
of the Act, which make the landlord liable, *at his own cost*, to:

(a) keep in repair the structure and exterior of the dwelling, including the drains,
gutters and external pipes;

(b) keep in repair and proper working order the installations in the dwelling for
the supply of water, gas, electricity and sanitation; and

(c) keep in repair and proper working order the installations in the dwelling for
space heating and hot water.

Since the landlord is liable to carry out such repairs *at his own cost*, he cannot
include those costs in any service charges levied on the tenant (LTA 1985,
s 11(5)).

The extent of these obligations is discussed below.

2.6.3 Parts of a building to which the landlord's statutory obligations apply

The reference in s 11(1)(a) of the LTA 1985 to 'structure and exterior', in
relation to a dwelling (such as a flat) which forms only part of a building, means
the structure and exterior of all those parts of the building belonging to the
landlord, and not just the structure and exterior of the demised premises
(s 11(1A)(a)). Similarly, the installations referred to in s 11(1)(b) and (c)
include those installations (such as central heating boilers) which serve the
demised premises directly or indirectly but are located elsewhere in the landlord's
building or are under the landlord's ownership or control (s 11(1A)(b)).
However, the provisions of s 11(1A) do not require the landlord to carry out any
works or repairs unless the disrepair or lack of working order affects the tenant's
enjoyment of the demised premises or any common parts which he is entitled to
use under his lease (s 11(1B)).

It should also be noted that the essential means of access to a dwelling has been
treated as part of the 'exterior' of that dwelling, although amenity areas, such as a
rear yard, have not (*Douglas-Scott v Scorgie* [1984] 1 All ER 1086; *Brown v
Liverpool Corporation* [1969] 3 All ER 1345; *Hopwood v Rugeley Urban District
Council* [1975] 1 WLR 373).

2.6.4   Extent of the landlord's obligations under s 11 of the LTA 1985

The obligations imposed by s 11 on the landlord do *not* require him:

(a) to carry out any works or repairs which would be covered by the tenant's duty to use the premises in a tenant-like manner;

(b) to rebuild or reinstate the premises after damage or destruction by fire or by tempest, flood or other inevitable accident; or

(c) to repair or maintain anything which the tenant is entitled to remove from the dwelling (s 11(2)).

In determining the standard of repair required of the landlord, regard shall be had to the age, character and prospective life of the dwelling and its locality (s 11(3)).

Furthermore, the obligation to keep the relevant parts of the building in 'repair' is itself a limited obligation, by reason of the restricted meaning given by the courts to the word 'repair' (see **1.4.2**). In *McDougall v Easington District Council* (1989) 58 P&CR 201, the Court of Appeal held that, by using the word 'repair', s 11 did not require the landlord to remedy major defects in the original construction and design of the dwellings which would have involved major structural alterations changing the character of the buildings. For the same reason, s 11 does not require the landlord to install new items which were not previously provided. Hence, it has been held that a landlord is not liable to install a damp-proof course where none had existed previously, nor to lag previously unlagged waterpipes against frost, nor to replace window-frames whose design made them prone to condensation (even though this resulted in dampness which damaged internal decorations) (*Wainwright v Leeds City Council* (1984) 270 EG 1289; *Wycombe Health Authority v Barnett* (1982) 264 EG 619; *Quick v Taff-Ely Borough Council* [1986] QB 809; *Eyre v McCracken* (2000) 80 P&CR 220, CA).

On the other hand, if internal redecoration is required as a consequence of repairs which the landlord is liable to carry out under s 11, the landlord is responsible for the necessary consequential redecoration and, if the landlord delays carrying out that redecoration, the tenant may be entitled to damages for the inconvenience of having to live in the premises in their poor decorative condition (*McGreal v Wake* (1984) 269 EG 1254; *Bradley v Chorley Borough Council* (1985) 275 EG 801).

The obligations to keep installations in proper working order have been the subject of some recent cases.

Examples

Sykes v Harry (2001) 17 EG 221, CA: A gas fire in a flat let on a shorthold tenancy was defective. The landlord did not enter into a service contract for its maintenance, had not inspected the flat and was unaware of the defect. Carbon monoxide poisoning made the tenant ill. **Held**: The landlord is liable in damages under the Defective Premises Act 1972, s 4 for personal injury caused by his failure to comply with his obligation to maintain installations under LTA 1985, s 11, even if he does not have actual notice of the defect, where he has not taken reasonable care.

O'Connor v Old Etonian Housing Association Ltd [2002] EWCA Civ 150 (unreported), CA: The landlord of a block of flats replaced old large water pipes with small bore pipes. Initially there was no problem, but later the mains water pressure decreased and the tenant's top floor flat, held on a short tenancy, ceased to get a proper supply, which would not have happened with the old larger pipes. The landlord could have installed a pump to rectify this, but did not. Six years later the water authority built a new pumping station which increased the mains pressure and solved the problem. Was the landlord liable in the meantime for breach of the covenant implied by LTA 1985, s 11(1)(b) to 'keep in . . . proper working order' the water pipes? **Held**: No; the small bore pipes were still in proper working order; when installed they had been properly designed and constructed and had worked effectively; at the time of installation a substantial long-term drop in water pressure could not have been reasonably anticipated.

2.6.5   Lettings of houses at low rents (sections 8 to 10 of the LTA 1985)

The LTA 1985 re-enacts some very old statutory rules concerning houses let at low rents. Sections 8 to 10 apply to a contract for the letting of a house if the rent does not exceed the amount set out in Table 1 below.

Section 8(6) provides that 'house' includes part of a house, but it is not clear whether it includes a flat in a purpose-built block.

TABLE 1

Date of making contract	Rent limit
Before 31 July 1923	In London: £40 Elsewhere: £26 or £16 (See Note (1))
On or after 31 July 1923 but before 6 July 1957	In London: £40 Elsewhere: £26
On or after 6 July 1957	In London: £80 Elsewhere: £52

Notes

(1)   The applicable figure for contracts made before 31 July 1923, is £26 in the case of premises situated in a borough or urban district which, at the date of the contract, had, according to the last published census, a population of 50,000 or more. In the case of a house situated elsewhere, the figure is £16.

(2)   The references to 'London' are, in relation to contracts made before 1 April 1965, to the administrative county of London and, in relation to contracts made on or after that date, to Greater London exclusive of the outer London boroughs.

The provisions of ss 8 to 10 of the LTA do not apply to a letting for three years or more if it contains an obligation on the tenant to put the premises into a condition reasonably fit for human habitation. For this purpose, a tenancy containing an option for either party to terminate the letting before the expiry of three years counts as a tenancy for less than three years. While, in some instances, a tenant's covenant to 'keep' premises in repair will be construed so as to include an obligation on the tenant to put the premises into repair at the outset of the letting (*Proudfoot v Hart* (1890) 25 QB 42), this appears to apply only where the premises are in disrepair at the commencement of the letting.

Since a lease is, in law, a 'contract', it would seem possible that, under the above rules, ss 8 to 10 of the LTA 1985 might apply to a long lease of a house granted at a premium and reserving a nominal ground rent if the tenant's repairing covenant is simply to 'keep' (and not 'put') the house in good repair. However, if the expression 'rent' is apt to include all sums payable to the landlord by the tenant under the terms of the tenancy, including a service charge, the effect would be, in many cases, to take the letting outside the rent limits set out in Table 1 above.

2.6.6   Effect of sections 8 to 10 of the LTA 1985

Tenancies to which ss 8 to 10 of the LTA 1985 apply carry an implied condition on the landlord's part that the house is fit for human habitation at the outset of the letting, and an implied obligation on the part of the landlord to keep it fit for human habitation during the letting. The cost of any works required to comply with these provisions cannot be charged to the tenant.

The criteria for fitness for human habitation are set out in s 10 of the LTA 1985. These are repair, stability, freedom from damp, internal arrangement, natural lighting, ventilation, water supply, drainage and sanitation conveniences, cooking and food preparation facilities and waste water disposal facilities. A house is to be regarded as unfit if (but only if) it is so defective in any one or more of these matters so that it is not reasonably suitable for occupation in that condition.

2.7   Service charge limits under Rent Act protected tenancies and right-to-buy leases

2.7.1   Rent Act protected tenancies

2.7.1.1   Introduction
Some short and periodic (eg quarterly) residential lettings constitute protected tenancies under the Rent Act 1977, as amended. The details of Rent Act protection, apart from those relating to service charges, are outside the scope of this book.

Until a rent is registered under the Rent Acts there is no limit on the amount of rent chargeable under a protected tenancy. However, once, and for so long as, a rent is registered the registration serves to specify the maximum which can be charged to the tenant by way of rent *and* service charge. The rent may either be registered as a fixed sum inclusive of a notional service charge, or with a separate variable service charge.

2.7.1.2 Registered rents with variable service charges

If the tenant's lease or tenancy agreement contains provisions for a variable service charge, and the rent officer or rent assessment committee considers that the terms of those provisions for variability of the charge are reasonable, the rent may be registered as a basic rent with an additional, separate, variable service charge (Rent Act 1977, s 71(4)). It must be remembered that service charges under a letting granted for a term of under seven years (including a periodic letting) cannot include the cost of works covered by ss 11 to 12 of the Landlord and Tenant Act 1985 (see **2.6**).

This power under s 71(4) is restricted to incorporating, in the rent registration, the *identical formula* for the variable service charge as that contained in the contractual tenancy. The rent cannot be registered with a different version of that formula. Accordingly, if, as is quite common, the contractual tenancy reserves, by way of service charge, a proportion of the amount by which the service expenditure may increase above the expenditure in a specified base year, the variable service charge can only be incorporated in the rent registration using exactly the same formula *including the same base year* (*Wigglesworth v Property Holding & Investment Trust Ltd* (1984) 270 EG 555; *Betts v Vivamat Properties Ltd* (1984) 270 EG 849).

In *Firstcross Ltd v Teasdale* (1983) 265 EG 305 the court considered that when determining the reasonableness of the contractual variability provisions contained in the lease or tenancy agreement, the court was bound to take into account the implied limitation of reasonableness laid down in *Finchbourne v Rodrigues* [1976] 3 All ER 581, CA (see **1.10.3**). However, in *Wigglesworth v Property Holding & Investment Trust Ltd* (above) the court took a different view and considered that s 71 required the contractual provisions of the lease or tenancy agreement to be considered on their own, to see whether they passed the test of reasonableness under that section.

In a case where the landlord was a co-operative which was owned by the tenants and incorporated under the Industrial and Friendly Societies Act 1965, it was held reasonable to have a clause which provided for the service charge to be a sum fixed each year by the annual general meeting of the co-operative, the rules of which (together with statutory provisions) provided for annual meetings, audited accounts, and other proper arrangements (*Re Heathview Tenants' Co-operative Ltd* (1981) 258 EG 644).

A rent registration is not to include a service charge where the services are provided by a company which is separate from a landlord (even if it is in the same group) and where the tenant pays for the services separately from the rent and the landlord is not personally liable to provide or procure the provision of the services (*Eaton Square Properties v Ogilvie* (2000) 16 EG 143, London Rent Assessment Committee).

2.7.1.3 Registered rents inclusive of service charges

If the contractual tenancy does not include a variable service charge clause (or if it does, but the Rent Officer or Rent Assessment Committee considers that the variability provisions of the clause are not reasonable), an inclusive rent will be registered incorporating a fixed service charge element. Under s 67 of the Rent Act 1977, as amended by s 59 of the Housing Act 1980, the landlord must, when applying for registration of a fair rent, submit details and calculations of the service costs referable to the particular dwelling. Once again, these cannot include the cost of works falling within ss 11 to 12 of the LTA 1985 where applicable (see **2.3**).

The Rent Officer is not bound by a mathematical calculation of the service costs in cases where this might result in an unrealistic figure. For example, in the case of a centrally heated flat in a block in which most other flats had been disconnected from the heating system, the actual mathematical cost of supplying the heating to that flat might be excessively high and will then be substituted by a typical, reasonable, heating charge (_R v London Rent Assessment Panel, ex parte Cliftvylle Properties Ltd_ (1983) 266 EG 44).

The landlord is entitled to include in his calculation of the service element, an allowance for depreciation of the service equipment (boilers, lifts, tanks, etc) and an element in respect of profit to the landlord on the provision of services (_Regis Property Co Ltd v Dudley_ [1959] AC 370; _Metropolitan Properties Co (FGC) Ltd v Lannon_ [1968] 1 All ER 354; _Metropolitan Properties Co (FGC) Ltd v Good_ (1981) 260 EG 67; _Metropolitan Properties Co Ltd v Noble_ [1968] 2 All ER 313; _Perseus Property Co Ltd v Burberry_ (1984) 273 EG 405). This 'profit' is intended to go towards the landlord's costs of financing the provision of the services and providing the capital money for the purchase of the service equipment.

If a rent is registered with a fixed charge element based on estimates and, subsequently, it is found that the actual service costs are less than the estimates, the tenant nevertheless, cannot have the rent registration varied or set aside (_Legal and General Assurance Society v Keane_ (1979) 38 P&CR 399). But where there is an appeal from the Rent Officer's determination to the Rent Assessment Committee, the landlord is entitled to place, before the committee, updated details of service costs which were not available at the time of the rent officer's consideration of the matter (_Daejan Properties Ltd v Chambers_ (1986) 277 EG 308).

2.7.1.4 Statutory tenancies on expiry of long leases

Part I of the Landlord and Tenant Act 1954 contains provisions for certain residential tenants to become assured tenants under the Housing Act 1980 (as amended), on the expiry of a long lease at a low rent. The detailed rules are outside the scope of this book.

Where the long lease reserved a service charge, any service charges payable in respect of a period prior to the commencement of the statutory tenancy will be recoverable from the tenant, even after that date, since the proviso to s 10(1) of the Landlord and Tenant Act 1954 excludes, from the extinguishment of past liabilities, sums payable in respect of parts of the building other than the demised premises (*Blatherwick (Services) Ltd v King* [1991] 2 EGLR 39, CA).

2.7.2 Right-to-buy leases

2.7.2.1 Introduction

The grant of long, shared-ownership leases under the right-to-buy legislation is governed by ss 143 *et seq* of the Housing Act 1985, the details of which go beyond the scope of this book. However, the Sixth Schedule to the Housing Act 1985 contains provisions restricting the service charges which can be imposed under such leases.

2.7.2.2 Service charge provisions

The Sixth Schedule to the Housing Act 1985 sets out limitations upon service charges under shared ownership leases granted in pursuance of the right to buy, and these are summarised (in outline only) below.

(1) Where the premises comprise a flat, the tenant can be required to pay a 'reasonable part' of the costs of discharging or insuring against the obligations imposed by the covenants implied by para 14(2) of the Sixth Schedule (which covers the repair of the structure and the exterior of the building, the making good of defects in the structure, the repair of common parts, the maintenance at a reasonable level of the services to which the tenant is entitled, and the repair of installations connected with those services) (para 16A(1)(a) of the Sixth Schedule).

The lease can, however, require the payment of a service charge contribution of a *fixed* sum with increases being index-linked; the provisions of para 16B only apply to service charges which vary according to the amount of costs incurred (*Coventry City Council v Cole* [1994] 1 WLR 398, CA).

(2) The tenant can, in the case of a house or a flat, be required to pay a 'reasonable part' of the costs of insuring against the obligation implied by para 14(3) (which covers rebuilding or reinstating the building in the event of damage by fire, tempest, flood or other normally insured peril) (para 16A(1)(b) of the Sixth Schedule).

(3) However, the amount recoverable from the tenant of a flat in respect of the cost of repairs (including making good structural defects) during the 'initial period' of the lease (generally the first five accounting years – see para 16B(4)) is restricted by reference to the amount of estimated cost notified to the tenant by the landlord's notice under s 125 of the Housing Act 1985 plus an inflation allowance (para 16B(1) to (3) of the Sixth Schedule).

(4) The lease of a flat can require the tenant to pay towards improvements to be carried out to the flat, the building or other land, if notified in the s 125 notice, and during the 'initial period' (generally the first five years of the term – see para 16C(4)) the amount recoverable in this respect is limited by

reference to the estimate contained in the s 125 notice, plus an inflation allowance (para 16C(1) to (3) of the Sixth Schedule).

2.8 Notices, service charge demands and time-limits

2.8.1 Need for notice of landlord's address for service

Section 48 of the LTA 1987 provides that no rent or service charge will be due from any tenant of premises which are or include a dwelling (except those within Part II of the Landlord and Tenant Act 1954 – relating to business premises) unless the landlord has served on the tenant a written notice giving the tenant an address in England or Wales at which notices (including notices in proceedings) can be served on the landlord by the tenant.

In *Dallhold Estates (UK) Pty Ltd v Lindsay Trading Properties Inc* [1994] EGLR 99, the Court of Appeal held that this meant that the rent was not due until the s 48 notice was served, at which time any rent which would otherwise have been in arrears became due immediately.

The section does not make it clear exactly when a notice needs to be served, but it seems appropriate that every residential tenant should be served with a s 48 notice well before any rent or service charge falls due or is to be demanded, and that each assignee should be given one as soon as the landlord or his agent learns of the assignment.

A specimen notice is given in **Appendix 2**. Formality of wording is not required (*Rogan v Woodfield* [1994] EGCS 145, CA) and strictly there is no need to state expressly that the address is being given 'for service' (*Drew-Morgan v Hamid-Zadeh* (1999) EGCS 72, CA). However, new statutory provisions for service charge demands may require particular wording to be used (see **2.8.2**).

2.8.2 Forms of service charge demand

In *addition* to the above requirement, ss 46 and 47 of the LTA 1987 impose requirements for rent and service charge demands addressed to those tenants. The requirements are that every demand must set out:

(1) the name and address of the landlord; and

(2) if that address is not in England or Wales, an address in England or Wales at which notices (including notices in proceedings) may be served on the landlord by the tenant.

Unless a receiver or manager is administering the service charge under a court order, no service charge will be payable on a demand which omits the above information until that information is supplied in writing (s 47(2) of the LTA 1987).

Further requirements for service charge demands will arise under the new s 21B of the LTA 1985, being inserted by the Commonhold and Leasehold

Reform Act 2002 as from a date to be fixed. When in force, this will require any demand for service charges to contain a summary of tenants' rights and obligations concerning service charges, in accordance with regulations to be made by the Secretary of State. If a notice is served without the summary, the tenant can withhold payment of the sum demanded until a fresh demand is served containing the summary (s 21B(3), (4)).

2.8.3 Time-limits

There is an extremely important time-limit imposed by s 20B of the LTA 1985. Where the Act applies, a service charge demand cannot include costs, even if the costs are within the scope of s 18 (see **2.1**), which are incurred more than 18 months before the demand for payment is served on the tenant, unless a written notice was given to the tenant during the 18 months beginning with the date when the costs were incurred, warning him that the costs were incurred and that he would, subsequently, be required to contribute to them through the service charge. It is essential that the notice specifies the amount of the costs incurred, otherwise they will be irrecoverable (*Westminster City Council v Hammond* [1995] LAG Bulletin, December, p 19, Central London County Court).

Where, under the terms of the tenant's lease, the demand cannot be made until a service charge certificate or account has been prepared, compliance with the above procedure will be important if the preparation of the certificate or account may be delayed.

A further extremely important time-limit is being introduced by the new s 21(2), to be inserted by the Commonhold and Leasehold Reform Act 2002 with effect from a date to be fixed. This imposes a deadline for the service of accounts and certificates (see **2.10.2** para (a)) and allows tenants to withhold payments in cases of default (see **2.12.3**).

As for the time-limits for making demands of former tenants and their guarantors, see **1.20.9**.

2.9 Interim charges

2.9.1 Common law position

The contractual position in respect of the entitlement to charge interim charges has been discussed at **1.15**. So far, there has been no reported case indicating any common law implied term that *interim* charges must be reasonable, but a court decision to that effect might not be entirely unexpected, having regard to the reasoning in *Finchbourne v Rodrigues* [1976] 3 All ER 58, CA (see **1.10**).

2.9.2 Statutory limits on interim contributions

Where s 18 of the LTA 1985 applies (see **2.1**), s 19(2) of that Act provides that, in respect of any service charge which is payable before the costs are incurred:

(1) no greater amount shall be so payable than is reasonable; and

(2) after the relevant costs have been incurred, any necessary adjustments shall be made by repayment, reduction in subsequent charges, or otherwise.

This would appear to permit both interim charges and reserve fund contributions, so long as the amounts demanded do not exceed a reasonable sum. The provisions of s 19(2) do not specify *how soon* 'after' the costs are incurred the adjustment must be made. The court might well imply that the adjustment must be within a reasonable time of the actual expenditure and, where the lease provides for annual accounting and certification, it is anticipated that the court would accept that procedure as complying with this requirement, assuming that the preparation and certification of the accounts were to be carried out within a reasonable time after the expiry of the accounting year.

Note also the time-limit provisions of s 20B of the LTA 1985 where a final demand may not be available to be served within 18 months of the costs being incurred (see **2.8.3**).

The procedure for the tenant to challenge the amounts demanded by the landlord is set out at **2.12.2**.

2.9.3   Inadequate interim charge provisions

If the lease fails to provide for sufficient interim charges, an application to the court to vary the lease should be considered (see **2.15**).

2.9.4   Trust of interim payments

Interim payments, until expended, are generally to be held on trust as described at **2.11**, although some landlords are exempt from that rule.

2.9.5   Designated accounts

The amendments made by the Commonhold and Leasehold Reform Act 2002, coming into effect on a date to be fixed, include a new s 42A to the LTA 1987.

This provides that interim payments (and other sums such as sinking funds) which are held on trust under the LTA 1987, s 42 (see **2.9.4** and **2.11**) must be held by the payee in a 'designated account' at a 'relevant financial institution'. The Secretary of State may make regulations identifying 'relevant financial institutions' and describing the type of account that can be used for this purpose. The institution must be notified in writing that the account is designated to receive the payments in question (ie sums collected by way of service charge from all those tenants who are contributing to the same service costs) and no other payments.

The contributing tenants have the right to be given reasonable facilities to inspect, or to be given copies of, documents evidencing compliance with these requirements (eg bank statements). This right can also be exercised by the secretary of a recognised tenants' association (see **2.2.6**). They can exercise this right by giving written notice to the landlord or the rent collector and the inspection facilities or copies must be provided to them within 21 days. A reasonable charge can be made for supplying copies. No charge can be made for being given inspection facilities, but any costs incurred by the payee in providing those facilities can be treated as part of his costs of management, so such costs could be included in the service charges if management costs are chargeable under the terms of the relevant leases.

Tenants may withhold further service charge payments if they have reasonable grounds for believing that the payee is not complying with the duty to pay the sums into a designated account with a relevant financial institution. Any provisions of the tenant's lease which would apply to the non-payment (eg landlord's right of forfeiture) or late payment (eg landlord's right to charge interest) of the amount withheld are suspended in relation to that amount during the period in which the tenant is allowed to withhold payment.

Failure to comply with the requirements of s 42A without reasonable excuse is the commital of an offence (LTA 1987, s 42B). Where the payee is a company or other corporate body, the offence will be committed personally by any director, manager, secretary or similar officer of the body who has consented to or connived in the offence. This also applies to members of the body who manage its affairs. Proceedings under these provisions can be brought by a local housing authority (within s 1 of the Housing Act 1985).

The Secretary of State may make regulations which exclude certain categories of landlords from these requirements (LTA 1987, s 42A(9A)).

2.10 Preparation and certification of accounts

2.10.1 Requirements of the lease

Requirements of the lease are discussed at **1.16**. Where statutes impose requirements in respect of the preparation and certification of accounts (see below), those will normally be *in addition* to, rather than replacing, the contractual requirements of the lease.

2.10.2 Provision of statements of account

Where s 18 of the LTA 1985 applies (see **2.1**), the landlord must supply, to each tenant who is liable to pay a service charge, a written statement of account for every accounting period (s 21). Until the amendment to s 21 made in 2002 comes into force, this duty only arises upon the tenant (or the secretary of a recognised tenants' association) making a request for the accounts.

A new requirement for the landlord, without request, to issue regular statements is imposed by the amended version of s 21 as from a date to be fixed, and the following rules will apply.

(a) Each accounting period must be of not more than 12 months and must start immediately after the previous accounting period, except that the first accounting period under this regime must start on the date on which service charges are first payable under any of the relevant leases or (if later) on the date when s 152 of the Commonhold and Leasehold Reform Act 2002 comes into force. Where the landlord is already operating annual accounting, he should be able to deal with this by having the first period under this regime as a period of less than a year running from the prescribed starting date to the end of his current accounting period.

(b) Each statement must specify:

    (i)   the total service costs of the relevant accounting period;

    (ii)   the service charges payable in respect of them by the tenant to whom it is being given and by other tenants who contribute to the same service costs;

    (iii) any service charge amounts in hand at the beginning of the accounting period;

    (iv) any service charge amounts to remain in hand at the end of the accounting period;

    (v)   any related matters; and

    (vi) any further matters that may be prescribed by regulations.

(c) The landlord must also supply to the tenant:

    (i)   an accountant's certificate as described at **2.10.3**, unless this requirement is exempted by regulations; and

    (ii)   a summary of the rights and obligations of tenants of dwellings in relation to service charges.

(d) The statements must be issued within six months of the end of the relevant accounting period.

(e) The statement, accountant's certificate and summary of rights and obligations must be supplied to the tenant at any address in England or Wales that the tenant may have given to the landlord or his agent for that purpose. If no such address has been given, they presumably may be given to the tenant at the flat.

The Secretary of State has power to make regulations dealing with the form and content of the statements of account, auditors' certificates and summaries of tenants' rights and obligations (s 21(4)) and exceptions to the need for auditors' certificates (s 21(5)).

Failure to comply with these requirements may result in the tenant being entitled to withhold payments of service charges (see **2.12.3**).

2.10.3   Certification of statements of accounts

The accountant's certificate under the amended s 21 will have to state:

(a)   that in his opinion the statement of account deals fairly with the matters with which it is required to deal under s 21 of the LTA 1985; and

(b)   that the costs stated in the summary are sufficiently supported by accounts, receipts and other documents which have been produced to him.

Regulations may impose further requirements for these certificates (see **2.10.2**).

Apparently, the accountant is *not* required to consider whether the costs were incurred in accordance with the reasonableness and consultation requirements of ss 19 and 20 of the LTA 1985.

The qualifications of the accountant must fall within s 28 of the LTA 1985. He must be a member of either the Institute of Chartered Accountants in England and Wales, the Institute of Chartered Accountants of Scotland, the Association of Certified Accountants, the Institute of Chartered Accountants in Ireland, or any other body established in the United Kingdom and recognised by the Secretary of State for the purposes of the Companies Act 1985, s 389(1)(a). Alternatively, he can be a person authorised by the Secretary of State under s 389(1)(b) of the Companies Act 1985 as being a person with similar qualifications obtained outside the United Kingdom. These references to the Companies Act 1985 include references to the corresponding provisions of the Companies Act 1948. However, a body corporate (except a Scottish firm), an officer or employee of the landlord or of a company in the same group as the landlord, or a person who is a partner or employee of any such officer or employee, cannot act as accountant for these purposes. Special rules apply where the landlord is one of certain specified public bodies listed in the LTA 1985 (s 28(6)).

2.10.4   Advance warning of late demands

As mentioned at **2.8**, the LTA 1985 precludes a demand from including relevant costs incurred more than 18 months prior to the service of the demand on the tenant, unless a warning notice under s 20B was given to the tenant within that period of 18 months.

2.10.5   Tenants' inspection of invoices

Some leases give the tenant the right to inspect the service charge records, books, invoices and vouchers. In addition to any such contractual rights, where s 18 of the LTA 1985 applies, a tenant who is entitled to receive a statement of account pursuant to s 21 has the right under s 22 of the LTA 1985 to be given reasonable facilities to inspect and copy (or take down extracts from) the accounts, receipts and other documents relevant to the matter to be dealt with in the statement of account (see **2.10.2**).

The inspection and copying facilities must be made available within 28 days of the tenant making a written request. The tenant must make his request within 12 months of the end of the relevant accounting period, except where the landlord issues the statement of account (exactly or substantially conforming to the requirements of s 21) more than six months after the end of the accounting period, in which event the tenant's time to request inspection of the vouchers and other supporting documents is extended to the date six months after the statement is actually issued to him. The request can be served on the landlord or the person who collects rent on his behalf (or on his agent specified in the rent book or similar document). Where there is a recognised tenants' association, a tenant may authorise the secretary of the association to carry out the inspection on his behalf.

The inspection facilities must be made available, free of charge, to the person inspecting, although this does not preclude the costs so incurred by the landlord being charged in the service charges as management costs if the service charge clause in the lease permits. The landlord is, however, entitled to make a reasonable charge for providing copying facilities.

These provisions are being amended by Sch 10 to the Commonhold and Leasehold Reform Act 2002 to ensure that they apply to service charge payments provided by just one tenant as they apply to contributions from two or more tenants.

2.10.6   Service of tenants' requests under s 22 of the LTA 1985

By virtue of s 22(5) of the LTA 1985 (as existing and also as to be amended by the Commonhold and Leasehold Reform Act 2002), the tenant's written request for inspection of accounts, receipts and other supporting documents may be served either on the landlord, or on the person who collects rent on behalf of the landlord, or on any other agent of the landlord named as such in the rent book or similar document.

2.10.7   Service charges levied by superior landlords

Where the landlord's own interest in the property is leasehold, the service costs incurred by the landlord may have been paid (wholly or partly) to the superior landlord. In such circumstances, if the landlord needs information from the superior landlord in order to prepare the statement of account and obtain the accountant's certificate under s 21, he can require that information from the superior landlord, who must comply within a reasonable time (s 23(1)). Similarly, if the landlord receives a request under s 22 from his tenant, he can, in turn, make a similar request to his own landlord, who is obliged to comply with the request within a reasonable time (s 23(2)). If there is a chain of leases, s 23 enables the request to be repeated as far up the chain as necessary. It will be appreciated that the provisions of s 23 are necessary because the immediate landlord may not have the benefit of the LTA 1985 *vis-à-vis* his own landlord.

Under the new s 23A, where the landlord or superior landlord parts with his interest in the premises while obligations under ss 21 to 23 remain outstanding, the obligations will be enforceable against his successor so far as he becomes able to fulfil them.

2.11 Trust of service charge funds

2.11.1 Service charges to which the statutory provisions apply

This is governed by s 42(1) of the LTA 1987, and covers payments in respect of service charges to which s 18 of the LTA 1985 applies (see **2.1**) but does not apply to payments by tenants of 'exempt landlords' (see **2.11.2**). Currently these provisions apply to funds contributed by two or more tenants, but amendments are being made by the Commonhold and Leasehold Reform Act 2002, Sch 10, which will apply these provisions even where there is only one contributing tenant.

2.11.2 Funds to be held on trust

Any sums paid by the contributing tenants by way of service charges, and any investments representing those sums, must (together with any accruing income) be held by the landlord (or other person to whom the service charges are paid) either as a single trust fund or in two or more separate trust funds, on trust to defray costs incurred (by himself or any other person) in connection with the matters for which the service charges were payable, and any balance being on trust for the persons who are the contributing tenants for the time being (LTA 1987, s 42(2) and (3)). However, this does not apply to contributions made by tenants of 'exempt landlords' as defined in the LTA 1987, s 58(1), which are principally local councils, development corporations, housing action trusts, charitable housing trusts, registered housing associations and unregistered fully mutual housing associations.

As to the requirements for designated accounts for funds held on trust, see **2.9**.

2.11.3 Investment of funds

Section 42(5) of the LTA 1987 gives power to the Secretary of State to make Orders as to how these trust funds must be invested.

The Service Charge Contributions (Authorised Investments) Order 1988, SI 1988/1284, which came into force on 1 April 1989, provides that any sums standing to the credit of any trust fund under s 42 of the LTA 1987 may be:

(a) deposited at interest with the Bank of England; or

(b) deposited in the UK at interest with a person carrying on, in the UK, a deposit-taking business (within the meaning of the Banking Act 1987); or

(c) deposited at interest with, or invested in shares in, a building society (within the meaning of the Building Societies Act 1986).

Paragraph (b) would encompass authorised banks and licensed deposit-takers.

2.11.4   Ultimate entitlement to the funds

On the termination of the lease of a contributing tenant, the tenant cannot withdraw his share of the fund, but:

(a) if at that time there are other contributing tenants whose leases are continuing, the whole fund will continue to be held on trust, for those remaining contributing tenants, to meet the relevant costs (LTA 1987, s 42(6));

(b) once all contributing tenants' leases have terminated, any remaining trust fund is to be dissolved as at the termination date of the last lease, and any assets in the fund will belong to the landlord (LTA 1987, s 42(7)).

However, by s 42(8) the above is subject to any provisions in the tenant's lease which may provide otherwise.

2.12   Disputes over service charges

2.12.1   Tenancies to which the rules apply

The rules set out below apply to service charges to which s 18 of the LTA 1985 applies (see **2.2**).

2.12.2   Determination of disputes

2.12.2.1   Present regime
Currently, the LVT has jurisdiction (given to it in 1997) to make a determination, upon an application by either the landlord or the tenant, on the following questions arising under s 19 of the LTA 1985:

(a) whether particular costs incurred on services, repairs, maintenance, insurance or management were reasonably incurred;

(b) whether particular services or works were of a reasonable standard;

(c) whether particular interim service charges were reasonable;

(d) whether, if certain costs were incurred on services, repairs, maintenance, insurance or management, they would be reasonably incurred;

(e) whether a certain specification of work or service would be to a reasonable standard; and

(f)   whether a certain amount of interim charge would be reasonable.

Any agreement by the parties to determine these issues by a particular procedure or on particular evidence is void, except for an agreement to refer the issue to arbitration (LTA 1985, s 19(3)).

This jurisdiction was given to the LVT by s 19(2A) and (2B) of the LTA 1985, which were inserted by HA 1996. Prior to those amendments, which came into force in 1997, only the county court had jurisdiction and that jurisdiction only covered issues (a) to (c). The statutory provision which formerly gave jurisdiction to the county court on those matters has been repealed, but the general view is that, whilst a separate application to the county court on matters (a) to (f) in isolation may no longer be possible (such jurisdiction being given now only to the LVT), there is nothing to prevent the county court from determining issues under s 19 when it is dealing with other proceedings in which those issues are relevant, such as proceedings for recovery of arrears of service charges. If it does so, the s 19 issue decided by the county court cannot then be referred to the LVT (s 19(2C) – see below). On the other hand, the court is not obliged to decide a s 19 issue arising in the course of court proceedings; the court may instead refer the s 19 issue to the LVT and adjourn the court proceeding until the LVT has determined it (s 31C).

No application can be made to the LVT under s 19(2A) or (2B) in respect of a matter which has been agreed or admitted by the tenant, or which has already been determined by a court or arbitral tribunal, or which is to be referred to arbitration under an arbitration agreement to which the tenant is a party (s 19(2C)). Currently, this includes arbitration taking place under a provision in the lease in which the parties agree to refer service charge disputes to arbitration. Further, currently an application cannot be made by the tenant if he has already paid the service charge in question (see *Daejan Properties Ltd v London Leasehold Valuation Tribunal* [2001] EWCA Civ 1095, (2001) *The Independent*, 12 July, CA).

Further, even the changes in LVT jurisdiction introduced in 1997 left the court, and not the LVT, with jurisdiction to make determinations on the correct interpretation of a lease, including determining whether a particular item of cost falls within the contractual provisions of the service charge (*Gilje and Others v Chalgrove Securities Ltd* [2001] EWCA Civ 1777 (unreported), CA). Currently, the LVT jurisdiction is only concerned with the statutory regime under the LTA 1985 (see **2.1**), and to avoid delays at LVT hearings if the tenant claims that a particular cost is outside the contractual scope of the service charge, it has been suggested by the Lands Tribunal that the reference in s 19(2A) to service charges which are 'alleged' to be payable enables the LVT to make a determination under the statutory test of reasonableness based on a provisional view as to the landlord's contractual right to charge for the item in dispute, leaving final determination on that point to be decided by the court if the parties cannot agree.

2.12.2.2   *New regime*
Under the LTA 1985, s 27A, which is inserted into the LTA 1985 by the Commonhold and Leasehold Reform Act 2002 with effect from a date to be

fixed, and which replaces s 19(2A) to (3), the LVT will have jurisdiction to determine the matters listed below. The implication is that the LVT can interpret and apply not only to the statutory tests of reasonableness (see **2.1–2.4**) and other statutory limitations (see **2.5–2.10**) but also the terms of the lease (see **Chapter 1** and **2.2.2**). The latter is a major change from the previous position under which interpreting the terms of the lease was a matter for the courts and not the LVT.

The revised jurisdiction of the LVT under s 27A gives the LVT power to decide whether a service charge is payable and the LVT can be asked to decide:

(1) who has to pay;

(2) who is to receive the payment;

(3) how much is payable;

(4) when it has to be paid; and

(5) how it is to be paid.

The LVT can also be asked to decide in advance:

(6) whether a service charge would be payable for the cost of specific proposed services, repairs, maintenance, improvements, insurance or management; and if so:

(7) who would have to pay;

(8) who would be entitled to receive the payment;

(9) how much would be payable;

(10) when it would be payable; and

(11) how it would be payable.

However, no application can be made to the LVT under s 27A in respect of anything which:

(a) the tenant has agreed or admitted (but merely paying an amount demanded is not itself an admission or agreement of liability);

(b) has been, or is to be, referred to arbitration under an agreement to arbitrate that the parties in dispute have entered into after the dispute has arisen (arbitration clauses in the lease no longer prevent the LVT deciding the dispute);

(c) has been decided by a court; or

(d) has been decided by an arbitral tribunal under an agreement to arbitrate entered into after the dispute arose.

The new provision that payment of the amount demanded is not an admission or agreement of liability, coupled with other textual changes, should avoid the effect of *Daejan Properties Ltd v London Leasehold Valuation Tribunal* [2001] EWCA Civ 1095, (2001) *The Independent*, 12 July.

It appears that the court will also have jurisdiction to determine whether service charges are recoverable under the terms of the lease and under the LTA 1985 (see new s 27A(7)).

2.12.2.3 *Procedure*

Section 31A of the LTA 1985, governing the current regime, provides that the jurisdiction of the LVT is exercisable by a Rent Assessment Committee and the Secretary of State has power to make regulations in connection with proceedings before the LVT (see the Leasehold Valuation Tribunals (Service Charges, Insurance or Appointment of Managers Applications) Order 1997, SI 1997/1853, summarised at **2.12.3**). Under the new regime, the procedure is governed by Sch 12 of the Commonhold and Leasehold Reform Act 2002 and regulations made under it.

Under the current regime, an appeal may be made from an LVT determination to the Lands Tribunal, but only with the leave of the LVT or the Lands Tribunal (s 31A(6)). A similar rule applies to the new regime under s 175 of the 2002 Act. The Lands Tribunal has expressed the view, in a case under s 20C (see **2.5.2**), that such an appeal should not be a rehearing but should be handled as a true appeal in which the LVT's discretion, if properly exercised, should not ordinarily be interfered with (*Barrington Court Development Ltd v Barrington Court Residents Association* [2001] 29 EG 128, Lands Tribunal).

Whilst the LVT currently has no power to make an award of costs in relation to such proceedings before it, it has been held under the current regime that the Lands Tribunal has such power in respect of proceedings before it, including appeals and applications for leave to appeal, but may order a party to pay a fixed sum of reasonable amount towards the other party's costs where the costs he is claiming are disproportionate (*Barrington Court Developments Ltd v Barrington Court Residents Association* (above)).

Under the new rules, the LVT will be able to award costs against a party whose application is refused because it is frivolous, vexatious or an abuse of process, or where the party has acted frivolously, vexatiously, disruptively or otherwise unreasonably in connection with the proceedings. In such cases, there is a maximum award of £500 or other maximum sum prescribed by regulations (Commonhold and Leasehold Reform Act 2002, Sch 12, para 10).

It is possible that the 'tenant' who may apply to the LVT can include a former tenant who is liable to pay the service charge where the present tenant has defaulted (see *Re Sarum Properties Ltd's Application* [1999] 2 EGLR 131, Lands Tribunal).

2.12.3 Tenant's right to withhold payment

The provisions of ss 21A and 21B of the LTA 1985 (introduced by the 2002 amendments) will, when they are in force, give tenants the right to withhold payment of service charges in certain situations. These are:

(a) where the landlord fails to supply the prescribed notice with the service charge demand, as required by the new s 21B (see **2.8.2**); or

(b) where the landlord fails to supply a statement of account (or, where required, an accountant's certificate) by the time-limit specified in the new s 21 (see **2.10.2**); or

(c) where the form or content of the statement or certificate purportedly supplied under the new s 21 does not exactly or substantially conform to the requirements of the relevant regulations (see **2.10.2** para (b)(iv)).

In the case of (a), the amount demanded by the service charge demand can be withheld until s 21B has been complied with. In cases (b) and (c), the maximum amount that the tenant may withhold from current and future payments of service charges is the aggregate of:

(1) a sum equal to the amount he paid by way of service charges in the accounting period which is covered by the missing or incorrect statement or certificate; and

(2) the credit balance (if any) at the beginning of that accounting period from his earlier payments in respect of service charges.

Any amount withheld under s 21A must be paid:

(a) immediately upon the correct statement or certificate being supplied; or

(b) upon the landlord obtaining a ruling from the LVT that he had reasonable excuse to fail to provide the statement or certificate.

Any provisions of the tenant's lease which would apply to the non-payment (eg landlord's right of forfeiture) or late payment (eg landlord's right to charge interest) of the amount withheld are suspended in relation to that amount during the period in which s 21A allows it to be withheld (s 21A(5)).

See also **2.9.5** for other circumstances in which tenants can withhold payment.

2.12.4 Applications to the LVT

The forms of applications to the LVT concerning service charges under the LTA 1985 are currently governed by the Leasehold Valuation Tribunals (Service Charges, Insurance or Appointment of Managers Applications) Order 1997, SI 1997/1853, the relevant parts of which are reproduced in **Appendix 3**. This came into force on 1 September 1997.

If the landlord wishes to apply to the LVT for a determination under LTA 1985, s 19(2A) in relation to costs already incurred or advance payments, or under s 19(2B) in relation to proposed expenditure (see **12.2.2**), his application must contain the particulars specified in Part I of Sch 1 to the Order.

If the tenant wishes to make an application under either or both of those sections, the required particulars are set out in Part II to that Schedule.

Applications by a tenant under LTA 1985, s 20C, seeking an order directing that costs incurred by the landlord in connection with service charge proceedings are not to be included as relevant costs in his service charge, are to specify the matters set out in Part II of Sch 1 to the Order.

If either party wishes to appeal to the Lands Tribunal from a decision of the LVT, the leave of the LVT will be required and the application for leave must contain the matters listed in art 2(7) of the Order.

New rules for LVT applications are introduced by s 168 of and Sch 12 to the Commonhold and Leasehold Reform Act 2002 with effect from a date to be fixed to take into account the amendments made by that Act.

2.12.5 Recovery of overpayment

The LVT is concerned only with the validity of service charges, not with repayment of sums wrongly paid. If the tenant is successful at the LVT and wishes to recover an overpayment from the landlord, the tenant would have to bring court proceedings against the landlord for repayment and any question of limitation would then be considered by the court (see *R v London Leasehold Valuation Tribunal, ex parte Daejan Properties Ltd* [2000] EGCS 108, QBD, and see **1.21**). Whilst the ambit of the LVT's jurisdiction is being widened (see *2.12.2.2*), the LVT is not being given jurisdiction to issue money judgments, but the county court is given power to enforce the LVT's determinations (Commonhold and Leasehold Reform Act 2002, Sch 12, para 11).

2.13 Recovery of arrears and other remedies

2.13.1 Tenant withholding payment

No steps can be taken to obtain payment of sums that the tenant is lawfully withholding under the LTA 1985, s 21A (see **2.12.3**) or s 21B (see **2.8.2**).

2.13.2 Limits on distress

The normal remedies are discussed in **1.20**. However, in the case of a residential tenancy which is a protected or statutory tenancy under the Rent Acts (and in the case of lettings for terms not exceeding 21 years, for the purpose of the two-thirds rateable value rule, the 'rent' includes any service charge), the remedy of distress is not available without leave of the court (Rent Act 1977, s 147).

2.13.3 Limits on forfeiture

Forfeiture by peaceable re-entry is not lawful in respect of premises which are being occupied as a residence (Protection from Eviction Act 1977). This restriction does not apply if the landlord believes, on reasonable grounds, that the residential occupier had ceased to reside in the property (Protection from Eviction Act 1977, s 1(2)). A mere temporary absence (eg on holiday) would not constitute ceasing to reside.

Forfeiture can otherwise be effected by court proceedings, and this is usually a far safer course for the landlord. However, no method of forfeiture of a lease of premises let as a dwelling is permissible on the ground of the tenant's failure to pay a service charge unless the amount of the service charge is agreed or admitted by the tenant or has been determined, at least 14 clear days previously, by a court or an arbitral tribunal (HA 1996, s 84(1), (2)). For this purpose 'service charge' has the same meaning as under s 18(1) of the 1985 Act (see **2.1**), but does not include a non-variable service charge element of a registered rent (HA 1996, s 77(4)). A service charge is 'determined' on the giving of the decision of the court or arbitral tribunal, even if that decision is susceptible to appeal or other legal challenge (HA 1996, s 81(3)). By an amendment to s 81 made by the Commonhold and Leasehold Reform Act 2002, s 170 (which will take effect on a date to be fixed), the determination by an arbitral tribunal which satisfies these requirements can only be under an agreement to arbitrate which the parties enter into after the dispute arises; a determination under an arbitration clause in the lease will not count for this purpose.

The above provisions apply whether the service charge is recoverable as rent or only under a tenant's covenant to pay it. In the latter case, the landlord's ability to serve a notice under s 146 of the Law of Property Act 1925 specifying the breach of covenant and requiring its remedy (which is a necessary step prior to forfeiture for breach of covenant (see **1.20.5**)) is not currently fettered but the notice must state that s 81 of the HA 1996 applies and must set out the effect of s 81(1). This notification must be no less conspicuous than the remainder of the notice, and the Secretary of State has power to make regulations prescribing a form of words for this purpose.

However, by the amendments to s 81 to be made by s 170 of the 2002 Act (see above), the landlord must not serve any notice under s 146 of the 1925 Act in respect of arrears of service charge before the amount of the charge has been agreed or determined under the above rules. In addition, these rules will equally apply to steps that the landlord might want to take to forfeit a lease on the ground of unpaid 'administration charges' as defined in Sch 11 to the 2002 Act (see **2.22**).

Furthermore, by s 167 of the 2002 Act, no forfeiture will be permitted for small amounts of arrears or where there is only a short period of delay in making payment. The threshold amounts and time periods are to be prescribed by regulations, but no such regulations had been made by the publication date of this book and these provisions have yet to be brought into force.

2.13.4 Sums in dispute

Where s 18 of the LTA 1985 applies, any dispute about whether individual items meet the requirements of s 19 or s 20 of that Act must be settled by the Leasehold Valuation Tribunal unless the dispute is covered by an arbitration clause or (under the 2002 amendments) by a post-dispute arbitration agreement (see **2.12.2**).

2.13.5 Preconditions

Currently, even if there is no dispute falling within those paragraphs, or such a dispute has been settled or determined, the question arises whether it is a precondition of suing for the arrears that the landlord must have supplied the tenant with a written summary of the costs under s 21 of the LTA 1985. Since the written summary need only be supplied if it is requested in writing by the tenant, it follows that delivery of such a summary cannot be a precondition of suing unless the tenant has made a written request for the summary. Even where the tenant has made such request, it is unclear whether or not this has the effect of precluding the landlord from suing for the service charge until he has supplied the summary; this point was left open by Stuart Smith J in *Woodtrek Ltd v Jezek* (1981) 261 EG 571.

To avoid arguments on this point it is good practice to ensure that the tenant is served with a proper certified summary of costs complying both with s 21 (if it applies) and the terms of the lease itself, before any action is brought against the tenant in respect of non-payment.

Following the coming into force of the 2002 amendments, payments of service charges will be incapable of being enforced if the new requirements for notices to accompany service charge demands (see **2.8.2**) or for statements of accounts and certificates (see **2.12.3**) have not been followed.

2.14 Consultation on appointment of managing agents

2.14.1 Leases to which the statutory rules apply

The following rules apply to premises where one or more of the tenants are represented by a 'recognised tenants' association', being an association recognised under s 29 of the LTA 1985 (see **2.2.6**).

Separate legislation provides for a management audit (see **2.16**).

2.14.2 The consultation rules

Consultation rules are set out in s 30B of the LTA 1985 and provide as set out below.

(1) The association may, at any time, serve notice on the landlord requesting him to consult the association on matters relating to the appointment or employment by the landlord of managing agents.

(2) If, at that time, no managing agents are employed, the landlord must, before appointing any agents, serve notice on the association specifying:

  (a) the name of the proposed managing agent;

  (b) those obligations of the landlord which he proposes to instruct the agents to carry out on his behalf;

(c) a period of at least one month (beginning with the date of service of the landlord's notice) within which the association may make observations;

(d) the name and address in the UK of the person to whom the observations are to be sent;

and the landlord shall have regard to any observations received during the specified period.

(3) If, however, at that time the landlord is employing a managing agent, the landlord must, within one month (beginning with the date of service of the association's notice) serve on the association a notice specifying:

(a) those obligations of the landlord which he has instructed the agents to carry out on his behalf;

(b) a reasonable period within which the association may make observations on the manner in which the agents are discharging those obligations and on the desirability of their continuing to discharge them;

(c) the name and address in the UK of the person to whom the observations are to be sent;

and the landlord shall have regard to any observations received during that period.

(4) If a notice under (1) above is served, then (in addition to complying with (2) or (3) above, as appropriate) the landlord must:

(a) at least once every five years, serve notice on the association specifying:

(i) any changes occurring, since the date of the last notice served by him on the association under s 30B, in the obligations which he has instructed the agents to carry out; and

(ii) a reasonable period within which the association may make observations on the manner in which the agents have discharged those obligations during that period and on the desirability of their continuing to discharge them;

(iii) the name and address in the UK of the person to whom the observations are to be sent;

and the landlord shall have regard to any observations received during that period;

(b) serve a notice complying with (2) above, whenever he proposes to appoint new managing agents, and have regard to any observations received during the specified period;

unless the association gives the landlord notice withdrawing its request to be consulted.

(5) On a change of landlord after service of a notice by the association under (1) above, the notice ceases to have effect but the association may serve a fresh notice on the new landlord.

2.15 Variation of defective service charge clauses

2.15.1 Statutory framework

Part IV of the LTA 1987 sets out two separate sets of procedures for seeking court orders to vary long leases of flats which contain allegedly defective provisions. They are subject to different rules.

Sections 35 to 36 of the LTA 1987 permit an application to be made to the court for a variation order in respect of just one lease, whilst s 37 allows an application to be made in respect of a group of leases.

Section 40 of the LTA 1987 applies certain of these provisions to dwellings other than flats, in respect of insurance clauses only.

Once a variation has been ordered by the court, it is binding not only on the current parties to the lease but also on all other persons, including successors-in-title, predecessors-in-title (LTA 1987, s 39(1)), and sureties (LTA 1987, s 39(2)).

By s 163 of the Commonhold and Leasehold Reform Act 2002, this jurisdiction will be transferred from the court to the leasehold valuation tribunal with effect from a date to be fixed.

The application of these rules to the Crown is to be governed by the Commonhold and Leasehold Reform Act 2002, s 172 as from a date to be fixed (see **Appendix 3**).

2.15.2 Leases of flats to which the provisions apply

These provisions apply to a *long lease* of *a flat*. 'Long lease' is defined in s 59(3) of the LTA 1987 to include:

(1) a lease granted for a term certain exceeding 21 years (even if terminable earlier by forfeiture or by a tenant's notice to quit);

(2) a perpetually renewable lease (which, by s 145 of the Law of Property Act 1922, is treated as a lease for 2,000 years) unless granted by subletting out of a lease which is not a long lease; and

(3) a lease granted under the right to buy provisions in Part V of the Housing Act 1985.

However, by the LTA 1987, s 35(6), these provisions do not apply to a lease:

(a) which demises three or more flats in the same building; or

(b)   which constitutes a tenancy to which Part II of the Landlord and Tenant Act
       1954 applies (ie a business tenancy).

Circumstances in (a) (above) might arise, for example, in those cases where a
developer of a block of flats grants a headlease of the block to a company which
will grant separate underleases of individual flats; the headlease will not fall within
these provisions.

The wording of (b) (above) is somewhat unclear as to whether the exclusion
relates to premises which at the time of the grant of the lease were premises to
which Part II of the Landlord and Tenant Act 1954 applied or whether the
exclusion only applies if the premises are protected by Part II of that Act at the
time of the application for a variation order. The existence of a business tenancy
depends not only on the terms of the tenant's lease, but also on his actually
occupying the premises for the purposes of a business, or for those and other
purposes. Therefore, a lease can, from time to time, move in and out of Part II of
the Landlord and Tenant Act 1954. Furthermore, a business tenancy can exist
under Part II of the Landlord and Tenant Act 1954 even where the terms of the
lease prohibit business use (ie if the landlord waives or acquiesces in a breach).

2.15.3   Application to vary an individual lease

'*Any party*' to the long lease of a flat can apply to the court to order that the lease is
varied (LTA 1987, s 35(1)). Thus, where the parties to the lease are, for example
(a) the landlord, (b) the tenant and (c) a management company, any one of those
three could make the application. Theoretically, if a guarantor for the tenant were
also a party to the lease, he too would be entitled to make an application for a
variation order.

2.15.4   Grounds for applying to vary an individual lease

The grounds for making an application are that the lease '*fails to make satisfactory
provision*' for one or more of the matters listed in s 35(2)(a) to (f) of the LTA
1987. Those paragraphs of s 35(2) which relate to service charges (and, thus, fall
within the scope of this book) are:

> '(e)   the recovery by one party to the lease from another party to it of expenditure incurred or to be
>   incurred by him, or on his behalf, for the benefit of that other party or of a number of persons
>   who include that other party; or
>
> (f)   the computation of a service charge payable under the lease.'

By an amendment inserted by the Commonhold and Leasehold Reform Act
2002, the Secretary of State will have power to make regulations adding
additional grounds on which applications to vary leases can be made under s 35.

'Service charge' is given the same meaning as under s 18(1) of the LTA 1985
(see **2.1.2**).

Section 35(4) of the LTA 1987 as amended in 1993 provides that, for the
purposes of s 35(2)(f), a lease fails to make satisfactory provision with respect to

the computation of a service charge if the lease requires the charge to be a proportion of the service expenditure and this, taken with the contributions payable by other tenants, results in the landlord recovering either less or more than the amount he expended, but see **1.3.4**. It is not completely clear from the wording of s 35(4) whether this is the *only* situation falling within s 35(2)(f), or whether other aspects of the 'computation' of a service charge can also fall within that paragraph, eg where one tenant's stated proportion is too high but is matched by another tenant's proportion being too low. It is submitted that s 35(4) should not be construed so as to restrict para (f), but there is no ruling on this to date.

By a further amendment inserted by s 162 of the Commonhold and Leasehold Reform Act 2002, a new s 35(3A) (which will come into force on a date to be fixed) provides that, for the purposes of s 35(2)(e), the factors for determining whether the lease makes satisfactory provision can include whether it provides for interest or other amounts to be payable in the event of late payment. This reflects the fact that some older leases do not expressly provide for interest to be paid on late payment.

2.15.5 Opposition to variation, and compensation for variation

The power of the court to order the lease to be varied is discretionary; LTA 1987, s 38(1) provides that, where a ground under s 35 is established, the court '*may*' make an order for the lease to be varied; and s 38(8) enables the court to order a variation in terms different from that specified in the application. However, these powers of the court are subject to the provisions of s 38(6) and (7), which allow the application to be opposed.

Section 38(6) provides that the court *shall not* make a variation order if it appears to the court:

(a) that the variation would be likely substantially to prejudice:

    (i) the respondent to the application (ie the landlord, if the application is made by the tenant, or vice versa); or

    (ii) any person who is not a party to the application,

    and that an award of compensation under s 38(10), would not be adequate; or

(b) that for any other reason it would not be reasonable to effect the variation.

These provisions enable a landlord or tenant to oppose a variation on the basis of substantial prejudice or unreasonableness.

Section 38(7) deals expressly with insurance, and provides that the court *shall not* make a variation order:

(a) which would terminate any existing right of the landlord, under the terms of the lease, to nominate the insurer; or

(b) which would require the landlord to nominate a selection of insurers from which the tenant could choose the insurer; or

(c) which, where the lease requires the tenant to insure with a specified insurer, requires the tenant to effect insurance otherwise than with another specified insurer.

If a court makes a variation order, it can also order compensation to be paid in respect of any loss or disadvantage which a person is likely to suffer as a result of the variation (LTA 1987, s 38(10)). In view of the provisions of s 38(6), this will apply only where such compensation will be adequate to compensate him; otherwise the variation will be refused.

2.15.6   Consequential variation of other leases

If an order is made varying the lease of one flat in a block, this may justify other leases being varied. For this reason, there are provisions in the LTA 1987, s 36 under which, if any party to a lease applies to the court for a variation order under s 35 of that Act, any other party to that lease can apply to the court asking that, if the court decides to vary the lease, it should also order the variation of the long leases of other specified flats. Those flats must have the same landlord, but need not be in the same building and need not be in identical terms (LTA 1987, s 36(2)).

By s 36(3), two criteria must be demonstrated to be fulfilled in this respect:

(a) each of those other leases must fail to make satisfactory provision with respect to the same matter or matters as are specified in the original application; and

(b) if a lease variation is made under the original application, it would be in the interests of the party applying under s 36, or in the interests of the other parties to these other leases, to have all the specified leases (including that comprised in the original application) varied *to the same effect*.

What is meant by 'to the same effect'? If the original application results in *decreasing* that tenant's service charge proportion because it was excessive for the size of his flat, would *increasing* the proportions payable by some or all of the other tenants, in order to retain 100 per cent recovery, be a variation *to the same effect*? It is hoped that this would be answered in the affirmative.

The power to make these consequential variations to other leases is discretionary and is limited by the same rights of objection under s 38 as discussed at **2.15.5** (s 38(2)).

2.15.7   Applications to vary multiple leases

Section 37 of the LTA 1987 enables a single application to be made requesting the court to order the variation of two or more leases, but subject to majority approval of all the parties.

An application under s 37 may be made by either the landlord or any of the tenants, but the following criteria must, in each case, be fulfilled:

(a) the leases must all be long leases of flats under which the landlord is the same person, but they need not be of flats in the same building and need not be in identical terms (s 37(2)); and

(b) the object to be achieved by the variation must only be achievable satisfactorily if all the specified leases are varied to the same effect (s 37(3)); and

(c) where the application involves eight or fewer leases, the application must have the consent of all, or all but one, of the parties concerned (s 37(5)(a));

(d) where the application involves nine or more leases, the application must have the consent of at least 75 per cent of the parties concerned, and must not be opposed by more than 10 per cent of them (s 37(5)(b)).

When counting the parties for the majority criteria of (c) or (d) (above), a person who is the tenant of more than one lease is counted as a separate party for each of his leases (s 37(6)(a)). The landlord is counted as one party (s 37(6)(b)).

These provisions, unlike those in s 35, do not confine the potential variations to a specified list of matters; the 'object to be achieved' could be any matter contained in (or omitted from) the leases. Presumably, this is justified by the requirements for majority consent to the application – an inappropriate proposed variation is unlikely to command majority support. (Variations on matters not relating to service charges are outside the scope of this book.)

Because of the 10 per cent provision for objectors, the procedure under s 37 would be a means of forcing a suitable lease variation on all the tenants in a block, notwithstanding a small number of objectors. However, these provisions are equally subject to the rights of opposition contained in s 38 (summarised at **2.15.5**), and could fail on grounds of substantial prejudice or unreasonableness (LTA 1987, s 38(3)).

2.15.8 Notification and cancellation

Under s 35(5) of the LTA 1987, rules of court have been made requiring notice of any application to be served on all persons likely to be affected by the proposed variation and entitling them to join in the proceedings.

If a person entitled to be served with notice of the proceedings was not served with the notice, he may, under s 39:

(a) sue the person who should have served the notice for damages; and/or

(b) apply to the court to cancel or modify the variation (s 39(3)).

2.15.9 Variation of insurance provisions in leases of dwellings other than flats

Whilst the provisions of LTA 1987, ss 35 to 39 apply as a whole only to long leases of flats, parts of those provisions are, by s 40, made to apply to long leases of dwellings other than flats (eg houses). This is where the lease fails to make satisfactory provision with respect to '*any matter relating to the insurance of the dwelling, including the recovery of the costs of such insurance*'. Leases of flats are excluded from these provisions (*John Lyon's Charity v Haysport Properties* (1995) NPC 165, ChD).

The provisions of s 36 (consequential variation of other leases) and s 38 (court discretion, objections, etc) are applied with the appropriate modification. Again the provisions do not apply to a lease consisting of three or more dwellings, or one which constitutes a business tenancy (s 40(4)). Further, a tenant who holds three or more dwellings under two or more separate long leases from the same landlord is also excluded (s 40(4A)) and, for this purpose if the tenant is a body corporate then this exclusion applies even if the other leases are held by associated companies (s 40(4B)).

2.16   Management audit

2.16.1   Purpose

The purpose of a management audit under Chapter V of the Leasehold Reform, Housing and Urban Development Act 1993 (the '1993 Act') is to ascertain whether the landlord's obligations towards the 'qualifying tenants' in respect of management functions are being discharged in an efficient and effective manner, and service charge monies payable by those tenants are being applied in an efficient and effective manner (1993 Act, s 78). The audit report may also facilitate an application by the tenants to the court for the appointment of a manager under the LTA 1987, s 24 (a detailed consideration of which is outside the scope of this book).

2.16.2   Qualifying tenants

Only 'qualifying' tenants are entitled to have the audit carried out on their behalf. To qualify, a tenant must hold a dwelling under a 'long lease' or a 'shared ownership lease' under which a service charge is payable. Tenants of business leases (defined in the 1993 Act, s 101 as leases to which Part II of the Landlord and Tenant Act 1954 applies) are excluded. 'Long lease' is defined in s 7(1) of the 1993 Act; broadly, it is a lease granted for a term of over 21 years. 'Shared ownership lease' is defined in s 7(7) of the 1993 Act and, broadly, is a lease acquired at a premium equal to a percentage of the value or cost of the dwelling.

If a dwelling is sublet and both the tenant and the subtenant would qualify under these rules, only the subtenant is given the right to demand the audit (1993 Act, s 77(4)).

2.16.3 Minimum number of qualifying tenants

If premises contain only one dwelling let to a qualifying tenant, that tenant can require the audit to be carried out (1993 Act, s 76(4), (5)).

Where premises (which the 1993 Act calls the 'relevant premises') contain two or more dwellings subject to a 'common service charge' – ie the tenants contribute by way of service charge to the same costs (1993 Act, s 76(8)) – then:

(a) if the relevant premises contain two dwellings let to qualifying tenants, either or both of them can demand the audit (1993 Act, s 76(2)(a));

(b) if the relevant premises contain three or more dwellings let to qualifying tenants, the audit has to be required by at least two-thirds of those qualifying tenants (1993 Act, s 76(2)(b)).

2.16.4 Appointment of auditor

The auditor is appointed by the qualifying tenants who wish to exercise these rights. Where three or more qualifying tenants demand the audit, the appointment must be made by at least two-thirds of them acting together (1993 Act, s 78(3)(ii)).

The auditor must be either a qualified accountant as defined in s 28 of the 1985 Act (see **2.10.3**) or a qualified surveyor being a fellow or professional associate of the Royal Institution of Chartered Surveyors or of the Incorporated Society of Valuers and Auctioneers or having some other qualification prescribed by regulations (1993 Act, s 78(5)).

2.16.5 Procedure

The appointed auditor serves a written notice on the landlord. By s 80 of the 1993 Act, the notice must:

(a) be signed by each of the tenants on whose behalf it is given;

(b) state the names of those tenants and their addresses at the relevant premises;

(c) state the name and address of the appointed auditor;

(d) specify any documents or description of documents which the auditor requires or wishes to inspect (see below);

(e) state the date (if any) on which the auditor wishes to inspect any common parts in the relevant premises or any appurtenant property, being a date between one and two months after the giving of the notice.

In addition to giving the notice to the landlord, the notice must also be given (so far as practical, at the same time) to any other person (the 'relevant person') who carries out the management functions, with a copy of that notice being given to the landlord (1993 Act, s 79(3)(b)).

The s 80 notice to the landlord may be given to the person who collects rent from the tenants on the landlord's behalf (1993 Act, s 80(5)).

The documents which the auditor can require to be supplied to him are the costs summaries which the tenants are entitled to require under s 21(1) of the 1985 Act (see **2.10.2** and **2.10.3**). The documents which the auditor can ask to be produced for his inspection are (a) the accounts, receipts and other documents supporting those cost summaries, and (b) any other documents the sight of which is reasonably required by the auditor for the purpose of carrying out his audit (1993 Act, s 79(2)).

When the provisions as to regular accounts and accountants' certificates under the amended version of s 21 (introduced by the Commonhold and Leasehold Reform Act 2002) comes into effect (see **2.10.2**), those documents will fall within this regime and the auditor will have the choice of inspecting and copying the documents or requiring the landlord to supply copies which (as the auditor decides) are to be sent to the auditor or left for him to collect.

Under s 87 of the 1993 Act, the Secretary of State may approve codes of practice to which, under s 78(2), the auditor must have regard when carrying out his audit. By the Approval of Codes of Management Practice (Residential Property) Order 1995, SI 1995/2782, the Secretary of State for the Environment and the Secretary of State for Wales approved The Association of Retirement Housing Managers' Code of Practice for the Management of Leasehold Sheltered Housing, but to be had regard to only in respect of matters occurring after the date on which the Order came into force. It is anticipated that other codes of practice may be approved on a similar basis. Failure by the landlord to comply with an approved code of practice is a ground on which tenants may apply to the court to appoint a manager of the building under the LTA 1987, s 24 as amended by the HA 1996, s 85.

The landlord and any 'relevant person' must comply with the notice, and the auditor can apply to the court under s 81(4) for an order compelling this.

The landlord cannot charge the auditor for providing facilities for him to inspect documents, but can make a reasonable charge for supplying documents to the auditor and for providing copying facilities in respect of other documents (1993 Act, s 79(5)). If the wording of the tenants' leases allows it, the landlord can include as management costs within the service charges any costs of providing the inspection facilities (1993 Act, s 79(6)).

If the landlord or relevant person claims that any documents specified by the auditor for production ought not to be inspected by him (presumably on the ground that sight of them is not reasonably required for the purposes of the audit), the landlord can give notice to the auditor to that effect and the matter can, if necessary, be decided by the court (1993 Act, s 81(1)(b)(ii)).

Section 82 of the 1993 Act makes provision for an immediate landlord who receives a s 80 notice to require relevant information and documents, where appropriate, from a superior landlord. The provisions of ss 81 and 82 of the 1993 Act have been amended by Sch 10 to the 2002 Act to match the amendments mentioned earlier and to clarify the procedures. Section 83 of the 1993 Act contains provisions dealing with the situation where the landlord, after receiving a notice under s 80, disposes of his interest in the dwellings.

2.17 Insurance information and choice of insurer

2.17.1 Insurance information

Where the service charge includes an amount payable directly or indirectly for insurance, the tenants have special rights to obtain information about the insurance from the landlord, in addition to any rights contained in their leases. These rights are granted by s 30A of and the Schedule to the LTA 1985, inserted by LTA 1987.

A request can be served on the landlord (or on an agent collecting the rent) requiring the supply of an insurance summary which must set out, in respect of every relevant policy, the insured amount or amounts, the name of the insurer, and the risks insured. The request for this summary can be made either by the tenant or by a recognised tenants' association. The summary must be supplied within one month of the request. This period will be reduced to 21 days under amendments made by Sch 10 to the Commonhold and Leasehold Reform Act 2002. Where two or more buildings are insured under the same policy, the summary need only be of the tenant's own dwelling and, if it is a flat, the building containing it. Where the tenant's dwelling is a flat, the insured amount specified in the summary must be that relating to the building containing the flat and, if specified in the policy, any amount insured for the flat itself. A full copy of the policy may be supplied instead of a summary.

After the tenant, or the secretary of the recognised tenant's association, has obtained an insurance summary or a copy of the relevant policy (whether under the above procedure or not), the tenant (or the secretary of the association with the consent of the tenant) may within six months request the landlord to give him reasonable facilities for inspecting the insurance policy and any accounts, receipts or other documents evidencing payment of the relevant premiums both for the current insurance period and for the immediately preceding period, and to provide facilities for taking copies or extracts.

As from the date when the amendments made by Sch 10 to the Commonhold and Leasehold Reform Act 2002 take effect, this right to inspect the insurance policy and related documents is exercisable at any time (not only after obtaining an insurance summary) and the landlord must comply within 21 days of a written request and must provide copying facilities, or supply a copy of the policy and other documents, to the tenant or the association secretary. The landlord can make a reasonable charge to that person for the copying; any costs he incurs in providing inspection facilities can be included in the service charges of the building as management charges if the wording of the lease so allows.

The Schedule to the LTA 1985 contains provisions dealing with the situation where the insurance is effected by a superior landlord. It also contains provisions allowing a tenant to serve directly on the insurer a notice of any damage to the dwelling (and, if a flat, any other affected part of the building) in respect of which a claim could be made under the insurance policy. These provisions will be subject to some minor and consequential amendments to be made by the

Commonhold and Leasehold Reform Act 2002, Sch 10, paras 8 to 13, as from a date to be fixed.

2.17.2   Choice of insurer

In addition, para 8 of the Schedule to the LTA 1985 (as amended by the HA 1996) contains provisions which apply where the lease requires the tenant (and not the landlord) to insure the building with an insurer nominated by the landlord; these provisions give the tenant the right to challenge the nomination of the insurer on the grounds that the insurance is unsatisfactory or the premiums are excessive. The procedures for challenging the landlord's choice of insurer, by applying to the Leasehold Valuation Tribunal, are currently set out in the Leasehold Valuation Tribunals (Service Charges, Insurance or Appointment of Managers Applications) Order 1997, SI 1997/1853.

These provisions will remain in force, but will in effect be superseded, in relation to leases of houses (not flats), by new provisions in s 164 of the Commonhold and Leasehold Reform Act 2002, coming into effect on a date to be fixed. The new provisions (see **Appendix 3**) will remove the landlord's right, under the lease, to nominate or approve the insurer of the house, giving the tenant freedom of choice. This will apply even if the landlord's insurer provided satisfactory insurance cover and charged reasonable premiums. The provisions contain safeguards for the landlord, for example by requiring the tenant's insurance to cover the landlord's interests as well as the tenant's.

More detail on this subject is outside the scope of this book.

2.18   Statutory management codes

Codes for managing private sector housing have been approved by the Secretaries of State for the Environment and for Wales, and the necessary order was laid before Parliament on 21 November 1996.

There are two codes which will apply to both landlords and their agents and they are designed to promote best practice. One deals with tenancies where rent only is paid with no separate reservation of a service charge. The second deals with the standard leasing situation which provides for a separate and variable service charge. There are some instances where this second code will apply to ordinary Regulated or Assured lettings, but only where these have a variable service charge. The codes place additional requirements on managers to ensure that they provide a professional, effective and responsive service and they can be used in evidence before a court or tribunal. The codes became operative on 17 March 1997.

2.19   Diplomatic and state immunity

In addition to the immunity (described at **1.22**) enjoyed by a tenant or occupier which is a foreign state or foreign diplomatic officer, special rules apply to residential premises used as the private residence of a foreign diplomatic officer. Such a residence enjoys the same protection and inviolability as a diplomatic mission, described at **1.22**, namely immunity against entry, execution, etc (Diplomatic Privileges Act 1964, Sch 1, Art 30).

This immunity prevents the landlord from exercising rights to enter the premises or seeking forfeiture of the lease, but would not prevent an action against the tenant for breach of the covenant to pay the service charge (see *Intpro Properties (UK) Ltd v Sauvel* [1983] 2 All ER 495, CA), subject to any personal immunity that the tenant may have (see **1.22.1** and **1.22.3**).

2.20 Social landlords

The Secretary of State has power, under ss 219 and 220 of the Housing Act 1996, to give directions to social landlords about service charges in respect of works of repair, maintenance or improvement. The directions may require the waiver or reduction of service charges where a grant or other financial assistance is given to the landlord by the Secretary of State, and may permit the waiver or reduction of service charges in other circumstances which the direction may specify.

'Social landlords' are those landlords (other than housing co-operatives) who can grant secure tenancies under s 80 of the Housing Act 1985, and registered social landlords who are registered under Part 1, Chap 1 of the HA 1996.

As to the application of the LTA 1985 to different types of social landlords, see **2.1.3**.

As to service charges under leases granted under the right-to-buy scheme, see **2.7.2**.

2.21 Managers and right-to-manage companies

2.21.1 Managers

Part II of the Landlord and Tenant Act 1987 ('LTA 1987') gives tenants a collective right to apply to the Leasehold Valuation Tribunal to appoint a manager to take over the management of their premises. Unlike the establishment of a right-to-manage company (see **2.21.4**), this right can only be exercised if the tenants can demonstrate the existence of specific grounds for complaint listed in the LTA 1987, s 24 about the landlord's existing management of the premises. The procedure is outside the scope of this book.

Certain landlords are exempt, including 'resident landlords' (defined in the LTA 1987, s 58(2) and (3)) and 'exempt landlords' listed in s 58(1) and including development corporations, housing action trusts and the Housing Corporation, registered housing associations and fully mutual unregistered housing associations. Certain premises held by charities are also exempt. The application of these provisions to the Crown is set out in the LTA 1987, s 56, which is to be amended by s 172 of the Commonhold and Leasehold Reform Act 2002 as from a date to be fixed (see **Appendix 3**).

The grounds for complaint in the LTA 1987, s 24 include where unreasonable service charges have been made or are proposed or are likely to be made. Here 'service charge' has the same meaning as in the LTA 1985, s 18(1), other than a fixed service charge in a registered rent. A service charge is 'unreasonable' if the amount is unreasonable having regard to the items for which it is payable, or if those items have been provided to an unnecessarily high standard, or if the items are of an insufficient standard with the result that additional service charges are or may be incurred (LTA 1987, s 24(2A)).

2.21.2 Manager taking over management

The order that the LVT can make may include (amongst other things):

(1) provisions with respect to such matters (including incidental or ancillary matters) as the LVT thinks fit in relation to the exercise by the manager of his functions, and the manager can subsequently apply to the LVT for directions with respect to any such matters (LTA 1987, s 24(4));

(2) provisions for the manager to take over from the landlord or other managing person any appropriate contracts (LTA 1987, s 24(5)(a)) and any appropriate contractual or tortious claims accruing before or after the date of the manager's appointment (LTA 1987, s 24(5)(b)); and

(3) provisions for the manager's remuneration to be paid by the landlord or by some or all of the tenants of the premises (LTA 1987, s 24(5)(c)).

The provisions mentioned at (1) might include ordering the landlord to hand over to the manager uncommitted service charge funds and to provide accounts of service costs spent since the last accounts were prepared.

The 'management functions' to which these orders can relate include (but are not limited to) the repair, maintenance or insurance of the premises (LTA 1987, s 24(11)).

2.21.3 Costs of application to appoint a manager

No order can be made in connection with the LVT proceedings under which one party can be required to pay the costs incurred by another party (LTA 1987, s 24A(5)). However, these provisions apparently do not prevent the landlord from seeking to include within the service charges his costs of opposing the application, if the wording of the lease is wide enough to encompass them, although any tenant can ask the LVT for an order prohibiting this under the LTA 1985, s 20C (see **2.5.2** and *Tenants of Langford Court v Doren Ltd* (2001) 5 March (unreported), Lands Tribunal).

If there is an appeal to the Lands Tribunal, that tribunal has jurisdiction under the Lands Tribunal Rules 1996, r 52(1) to award costs of all proceedings before it, and this includes proceedings under the LTA 1987 (see **2.5.2** above and *Barrington Court Developments Ltd v Barrington Court Residents Association* [2001] 29 EG 128, Lands Tribunal).

2.21.4 'Right-to-manage' companies

This new regime, created by Part 2 of the Commonhold and Leasehold Reform Act 2002 ('CLRA 2002'), gives tenants a collective right to take over the management of their premises. Unlike the appointment of a manager under the LTA 1987, this right can be exercised whether or not the landlord has been guilty of bad management.

The 'right to manage', as the CLRA 2002, s 71 calls it, will give the requisite number of qualifying tenants of flats in a block the right to set up a management company (called an 'RTM company') to take over the management of the building from the landlord. More detail about the requirements and procedure is outside the scope of this book.

2.21.5 Functions acquired by the RTM company

The RTM company will take over from the landlord (or an existing management company or manager) those obligations in the flat leases which constitute 'management functions', as well as certain other matters outside the scope of this book.

The 'management functions' are defined in the CLRA 2002, s 96. They are the functions of the landlord, management company or manager with respect to services, repairs, maintenance, improvements, insurance and management, but excluding functions relating exclusively to any flats or other units which are not let to qualifying tenants, and also excluding functions relating to re-entry or forfeiture of leases (CLRA 2002, s 96(5) and (6)). Regulations can be made amending both this list and these exclusions.

The RTM company takes responsibility for these matters in place of the persons previously responsible (CLRA 2002, s 96(2) and (3)) and owes this responsibility to the landlords as well as to the tenants (CLRA 2002, s 97(1)). The RTM company also takes over the power to exercise those rights under the leases that relate to these functions (CLRA 2002, s 97(4)), such as the right to collect service charges.

The persons from whom responsibility has been taken no longer have the power to exercise those rights (CLRA 2002, s 97(2)), although this does not prevent the landlord from effecting his own insurance of the premises at his own cost, if he wishes to do so (CLRA 2002, s 97(3)), nor does he lose the right to collect service charges relating to expenditure incurred before the management has passed to the RTM company (CLRA 2002, s 97(5)).

2.21.6 Statutory obligations affecting the RTM company

The rules relating to service charges in the LTA 1985, ss 18–30, the obligations under the LTA 1987, ss 42–42B to hold service charge funds on trust, and the restrictions on administration charges imposed by Sch 11 to the CLRA 2002, all apply as if the RTM company were the landlord (CLRA 2002, Sch 7, paras 4 and 11). They will apply even if any of them did not previously apply because the landlord was a local authority or other public body exempted by the

LTA 1985, s 26 (see **2.1.3**). Where the RTM company requires a landlord to pay towards service expenditure (as mentioned at **2.21.10**), the landlord has the same rights on these matters as if he were a tenant of the relevant flat.

The implied obligations under the LTA 1985, s 11 which require a landlord to carry out, at his own cost, certain repairs and provide certain amenities to flats let on short lettings (see **2.6**) will apply to the RTM company in relation to any flats which are let on such short lettings, but only in respect of those elements as do not relate exclusively to the flat (so, for example, the RTM company would be liable for providing space heating and hot water through a communal system being managed by the RTM company, but would not be responsible if the flat had its own individual heaters), and the RTM company will owe those obligations to all occupiers of such flats as well as to the tenant and, indeed, to the landlord (CLRA 2002, Sch 7, para 3).

The RTM company will be bound by the rights of tenants to seek information about insurance under the LTA 1985, s 30A and the Schedule to that Act (see **2.17**), and where the RTM company requires a landlord to pay towards insurance (as mentioned at **2.21.10**), the landlord also has these rights (CLRA 2002, Sch 7, para 5). The RTM company will be obliged to consult a recognised tenants' association on the appointment of new managing agents under the LTA 1985, s 30B (see **2.14**) but ignoring s 30B(6) of those provisions (CLRA 2002, Sch 7, para 6). The RTM company will be obliged to furnish tenants with details of names and addresses under the LTA 1987, ss 46–48 (see **2.8**) as if it were the landlord (CLRA 2002, Sch 7, para 12).

The tenants will have the right to impose a management audit on the RTM company under the Leasehold Reform, Housing and Urban Development Act 1993 (see **2.16**); and where the RTM company requires a landlord to pay towards service expenditure (as mentioned at **2.21.10**), the landlord has the same rights on these matters as if he were a tenant of the relevant flat (CLRA 2002, Sch 7, para 14). The right of a recognised tenants' association to appoint a surveyor to investigate service charge matters under the Housing Act 1996, s 84 and Sch 4 to that Act (see **2.2.7**) will apply in respect of service charges administered by RTM companies, but excluding Sch 4, para 7 (CLRA 2002, Sch 7, para 1).

2.21.7   Management contracts

Where contracts are in place with contractors for the provision of services or works falling within the management functions which are to be taken over by the RTM company, the RTM company may wish to try to take over some or all of these contracts. These contracts might include contracts of insurance, contracts with managing agents, cleaners, gardeners, maintenance companies, etc.

To facilitate negotiations concerning these contracts, the CLRA 2002, ss 91 and 92 contain provisions for various notices to be given to the interested parties in order to create an opportunity in which the parties might be able to negotiate a transfer of some or all of these contracts to the RTM company. However, the RTM company may not want to take them over or the contracting parties may not want that to happen, and there is no compulsion in the legislation for any of these contracts to be transferred.

It is assumed that any contracts which are not transferred to the RTM company will end under the legal doctrine of 'frustration' when the RTM company acquires the right to manage the premises, since the ability of the contracting parties to perform the contract will then be frustrated.

2.21.8   Provision of information to the RTM company

If the RTM company will be acquiring the right to manage it may need to obtain information and documents in order to take over the management, such as service expenditure records, copies of those flat leases which its members have been unable to provide, etc.

Under the CLRA 2002, s 93, the RTM company can require the landlord or other person currently handling the management to provide the company with any information in his possession or control which the company reasonably requires for this purpose, and requiring him to permit inspection of the relevant documentation by a person authorised by the company and to supply a copy.

2.21.9   Transfer of service charge funds to the RTM company

If the landlord or other party that has been managing the property has service charge contributions in hand, these must, to the extent that they are not required to meet committed service costs, be paid over to the RTM company on or as soon as practicable after the date when it acquires the right to manage or, if later, by the date four months after the date when the RTM company served notice of its claim to exercise the right to manage (CLRA 2002, s 94(4) and (5)).

The amount to be handed over is to be calculated by aggregating the contributions in hand from all tenants of the premises, including the value of any investments (and accrued interest) and deducting an amount equal to the aggregate amount required to meet costs incurred before the acquisition date and properly chargeable against those contributions (CLRA 2002, s 94(1) and (2)). Any dispute on these matters may be referred to the LVT (CLRA 2002, s 94(3)).

2.21.10   Landlord's liability for ongoing service charges

If the premises:

(a)   contain one or more flats or other units (called an 'excluded unit') not let to qualifying tenants (eg let on short lettings or undemised);

(b)   have a service charge regime under the leases of flats held by qualifying tenants by which each such tenant is liable to pay a service charge equal to a proportion of the service costs; and

(c)   the aggregate of the service charges payable by those qualifying tenants amounts to less than 100 per cent of the total service costs;

then the amount by which the service charges payable by the qualifying tenants falls short of the total service costs can be recovered by the RTM company from the following 'appropriate person' or persons, under the CLRA 2002, s 103(1) and (2).

The appropriate persons are:

(a) in respect of an excluded unit which is not let, the freeholder;

(b) in respect of an excluded unit which is subject to a lease, the landlord of the lease;

(c) in respect of an excluded unit which is let and sublet, the landlord of the most inferior of such leases (CLRA 2002, s 103(5)).

Where there is more than one excluded unit, the appropriate persons bear the shortfall between themselves in the proportions of the internal floor areas of their excluded units (CLRA 2002, s 103(3) and (4)).

2.22   Administration charges

2.22.1   Scope

This regime, created by Sch 11 to the CLRA 2002, will come into force on a date to be fixed.

It applies to 'administration charges'. This is defined to mean amounts payable by a tenant of a dwelling either as part of, or in addition to, rent, and which are payable directly or indirectly:

(1) for or in connection with applications for, or the grant of, approvals under the lease (eg consent for assignment, subletting, alterations or keeping pets);

(2) for or in connection with the provision of information or documents by the landlord or another party to the lease such as a management company (eg insurance or service charge documents);

(3) in respect of the tenant's failure to pay sums on their due date to the landlord or other party to the lease (eg interest on late payment of rent or service charges); or

(4) in connection with an actual or alleged breach of covenant under the lease.

However, it does not include any amount payable by a tenant whose rent is registered under Part 4 of the Rent Act 1977, unless the amount is registered as a variable amount under s 71(4) of that Act (see **2.7.1**).

The scope of the rules can be amended by an order of the appropriate Secretary of State.

2.22.2   Reasonableness tests

Where the amount of the administration charge is variable – that is, it is not fixed by the lease, either as a stated sum or by a formula for calculating one – the tenant does not have to pay more than a reasonable amount (CLRA 2002, Sch 11, para 2).

Any party can apply to the LVT under Sch 11, para 4 concerning amounts payable by way of administration charge; and the LVT can be asked to decide whether or not anything is payable and, if it is:

(1)   who has to pay;

(2)   who is to receive the payment;

(3)   how much is payable;

(4)   when it has to be paid; and

(5)   how it is to be paid.

However, no application can be made to the LVT in respect of anything which:

(a)   the tenant has agreed or admitted (but merely paying an amount is not itself an admission or agreement of liability);

(b)   has been, or is to be, referred to arbitration under an agreement to arbitrate that the parties in dispute have entered into after the dispute has arisen (arbitration clauses in the lease no longer prevent the LVT deciding the dispute);

(c)   has been decided by a court; or

(d)   has been decided by an arbitral tribunal under an agreement to arbitrate entered into after the dispute arose.

The jurisdiction of the LVT is not exclusive and the court can also decide the reasonableness of an administration charge (Sch 11, para 4(2)).

2.22.3   Varying leases which prescribe charges

Where the amount of the administration charge is fixed by the lease either as a stated sum or by a formula for calculating one, the tenant will have to pay the sum prescribed by the lease, but either party can apply to the LVT to vary the lease, or to order the parties to vary it, on the grounds that the fixed sum or formula is not reasonable (CLRA 2002, Sch 11, para 3). The variation may be as the applying party requests or such other variation as the LVT thinks fit. The provisions of Sch 11 do not state whether the variation can be backdated.

This jurisdiction is exclusive to the LVT and is not exercisable by a court.

Service Charges: Law and Practice

2.22.4 Information to tenants

The provisions of ss 47 and 48 of the LTA 1987, which prescribe information to be given to tenants (see **2.8.1** and **2.8.2**) also apply in connection with the charging of administration charges (CLRA 2002, Sch 11, paras 10 and 11).

Demands for administration charges will have to include a statement of the paying party's rights and obligations (CLRA 2002, Sch 11, para 3A). This will be prescribed in regulations yet to be made.

3   VALUE ADDED TAX

3.1   Basic VAT rules

3.1.1   The basic obligation to charge VAT

VAT is to be charged, at the standard rate or zero rate, as applicable:

(a)   on any supply of goods or services made in the UK;

(b)   by a person registered for VAT purposes;

(c)   if the supply is in the course or furtherance of any business carried on by that person; and

(d)   if the supply is not exempted by the Value Added Tax Act 1994 ('VAT Act 1994'), Sch 9.

'Goods and services' covers not only goods and services in the normal sense but also land and buildings.

'Business' is not specifically defined in the VAT Act 1994 but includes any trade, profession or vocation. The Sixth Council Directive of the European Union, art 4 indicates that VAT is to be charged by a person carrying out any 'economic activity' and defines that term widely so that it includes the exploitation for income of tangible or intangible property. Generally, therefore, any supply of goods or services made by a person registered for VAT purposes can be a taxable supply unless it is specifically exempted.

Subject to some complex rules on deemed consideration which are not relevant for the purpose of this book, VAT is charged at the appropriate rate (zero in certain circumstances – see VAT Act 1994, Sch 8) on the cash consideration received for the supply.

If the consideration is expressed to be 'exclusive of VAT' the appropriate rate is applied to the cash consideration (ie consideration of £100 exclusive of VAT results in a charge to VAT of £17.50 at the current standard rate of 17.5 per cent and, thus, a total price of £117.50). However, if the consideration is expressed to be 'inclusive of VAT' or does not refer to VAT at all, the cash consideration is deemed to include VAT (eg VAT-inclusive price of £100 includes VAT of £14.89 and, thus, incorporates a net consideration of £85.11). It is convenient to use the fraction $^7/_{47}$ when calculating the VAT element of the VAT-inclusive price.

3.1.2   The right to deduct input tax

'Input tax' is the VAT paid by a person when paying for goods or services supplied to him. For example, where he pays a VAT-inclusive sum of £117.50 for cleaning services, he will have paid input tax of £17.50.

A person is entitled, in principle, to deduct input tax suffered by him against VAT payable by him to HM Customs and Excise (or obtain a refund of input tax from HM Customs and Excise if the VAT for which he is accountable in that VAT period is too small) if:

(a) he is registered for VAT purposes; and

(b) the input tax relates to supplies made to him of goods or services used or to be used by him for the purposes of a business in which he makes *VAT taxable* supplies to his customers; and

(c) he obtains (subject to one or two minor exceptions) a proper VAT invoice for the input tax.

Having identified input tax in respect of supplies received for the purpose of the business, it is necessary to apportion that input tax between taxable and exempt (if any) supplies made by the business (only the former category being deductible). If all the supplies made by a business are taxable supplies (which, for this purpose, includes supplies which are zero rated), then that business can recover all its input tax. However, many businesses make both taxable and exempt supplies and, therefore, can recover only a proportion of the input tax they have suffered. This is known as 'partial exemption' and is discussed in more detail in **3.1.3**.

3.1.3 Partial exemption

As mentioned above, where a person registered for VAT purposes makes both taxable and exempt supplies, he may only be able to recover a proportion of input tax suffered on supplies made to him.

It is necessary for such a person to analyse the supplies of goods and services made to him and to attribute those supplies across the following categories:

(1) taxable supplies made by him (including both standard-rated and zero-rated supplies); and

(2) exempt supplies made by him; and

(3) 'mixed' supplies which are neither wholly taxable nor exempt (eg annual audit fee, telephone charges, etc).

The input tax attributable to category (1) is wholly deductible and that attributed to category (2) is not deductible. Input tax attributed to category (3) is apportioned to determine the amount deductible.

The rules concerning the apportionment of input tax falling into category (3) are contained in the Value Added Tax Regulations 1995, SI 1995/2518 ('the VAT Regulations 1995'). Input tax is apportioned in accordance with a fraction in which the numerator is the value of taxable supplies made by the person for the VAT period in question and the denominator is the value of total supplies made by that person for that period. The proportion of input tax falling within category (3) as determined by that fraction is deductible.

In determining the amount of total supplies for any period for the purpose of the fraction, certain exempt incidental outputs can be left out of account (see reg 101(3) of the VAT Regulations 1995). The most important of these is *exempt supplies of land*.

If only small amounts of exempt supplies are made, the registered person may fall within a de minimis limit of less than £625 per month on average of input tax attributable to exempt supplies made by him, provided that such input tax is no more than 50 per cent of all the input tax incurred per month. Therefore, a registered person may incur VAT-exclusive expenditure relating to exempt supplies made by him of up to £50,357 (at the current rate of VAT of 17.5 per cent) in any year without having partial exemption status, but only if further expenditure of at least the same amount is incurred in buying goods or services to be used in making taxable supplies. This effectively bars persons making wholly or substantially exempt supplies (such as dentists) from taking advantage of the de minimis limit.

3.1.4 Commercial lettings and the election to waive the VAT exemption

The letting of commercial and domestic property is exempted for VAT purposes by Group 1 of Sch 9 to the VAT Act 1994. Thus, prima facie the provision of premises by a landlord to a tenant under a lease represents an exempt supply, with the result that:

(a) VAT is not chargeable on the consideration (ie the rent); and

(b) input tax incurred by the landlord in respect of any expenses he incurs in relation to the property (eg VAT he pays on maintenance contractor's charges) is not deductible by the landlord.

However, from 1 April 1989 the UK has adopted provisions allowing a property owner to elect to waive this exempt status for commercial property. If he does so:

(a) any supply of the property (ie its letting or sale) made by the owner will become subject to VAT at the standard rate (currently 17.5 per cent); and

(b) input tax incurred by the owner in respect of any expenses he incurs in relation to the property will become deductible by him.

This election is made by virtue of the VAT Act 1994, Sch 10, para 2 and is revocable only within its first three months (subject to certain conditions) or after 20 years. The election must be notified in writing to HM Customs and Excise within 30 days of the election being made and in certain circumstances the prior written permission of HM Customs and Excise must be obtained (see C & E Notice 742, para 8.6 and Appendix H).

The election is capable of being exercised only in respect of commercial property and where a building is only partly commercial (eg a shop with a flat above) the election can only apply to that part of the building which is not residential accommodation. The rent on a letting of such a mixed-use building would have to be apportioned if there are not separate lettings of the commercial and residential parts, and HM Customs and Excise will accept an apportionment which has an objective basis and gives a fair and reasonable result.

Subject to the above rule concerning buildings with mixed uses, an election must have effect in relation to the whole of a building and all the land within its curtilage. Buildings linked internally or by a covered walkway and 'complexes' (ie units grouped around a fully enclosed concourse) are to be taken as a single building covered by the same election, if they are owned by the same person (or by companies in a single VAT group).

Although the provision of parking facilities is normally standard rated for VAT purposes, a letting of premises including parking space is indivisible and the VAT treatment for the rent follows the treatment of the premises generally (ie standard rated if an election has been made or exempt if no election has been made).

Landlords must take care in deciding whether or not to make an election in respect of any particular building because *any* supply made in connection with that building after the election has taken effect, whether by way of letting or sale, must carry VAT at the standard rate and landlords must remember that certain tenants, such as financial institutions, are able to recover only a small proportion of input tax charged on the rents or purchase consideration. Therefore, the ability of the landlord to deduct input tax (perhaps on a costly refurbishment) must be weighed against the possibility of alienating a species of valuable potential tenant.

Buildings occupied by charities for charitable purposes (other than as offices) are accorded the same status as domestic accommodation and the election to waive exemption cannot be made in respect of such buildings. A charity using premises for business purposes, eg as a shop, is not treated as occupying for charitable purposes.

It is, perhaps, unlikely that a building already subject to an election would become used wholly or partly as a dwelling or for charitable purposes. However, if this happens the election is effectively suspended in respect of the appropriate part of the property and supplies revert to being exempt from VAT until commercial use recommences.

Some organisations (eg banks) which are largely VAT exempt were exploiting the election to waive VAT exemption. They were procuring property developers to lease back buildings to them or were funding developers to buy land and lease the land to them after development. Thus, the developer could reclaim VAT on the purchase and construction costs and the VAT-exempt organisation suffered irrecoverable VAT only slowly on periodic rents and service charges. The Finance Act 1997 prevents this device. If a lease back is granted to a landlord or a developer grants a lease to a person funding a development and either of them, or anyone connected with them, occupies the land other than wholly or mainly for making taxable supplies, then any election made by the landlord is disabled. No

VAT will be chargeable on rent or service charges. More than 80 per cent of supplies made must be taxable to avoid the legislation applying.

It is important to note that, in a lease back, the developer's election is not affected and he must charge VAT on the rent and service charge payable by the ultimate landlord. However, the ultimate landlord's election is disabled and he can neither recover the VAT charged to him nor charge VAT on the rent and service charge payable by the developer. This legislation is extremely complex and more detailed advice should be sought if it appears likely that these rules may apply.

3.2 VAT and commercial lettings

3.2.1 The commercial landlord's VAT position

Service charges for the general upkeep of the structure and common areas of a tenanted commercial building, or for providing the tenants with the services of a person such as a caretaker, are regarded as part of the consideration for the letting, and the liability of the service charge follows that of the main rent. Therefore:

(a) if the landlord has *not* elected to waive exemption in respect of a property, both the rent and the service charge for the services provided under the terms of the lettings of the property will generally be exempt for VAT purposes; but

(b) if the landlord *has* elected to waive exemption, both the rent and the service charge will generally be subject to VAT at the standard rate.

The word 'generally' is used because the above rules apply only to charges for supplies of services which are inherent in the right of the tenant to occupy the premises, such as maintenance by the landlord of the main structure and common parts of a multi-let building.

Supplies such as heating, lighting or cleaning etc to the area occupied by a tenant are regarded as separate from any right to occupy the premises, and VAT is chargeable by the landlord at the appropriate rate for the particular supply concerned, irrespective of the VAT status of the letting. Almost all these supplies, such as cleaning, heating and lighting, reception services, telephone switchboard, are liable to VAT at the standard rate.

The treatment of supplies of gas and electricity is more complicated. If the landlord rents or owns secondary credit meters, the charges for the units of gas or electricity supplied through those meters by the landlord are standard rated for VAT purposes. However, if the landlord does not provide secondary credit meters to the tenants and simply makes a fixed charge for unmetered supplies of gas or electricity (as would be normal where the only supply is in respect of the common parts of the building – each tenant arranging for his own direct supply to the let premises) the charge follows the treatment of rent for VAT purposes, as described above.

As explained in **3.1.2**, the landlord can recover input tax charged to him in respect of services supplied on to the tenant, if the on supply is taxable and not exempt. Therefore:

(a) if the landlord *has* elected to waive exemption, all input tax in respect of supplies made to him for the let property should be deductible; but

(b) if the landlord *has not* elected to waive exemption, input tax deduction is restricted to input tax suffered on those items, if any, which are on charged to the tenant with VAT, eg cleaning services supplied by the landlord's contractor within the premises let to the tenant.

The deductibility of input tax by the landlord influences the way in which he bills the tenant for the service charges. Thus:

(a) where the landlord *does* recover his input tax, he will on charge the tenant for the net amount, ie excluding the input tax which he can recover from HM Customs and Excise (but he will have to charge the tenants VAT on top of the total net costs); but

(b) where the landlord does *not* recover his input tax, he will on charge the tenant for the gross amount, ie including the input tax (but not charge further VAT on top of it).

Example – communal services

The landlord owns a four-storey office building. Each floor is the same size and is separately let. The landlord can charge each tenant for 25 per cent of the costs of maintaining the communal lift. The landlord pays lift maintenance charges of £1,000 + £175 VAT = £1,175.

*(A) Where the landlord has **not** elected to waive the exemption*

The landlord cannot recover the £175 input tax from HM Customs and Excise. The landlord therefore bills each tenant for 25 per cent of £1,175, ie £293.75. He does not give them VAT invoices (and they cannot recover the VAT – see **3.2.2**).

*(B) Where the landlord **has** elected to waive the exemption*

The landlord can recover the input VAT of £175 from HM Customs and Excise. The landlord, therefore, bills each tenant for 25 per cent of £1,000, ie £250. He must charge VAT on top, so he charges them £250 + £43.75 VAT = £293.75, and provides them with VAT invoices for this (so that they can recover the VAT – see **3.2.2**).

Example – non-communal services

The same landlord as in the above example provides each tenant with office cleaning carried out by the landlord's contractors. The contractors charge the landlord £2,000 + £350 VAT = £2,350.

*(A) Where the landlord has **not** elected to waive the exemption*

Even though the landlord has not elected to waive exemption, so that the supply of the premises remains exempt from VAT, nevertheless the supply of office cleaning is standard rated. The landlord must charge VAT for supplying that service on to the tenants and can, therefore, recover the input tax of £350 from HM Customs and Excise. The landlord bills each tenant for 25 per cent of £2,000, ie £500. He must charge VAT on top, so he charges them £500 + £87.50 VAT = £587.50, and provides them with VAT invoices for this (so that they can recover the VAT – see **3.2.2**).

*(B) Where the landlord **has** elected to waive the exemption*

The fact that the landlord has elected makes no difference in practice except that, as a matter of convenience, the cleaning costs can be dealt with in the same computations as the lift maintenance costs, since their VAT treatment is the same (although for different reasons).

3.2.2 The commercial tenant's VAT position

A commercial tenant using the let premises for the purpose of a fully taxable business can deduct the whole of any input tax charged to him by a landlord in respect of rent and service charges. If the tenant uses the building for the purpose of a business which is partially exempt (as will be almost all financial institutions etc), a partial deduction can be claimed by the tenant in respect of input tax suffered on the rent and service charges. With some partially exempt businesses, the rate of deduction can be very small. If the tenant uses the building for the purpose of a business which is wholly exempt (as will be almost all medical services), no deduction can be claimed by the tenant in respect of input tax suffered on the rent and service charges.

Example – communal services

Using the same example as set out under **3.2.1**, where the landlord pays lift maintenance charges of £1,000 + £175 VAT = £1,175, and will charge this equally between four tenants. Assume that three of the tenants are traders carrying on businesses which involve making wholly taxable supplies to their customers, but the fourth tenant is a private doctor making wholly VAT-exempt supplies to his patients.

*(A) Where the landlord has **not** elected to waive the exemption*

The landlord charges each tenant £293.75 and does not give them VAT invoices. None of the tenants can recover any VAT, even though VAT was part of the sum paid to the lift company. The actual cost to each of them is therefore, £293.75.

*(B) Where the landlord **has** elected to waive the exemption*

The landlord charges each tenant £250 + £43.75 VAT = £293.75 and provides them with VAT invoices for this. The trading tenants can each recover £43.75 as input tax in their own VAT returns, so the actual cost to them is only £250 each. The fourth tenant, the doctor, cannot recover any input VAT, so the actual cost to him is the full £293.75.

Example – non-communal services

The earlier example of the office cleaning services may be taken again, but the same assumption about the four tenants as set out above can also be made.

*(A) Where the landlord has **not** elected to waive the exemption*

The landlord charges each tenant £500 + £87.50 VAT = £587.50 and provides them with VAT invoices for this. The trading tenants can each recover £87.50 as input tax in their own VAT returns, so the actual cost to them is only £500 each. The fourth tenant, the doctor, cannot recover any input VAT, so the actual cost to him is the full £587.50.

*(B) Where the landlord **has** elected to waive the exemption*

The fact that the landlord has elected to waive the exemption makes no difference.

If a tenant does not use the property for the purpose of his own commercial activity, but, instead, sublets it to subtenants, the rules indicated in **3.2.1** will apply to any service charges which he may recharge to his subtenants. The deductibility of input tax by the tenant in respect of service charges made by the landlord will depend on whether or not the tenant has, in turn, elected to waive exemption of the supply of the property to the subtenants. If the tenant has made such an election, the input tax may be fully deductible but the tenant must charge VAT at the standard rate in respect of the rent and service charges payable by the subtenants.

3.3 VAT and domestic and charitable lettings

3.3.1 The landlord's VAT position

Domestic (including charitable – see below) lettings have their own peculiar set of rules for VAT purposes and these differ from commercial lettings as follows:

(a) a landlord cannot elect to waive exemption and no supplies of domestic lettings can be taxable; and

(b) supplies of basic amenities such as electricity, gas, water and sewerage services are (at 1 March 2002) liable to VAT at a special lower rate of 5 per cent to a domestic tenant or to a landlord for on supply to domestic tenants. This includes supplies of gas or electricity by the landlord through a secondary credit meter and also supplies of heat, ventilation or air conditioning from a central plant operated by the landlord.

Again, it is necessary to examine the basic VAT treatment of rent in connection with domestic letting in order to ascertain the correct treatment of those service charges which follow the treatment of rent and also a landlord's entitlement to deduct input tax charged to him.

The supply by a person constructing a domestic dwelling (or a building to be used for charitable purposes) of a 'major interest' in the building (a lease exceeding 21 years) can be zero rated for VAT purposes. Zero-rated status is also offered to a person converting a commercial building to domestic use, providing certain qualifying conditions are met. However, where the consideration is represented by an annual rent rather than an initial premium, only the first payment of rent is zero rated and the remainder of rental payments are exempt for VAT purposes. All rents in respect of a letting of 21 years or less (or, in Scotland, less than 21 years) are exempt. Therefore, the landlord cannot recover input tax charged to him in respect of maintenance expenses incurred after the beginning of the letting, since those expenses will be attributed to exempt supplies.

As the landlord has no ability to elect to waive exemption in respect of the letting of domestic property, rental payments subsequent to the first payment will be exempt from VAT and those service charges which follow the treatment of rent and are made after the initial letting will also be exempt for VAT purposes.

Services for the general upkeep of the structure and common areas of the building, such as janitorial or porterage services, maintenance of communal gardens, and cleaning of the common parts, follow the same VAT treatment as for rent. For the reasons given above, these particular service charges will be exempt for VAT purposes, but this may be of no advantage to the domestic tenant. Unless the landlord uses direct labour, he will usually be charged VAT on the supply of the respective services to him and, since such input VAT will not be deductible by him in his own VAT returns (being attributable to an exempt supply to the tenants), the landlord will almost inevitably pass the cost of that VAT on to the tenants through the service charge by charging on the basis of the gross cost inclusive of the VAT. Thus, the domestic tenant would still bear the cost of the VAT.

Services supplied to the portions of the building occupied by tenants are regarded as supplies separate from the basic right to occupy the premises and, for any supplies other than the basic amenities mentioned above, the landlord must charge VAT at the standard rate on top of the total charges relating to that expenditure. The same rule applies for those basic amenities liable to the special lower rate of 5 per cent. Once again, the landlord can recover the input VAT for costs recharged with VAT, so VAT would be added only to each tenant's share of the basic net costs. Therefore, the tenant may notice little practical difference between charges for services provided in the tenant's premises and charges for services for the communal areas.

It should be noted that where charity tenants are referred to in this paragraph, it is assumed that the premises in question are occupied solely for charitable purposes. If the charity conducts a business on the premises, or part thereof, the comments above concerning commercial lettings apply also to the building. If the business activities are conducted on only part of the premises the service charges are apportioned between the respective parts, and the separate rules for commercial and domestic lettings apply accordingly. An office occupied by a charity is always regarded as occupied for the purposes of business activities and, therefore, 'charitable purposes' are, effectively, restricted to premises used as a home for beneficiaries, schools, etc.

3.3.2   The domestic/charitable tenant's VAT position

Unless the landlord uses direct labour for the provision of many services, the only costs incurred VAT-free by the domestic tenant (under the present rules) are the basic amenities of water and sewerage services. The other costs, on which the landlord will have been charged VAT at either the standard rate or the lower rate of 5 per cent, will be recharged to the tenant on a VAT-inclusive basis. The domestic tenant can be at a disadvantage compared with most commercial tenants who can be charged VAT directly by the landlord in respect of service charges and who can reclaim the VAT.

3.3.3   Services provided other than by landlords

The rules explained above apply only if the landlord is providing the services to the tenants. The correct VAT treatment where the services are supplied by a third party (eg the trustee of a maintenance trust, even if the landlord is the trustee) is more complicated and has been the source of much confusion. The House of Lords has laid down guidelines in *Nell Gwynn House Maintenance Trustees v HM Customs & Excise* [1999] STC 79.

3.3.3.1   The Nell Gwynn House case
Nell Gwynn House is a block of 435 apartments. Many years ago, the tenants were concerned at the large sum of money held by the head lessee in collected

service charges. In order to allay this concern, a fund to pay for the maintenance of the building was established by trust deed to which each tenant contributes under the terms of his or her lease. The independent trustees of the fund employ 17 maintenance staff.

The trustees are paid a fee, agreed by all parties to be VAT standard rated. HM Customs and Excise accepted that the trustees should not charge VAT on the part of their service charges which recovers the cost to the fund of obtaining maintenance services from third party contractors, as the trustees had no opportunity of making any profit on this cost. However, HM Customs and Excise maintained that the trustees should charge the tenants VAT at the standard rate on the balance of the service charges levied (used to pay staff salaries and the trustees' fees out of the fund), arguing that the balance represents consideration for a supply of services. The trustees maintained that VAT is not chargeable on the service charges (except to the extent of their fees), either because the charges represent contributions to a trust fund by the beneficiaries of the trust, or because the service charges are part of an exempt supply of property (ie that the treatment of service charges follows the treatment of the rent for each apartment).

Both grounds were rejected by the VAT Tribunal and the High Court:

(1) the first on the ground that the 'mutuality' principle which has effect for direct tax purposes does not prevent a chargeable supply of services arising for VAT purposes; and

(2) the second on the ground that the trustees could not make a supply of property because they constitute a separate legal entity from the landlord and cannot be equated with the landlord (even if the landlord also acts as the trustee of the maintenance trust).

Undaunted, the trustees appealed to the Court of Appeal with a new argument that no part of the service charge, other than their fee, constitutes consideration under European law because the trustees are not themselves at liberty to deal with the money. This argument was accepted by the Court of Appeal. However, the House of Lords rejected this argument completely and restored the decision of the lower courts. The trustees' application for a reference to the European Court of Justice was refused, although only after the Law Lords deliberated for nine months! The Law Lords brushed aside the trustees' argument that a restoration of the decision of the VAT Tribunal would result in all the service charges being VAT standard rated (whereas HM Customs and Excise was arguing that only the recharge of salaries and the trustees' fees are standard rated), Lord Slynn stating that any concession by HM Customs and Excise in respect of this claim cannot affect the true legal position.

The three difficulties with the decision of the House of Lords are as follows.

(1) Their Lordships applied English trust law in deciding that the trustees are not the agents of the beneficiaries. It is submitted that the proper law to apply is European law, in which trusts are hardly known, but mutual funds are recognised. It is likely that on a proper application of European law the

trustees would have been regarded as the agent of the beneficiaries and the services as provided by an agent to its principal. This would have removed the liability to VAT on the service charges.

(2) Their Lordships' decision ignored a line of European Court of Justice cases holding that the consideration for a supply is limited to the amount that can be retained by the supplier and any amount that the supplier is mandated to pay away to a third party is to be ignored.

(3) Their Lordships held that the tax point of the supply of staff by the trustees occurs when money is removed from the fund to pay the staff. This decision is difficult to understand because it appears that if the main decision on liability is correct, the only possible tax point is the date of receipt by the trustees of service charges or the date of issue of a tax invoice to a tenant, whichever occurs earlier.

Nevertheless, there is no appeal from the decision of the House of Lords, the the European Court of Justice being unable to intervene without a reference from a national court.

3.3.3.2   The effect of the Nell Gwynn House case – commercial letting

Service charges for the common parts of a building will be VAT exempt only if:

(1) they are paid to the landlord acting in his capacity as such and not as the trustee of a maintenance trust; and

(2) the landlord has not elected to waive exemption from VAT in respect of the property.

3.3.3.3   The effect of the Nell Gwynn House case – domestic letting

As all service charges for domestic letting are held in a statutory maintenance fund trust (by virtue of the Landlord and Tenant Act 1987, s 42), then on a strict interpretation of this decision it would appear that all such service charges are VAT standard rated. This is so even if the landlord of the property acts as the trustee of the statutory trust, because when acting as trustee he would be deemed to be a separate legal person for VAT purposes. This was made quite clear in the *Nell Gwynn House* judgment in both the High Court and the House of Lords.

HM Customs and Excise's view on domestic service charges was set out in Business Brief 3/94, which announced a concession in respect of service charges for the common areas of estates of dwellings and blocks of apartments from 1 April 1994. Until any further public announcement is made, this remains HM Customs and Excise's position. As the House of Lords restored the decision of the lower courts in *Nell Gwynn House*, no significant further announcement is expected from HM Customs and Excise. Business Brief 3/94 is reproduced below:

'Service charges relating to the upkeep of the common areas of dwellings, or the common areas of a domestic dwelling if it is multi-occupied, are exempt from VAT under the general exemption for land, if they are paid by leasehold owners of property under the terms of the lease, or by people renting the property, and these charges are paid to the lessor or the ground landlord.

Previously service charges paid by freehold owners of domestic property, and by anyone for services which are not supplied by or under the direction of the lessor or ground landlord, have been taxable. This was because they could not be consideration for any supply of land.

This has led to an anomaly for the occupants of residential property, since the liability of the service charges they pay towards the upkeep of the common area does not depend on the services provided, but instead on the tenure of their residence and on the status of the supplier.

The new concession means that the liability of the service charge will no longer depend upon the tenure of the residence or on the status of the supplier. What will be important is whether each resident is obliged to accept the service because it is supplied to the estate of buildings or blocks of flats as a whole. Optional services supplied personally to a resident, such as carpet cleaning and shopping continue to be taxed in their own right.

This extra-statutory concession does not affect the VAT treatment of service charges paid by the occupants of non-domestic property such as shops, offices, industrial units etc, which will continue to depend on the tenure of occupation, on the status of the supplier and on whether any landlord supplying the service has elected to waive exemption in relation to the property.

It also does not affect the VAT treatment of service charges paid in respect of holiday accommodation which remain standard rated.'

3.3.3.4   Planning point

The effect appears to be to maintain the pre-*Nell Gwynn House* position with respect to domestic letting, but by concession only! Service charges for services to the common parts will be VAT exempt. Of course, as demonstrated above, the effective cost to a domestic tenant of service charges does not, in practice, depend on their VAT status, unless the landlord has incurred no VAT in providing them (as in *Nell Gwynn House*).

3.4   VAT and mixed-use buildings

Where service charges are made by a landlord to both commercial tenants and domestic tenants in the same property (for example a parade of shops with flats above) and the costs giving rise to the service charges need to be apportioned to arrive at the separate service charges for the commercial tenants and the domestic tenants, HM Customs and Excise will accept a reasonable apportionment. If the apportionment is not specified in the relevant leases, it may be based on respective floor space, although weighting adjustments will be permitted if floor space alone does not provide a just and reasonable apportionment.

After making the apportionment of the cost, the part apportioned to the commercial tenant is to be dealt with in accordance with **3.2** and that apportioned to the residential tenants is to be dealt with in accordance with **3.3**.

Example

A landlord spends £120,000 plus £2,100 VAT, totalling £14,100, on repairing the exterior of a four-storey building containing a retail shop on the ground floor and a residential flat on each of the three upper floors. The shop is let on a ten-year commercial lease and the three flats were sold on long leases. All the leases reserve service charges in equal proportions (25 per cent each) and include the cost of external repairs. The landlord has elected to waive exemption from VAT in respect of the building. The position is:

(a) the landlord can recover 25 per cent of the VAT he incurred on the cost of repairing the exterior (ie £525) since that proportion of the cost is attributable to the commercial service charge which is VAT standard rated;

(b) the remaining VAT of £1,575 is not recoverable as it is attributable to the three VAT-exempt domestic service charges;

(c) the commercial tenant's service charge will include 25 per cent of the cost of the works ignoring VAT (ie a charge of £3,000) and the landlord will charge him VAT on that service charge;

(d) the domestic tenants' service charge will each include 25 per cent of the cost of the work inclusive of its irrecoverable VAT (ie a charge of £3,525 each) on which VAT will not be chargeable by the landlord.

3.5 VAT and shared premises

3.5.1 General

Sometimes, a landlord will occupy premises with his tenants or a tenant will agree to discharge bills for utilities and collect appropriate proportions of the costs from other tenants. This amounts to a sharing of costs and has the following VAT consequences.

3.5.2 Arrangements between occupiers to share cost of utilities

Tenants may enter into an agreement concerning the discharge of costs for utilities etc, under which a 'lead' tenant will collect payments from the other occupants of their share of the costs. The 'lead' tenant can treat these collected costs as disbursements and so the other occupiers' shares of these amounts are ignored in determining the VAT position of the 'lead' tenant.

If his business is fully taxable, the 'lead' tenant will be able to claim a deduction for his share of any input tax but not for the other occupiers' shares. He will recoup the other tenants' shares of the total costs from them on a VAT-inclusive basis, and they will not be able to deduct input tax because they will have no tax invoice from the 'lead' tenant to support the claim.

Example

Alan, Bill, Colin and Douglas are all tenants in a small building. There is one electricity meter for the whole building. Alan agrees to be the subscriber and to recharge the others so that they all share the charges equally. Alan receives an electricity bill for £200 + £35 VAT = £235. The position is:

(a) Alan is entitled to recover his one-quarter share of the £35 VAT in his own tax returns, ie £8.75;

(b) Alan asks each of the others to reimburse him for one-quarter of the total bill of £235, ie £58.75 each, but he does not give them VAT invoices;

(c) the actual cost to Alan is £58.75, less his recovered input tax of £8.75, ie £50. Bill, Colin and Douglas have to pay £58.75 each and cannot recover any of the VAT.

Generally, therefore, this type of arrangement is suitable only where no VAT is chargeable by the particular utility supplier (now restricted to only non-industrial water and sewerage charges), or where the other tenants are not entitled to reclaim input tax in any event.

3.5.3 Landlord in occupation providing services to tenants

Where the landlord in occupation provides services to tenants, the costs recharged to tenants by a landlord (including a tenant granting subleases) generally follow the basic rules in **3.2** and **3.3**, as appropriate. The additional points to note where the landlord himself occupies the building and shares his own facilities with his tenants are as follows:

(1) *Reception and switchboard*
A charge for part of the cost of operating reception or switchboard facilities (eg based on the wages of the receptionists or telephonist) follows the treatment of rent, and, thus, will be exempt from VAT unless the landlord has elected to waive the exemption.

(2) *Office staff and services*
A charge for part of the cost of employing office staff (eg secretaries) *other than staff concerned with maintaining the building* is standard rated for VAT purposes, as is the recharge of other office services, such as the provision of photocopying facilities.

(3) *Car parking*
A charge of part of the cost of car parking is standard rated.

(4) *Staff facilities*
A charge for the provision of facilities for use by staff (eg recreation rooms or sports facilities) in the common parts of the building is the same as the VAT treatment for the rents. A charge for the costs of other shared staff facilities (eg canteen, vending machines, sports facilities away from the building) is standard rated for VAT purposes.

A charge for building maintenance staff (mentioned in (2) above) is covered by the normal rules in **3.2** and **3.3**.

3.5.4   Associated companies sharing occupation

It is not uncommon for a company to take a lease of premises and then to allow associated companies (perhaps companies in the same group) to occupy parts of the premises without themselves entering into arrangements directly with the landlord or entering into formal subleases or licences with the actual tenant.

This grant of an informal right to use a part of the premises is a standard-rated supply for VAT purposes and any charge made by the actual tenant is subject to VAT. This applies even if the tenant is simply passing on an appropriate share of costs, such as rent, business rates, insurance, etc. As the actual tenant is making standard-rated supplies, he is able to deduct any input tax charged by the supplier of services in respect of which a recharge with VAT is made to the associated companies.

The necessity for this charge to VAT can be avoided if the tenant and the associated companies can enter into a group VAT registration within the meaning of s 43 of the VAT Act 1994. (The details of that topic are outside the scope of this book.) Alternatively, the tenant could grant a licence of a specified area to its associate (see para 2.7 of Customs and Excise Notice 742).

3.5.5   Serviced offices

The proliferation of buildings dedicated to providing serviced office facilities has increased as landlords have been faced, in a recessionary property market, with buildings that cannot be sold and for which an income-generating use must be found.

A landlord providing serviced office facilities sometimes separates the charge for facilities from the charge for office space, and sometimes separate contracts are entered into for each of those supplies. The VAT Tribunal has considered the effects of this treatment in the following cases.

Business Enterprises (UK) Ltd v Commissioners of Customs and Excise (1998) VATTR 160 (3161): The appellant company supplied, as a package, serviced office accommodation at a time before the introduction of the election to waive exemption, so that all supplies of property were VAT exempt. The services included furniture, use of a telephone switchboard and cleaning, etc. The company contended that the supplies were taxable at the standard rate (so that it could recover input tax incurred by it in providing the services), but HM Customs and Excise contended that the company made only supplies of exempt licences to occupy land. The VAT Tribunal held that the company predominantly supplied exempt licences to occupy land and the facilities provided were ancillary and subservient to that predominant supply. The company could not recover any input tax.

Sovereign Street Workspace Ltd v Commissioners of Customs and Excise MAN/91/403 (9550): *Business Enterprises (UK) Ltd* was distinguished in a subsequent case in which the VAT Tribunal held that a company which supplied serviced office accommodation (and had not elected to waive exemption over the building) was making multiple and separate supplies comprising of:

- the grant of exempt licences to occupy land; and

- the supply of the use of facilities including telephone answering services and mail handling which were independent of the land (and taxable at the standard rate of VAT).

The VAT Tribunal held that the consideration paid by the tenants had to be apportioned between the two separate supplies and, accordingly, VAT was chargeable at the standard rate for the use of the facilities.

First Base Properties Ltd v The Commissioners of Customs and Excise LON/93/ 3122A (11598) (unreported): First Base took a lease of office space and then, after partitioning the premises into smaller offices, furnished the offices with business equipment and furniture. The offices were rented to customers as serviced offices but First Base did not elect to waive VAT exemption over the building. Customers were charged £15 per square foot for the right to occupy the individual office space allocated to them and £40 per square foot for the services and use of the equipment and furnishings. A customer could rent an unfurnished office without services if he so wished.

First Base attempted to recover the input tax incurred on the equipment and furnishings on the basis that the £40 per square foot rent was a separate taxable supply at the standard rate of VAT. HM Customs and Excise resisted on the grounds that one single VAT-exempt supply of a licence to occupy the accommodation was being made.

The VAT Tribunal had to decide whether the services and use of the equipment and furnishings was an integral part of the supply of the accommodation or a separate supply for a separate consideration. It distinguished *Business Enterprises (UK) Ltd* on the grounds that First Base specified a separate charge for the services and use of the equipment and furnishings in the rental agreements and there were no supplies of unfurnished offices involved in *Business Enterprises (UK) Ltd*. The fact that First Base offered, and did actually supply, unfurnished accommodation without services appears to have influenced the VAT Tribunal.

Therefore, the VAT Tribunal considered that the charge for the supply of the services and use of the equipment and furnishings was standard rated and that input tax recovery could be made in respect of the purchase of equipment and furnishings. However, First Base was not entirely successful as a charge for cleaning was held to be an integral part of the supply of accommodation and VAT exempt.

Assuming that no election to waive exemption has been made by the landlord (because such an election would render all supplies of both accommodation and facilities liable to VAT at the standard rate), the conclusions to be drawn from these cases are:

- if a single charge is made for the accommodation and the office facilities, then the charge should be exempt from VAT as consideration for a licence to occupy land; unless

- the services provided are of significant value, in which case an apportionment between exempt accommodation and standard-rated services may be necessary; but

- if a separate charge is made for the office facilities, preferably with separate supporting documentation, then that separate charge is most likely to be VAT standard rated and the charge for the accommodation is most likely to be exempt from VAT as consideration for a licence to occupy land; and

- this treatment is more certain if unfurnished office accommodation, without office facilities, is also let to tenants.

3.6   General points on VAT

3.6.1   Accounting for VAT on service charges

VAT becomes chargeable and accountable by reference to a VAT 'tax point'. The basic tax point for rent and for service charges which follow the treatment of the rent, is the earlier of:

(1) the issue of a VAT invoice (which must conform with particular requirements); or

(2) the receipt by the landlord of payment.

Service charges which do not follow the treatment of the rent (as described above) should, nevertheless, follow the same rule; whilst normally a tax point for an individual item of service will be the date the item of service is completed, service charges are treated as continuing services in respect of which reg 90 of the VAT Regulations 1995 provides that the normal linkage of the tax point to the completion of the service is disapplied.

A landlord is permitted, by the VAT Regulations 1995, to send out a VAT invoice covering a period of up to one year in advance, setting out the payments due from the tenant in that period. The tax point in respect of each payment covered by the VAT invoice is then fixed at the earlier of the due date for, or receipt of, the payment.

However, many landlords do not adopt this procedure because it fixes a tax point at the due date, even if a tenant is late in paying. Instead they send out a 'reminder' for rent and service charges, in a form which does not constitute a VAT invoice, eg by the omission of the VAT number and stating 'This is not a VAT Invoice'. It is important to note that the 'reminder' must not show VAT separately (see VAT Act 1994, Sch 11, para 5(2)). The tax point is then fixed at the time of receipt of actual payment from the tenant and the landlord sends the tenant a VAT invoice after (but within 30 days of) receiving the payment (as required by reg 13(1) and (5) of the VAT Regulations 1995).

This procedure is not always popular with tenants since they are not entitled to deduct the input tax in their VAT returns until they receive the VAT invoice, and there may be a delay in obtaining a deduction if they make the payment in the last few days of a VAT period and the VAT invoice is not received from the landlord until later. However, as this particular procedure crystallises a tax point only on receipt of payment by the tenant, the tenant cannot, in law, demand a VAT invoice in advance of making payment.

The introduction of the election to waive exemption had the effect of applying VAT to certain rents and service charges which were reserved by leases or other contractual obligations entered into before VAT was generally applied to land and which may, therefore, be silent as to the tenant's liability to pay VAT. Section 89 of the VAT Act 1994 provides that unless the lease or contractual arrangements specify otherwise, the landlord is able to require the tenant to pay VAT in addition to the rents and service charges, as from the date of the election to waive exemption. For this purpose, a lease (but not other contractual arrangements) 'specifies otherwise' only if a specific reference to VAT is made in the clause concerned. Thus, a generally worded provision that the tenant is not liable to pay tax on the rent will be insufficient to avoid the tenant having to pay VAT on the rent.

It should be noted that s 89 applies only to a lease or contractual arrangement in existence at the time that the election to waive exemption takes effect. If VAT is to be chargeable on rent and service charges reserved by a lease or contractual arrangement granted or entered into after the election, the lease or contract must expressly state that the sums reserved are 'exclusive of VAT' or contain some other express provision for VAT to be paid in addition to the stated amounts. If this is not done the tenant need pay no more than the stated sums, but the receipts by the landlord will be deemed to include VAT for which the landlord must account to HM Customs and Excise.

3.6.2 Interaction with stamp duty

The Inland Revenue Stamp Office maintains that, in stamping the grant of a lease, stamp duty is chargeable on the total of rent and VAT where the landlord has elected to waive exemption. It should be noted that if the lease provides for a single inclusive sum for both rent and service charges stamp duty under para 12(3) of Sch 13 to the Finance Act 1999 will be chargeable on the sum, including service charges. If, however, the service charges are reserved separately, they will be ignored for stamp duty purposes.

If a lease is granted without an election to waive exemption having being made by the landlord, the Stamp Office charges stamp duty on hypothetical VAT which would be charged on future rents, if an election were to be made, unless the landlord covenants never to make the election.

If VAT is reserved, not as additional rent but as a separate payment in a lease, it is ignored for the purpose of the 'lease or tack' charge but will be charged to stamp duty separately as a period payment under s 56 of the Stamp Act 1891. This treatment can increase the total stamp duty in comparison with VAT reserved as rent if the lease period does not exceed 100 years.

3.6.3 VAT procedure for managing agents

HM Customs and Excise will not accept a managing agent as being responsible for the landlord's VAT affairs and, therefore, it is not possible for a managing agent to assume sole responsibility for invoicing and accounting for VAT where a landlord has exercised the option to waive exemption and must account for VAT on rents.

However, in the circumstance that VAT is chargeable on rents and/or service charges, it is understood that the following invoicing procedures are acceptable to HM Customs and Excise:

(a)   the landlord issues rent 'reminders' and/or VAT invoices directly to the tenant; or

(b)   the managing agent invoices the tenant in his own name and using his own VAT registration number. The supply is treated as being made by the landlord to the managing agent and then by the managing agent to the tenant (s 47(3) of the VAT Act 1994). The landlord will issue a VAT invoice to the managing agent and the managing agent will reclaim input tax on it. In turn, the managing agent will issue a VAT invoice to the tenant. However, the involvement of a managing agent cannot change the nature or timing of a supply (which remains that of landlord to tenant in basic law (*Metropolitan Borough of Wirral v C&E* [1995] STC 597)) and the VAT invoices issued by the landlord and the managing agent, therefore, should have the same tax point. This arrangement can make the issue of 'reminders' followed by a VAT invoice after receipt of payment from the tenant somewhat cumbersome; or

(c)   the arrangement in (b) above may be short-circuited somewhat by concession from HM Customs and Excise. The managing agent may be regarded as an independent principal and under this arrangement there is no timing linkage between the VAT invoice issued by the landlord to the agent and the VAT invoice issued by the agent to the tenant. The agent does not invoice the landlord separately for his fee or commission but instead the supply from the landlord to the agent is deemed to be net of that fee or commission. This avoids the timing problem but it may be confusing for landlords to have to bill the agent for rent net of the agent's fee or commission and so is still cumbersome to an extent; or

(d)   the managing agent issues a 'reminder' and/or VAT invoice using the landlord's name, address and VAT registration number. In this case the name and address of the managing agent may appear on the documentation only as an instruction to the tenant as to whom the actual payment should be made.

Whichever method of accounting is adopted, the managing agent must ensure that the landlord is kept fully informed as to matters concerning its VAT affairs. In particular, where method (d) (above) is adopted, the landlord must be sent promptly copies of any invoices issued in the name of the landlord to ensure that the VAT charged is appropriately entered in the landlord's VAT return.

In respect of services obtained by the landlord for the premises, the managing agent can either:

(a) arrange for VAT invoices to be issued to him and then himself invoice the landlord accordingly (ensuring that both invoices have the same tax point), the managing agent reclaiming the input tax on the VAT invoice sent to him; or

(b) arrange for contractors to invoice the landlord directly.

It should be noted in option (b) (above), that the invoices can still be sent to the managing agent for processing as long as the landlord is shown on the invoice as the recipient of the supply of services and is informed accordingly so that the appropriate reclaim of input tax can be made by the landlord.

Whatever arrangement is adopted, and whether or not 'reminders' are sent before VAT invoices are issued, any failure to operate the chosen procedure correctly may lead to the imposition of a misdeclaration penalty and/or default interest on either or both of the managing agent and the landlord. Where the landlord has a penalty or interest levied against him due to misapplication of procedures by the managing agent, the landlord may seek to hold the agent liable in negligence.

The managing agent should remember to charge VAT at the standard rate on his fees, in all circumstances, other than in (c) above.

4 RESERVE FUNDS AND SINKING FUNDS

4.1 Different types of funds

Traditionally, there has been a distinction between reserve funds and sinking funds. Reserve funds were established for the purpose of meeting recurring expenditure (such as periodic redecoration of the exterior and common parts of a building) whilst evening out the annual service costs, whereas sinking funds were to provide for expenditure which might only be incurred once or twice during a lengthy lease term on quite specific items (eg replacement of lifts or reroofing). In recent years, this distinction appears to have become blurred, perhaps because some of the plant and equipment now being manufactured has a much shorter life than was formerly the case.

The Nugee Committee found that funds were useful because they helped to avoid enormous service charges being demanded in the years in which these types of major expenditure took place, but that funds had not been established for many blocks because either the leases did not make provision for it or because of bad management. The Nugee Committee also found that some funds were 'raided' by managing agents or tenants, to avoid service charges being increased, for expenditure other than that for which the funds had been established.

4.2 Principles of operation

4.2.1 Specific purpose clauses

Some clauses provide for the establishment of a reserve or sinking fund in order to provide for specific types of expenditure, particularly renewals or replacements, but occasionally for more frequently recurring items such as redecoration, for example:

'The establishment and maintenance of a sinking fund for the replacement from time to time of the *lifts, boilers or other central heating apparatus, hot water supply systems, air conditioning systems appliances, fire-fighting equipment, pumps and all other plant equipment machinery and apparatus* serving the Building.'

In the event that the provisions of the lease are specific in this way, the fund can only be established and used in order to provide for the stated items.

4.2.2 Non-specific clauses

Some reserve or sinking fund clauses are silent or wide-ranging on the types of expenditure for which the fund is to be built up. Others expressly give the landlord or his managing agents discretion on the subject, for example:

'To set aside as a reserve such sums as the Landlord shall reasonably require to meet such future costs as the Landlord shall reasonably expect to incur in *replacing maintaining and renewing those items which the Landlord has hereby convenanted to replace maintain and renew*.'

This clause limits the purpose for which the fund can be built up to those items of replacement, maintenance and renewal which are within the landlord's covenants, and the landlord would not be entitled to build up the reserve fund for anything which fell outside his covenants. In the above example, the landlord is contractually obliged to act reasonably in estimating and demanding the reserve fund contributions.

4.2.3   Calculation of funds

Sinking or reserve funds fall into two types and it is recommended that a different approach is taken for each of these, for the purposes of collecting the relevant payments. The two types are:

(1) funds required for regular periodic items, such as redecoration of the exterior;

(2) funds required for the replacement of major capital items where the anticipated life is in excess of 10 years.

These different types of fund are discussed in the next two sections.

4.2.4   Funds for periodic items

It should be possible to draw up a five-year plan for any major block under management and to show the incidence of regular, periodic requirements, such as painting of the exterior or interior common parts of a building. The costs involved in this work are generally quantifiable and, under normal circumstances, are not unduly subject to the ravages of inflation. The periods involved are comparatively short, so that interest on the fund is not a major consideration and, consequently, it should be simple to calculate the amount required for the fund to take account of the relevant needs. The five-year plan should be a rolling plan, so that the annual cost can be recalculated in the light of both inflation and interest.

Example

In a block of flats the only periodic items are the painting of the exterior every three years and the painting of the interior common parts every five years. Assuming that the current cost of painting the exterior is £20,000 and the current cost of the painting of the interior common parts is £10,000, the five-year cash-flow requirements are as follows:

Year 1	Nil
Year 2	Nil
Year 3	Paint exterior £20,000
Year 4	Nil
Year 5	Paint interior £10,000

If interest and inflation are ignored the annual payments to provide sufficient funds for this work amount to £8,666, so that after five years the total income on this simple basis will have been £43,330 and the total expenditure £30,000 leaving, £13,330 towards the next exterior painting in Year 6. However, this is too simple an approach and the reality is shown in Table 2 (below), where the following assumptions have been taken:

(1) interest has been added yearly at 4 per cent per annum net of tax, giving an annual rate of 5.13 per cent (for a basic rate tax payer);

(2) the expenditure has been inflated at 3 per cent per annum compound;

(3) the contributions are received at the beginning but the expenditure is made at the end of each financial year.

TABLE 2

Year	Income £	Interest £	Total £	Expenditure £	Balance c/f £
Year 1	8,666	347	9,013	–	9,013
Year 2	8,666	707	9,373	–	18,386
Year 3	8,666	1,082	9,748	21,855	6,279
Year 4	8,666	598	9,264	–	15,543
Year 5	8,666	968	9,634	11,593	13,584
Year 6	8,666	890	9,556	23,881	-741

It will be seen that the two expenditures can be met from the balance being held in the account, so that at the end of Year 5 there is a balance of £13,584. However, the expenditure on external painting is due in Year 6 and this produces a deficit at the end of Year 6 of £741. If interest runs ahead of inflation this deficit is not important since the position will rectify by itself at the beginning of Year 7, but this will not be the case if the reverse happens.

4.2.5 Funds for long-term capital expenditure

Long-term capital expenditure is not radically different from the situation given above, except that the actual expenditure is much more difficult to predict, owing to the long periods involved. It will, therefore, be necessary to check the calculations periodically to see that the sinking fund scheme is on target. Two schemes can be devised:

(a) constant payment scheme;

(b) increasing annual costs scheme.

A simple example can be used to indicate the two approaches.

Service Charges: Law and Practice

Example

A fund is required to replace a lift. The current cost of providing a new lift is
£25,000 and the anticipated life of the lift is 15 years. Assuming as in the above
examples that cost inflation is 3 per cent per annum and that interest on the
sinking fund is at 4 per cent per annum compound, the cost of the new lift is 15
years' time will be £25,000 multiplied by the amount of £1 for 15 years at 3 per
cent = £35,950.

4.2.5.1 Constant payment scheme

In order to find the annual sum with constant payments, the anticipated
replacement cost must be divided by the annual sinking fund for 15 years at 4 per
cent per annum = £2,130. The calculation should be tested after five years to
check that the sinking fund is on target and no action needs to be taken. If,
however, the actual cost is found to be higher, it will be necessary to predict the
anticipated replacement cost after a further 10 years and this new cost, minus the
balance in the fund to date, must be amortised over the remaining 10 years and
the new annual cost found. Of course, the reverse could be true and, therefore, it
could be found that the anticipated repayment cost had fallen so that the
adjustment would be downwards. The advantage of this scheme is that there is a
constancy of payments, but the disadvantage is that the cost is high in the early
years and low in the later years, so that the actual percentage of disposable
income applicable to this fund is falling. The second method provides for the
opposite effect.

4.2.5.2 Variable annual payments

Table 3 (below) has been calculated by taking the current cost of a new lift as
£25,000 and dividing this by 15, to give a required sinking fund in Year 1 of
£1,666. The sinking fund payments should have then been increased by 3 per
cent per annum to give the figure shown. It will be seen that, at the end of 15
years, the total amount in the fund is just under £39,000, which compares very
favourably with the required amount of £38,650. It is not worth adjusting the
percentage increase to allow for the very small difference between the two
relevant figures. The advantage of this scheme is that the payments will rise in
pace with inflation rises so that the percentage of disposable income should
remain constant. Again, the calculations can be tested on a regular basis and
recalculations made, if it is found that the anticipated replacement cost is higher
or lower than the originally calculated figure. In these examples, it has been
assumed that the sinking fund payments will be made yearly in advance and that
interest will be credited at the end of each year in arrears. In any sinking fund
scheme there must be some assumption about the interest and inflation, and
account must also be taken of ability to pay, as well as the actual mathematical
calculations. If the Tables are presented to the tenants in advance so that they are
aware of the anticipated annual increases, there should be fewer problems in
collecting the funds.

TABLE 3

Year	Income £	Interest £	Total £	Expenditure £	Balance c/f £
Year 1	1,666	67	1,733	–	1,733
Year 2	1,716	138	1,854	–	3,587
Year 3	1,767	214	1,982	–	5,568
Year 4	1,820	296	2,116	–	7,684
Year 5	1,875	382	2,257	–	9,942
Year 6	1,931	475	2,406	–	12,348
Year 7	1,989	573	2,563	–	14,911
Year 8	2,049	678	2,727	–	17,638
Year 9	2,110	790	2,900	–	20,538
Year 10	2,174	908	3,082	–	23,621
Year 11	2,239	1,034	3,273	–	26,894
Year 12	2,306	1,168	3,474	–	30,368
Year 13	2,375	1,310	3,685	–	34,053
Year 14	2,447	1,460	3,907	–	37,960
Year 15	2,520	1,619	4,139	38,650	3,449

4.2.6 Crediting the tenants with reserves

When funds held in a reserve fund are taken out in order to be applied towards the expenditure for which they have been set aside, it is proper practice for the service charge to be computed by charging each tenant individually with his appropriate share of the costs and crediting him with his share of the funds taken from reserve.

Some surveyors merely credit the total sum taken from reserve against the total amount of the relevant expenditure, and then allocate the net cost among the tenants. However, this will be unfair and inappropriate where tenants have not contributed to the reserve in the same proportions as their current service charge liability; this might arise, for example, where some parts of the building were let to tenants who paid contributions to the reserve fund at a time when other parts were unlet or were let to tenants who had no such liability.

The individual method of crediting tenants is almost certainly obligatory under the statutory trust regime created by s 42 of the 1987 Act.

4.2.7 Depreciation

If the lease entitles the landlord to include in the service charge a sum for 'depreciation' in respect of plant and machinery, this is a sum which can be retained by the landlord, although it may be implied that, for the purpose of calculating the service charges if and when the relevant plant is actually replaced during the term of the lease, credit for the depreciation amount is to be given against the actual cost of replacement.

Example

Secretary of State for the Environment v Possfund (North West) Ltd [1997] 39 EG 179, ChD: The lease did not entitle the landlord to create a reserve fund, but it did entitle him to charge depreciation in respect of plant and machinery. The landlord obtained payments from the tenant, ostensibly towards the future replacement of the air conditioning system. The system was not replaced by the end of the lease and the tenant sought a refund of the payments. **Held:** The payments were attributable to the depreciation charge and so the amount contributed by the tenant belonged to the landlord and was not refundable, but the landlord 'would ordinarily be expected' to give credit for the depreciation sum against the cost of new plant and machinery if it was replaced during the term.

4.3 Investment of funds

4.3.1 Basic principles

The provisions of the lease may expressly require the fund to be invested and the interest earned to be accumulated. The lease may state specifically that the fund is to be held on trust, in which case there is a clear duty to invest the fund in appropriately safe investments, such as in a bank deposit account or building society account. Even in the absence of an express direction to invest or an express trust, there is possibly an implied duty that the fund should be invested so as to earn interest (see *Yorkbrook Investments Ltd v Batten* (1985) 276 EG 545). It is, in any event, good practice for service charge monies to be held in a separate bank account identified as being the service charge (or sinking or reserve) fund for the particular building.

4.3.2 Where the LTA 1985 and the LTA 1987 apply

In the case of residential service charges to which s 18 of the LTA 1985 applies (see **2.1**), there is a statutory requirement for the investment of such monies as trust funds (s 42 of the LTA 1987 and Orders made under that section – see **2.11**).

There are also new provisions as to designated accounts in which funds are to be held (s 42A of the LTA 1987, inserted by the Commonhold and Leasehold Reform Act 2002 as from a date to be fixed) as set out at **2.9.5**.

4.4 Security problems with reserve funds

If the fund is not held as trust money or identified as being money held for a specific purpose, there is a danger that if the landlord (or its agent) holding the funds in its own name were to become bankrupt or go into liquidation, the fund might form part of the general assets of the landlord (or agent) and the tenants would then have to prove in the bankruptcy or liquidation in order to recover the fund, and rank in priority after preferential creditors.

For these reasons, it is preferable for the funds to be held in a separate, designated bank or building society account and identified as being the reserve or sinking fund for the particular building (see *Re Chelsea Cloisters Ltd* (1980) 41 P&CR 98; *National Westminster Bank v Halesowen Presswork* [1972] AC 785; *Re Arthur Sanders Ltd* (1981) BLR 125).

4.5 Tax problems with reserve and sinking funds

4.5.1 Introduction

4.5.1.1 *Landlords' tax position*

Service charges levied by a landlord will, in most cases, form part of the landlord's income arising from ownership of land and be assessable to income or corporation tax under Schedule A. Services provided by the landlord for which the charges are made will rarely be sufficiently intensive to form a trading activity from which the service charges comprise trading receipts. It should be noted that references in this section to a landlord refer only to the person holding the freehold or superior interest in the property, unless specific reference is made otherwise.

Service charges are levied to meet specific expenditure incurred by the landlord in providing services to tenants and performing the obligations imposed upon the landlord under the lease. Revenue expenditure so incurred by the landlord will be deductible under the normal rules of Schedule A. The position with regard to expenditure on plant and machinery (eg provision of a new lift) is more complicated but, generally, capital allowances may be granted to the landlord under ss 11 and 16 of the Capital Allowances Act 2001. However, as capital allowances for plant and machinery are given at a rate of 25 per cent per annum on a reducing balance basis, a mismatch can occur between service charge receipts and the capital allowance for any period of assessment, so that a portion of the service charge receipts relating to expenditure on machinery and plant may remain taxable in the year of receipt.

Strictly, capital allowances are not available for plant and machinery utilised in common parts of the building, possession and control of which are retained by the landlord. In practice, capital allowances are often given but if the common parts are let to a third party responsible for their upkeep and maintenance, the validity of a claim to capital allowances is put beyond doubt. This is one reason why, in many cases, the landlord passes responsibility for upkeep and mainten- ance to a management company.

4.5.1.2 Tenants' tax position

A commercial tenant occupying leased premises for the purpose of his trade or business will be entitled normally to deduct the service charges paid in computing trading profits. This is so whether or not the landlord immediately expends the funds or creates a sinking fund, providing the tenant has divested himself absolutely of the sum in question. A more difficult point is the classification of the payment of service charge by the tenant into revenue or capital expenditure.

The fact that a service charge is payable at regular intervals and may be reserved as rent in the lease is support for the view that the payment represents revenue expenditure, no matter how the landlord expends the sum in the upkeep of the building. Further, the service charge will usually be levied by the landlord with a view to a mix of anticipated expenditure, both revenue and capital, in the course of upkeep and maintenance. However, this does not prevent the payment of a service charge representing capital expenditure by the tenant if it is to meet specific capital expenditure by the landlord and caution must be taken in drafting clauses providing for the payment of service charges.

If certain payments of service charges are unavoidably classified as capital expenditure by the tenant, it would appear that there is insufficient nexus between the levying of the service charge and the capital expenditure by the landlord, so that the expenditure of the tenant would not be a 'capital contribution' within s 537 of the Capital Allowances Act 2001 entitling the tenant to capital allowances. The provisions of s 183 of the Capital Allowances Act 2001 permitting a transfer of capital allowances from a lessor to a lessee will not be of help as the plant and machinery in the common areas of the building will not be subject to any lease but will be retained by the landlord.

The writer recently conducted a long argument with the Inland Revenue concerning the tax treatment of sizeable service charges paid by a head lessee. The freeholder had instituted a programme of refurbishment to the building which included substantial capital expenditure on the lifts etc. The Inland Revenue argued that a proportion of the head lessee's service charges were disallowable in the head lessee's Schedule A computation because of the capital works on which the freeholder had spent the service charges collected. The Inland Revenue also wished to disallow a similar proportion of the service charges levied by the head lessee on its subtenants, so that the disallowance would have been repeated several times over! Of course, this was a nonsense as on a properly constructed lease only the freeholder should have suffered a disallowance in its Schedule A computations for the capital expenditure.

The construction of the relevant leases required the head lessee to pay a single service charge with no direct apportionment to any particular expenditure by the freeholder, over which the head lessee had no control. After referring the matter to the appropriate technical office of the Inland Revenue, the Inspector of Taxes conceded that the service charges were wholly allowable in the head lessee's Schedule A computation.

4.5.2   Sinking funds – problems of timing

If a landlord is beneficially entitled under the lease (as opposed to a trust arrangement – see below) to a service charge calculated so as to exceed current expenditure, the service charge remains assessable under Schedule A. Even though the receipts, or part of them, may be set aside by the landlord into a sinking fund, the landlord will not be able to avoid bringing the receipts into account as income for Schedule A purposes in the relevant period of assessment.

Further, no deduction may be made for tax purposes for sums set aside in the sinking fund as there will have been no *payment* of a deductible expense nor the *incurring* of expenditure on the provision of machinery or plant.

Of course, payments out of the fund will be deductible for tax purposes but if the fund is set aside to meet occasional substantial expenditure (eg the refurbishment of the whole of the outside of the building), the expenditure will exceed the service charge receipts for the lease in question for the period of assessment in which the expenditure is incurred and the landlord will need to set the excess expenditure against other sources of Schedule A income. If the landlord has insufficient sources of income, the calculation of service charges over the period of the sinking fund will need to take into account the restriction on tax relief available to the landlord when the fund is expended.

4.5.3   Tax problems with trust arrangements

4.5.3.1   General
Some leases provide for service charge sinking funds to be held in an express or implied trust for the benefit of the tenants from time to time. It is important that the fund is held for the benefit of the tenants, because for a trust to be validly created there must be one or more beneficiaries in whose favour the court can decree performance. The trust may provide for the fund to be held for the purpose of maintaining the building without being an invalid purpose trust, provided that there is at least one beneficiary who is able to enforce the trust for the purpose of maintaining the building.

4.5.3.2   Payment into the trust
The classification of payments of service charges made by tenants to the landlord acting as trustee is complex and there is no specific authority. The main possibilities for classifying the receipts of the trustees are:

(1)   income taxable under Schedule A; or

(2)   income assessable under the residual head of Schedule D, Case VI; or

(3)   an annual payment assessable uner Schedule D, Case III; or

(4)   a capital payment.

It is not thought that the income is assessable under Schedule A as the landlord *qua* trustee does not have any interest in the property from which to derive income. In order to constitute an annual payment the receipt must be 'pure income profit' in the hands of the trustee. In other words, the trustee must receive the sum without any obligation to do anything in return. It is thought that, in the hands of the trustee, the payments from tenants are not pure income from which it then meets incidental expenses but rather that the receipts are one element of the overall determination of income and expenditure. Thus, the receipts would not be annual payments and the tenants would not be entitled to deduct them as a charge on income. However, if the obligation to maintain the building is placed on the landlord and the trust exists simply to reimburse the landlord for the cost of meeting his obligations, the receipts may represent 'pure income profit' in the hands of the trustee because the trust will not actually perform any obligation for the receipt of payment from the tenant. The taxation treatment may depend on whether or not the obligation of maintaining the building is placed on the landlord or the trustee (albeit he is the same person as the landlord).

This leaves the possibility of assessment on the trustee under the residual head of Schedule D, Case VI or the possibility that payments by the tenants represent capital contributions to the trust, in effect sums settled on trusts.

4.5.3.3 Possibility of payments into trust being capital

There is a strong argument that receipts from the tenant would be assessable in the hands of the trustee under Schedule D, Case VI and, in that event, there may be a liability to income tax in the early years of the sinking fund from which subsequent expenditure could not be deducted. However, it may be possible to argue that the receipts are capital contributions from the tenants (although that would destroy any possibility of a tax deduction for commercial tenants) following the line of argument in the case of *IRC v The Forth Conservancy Board (No 2)* (1931) 16 TC 103, which concerned the assessability of a surplus of receipts over expenditure of a statutory body charged with the maintenance of the River and Firth of Forth. The decision tends to indicate that the 'mutuality' principle (that one cannot make a profit out of onself) which applies to members' clubs etc, can apply in circumstances similar to a sinking fund held in trust. The argument is that the tenants are both settlors and beneficiaries of the trust and as such the trustee, as custodian of the fund, cannot be assessable to income tax in respect of surpluses arising. On this basis, the payments by tenants to the trust represent the settling of additional capital sums which do not have the quality of income in the hands of the landlord as trustee.

4.5.3.4 Summary of taxation of payments into trust

It can be seen that there was no one clear line of authority concerning the taxation of the payment of service charges by tenants into a trust. However, in its Tax Bulletin No 37, the Inland Revenue was prompted by the introduction of reforms to the taxation of Schedule A income to provide its opinion on the taxation of service charge trusts. The opinion (which is not binding and can be retracted at any time) refers specifically to tenant-owned flat management companies but should apply to all service charge and sinking fund trust arrangements. However, it is necessary for a reader to be absolutely certain that a trust arrangement actually exists (see **2.11**).

The Inland Revenue's view is that from 1 April 1998, service charges received by a trustee ordinarily will be outside the scope of Schedule A. The Inland Revenue's reasoning is that, under proper accountancy principles, usually it will not be correct to tax under Schedule A sums to which the landlord is not beneficially entitled. Consequently, service charges received by a trustee will ordinarily be received as capital in the landlord's capacity as trustee (under either a common law or s 42 of the LTA 1987 statutory trust). If the trust includes a power to accumulate income, then investment income arising on the fund will be chargeable on the trustee at the income tax rate applicable to trusts. Note that s 42 of the LTA 1987 contains an implied power to accumulate in the case of all statutory trusts.

Any rent receivable by a landlord in his capacity as such, rather than as a trustee of a service charge or sinking fund trust, is outside any trust arrangement and remains chargeable on the landlord under Schedule A.

The opinion published by the Inland Revenue in its Tax Bulletin No 37 endorses the view that payments by tenants into a service charge or sinking fund trust are capital in nature. Rent received by a landlord in his capacity as landlord is chargeable to tax under Schedule A in the usual manner.

4.5.3.5 *Commercial tenants' tax position*
The opinion expressed by the Inland Revenue and set out above determines the tax deductibility of a commercial tenant's payments into a service charge or sinking fund trust. Regrettably, as far as the commercial tenant is concerned, the opinion is fatal to the tenant's ability to claim a tax deduction for the payments. This is because the payments are classified as capital contributions to the trust and the payments lack the necessary revenue nature for a tax deduction.

4.5.3.6 *Inheritance tax*
No review of a trust is complete without considering the incidence of inheritance tax. It is arguable that a trust arrangement for a sinking fund is wholly commercial and involves no element of bounty in its creation. However, it is understood that the Inland Revenue regards a sinking fund trust as within the inheritance tax provisions and, as no single beneficiary has an immediate right to income or capital, the treatment is that of a discretionary trust. Accordingly, there would be a potential charge to inheritance tax on property leaving the settlement (other than by way of the payment of expenses, eg on the determination of the trust) and on each 10-year anniversary of its creation. This latter, potential charge could have serious effects on a large property with a sinking fund for long-term projects.

4.5.4 Maintenance companies

4.5.4.1 General

The landlord may create a company specifically responsible for the upkeep and maintenance of the property, with or without a transfer of the freehold reversion to the company. With residential properties, each tenant may be a shareholder in the company, the landlord having no interest and, in that event, the tenant would transfer his share in the company to an assignee of the lease on a sale.

If the company does not hold the freehold reversion to the building, receipts of service charges cannot be assessable under Schedule A in respect of land and, usually, the company will be regarded as carrying on a trade of providing maintenance services. If the company receives service charges as a trustee of a trust for a sinking fund, the tax considerations set out above will apply. This is particularly relevant in connection with service charges for residential blocks of flats, for which, in most cases, s 42 of the Landlord and Tenant Act 1987 creates, by statute, a trust arrangement for the sinking fund (but see **4.5.5**).

4.5.4.2 Mutuality

Where there is no trust arrangement, it is likely that the principle of mutuality will apply if the tenants are the only shareholders. This principle is based on the maxim that a person cannot make a profit from himself and, following *Styles v New York Life Insurance Company* (1889) 2 TC 460, the fact that the mutual activity is carried out through a company does not prevent the mutuality principle applying. In this case, the service charges will not be assessable to corporation tax, although interest income arising on the fund will be assessable.

4.5.4.3 Tenants' tax position

Notwithstanding the mutuality principle, a tenant of commercial property should be able to deduct, as a trading expense, the service charges paid, following the principle in *Thomas v Richard Evans & Co Ltd* (1927) 10 TC 790, which concerned a mutual insurance reserve fund and bears strong resemblances to a sinking fund for service charges. However, the comments above concerning the possible identification of a capital element to the service charges should be borne in mind.

If a surplus of funds is returned to members on the liquidation of a mutual company, the receipts may be subject to tax under Schedule D, Case VI, to the extent that the service charges were claimed as trading expenses.

4.5.4.4 Summary

In summary, it is likely that service charges paid to management companies will be either payments under trust arrangements, attracting the same difficulties with regard to tax which are outlined above or the management company will be a mutual company, so that the surplus on the sinking fund is not immediately taxable. However, many management companies which are likely to be mutual will operate in respect of domestic property and, following the establishment of mandatory trust arrangements under s 42 of the Landlord and Tenant Act 1987, it is possible that the incidence of mutual companies will diminish.

4.5.5 Section 42 of the Landlord and Tenant Act 1987 – perpetuity period

There is an apparent dichotomy between s 42 of the Landlord and Tenant Act 1987 and the normal rule of trust law which prevents trusts continuing indefinitely. A valid trust must not be capable of continuing beyond the expiry of a 'perpetuity period'. A s 42 trust determines on the expiry of the last remaining lease for the property concerned, which can, *in extremis*, be 999 years from the creation of the trust. Thus, s 42 trusts potentially offend against the perpetuity principle and are invalid.

However, there is a basic presumption that Parliament cannot have intended to legislate for invalid trusts and that the provisions of s 42 are intended to overrule the law on perpetuities. If this presumption is incorrect and a trust is invalid, the fund remains the property of the tenants in the proportions to which they have contributed. Any income arising on the fund is apportioned amongst those tenants and no tax relief is available for commercial tenants in respect of contributions to the fund until the fund is expended.

4.6 Drafting points

When drafting leases which have to make provision for such funds, lawyers must not only take account of the tax and security problems associated with reserve and sinking funds, but also the problems which are posed by the law of trusts. A full discourse on the subject is beyond the scope of this book, but a few basic points should be noted.

A 'purpose trust' (a fund for a specific purpose which does not have individuals as beneficiaries) cannot validly be created, except for solely charitable purposes, unless it can be seen, ultimately, to have persons as beneficiaries (*Re Denley's Trust Deed* [1969] 1 Ch 373).

Furthermore, a trust for beneficiaries must vest the fund in them before the expiry of the 'perpetuity period', which can be measured either by reference to someone's life (hence the commonly found 'Royal Lives' clauses), or be a stated, fixed period of up to 80 years under the Perpetuities and Accumulations Act 1964, s 1.

However, once trust property becomes vested absolutely in a group of adult beneficiaries, they can put an end to the trust and call for the fund to be distributed amongst themselves (*Saunders v Vautier* (1841) 4 Beav 115). This would be most inconvenient if the vesting of a reserve fund occurred before the end of the leases, when major expenditure on repairs and renewals was still pending.

Some of the questions which arise for the draftsman are, therefore as follows.

(1) Should the lease declare an express trust of the fund or remain silent on the point?

(2) If a trust is expressed, should this be a 'purpose trust' or specify the tenants as beneficiaries?

(3) What perpetuity period should be applied?

It has been suggested that an acceptable formula would be to provide that the landlord will hold the fund on trust to expend it on the specified categories of works during the perpetuity period, and that any surplus at the end of the period would be held for the then tenants in the same proportions as their liability to pay service charges. The perpetuity period would be as long as possible, unless, perhaps, the existing building had a limited life after which it was to be demolished or reconstructed at the landlord's cost, in which case the period should end prior to that time. However, the tax problems outlined in **4.5** must be remembered, and there seems to be no simple way to resolve the conflicting factors of tax and trust law. This may explain why many landlords shy away altogether from establishing reserve or sinking funds.

5 SERVICE CHARGES – FREEHOLD AND COMMONHOLD PROPERTIES

5.1 The legal problems with freeholds

5.1.1 Inability to enforce positive covenants

Unlike the tenant's covenants in a lease, which are usually automatically binding on (and, thus, enforceable by the landlord against) every assignee of the lease (see **1.18.2**), positive covenants given by a purchaser of freehold land are not directly enforceable by the covenantee (the person to whom the covenants are given, ie the vendor who imposed them) against a person acquiring the land from the purchaser. The original person giving a positive covenant remains liable to perform it (unless the terms of the covenant free him from liability when he parts with the property) and, often, the person acquiring the property from him will expressly covenant to indemnify him in respect of the liability. Nevertheless, unless further provisions of the types mentioned in **5.1.2** are used, the covenantee cannot sue the new owner in respect of positive covenants.

Accordingly, if the freehold of a property is sold and, in the transfer or conveyance, the purchaser simply covenants to pay a service charge towards the cost incurred by the vendor in, for example, maintaining private roads or amenity areas, if the purchaser subsequently resells the property, the vendor cannot sue the new owner for the service charge. He can only sue the original purchaser, if he can find him.

5.1.2 Solutions

The problem outlined in **5.1.1** can be tackled in a number of ways.

(1) By providing, in the original transfer or conveyance, a further positive covenant that, when the purchaser sells the property, he will procure that the new owner gives a direct covenant to the covenantee that he will perform the positive covenants in the original transfer or conveyance (including the covenant as to obtaining direct covenants on a further sale).

(2) By providing, in the original transfer or conveyance, that the use of the roads or amenities is conditional on the owner of the property having paid the service charges.

(3) By reserving the service charges as an estate rentcharge under the Rentcharges Act 1977.

(4) By disposing of premises on a commonhold, rather than a freehold, basis (see **5.4**).

Method (1) can break down if, contrary to the covenant, an owner fails to ensure that his successor gives the direct covenant to the covenantee, as occurred in *Thamesmead Town Ltd v Allotey* [1998] 37 EG 161, CA, where the estate company had no right to sue the new house owner for payment of certain estate costs. This can usually be avoided by providing for the registered title of the property to contain a restriction against registration of any transfer without the direct covenant being given by the transferee.

Method (2) is hard to enforce because clearly it is difficult physically to prevent one owner of a property on an estate from using the roads or other amenities without affecting their use by other owners who have paid their service charges. It would be possible to seek an injunction against the defaulting owner but this is a costly and uncertain remedy. The estate rentcharge under method (3) is, in many respects, better, but it has its limitations. These are considered below.

5.2   Estate rentcharges

5.2.1   The Rentcharges Act 1977

The Rentcharges Act 1977 enables the vendor of a freehold property to reserve:

(a)   a nominal rentcharge for the purpose of making positive covenants given by the purchaser enforceable against the purchaser's successors-in-title (s 2(4)(a)); and/or

(b)   a variable rentcharge which will be payable by the purchaser and his successors in title (s 2(4)(b)).

The variable rentcharge can only cover the costs of the performance by the rent owner of covenants for:

(1)   the provision of services;

(2)   the carrying out of maintenance or repairs;

(3)   the effecting of insurance; or

(4)   the making of any payment by him for the benefit of the land subjected to the rentcharge (or that and other land).

Item (4) enables the rent owner to include in the rentcharge sums such as rates and similar outgoings levied on common parts which are used by the paying parties (*Orchard Trading Estate Management Ltd v Johnson Security Ltd* [2002] EWCA Civ 406 (unreported), CA).

However, the rentcharge can only be reserved if the transfer or conveyance includes express covenants by the rent owner (usually the vendor, but possibly a management company) to provide the services or other matters for which the charge is to be made.

By s 2(5) of the Rentcharges Act 1977, an estate rentcharge will be valid only if 'it represents a payment for the performance by the rent owner of any such covenant . . . which is reasonable in relation to that covenant'. In *Orchard Trading* (above), the Court of Appeal held that this meant that the clauses of the deed creating the rentcharge had to be reasonable. The court considered that provisions under which the rent owner would recoup his actual expenditure were reasonable (and therefore valid) even if they did not expressly limit the charge to 'reasonable' amounts, whereas provisions which, for example, imposed an excessive fixed payment would not be reasonable (and therefore would be invalid). Having decided that the rentcharge clauses need not contain an express test of reasonableness, the court left open the question whether a reasonableness test would be implied into the actual operation of the clauses.

5.2.2 Application

The scheme under the Rentcharges Act 1977 is extremely useful where a developer is selling the freeholds of houses on a residential estate, or units on an industrial or warehousing estate, and requires to reserve a service charge to cover the cost of maintaining private roads, services or amenities. The estate rentcharge can be created in one of two ways:

(1) by granting the rentcharge to a management company before selling off the units or plots, and selling them subject to the rentcharge; or

(2) by reserving the rentcharge on the sale of each unit or plot.

In either case there should be a separate rentcharge created or reserved in respect of each unit or plot equal to its proper proportion of the total estate costs.

5.3 Right-to-buy houses

5.3.1 Introduction

The sale of freehold houses under the 'right-to-buy' legislation is governed by ss 118 *et seq* of the Housing Act 1985 and, in relation to 'registered social landlords' such as housing associations, by ss 16 *et seq* of the Housing Act 1996, the details of which are beyond the scope of this book. However, there are provisions which include matters relating to service charges and insurance contributions.

5.3.2 Provisions relating to service charges etc

Under s 139 of the Housing Act 1985 (which also applies to sales under the 1996 Act) the conveyance must comply with the provisions of Parts I, II and IV of the Sixth Schedule to that Act. These include a number of relevant matters, which can be summarised in outline as follows.

(1) The conveyance can contain such covenants and conditions which are reasonable in the circumstances (para 5 of the Sixth Schedule). Presumably this enables terms to be included for the payment of service charges or maintenance contributions.

(2) The freehold can be conveyed subject to an estate rentcharge (para 21(3) of the Sixth Schedule). The use of estate rentcharges is discussed at **5.2**. Under para 21(3)(a) of the Sixth Schedule the transferor must indemnify the transferee if the rentcharge also affects other land; this could be avoided if the transferor created individual rentcharges (eg in favour of a management company) issuing out of each separate house prior to the right-to-buy being exercised.

5.3.3 Limitation of service charges

Where the freehold of a house has been conveyed by a 'public sector authority' and the terms of the conveyance enable the vendor to recover from the purchaser a service charge, the service charge is limited by ss 47–51 of the Housing Act 1985, which contains provisions quite similar to some of those applied to tenants' service charges by the LTA 1985 as originally enacted.

The term 'public sector authority' is defined in s 45(2) of that Act as including a local authority, a National Park authority, a new town corporation, an urban development corporation, a housing action trust, the Development Board for Rural Wales, the Housing Corporation, and a registered social landlord.

In such cases, costs can only be taken into account in determining a service charge to the extent that they are reasonably incurred and, where they are incurred on the provision of services or the carrying out of works, only if the services or works are of a reasonable standard (Housing Act 1985, s 47). Further, where sums are payable on account before the relevant costs are incurred, no greater amount than is reasonable is payable and any necessary adjustment must be made by repayment, reduction of subsequent charges or otherwise once the actual costs have been incurred.

Apart from an arbitration agreement, any agreement by the payer will be void so far as it purports to provide for a determination in a particular manner or on particular evidence of any issue as to whether costs have been reasonably incurred, interim charges are of a reasonable amount, or the services or works are of a reasonable standard.

Under s 48, the payer is entitled to request in writing that the payee supplies him with a written summary of the costs which are relevant to the service charges, and the payee must comply with the request within one month or within six months from the end of the relevant accounting period, whichever is later, provided that the accounting period does not exceed 12 months. The summary must set out the costs in a way showing how they are or will be reflected in demands for service charges and they must be certified by a qualified accountant (defined in s 51) as being, in his opinion, a fair summary complying with these requirements and as being sufficiently supported by accounts, receipts and other documents which have been produced to him.

Where the payer has obtained a summary, he may within six months of obtaining it require the payee in writing to give him reasonable facilities for inspecting the accounts, receipts and other documents supporting the summary and taking copies or extracts from them, and the payee must make these facilities available for a period of two months beginning not later than one month after the request is made.

In cases where a grant has been or is to be paid under s 523 of the Housing Act 1985 by way of assistance for the provision of separate service pipes for water supply, or under Chapter 1 of Part 1 of the Housing Grant, Construction and Regeneration Act 1996, any costs summary must state this fact and credit for the relevant grant must be given against the relevant service costs when calculating the service charge.

5.4   Commonhold houses and flats

5.4.1   Introduction

Commonhold is a new type of land ownership which is being introduced, from a date to be fixed, by the Commonhold and Leasehold Reform Act 2002 (CLRA 2002). Houses, flats and other 'units' can be sold as commonhold units if they are part of a freehold estate which has been registered as commonhold land at the Land Registry.

The estate is to be administered by a commonhold association, which must be a company limited by guarantee. The estate is to be regulated by a commonhold community statement. All unit-holders are to be members of the association.

The community statement and the memorandum and articles of the commonhold association must conform to requirements set out in the CLRA 2002, ss 31 and 34 and Sch 3 (the details of which are outside the scope of this book), and must also conform to requirements to be laid down by regulations to be made by the Secretary of State under the CLRA 2002, s 32, but no regulations had been made by the publication date of this book.

5.4.2   Service charges

The CLRA 2002 does not set out much detail about service charges payable by unit-holders. Section 31(5) permits the commonhold community statement to impose duties on unit-holders which may include the duty to pay money to the commonhold association and to pay interest in the event of late payment.

Whilst the Secretary of State has the power to make regulations as to the contents of community statements, it is understood that the government is not currently proposing to require any provisions to be included which would impose reasonableness criteria or consultation procedures in respect of the costs incurred by commonhold associations on works and services. The government takes the view that it is sufficient that the association will be run by the unit-holders and that any differences of opinion should be settled by majority voting without any external interference.

It also remains to be seen if and how regulations will provide for disputes about service charges to be resolved. The CLRA 2002, s 37(2)(i) allows regulations to prescribe specific forms of arbitration, mediation or conciliation procedures before legal proceedings may be brought in relation to disputes over rights and duties arising out of provisions of the community statement or the memorandum and articles of the commonhold association. The CLRA 2002, s 42 allows regulations to prescribe that disputes may be referred to an approved ombudsman scheme. No such regulations had been made at the publication date of this book.

5.4.3 Reserve funds

The CLRA 2002, s 39 allows regulations to be made requiring community statements to contain provisions about reserve funds to be used only for specified activities. No such regulations had been made at the publication date of this book.

5.5 Residential estate management schemes

5.5.1 Introduction

It is common for estate management schemes to require the owners of enfranchised houses and blocks of flats to pay service charges towards the cost of maintaining unadopted roads, communal gardens, private sewers and other shared amenities.

The Commonhold and Leasehold Reform Act 2002 (CLRA 2002) has introduced reasonableness tests which are to apply, as from a date to be fixed, to payments (which are called 'estate charges') which arise under schemes made under the statutory provisions of the Leasehold Reform Act 1967, s 19 and the Leasehold Reform, Housing and Urban Development Act 1993, Part I, Chapter 4. These relate to the purchase of the freeholds of houses and blocks of flats. The scope of matters for which the 'payments' arise is not limited and these rules are not therefore confined to repairs, services etc.

5.5.2 Reasonableness test for variable estate charges

Section 159(2) of the CLRA 2002 provides that variable estate charges – those which are not fixed by the scheme as either a specific sum or by a formula for calculating one – are only payable up to a reasonable amount.

Any party can apply to the LVT under s 159(6) to determine whether a variable estate charge is payable and the LVT can be asked to decide:

(1) who has to pay;

(2) who is to receive the payment;

(3) how much is payable;

(4) when it has to be paid;

(5) how it is to be paid.

However, no application can be made to the LVT under s 159(6) in respect of anything which:

(a) the paying party has agreed or admitted (but merely paying the amount demanded is not itself an admission or agreement of liability);

(b) has been, or is to be, referred to arbitration under an agreement to arbitrate that the parties in dispute have entered into after the dispute has arisen (arbitration clauses in the scheme documents do not prevent the LVT deciding the dispute);

(c) has been decided by a court; or

(d) has been decided by an arbitral tribunal under an agreement to arbitrate entered into after the dispute arose.

The fact that a payment in respect of the charge has been paid does not prevent the LVT determining the matter (CLRA 2002, s 159(7)).

The jurisdiction given to the LVT is in addition to any jurisdiction of a court, so if there are court proceedings as to whether costs are chargeable under the terms of the scheme documents, the court could determine the matter and need not refer it to the LVT.

5.5.3 Varying schemes which prescribe estate charges

Where the amount of an estate charge is fixed by the scheme as either a specific sum or by a formula for calculating one, the amount prescribed at any time will be payable, but the paying party can apply to the LVT for an order varying the scheme on the grounds that the amount specified, or the formula, is unreasonable (CLRA 2002, s 159(3)). The variation may be as the applying party requests or such other variation as the LVT thinks fit. The provisions do not state whether the variation can be backdated to catch sums already payable.

This jurisdiction to vary schemes is exclusive to the LVT and cannot be exercised by the court.

6   ENVIRONMENTAL MATTERS

6.1   Introduction

The emergence of a distinct body of law relating to the environment, both from common law and statute, is increasingly affecting the practice of property management. The pace at which property managers are able to respond to environment regulation, or to adopt a wide range of voluntary initiatives, is directly affected by service charge clauses and the ability to recover the additional costs involved. Voluntary initiatives are unlikely to be adopted unless they will produce long-term, economic benefits, such as ongoing running cost savings deriving from installing energy-efficient equipment.

It is becoming more widespread to construct buildings in accordance with good environmental practice – at least, where this can be achieved without excessive cost. It therefore makes sense for service charge clauses to contemplate, and require, that parallel requirements be imposed throughout the life of the property.

In some cases, compliance with environmental legislation will involve professional time being spent on environmental compliance issues. It may be possible to include the fees for this in the service charge where the charge is expressed to cover the cost of compliance with legislation or the cost of proper management and related professional fees.

With regard to the voluntary practices which the property industry is being encouraged to adopt but which are not *per se* required by legislation, such as compliance with British Standard BS EN ISO 14001: 1996 (discussed at **6.4**) or carrying out periodic environmental assessment of properties (considered at **1.6.3**), whether landlords can be required to adopt them, and whether tenants can be required to pay for them, will depend on the relevant provisions of the lease.

6.2   Statutory duties relating to environmental matters

6.2.1   Costs of compliance

A well-drawn service charge clause will expressly include the costs incurred by the landlord in complying with statutory obligations in respect of such matters as common parts and communal services, and (in relation to multi-occupied buildings) the main structures. In the absence of an express provision, the costs concerned may, nevertheless, be recoverable under a sweeping-up clause (see **1.2.3**) or be the subject of a specific statutory provision entitling the landlord to apply to the court to order the tenants to contribute towards the costs.

If a landlord has to meet the costs of dealing with a statutory requirement, either directly or by reimbursing the costs expended by an authority (eg local authority's costs of abating a nuisance), and this liability arises because of a tenant's acts or omissions which constitute a breach by him of the covenants in his lease (as will often be the case, for example, under the usual covenant to comply with statutes), the landlord may be able to recoup his expenditure from that tenant in damages for breach of covenant. In addition, many leases contain separate provisions expressly requiring the tenant to meet certain costs of this type, particularly the cost of abating a nuisance from the demised premises.

6.2.2   Risk of prosecution and fines

Many new environmental offences have been created in the past few years which are often strict offences. There are a number of examples where landlords or property management companies, or the individuals involved in them, could be prosecuted under environmental legislation. Substantial fines could be imposed, even on companies or individuals with few assets. The ability of the management company or landlord to obtain an indemnity from the tenants could, therefore, be crucial to the survival of the company.

The landlord should be wary of failing to comply with a statutory requirement in the belief that he will be able to recoup a fine from the tenants. Even if the lease clearly provided for this, any attempt to recover from the tenants the amount of a fine imposed on the landlord would, in effect, be seeking indemnity against the consequences of a criminal offence. In some circumstances, the common law, for reasons of public policy, renders contractual provisions for that type of indemnity unenforceable. This topic is complex and falls outside the scope of this book, but, briefly, the courts have in some instances distinguished criminal acts involving individual negligence or wilful default from those of strict liability involving no fault on the part of the offender. In the former case, an indemnity against the criminal penalty will almost always be void; in the latter case, it may, in some situations, arguably be valid. Furthermore, however, if the landlord was in breach of a covenant in the lease requiring him to observe statutory requirements or good estate management in relation to common parts, communal services, main structures, etc, and the fine arose as a result of his failure to fulfil his covenant, he might be barred from seeking to recover the fine from his tenants under the principle that one cannot benefit from one's own breach of obligation (see *Alghussein Establishment v Eton College* [1991] 1 All ER 267, HL).

6.2.3   Waste disposal

Section 34 of the Environmental Protection Act 1990 places a duty of care on any person who produces, stores, transports, treats or disposes of controlled waste or who acts as a broker of controlled waste. 'Controlled waste' covers commercial, industrial and household waste.

An individual residential occupier is not under this duty as regards his own household waste. However, his landlord, if he manages the disposal of the waste, will be under the duty of care. The statutory duty, therefore, applies to any landlord (or management company) which has obligations related to waste, whether in respect of an industrial estate, office block, shopping centre or a block of flats.

Landlords must take reasonable measures to comply with the duty of care as it applies to them in relation to the particular obligations which they are given. The duty of care has the effect of imposing obligations which include:

(1) a duty to prevent the escape of waste from the control of the person subject to the duty of care, or from the control of any other person;

(2) keeping waste safe against corrosion, wind, accidental spillage or leakage, scavenging or thieves;

(3) storing waste in containers which are suitable, given the nature of the waste;

(4) segregating categories of waste which are incompatible (for example because they react with one another) and to label waste containers appropriately;

(5) ensuring that the waste is transferred only to an authorised person (as defined in s 34 of the Environmental Protection Act 1990 as amended by Sch 22 to the Environment Act 1995) or to a person for authorised transport purposes, and completing a transfer note on transfer of the waste.

Additional regulations apply to certain specific wastes, such as 'special' or hazardous wastes. Breach of the duty of care is a criminal offence which carries a maximum penalty of an unlimited fine if convicted.

Section 59 of the Environmental Protection Act 1990 gives waste regulation and collection authorities the power, in certain circumstances, to take remedial measures in respect of controlled waste which has been deposited illegally. The necessary cost of the measures may then be recovered from any person who deposited or knowingly caused or knowingly permitted the deposit of any of the waste.

Section 33(1)(c) of the Environmental Protection Act 1990 provides that it is an offence to treat, keep or dispose of controlled waste in a manner likely to cause pollution of the environment or harm to human health. The maximum penalty on conviction on indictment is imprisonment for a term not exceeding two years or a fine or both. Stiffer penalties apply to an offence committed in relation to 'special' waste.

6.2.4 Effluent and pollution

Section 85 of the Water Resources Act 1991 provides that it is an offence for any person to 'cause or knowingly permit any poisonous, noxious or polluting matter or any solid waste matter to enter any controlled waters'. Most watercourses come within the definition of 'controlled waters'. It is also an offence to cause or knowingly permit any trade or sewage effluent to be discharged into any controlled waters in contravention of a relevant consent. On conviction on indictment, the maximum penalty for an offence under s 85 is imprisonment for a term not exceeding two years or a fine or both.

Section 118 of the Water Industry Act 1991 makes it an offence for the 'occupier' of premises to discharge 'trade effluent' into public sewers without a consent. 'Trade effluent' is defined in s 141 of that Act and includes liquid (with or without particles of matter in suspension) produced in the course of any trade or industry carried on at trade premises. 'Occupier' is likely to include any person having a degree of control over the activities of persons on the premises. In the case of effluent emanating from the communal drainage system of an industrial estate, the occupier might be the landlord or management company.

Section 161 of the Water Resources Act 1991 gave the National Rivers Authority power to carry out certain anti-pollution works and operations where it appears to it that any poisonous, noxious or polluting matter is likely to enter any controlled waters or to have been present in controlled waters. By s 2 of the Environment Act 1995, this function has devolved upon the Environment Agency. The reasonable costs of carrying out the works can be recovered from any person who caused or knowingly permitted the matter in question to be present in the relevant place.

These provisions could lead to substantial liabilities being incurred by landlords and other property managers. It is, for example, relatively common-place for the landlord of an industrial estate or a management company to be responsible for operating and maintaining private sewage or effluent treatment works. Those landlords should ensure that they seek to obtain trade effluent discharge consents, and should install and maintain treatment plant which is able to cope with the nature and volume of effluents emanating from the tenants' units. Whilst many leases of industrial premises impose obligations on the tenants not to discharge corrosive or pollutant substances into the drains or sewers, this is not universal and many industrial tenants expect the communal drainage system to be able to cope with a wide range of effluent.

Additional provisions inserted into the Water Industry Act 1991 by the Environment Act 1995 impose a duty on water undertakers to promote the efficient use of water by their customers.

6.2.5 Statutory nuisances

Section 79 of the Environmental Protection Act 1990 as amended by the Environment Act 1995 defines those matters which constitute a 'statutory nuisance'. They are wide ranging and include:

(1) premises in such a state as to be prejudicial to health or a nuisance;

(2) emission of smoke, fumes, gases or noise from premises so as to be prejudicial to health or a nuisance;

(3) dust, steam, smell or other effluvia arising on industrial, trade or business premises and being prejudicial to health or a nuisance,

but do not include land contamination which is covered by separate provisions of the 1995 Act.

Local authorities can prohibit, restrict or require the abatement of, a statutory nuisance, by serving an abatement notice under s 80 of the Environmental Protection Act 1990. The notice can require the execution of works where they are necessary for the prohibition, restriction or abatement of the statutory nuisance. If the nuisance arises out of a defect of a structural nature, the notice is served on the owner of the premises. If the person responsible for the nuisance cannot be found or the nuisance has not yet occurred, the notice is served on the owner or occupier of the premises. Failure without reasonable excuse to comply with the notice is an offence, rendering the person liable to a fine, and it also enables the local authority to take steps to abate the nuisance and do whatever may be necessary in execution of the notice. Section 81(4) provides that the local authority may recover any expenses reasonably incurred in abating or preventing the recurrence of a statutory nuisance from the person by whose acts or defaults the nuisance arose. If that person is the owner of the premises, reasonable expenses may be recovered from any person who is the owner for the time being.

6.2.6 Air conditioning systems

Cooling towers which form part of an air conditioning system can harbour legionella, as, indeed, can water systems generally. A Health and Safety Commission Approved Code of Practice on the prevention or control of legionellosis (including legionnaire's disease) contains guidance on the application of relevant provisions of the Health and Safety at Work Act 1974 and of the Control of Substances Hazardous to Health Regulations 1988, SI 1998/1657, to the risk of legionellosis. It is not an offence, as such, to fail to comply with the provisons of the Code of Practice, but failure to comply can be taken into account by a court in criminal proceedings for breach of the Health and Safety at Work Act 1974 or of the Control of Substances Hazardous to Health Regulations.

The Notification of Cooling Towers and Evaporative Condensers Regulations 1992, SI 1992/2225, require any person who has, to any extent, control of non-domestic premises containing wet cooling towers and/or evaporative condensers to notify their local authority's Environmental Health Department that they have that equipment.

6.2.7 Contaminated land

Part II of the Environment Act 1995 inserted new ss 78A to 78YC into the Environmental Protection Act 1990 (the 'EPA 1990') in respect of contaminated land. This is defined as land having substances in, on or under it, and as a result significant harm is being caused (or there is a significant possibility of such significant harm being caused) to the health of living organisms, the ecological system, or property, or pollution of controlled waters is being caused or is likely to be caused.

The procedure under these provisions is that the local authority will inspect land in its area, identify contaminated land, and notify the Environment Agency and also the 'owner' of the land, its occupier, and any 'appropriate person'. After a consultation period of at least three months, a Remediation Notice is to be served by the local authority on the 'appropriate person' and an entry made on a register. If land is believed to fall into the category of a 'special site' (as designated by regulations), the steps towards securing remediation will be taken by the Environment Agency instead of the local authority. The statutory framework is supplemented by the Contaminated Land (England) Regulations 2000, SI 2000/227 and the DETR Circular 2/2000 on Contaminated Land.

The 'appropriate person' is the person who caused or knowingly permitted the substance to be present. 'Knowingly permitted' is not defined but existing case-law indicates that it means having knowledge of the presence of the substance, having power to procure its remediation (eg its removal, treatment or encapsulation) and the elapse of adequate time to do this. If there is no person liable under the foregoing, the Remediation Notice is served on the 'owner'. The 'owner' is the person entitled to receive the rack rent of the land (or would be if the land were let) and so will normally exclude a tenant who is paying a market rent. 'Owner' does not include a mortgagee unless he is in possession.

In the DETR Guidance, which has statutory force, the person who caused the substance to be present and the person who knowingly permitted the substance to be present are termed Class A persons and those who are neither but are simply owners or occupiers are termed Class B persons. Under the EPA 1990, s 78H and Part D of the Guidance, no person in Class B (*owner or occupier*) is to be liable for remediation if a person is found within Class A (*causing or knowingly permitting*). A person's potential liability as 'owner' or 'occupier' in Class B may arise if the enforcing authority cannot find anyone liable within Class A. In that case, as between the owner and the occupier within Class B, a tenant will not be an 'owner' if he pays a full rent; a tenant as 'occupier' will be excluded under para D89(a) of the DETR Circular if he is a mere licensee and will be excluded under para D89(b) if he pays a full rent and has no beneficial interest in the land beyond his tenancy; and thus it may leave the landlord (as owner) carrying the liability.

Where substances escape from one person's land onto another's, the Remediation Notice may be served on the person who caused or knowingly permitted the substance to be on the source land as well as being served on any person who caused or knowingly permitted it to be on the affected land.

An appeal against a Remediation Notice is possible to the magistrates' court or the Secretary of State. If properly required remediation work is not done, an offence is committed by the recipient of the notice. Furthermore, the local authority or Environment Agency can carry out the work and the costs incurred plus interest can be recovered from him.

6.3 Civil liability for pollution etc

6.3.1 Statutory liability for damage caused by waste

Where a person has illegally deposited or knowingly caused or permitted the deposit of waste, s 73(6) of the EPA 1990 imposes liability for any damage caused by that waste, on that person. There are exceptions to provide for situations where the damage was due wholly to the fault of the person who suffered it, or was suffered by a person who voluntarily accepted the risk of the damage being caused.

6.3.2 Common law liability for damage caused by escapes

Civil liability for damage caused to the environment can arise as a result of the application, to cases involving pollution or environmental degradation, of common law rules relating to trespass, nuisance, or the rule in *Rylands v Fletcher* (1868) LR3 HL 330 (which makes a person liable for the escape from his land of any substance derived from a non-natural use of that land). Further detail on these matters is outside the scope of this book, but the damages awards in actions brought on the basis of these common law rules can be quite substantial.

A leading decision on this subject is *Cambridge Water Company v Eastern Counties Leather plc* [1994] 1 All ER 53, in which the leather tannery was found to have polluted an underground aquifer as a result of accidental spillages occurring, possibly, before 1976, the result of which was that the water extracted from the water company's borehole 2 km away failed to meet the stricter purity standards imposed by an EC Directive in August 1982. The House of Lords, overruling the Court of Appeal, held that the tannery was not liable in law to the water company since, at the time of the spillages, the possibility of causing harmful pollution was not reasonably foreseeable. The result would have been different if the harm had been foreseeable.

Landlords should consider the possibility of insuring against such liabilities as well as making adequate provision in their leases for the recovery of any such damages from any tenant who may be responsible for the problem.

6.4 Voluntary initiatives

6.4.1 ISO 14001:1996 Eco-management and Audit Scheme

The landlord of a major development may wish to demonstrate his commitment to maintaining an environmentally sound management system by seeking accreditation under British Standard BS EN ISO 14001:1996 on Environmental Management Systems. The standard sets out the elements of an environmental management system. It includes requirements relating to the adoption of an

environmental policy, emergency measures, training, testing, record-keeping
and personnel and environmental management audits and reviews. The
Standard requires that a record be kept of legislative, regulatory and policy
requirements relating to the organisation's activities.

6.4.2   Other voluntary practices

A number of practice guidelines have been promulgated or are at discussion
stage and, undoubtedly, the property industry will, over the next few years, be
encouraged to comply with new recommended practices and standards.

7 COMMERCIAL CODES OF PRACTICE

7.1 Service Charges in Commercial Properties – A Guide to Good Practice

This concise guide, now in its second edition (August 2000) is published by seven bodies including the Royal Institution of Chartered Surveyors, the Incorporated Society of Valuers and Auctioneers, the British Property Federation and the Property Managers Association.

It encourages the property owner to monitor and review the quality and cost of services, to adopt sound management procedures, and to act in an efficient and economic manner. It provides straightforward guidelines covering a variety of matters including the bearing of initial capital costs, providing value for money, apportioning costs between tenants, consulting with tenants, preparing estimates, and producing accounts.

The guide appears in **Appendix 4**.

7.2 Code of Practice for Commercial Property Leases in England and Wales

This was first published in 1995, but a new Code was issued in April 2002. Prepared by a joint working group (chaired by one of the authors of this book) which comprised delegates from bodies representing property occupiers, owners, investors and funders as well as property professionals (both surveyors and lawyers), the new Code is a response to the government's pressure on landlords to provide tenants with more flexible lease terms.

The new Code contains 23 recommendations covering the negotiation of a new lease and conduct during the term of a lease. The following recommendations apply to service charges and related matters:

- **Negotiating a business tenancy**
  Recommendation 2: Parties intending to enter into leases should seek early advice from property professionals or lawyers.
  Recommendation 3: Landlords should provide estimates of any service charges and other outgoings in addition to the rent . . .
  Recommendation 7: The tenant's repairing obligations, and any repair costs included in service charges, should be appropriate to the length of the term and the condition and age of the property at the start of the lease. Where appropriate the landlord should consider appropriately priced alternatives to full repairing terms.

Recommendation 8: Where the landlord is responsible for the property insurance, the policy terms should be competitive. The tenant of an entire building should, in appropriate cases, be given the opportunity to influence the choice of insurer. If the premises are so damaged by an uninsured risk as to prevent occupation, the tenant should be allowed to terminate the lease unless the landlord agrees to rebuild at his own cost.

- **Conduct during a lease**

  Recommendation 11: Landlords and tenants should deal with each other constructively, courteously, openly and honestly throughout the term of the lease and carry out their respective obligations fully and on time. If either party faces a difficulty in carrying out any obligations under this lease, the other should be told without undue delay so that the possibility of agreement on how to deal with the problem may be explored. When either party proposes to take action which is likely to have significant consequences for the other, the party proposing the action, when it becomes appropriate to do so, should notify the other without undue delay.

  Recommendation 20: Landlords should observe the Guide to Good Practice on Service Charges in Commercial Properties. Tenants should familiarise themselves with that Guide and should take professional advice if they think they are being asked to pay excessive service charges.

  Recommendation 21: When disputes arise, the parties should make prompt and reasonable efforts to settle them by agreement. Where disputes cannot be settled by agreement, both sides should always consider speed and economy when selecting a method of dispute resolution. Mediation may be appropriate before embarking on more formal procedures.

APPENDICES

Appendix 1 SPECIMEN SERVICE CHARGE CLAUSES

A Introduction

A.1 Drafting in context

These specimen clauses are intended to illustrate points made in the text of this book, and the footnotes provide the appropriate text references.

While certain provisions of these clauses may be considered to attain a reasonable balance between the interests of the landlord and the tenant, others are weighted in favour of one party or the other. In some instances, alternative provisions have been included.

The clauses should not be adopted as precedents without careful consideration, editing and adaptation to the particular facts of the situation and having regard to the provisions and terminology of the lease as a whole. The specimen clauses assume, for example, that insurance premiums are recouped by additional rent and not through the service charge. Furthermore, the provisions are detailed and reasonably comprehensive (although not exhaustive) and, whilst they might need little adaptation for use in, for example, a standard lease of a shop unit in a shopping mall, they would need heavy editing in order to make them suitable for more modest premises. Indeed, many prospective tenants would find the lists of potentially chargeable items quite daunting.

A.2 Method of reservation of service charge

The draftsman must choose between reserving the service charge as additional rent and simply having a covenant by the tenant to pay the service charge. The resulting differences in the remedies available to the landlord in the event of non-payment were discussed at **1.20** and these should be taken into account when making the choice.

There may also be a stamp duty consideration (see **3.5.2**).

A.3 Scope of services

Paragraphs 9 to 11 of the specimen clauses deal with the scope of the services the costs of which can be included in the service charge. If used as a precedent, these provisions should be adapted to meet the facts and circumstances.

A.4 Reserve or sinking funds

For the special additional covenants and declarations required in connection with reserve or sinking funds, see **Chapter 4**.

A.5 Management company

The specimen clauses have assumed that the landlord will provide the services, but could be adapted if a management company is to do so. In that event, elsewhere in the lease there should be provision that when the lease is assigned the assignee will enter into a deed of direct covenant with the management company, in which the parties mutually covenant with each other to comply with the terms of the lease as to the provision of services and the payment of the service charge. This is because there is no privity of estate between the tenant and a management company which is not the landlord and the effect of s 12 of the Landlord and Tenant (Covenants) Act 1995 is not completely clear in relation to the need for mutual covenants in this context.

A.6 Penalties

No attempt has been made to incorporate an indemnity against fines or other penalties which may be imposed on the landlord in respect of the building or anything escaping from it, in view of the difficulties summarised at **6.2.2**.

A.7 Style of the specimen clauses

The specimen clauses are drafted on the assumption that it will be most user-friendly to set out the service charge clauses in a separate schedule in the lease. A modern style of phraseology has been adopted, but this could be altered to blend in with a more traditionally drafted lease.

B The specimen clauses

B.1 Reservation or covenant for payment

[If the service charge is to be reserved as rent][1]
... and paying as additional rent an Interim Charge and a Service Charge in accordance with the provisions of Schedule [   ] to this Lease.

[If the service charge is to be a covenanted payment][1]
To pay to the Landlord an Interim Charge and a Service Charge in accordance with the provisions of Schedule [   ] to this Lease.

B.2   The service charge schedule

Schedule [   ]
(Service charges)
Part I – Computation, certification and payment

1   Purpose of Service Charge[2]

The Tenant shall pay to the Landlord a Service Charge (and an Interim Charge on account) in accordance with the following provisions, the purpose of which is to enable the Landlord to recover from the Tenant the Tenant's due proportion of all expenditure overheads and liabilities which the Landlord may incur[3] in and in connection with carrying out works on the Building and providing present and future services to its occupiers (but not including expenditure on those parts of the demised premises which the Tenant is liable to repair and maintain under the terms of this Lease and the corresponding parts of the other lettable premises in the Building).

2   Definitions

In this Schedule the following definitions apply:

'Accounting Date':   the   day of   in each year (or such other date as the Landlord may from time to time substitute for that date);

'Accounting Period':   the period commencing on the day immediately after each Accounting Date and ending on the following Accounting Date;

'Certificate':   a certificate issued under the provisions of paragraph 5 of this Schedule;

'Commencement Date':   [the date of this lease] *or* [the   day of 20   ];

'Estimate':   an estimate prepared under the provisions of paragraph 3.1 of this Schedule;

'Initial Interim Rate':   £   per year;

'Interim Charge':   the Tenant's Proportion of the amount of the Estimate for each Accounting Period;

'Payment Days':   the [usual quarter days] in each year;

'Reserve Fund':   a fund that the Landlord may[4] decide to establish in
                               order to meet future expenditure which he expects to
                               incur in maintaining replacing rebuilding or renewing
                               those items which he is obliged or entitled to maintain
                               replace rebuild or renew under the terms of this
                               Lease;

'Service Charge':   the Tenant's Proportion of the amount of Service
                               Costs for each Accounting Period;

'Service Costs':   the amounts specified in Part II of this Schedule;

'Supplemental Interim
Charge':   the payment mentioned in paragraph 4.4 below;

'Tenant's Proportion':   .....% (or such other proportion[5] as may from time to
                               time be substituted for it under the provisions of
                               paragraph 7 of this Schedule).

3 Preparation of the Estimate

3.1   On or before (or, if that shall be impractical, then as soon as practicable
      after) each Accounting Date the Landlord shall prepare an Estimate in
      writing of the Service Costs which he expects to incur or charge during or
      in respect of the Accounting Period commencing immediately after that
      Accounting Date.

3.2   The Estimate shall contain a summary of those estimated Service Costs.

3.3   Within 14 days after preparation, a copy of each Estimate shall be served
      by the Landlord on the Tenant together with a statement showing the
      Interim Charge payable by the Tenant on account of those estimated
      Service Costs.[6]

4 Payment of Interim Charge[7]

4.1   The Interim Charge for each Accounting Period (together with Value
      Added Tax,[8] if payable) shall be paid by the Tenant by [four] equal
      instalments on the Payment Days during that Accounting Period.

4.2   The initial Interim Charge shall be calculated at the Initial Interim Rate
      and the first payment shall be made on the date of this Lease and shall be
      an apportioned part for the period from the Commencement Date until
      the next Payment Day.

4.3   If the Interim Charge for any Accounting Period is not ascertained and
      notified to the Tenant by the first Payment Day in that Period:

      (a)   until the Payment Day following the ascertainment and notification
            to him of the new Interim Charge, the Tenant shall pay on account a
            provisional interim charge at the rate previously payable;

(b) commencing on that Payment Day, the Tenant shall pay the new Interim Charge; and

(c) on that Payment Day, the Tenant shall also pay the amount by which the new Interim Charge for the period since the commencement of that Accounting Period exceeds the amount paid on account (but if the amount paid on account exceeds the new Interim Charge for that period, the Landlord shall give credit for the overpayment).

4.4 If at any time during an Accounting Period it appears to the Landlord that (whether due to the need arising to incur a cost which was not included in the Estimate, or for any other reason whatsoever) the Interim Charges payable by the Tenant shall be insufficient to meet the Service Charge for that Accounting Period, the Landlord shall be entitled to serve on the Tenant a demand for a Supplemental Interim Charge[9] of such amount as the Landlord may [reasonably] specify, accompanied by a written explanation of the reason for it, and the Tenant shall pay the amount demanded within [fourteen days] of service of the demand.

5 Preparation and Service of the Certificate[10]

5.1 The Landlord or its managing agents shall keep proper books and records of the Service Costs and as soon as practicable[11] after each Accounting Date the Landlord or its managing agents shall prepare a certificate of the Service Costs of the Accounting Period ending on that Accounting Date.

5.2 The Certificate shall contain a summary of the Service Costs to which it relates.

5.3 If a Reserve Fund exists or is to be established, the Certificate shall also state any amount in the Reserve Fund at the commencement of the Accounting Period, any expenditure from the Reserve Fund during or in respect of that Accounting Period, and any sums included in the Service Costs to be added to the Reserve Fund.

5.4 [The Certificate shall be signed by the Landlord or its managing agents and shall include a certificate by him or them that it sets out a true and accurate account of the Service Costs to which it relates.][12]
or, in the case of residential leases
[The Certificate shall be signed by an accountant or firm of accountants (who shall be qualified as specified in section 28 of the Landlord and Tenant Act 1985) and shall include a certificate by him or them that the summary of Service Costs set out in the Certificate is a fair summary and that the Service Costs are sufficiently supported by accounts, receipts and other documents which have been produced to him or them.][13]

5.5 Within 14 days of signing, a copy of each Certificate shall be served upon the Tenant together with a statement showing:

(a)   the Service Charge payable by the Tenant in respect of the Accounting Period to which the Certificate relates;

(b)   the Interim Charge (and Supplemental Interim Charge, if any) paid by the Tenant on account of that Service Charge; and

(c)   the amount (if any) by which the Service Charge exceeds or falls short of the aggregate of the payments received by way of Interim Charge and Supplemental Interim Charge.

5.6   Within 14 days from the service of each statement under paragraph 5.5 above, the Tenant shall pay to the Landlord (together with value added tax, if payable) the amount (if any) by which the stated Service Charge exceeds the Interim Charges stated to have been received on account.

5.7   During the two months commencing on the date of service of each Certificate, the Tenant or its authorised representative shall be entitled to inspect the books, records, invoices and accounts relating to the Service Costs included in such Certificate during normal office hours at the offices of the Landlord or its managing agents on the Tenant giving to the Landlord or its managing agents not less than two working days' written request for such inspection.[14]

5.8   So far as permitted by law,[15] each Certificate shall be conclusive of the matters which it purports to certify, and no invalidity of a part of any Certificate shall affect the validity of any other part of the Certificate.

6   Commencement and Expiration of Term

6.1   The Service Charge for the Accounting Period during which this Lease is granted shall be apportioned as from the Commencement Date.

6.2   The provisions of this Schedule shall remain in force notwithstanding the expiration or earlier determination of the term created by this Lease and the Service Charge for the Accounting Period during which the date of such expiration or determination falls shall be apportioned down to that date.

6.3   The apportionments mentioned in paragraphs 6.1 and 6.2 above shall be computed as if the total Service Costs for the relevant Accounting Periods were incurred by equal daily amounts throughout each such Accounting Period.

7   Variation of Proportion[16]

7.1   The Landlord shall be entitled by giving written notice to the Tenant to vary the Tenant's Proportion from time to time as a consequence of any alteration or addition to the Building or any alteration in the arrangements for provision of services in or to the Building or any other relevant circumstances.

7.2 Any variation in the Tenant's Proportion shall take effect from such date as the Landlord may specify in such written notice having regard to the date of occurrence of the reason for such variation.

8 Disputes[17]

8.1 [Any dispute arising out of this Schedule shall be referred to the determination of an independent surveyor [acting as an arbitrator in accordance with the provisions of the Arbitration Act 1996] *or* [acting as an expert whose decision shall be final and binding on the parties and who shall have power to determine the proportions in which the costs of his determination shall be borne between the parties.][18]

8.2 The said surveyor shall be appointed [by the Landlord but he shall not be a member or employee of the Landlord or of its managing agents] *or* [on the application of either party by or on behalf of the President for the time being of the Royal Institution of Chartered Surveyors].

8.3 In the event of there being disputes between the Landlord and two or more tenants in the Building with respect to the same Certificate, the Landlord shall be entitled to require all such disputes to be consolidated before the same independent surveyor.

8.4 The Tenant shall not be entitled to dispute or question the amount of any item in the Service Costs on the sole ground that it exceeds the amount shown in the relevant Estimate nor [(save in the event of manifest extravagance)] on the ground that it could have been provided or performed at lower cost.[19]

8.5 No dispute or question in relation to the contents of any Certificate shall be valid unless made by the Tenant in written notice specifying the item or items disputed or questioned and served on the Landlord within [two months] of the service of the Certificate (time being of the essence).

8.6 No dispute or question affecting any Certificate shall entitle the Tenant to withhold payment of the sums specified in paragraph 5.6 or any other sums payable under the terms of his lease but if it shall be ascertained (by virtue of a determination under paragraphs 8.1 to 8.3 or otherwise) that the Tenant has made any overpayment in respect of the Service Costs the Landlord shall repay the amount of the overpayment to the Tenant within 14 days.

Part II – Service costs

9 Basic Service Costs

9.1 The Service Costs of any Accounting Period are all the expenditure liabilities and overheads (including Value Added Tax to the extent to which it is not recoverable by the Landlord as input tax) paid or incurred by or on behalf of the Landlord during or in respect of that Accounting Period of and incidental to:

(a) [the performance of the Landlord's obligations under clause ... of this Lease] [and] [the carrying out of the works and the provision of the services specified in paragraph 11.1 below in or on the Building] [in such manner as to such standard as the Landlord or its managing agents shall determine in their absolute discretion];[20]

(b) the carrying out of such other works in or on the Building and the provision of such other services to the occupiers of the Building as the Landlord or its managing agents may from time to time [reasonably] *or* [in their absolute discretion] consider appropriate or necessary or beneficial to those occupiers as a whole;[21]

(c) the cost of employing managing agents for the general management and administration of the Building;[22]

(d) the cost of employing managing or other agents, architects, surveyors or other professional persons to arrange and supervise the execution of any works or the provision of any services in or on the Building;[23]

(e) the cost of keeping the books and records of the expenditure comprised in the Service Costs and of preparing and (if applicable) auditing and certifying the Service Costs;
     add in the case of a tenants' management company or tenants' nominee landlord company:
     [and the cost of maintaining the books and records of the Landlord pursuant to the Companies Acts and the cost of preparing and filing returns and accounts under those Acts];

(f) the payment of all existing and future rates, assessments, impositions and outgoings charged or imposed or payable on or in respect of [staff accommodation and] the Building as a whole or the common parts;

(g) the payment of all liabilities in respect of the cost of repairing, maintaining, cleansing and renewing any party or other walls, fences and structures and service media, roadways, paths, yards and other things common to the Building and other adjacent or neighbouring premises;

(h) the cost of employing or engaging solicitors, counsel and other professional persons in connection with the management of the Building and the administration and collection of the Service Charge payable by the Tenant and by the other tenants in the Building;[24]

(i) the cost of enforcing or attempting to enforce against the Tenant the covenants and restrictions imposed on the Tenant by this lease and the cost of enforcing or attempting to enforce against other tenants in the Building similar covenants and restrictions imposed on them, but only so far as such costs shall not be recovered from the person against whom such enforcement is made or attempted or from the person requesting such enforcement;

(j) the cost of opposing or making representations in respect of the provisions or requirements of any statutory notice served on the Landlord by a competent authority in respect of the Building or the common parts or service media;

(k) the cost of opening and maintaining one or more bank accounts and the cost (including interest) of borrowing funds (by loan or on over-draft) in order to provide the amount by which the monies in hand from the Interim Charges and Service Charges actually received from the Tenant and from the other tenants in the Building are insufficient to cover the expenditure liabilities and overheads mentioned above (and for this purpose the monies in hand shall be assumed to include Interim Charges and Service Charges contrib-uted by the Landlord, corresponding to those payable by the Tenant under this Lease, in respect of any lettable parts of the Building which are not for the time being let on leases under which such Interim Charges and Service Charges are payable by the tenants).[25]

9.2 If the Landlord shall require its employed staff to perform the functions mentioned in paragraphs 9.1(c) and/or (d) instead of managing agents, agents, architects, surveyors or other professional persons (as the case may be), then the Service Costs shall include a reasonable charge by the Landlord for providing those functions.[26]

9.3 If the Landlord shall itself provide any labour or materials for the provision of any services or for the carrying out of any works falling within paragraph 9.1, then the Service Costs shall include a proper payment for such labour or materials [including [a reasonable element of] *or* [.... %] profit for the Landlord].

9.4 If the Landlord in its discretion shall provide accommodation (in the Building or elsewhere) for any staff employed in or in connection with the Building, the Service Costs shall include a reasonable rent to the Landlord for that accommodation and all rates, water charges and other assess-ments and outgoings of that accommodation.[27]

9.5 If the Landlord decides to establish a reserve fund, the Service Costs shall also include such sums as the Landlord may from time to time require to put into the reserve fund.

9.6 If the Landlord in its discretion shall so decide, the Service Costs for any Accounting Period ('the current Accounting Period') shall include a proper proportion (apportioned on a daily basis) of:

(a) costs expended in the preceding Accounting Period on works or services supplied in respect of a period falling partly in that Accounting Period and partly in the current Accounting Period;

(b) costs expended in the current Accounting Period on works or services supplied in respect of a period falling partly in the current Accounting Period and partly in the next Accounting Period.[28]

10 Supplemental

10.1 The costs and expenses of any works or services shall (but not by way of limitation) include:

(a) the wages of any staff employed by the Landlord to arrange them, supervise them, or carry them out, including all payments made by the Landlord in respect of any tax on employment or services which has been or may be imposed in respect of any such staff and the Landlord's contributions to the National Insurance of such staff and the cost of provision of pensions for such staff (and where any staff are employed for those functions and also for other functions not falling within the Service Costs, the foregoing costs and expenses shall be fairly apportioned for this purpose);

(b) the cost (or a fair apportionment, if appropriate) of providing any uniforms, working clothes, tools, appliances, equipment and materials used in connection with those works and services;

(c) the cost of electricity, gas, oil or other fuel used for the works or services;

(d) the cost of leasing or hiring machinery plant and equipment;

(e) the cost of inspections, examinations, surveys and insurance valuations.

10.2 For the avoidance of doubt, nothing in this paragraph shall require the Landlord to employ staff to arrange, supervise or carry out any work or service if the Landlord at his discretion deems it desirable to engage agents, architects, surveyors or other professional consultants and/or independent contractors for that purpose.

11 Works and Services

11.1 The works and services mentioned in paragraph 9.1(a) above are:

(a) Structure etc

maintenance, repair, cleaning, redecoration, replacement, renewal and rebuilding (whenever necessary or desirable) of, and compliance with codes of practice and the requirements of statutes and regulations affecting, main structures, roofs, foundations, external walls, party walls and structures, boundary walls, fences and railings, windows, window frames, doors, door frames, balconies and terraces and their surrounds;

(b)   External areas

maintenance, repair, lighting, cleaning, rebuilding and resurfacing (whenever necessary or desirable) of, and compliance with the requirements of codes of practice and statutes and regulations affecting, yards, car parking areas, drives, paths, lightwells and open areas;

(c)   Service media

maintenance, repair, redecoration, replacement and renewal (whenever necessary or desirable) of, and compliance with codes of practice and the requirements of statutes and regulations affecting, drains, effluent treatment plant, sewers, pipes, gutters, wires, tanks, traps, meters, vents, ducts, chutes, manholes, refuse enclosures and sanitary equipment;

(d)   Common parts

maintenance, repair, redecoration, furnishing, replacement and renewal (whenever necessary or desirable) and lighting, heating and cleaning of, and compliance with codes of practice and the requirements of statutes and regulations affecting, entrances, halls, landings, staircases, smoke lobbies, fire escapes, lifts, escalators, toilets, tea-making rooms and other parts of the Building available for use by the Tenant in common with other occupiers of the Building, and the provision and laundering of towels for such toilets and tea-making rooms;

(e)   Plant and equipment

operation, maintenance, repair, redecoration, replacement and renewal (whenever necessary or desirable) of, and compliance with codes of practice and the requirements of statutes and regulations affecting, lighting, lift machinery, escalator machinery, boilers, hot water systems, space heating systems, air conditioning and air handling and ventilation systems, fire alarm systems, sprinkler systems, security systems, entry-phone systems, internal telephone systems, public address systems, piped music systems, television and radio relay systems, and traffic control systems;

(f)   Gardens etc

landscaping, gardening and the provision and cultivation of plants, shrubs and flowers in, and compliance with codes of practice and the requirements of statutes and regulations affecting, gardens, landscaped areas, window boxes, entrance halls and other common parts;

(g)   Hot water and space heating

provision of hot water to the basins in the demised premises and (when, in the Landlord's opinion, outside temperatures so require) space heating from the radiators in the demised premises;

(h) Porterage etc

provision of porterage, caretaking and reception services at such times and in such manner as the Landlord shall consider desirable;

(i) Staff accommodation

maintenance, repair, redecoration, furnishing, lighting, heating and cleaning of, and compliance with codes of practice and the requirements of statutes and regulations affecting, any flats in the Building [or elsewhere] for the accommodation of porters, caretakers or other staff employed in connection with the Building.

11.2 Provided that (for the avoidance of doubt) nothing contained in paragraph 11.1 shall:

(i) impose upon the Landlord any obligation to carry out any works or provide any services beyond the matters set out in clause ... of this Lease; or

(ii) extend the Service Costs to include the cost of any works, acts, matters or things to or in respect of any parts of the demised premises for which the Tenant is liable under the terms of this Lease or the corresponding parts of the other lettable parts of the Building.

NOTES

1 See paragraph **A.2** of the Introduction to this Appendix.
2 See **1.2.2**.
3 See **1.3.5**.
4 See **Chapter 4**.
5 See **1.13**.
6 See **1.15.3**.
7 See **2.9** (residential lettings only).
8 See **Chapter 3**.
9 See **1.15.3**.
10 See **1.16** (and, for residential lettings, **2.10**).
11 See **1.16.4** (and, for residential lettings, **2.8.3**).
12 See **1.16.3**.
13 See **2.10.2** and **2.10.3** (residential lettings only).
14 See **1.16.6** (and, for residential lettings, **2.10.5**).
15 See **1.16.5**.
16 See **1.13.5**.
17 See **1.17**.
18 See **2.12.2** (not appropriate for residential lettings).
19 See **1.10.1**.
20 See **1.4.3** and **1.10.1** to **1.10.3** (and, for residential lettings, **2.3**).
21 See **1.2.3** and **1.3.3**.
22 See **1.6.1**.
23 See **1.6.2**.
24 See **1.6.4** (and, for residential lettings, **2.5.1**).
25 See **1.11.2**.
26 See **1.7.1** (and, for residential lettings, **2.5.1**).
27 See **1.8**.
28 See **1.16.2**.

Appendix 2   SPECIMEN NOTICES, DEMANDS, ACCOUNTS AND CERTIFICATES

1 Notice under section 48 of the Landlord and Tenant Act 1987

To: (*Name of tenant*)
        (*address of tenant*)

being the tenant of premises known as (*address of premises*).

We (*name and address of landlord's solicitors or agents*), on behalf of your landlord (*name of landlord*), give you notice pursuant to section 48(1) of the Landlord and Tenant Act 1987 that the address of your landlord for service of notices (including notices of proceedings) is:

(*landlord's address for service*)

Signed: ....

Date: .... 200....

2   Specimen summary of service costs

[*Issued under paras 5.1 to 5.4 of the specimen service charge clause in the form set out in Appendix 1.*]

RE: ABC HOUSE, ALPHABET STREET, ANYTOWN

CERTIFICATE OF SERVICE COSTS FOR THE ACCOUNTING YEAR ENDED 30 JUNE 2001

	£	p
Cleaning of common parts	1 005.70	
Gardening	500.00	
Boiler fuel and maintenance	4 705.60	
Lift maintenance	520.34	
Security	299.17	
Porters and other staff	4 074.81	
Telephone and entryphone	198.33	
Window cleaning	360.00	
Internal maintenance	264.66	
Fire equipment hire	111.74	
Exernal redecoration	19 828.42	
External repairs	4 222.52	
Management fees	4 120.82	
	40 212.11	
Less taken from reserve	22 000.00	
	18 212.11	
Add provision for reserve fund	4 500.00	
TOTAL EXPENDITURE	22 712.11	
Reserve fund at 1 July 2000	27 715.25	
Interest accrued	1 247.19	
Sums taken as above	22 000.00	
	6 962.44	
Reserve fund provision	4 500.00	
Reserve fund at 30 June 2001	11 462.44	

All the above sums are [inclusive] [exclusive] of value added tax.

(*Landlord's, agent's or accountant's certificate of correctness to be added – see Specimens 3 and 4 below.*)

3 Specimen certificate of service charge under terms of lease

[Issued under para 5.4 of the specimen service charge in the form set out in Appendix 1.]

[This form represents the certificate of the landlord or managing agent under the first of the alternative provisions set out in para 5.4 of the specimen clauses contained in Appendix 1. It will be observed that the wording below closely follows that contained in the part of the service charge clause or schedule which provides for the issue of the certificate. This is the proper basis for drafting any certificate to be issued under the express terms of a lease: the wording of the relevant clause should be followed as closely as possible.]

We hereby certify that the above is a true and accurate account of the service costs referred to in [clause   ] [Schedule   ] of the leases of the above-mentioned property in respect of the accounting period ended [   ].

Signed: ....

Date: .... 200 ....

4 Specimen certificate of service charge under the Landlord and Tenant Act 1985

[*To conform with s 21 of the Landlord and Tenant Act 1985 until the amendments made by the Commonhold and Leasehold Reform Act 2002 come into effect. After that time, this certificate would have to be redrafted so as to comply with the new s 21(3) and regulations made under the new s 21(4)(b) and (c).*]

I hereby certify that in my opinion the above is a fair summary complying with Section 21(5) of the Landlord and Tenant Act 1985 of the costs incurred by or on behalf of ..... (*landlord*) .... in connection with the matters for which the service charge is payable, and is sufficiently supported by accounts, receipts and other documents which have been produced to me.

Signed: .... Accountant

Date: .... 200 ....

5   Specimen statement of service charge

[*Issued under para 5.5 of the specimen service charge in the form set out in Appendix 1.*]

ABC LANDLORDS LIMITED   (*landlord's address*)

RE: ABC HOUSE, ALPHABET STREET, ANYTOWN

To:

STATEMENT OF SERVICE CHARGES DUE FROM YOU AS
TENANT OF OFFICE SUITE X FOR THE ACCOUNTING YEAR
ENDED 30 JUNE 2000

	£ p
Total Expenditure as per attached Accounts	22 712.11
Total service charge payable (14.3% of £22,712.11)	3 247.83

Less interim charges received:

29.9.1999	£750
25.12.1999	£750
25.3.2000	£750
24.6.2000	£750

	−3 000.00
BALANCE DUE	247.83

All sums are [inclusive] [exclusive] of value added tax.

6   Specimen prescribed notice under the Landlord and Tenant (Covenants) Act 1995

Landlord and Tenant (Covenants) Act 1995 (Notices) Regulations 1995 Form 1

LANDLORD AND TENANT (COVENANTS) ACT 1995
Section 17

Notice to Former Tenant or Guarantor of Intention to Recover Fixed Charge

To

IMPORTANT – The person giving this notice is protecting the right to recover the amount(s) specified from you now or at some time in the future. There may be action which you can take to protect your position. Read the notice and all the notes overleaf carefully. If you are in any doubt about the action you should take, seek advice immediately, for instance from a solicitor or citizens advice bureau.

---

1.   This notice is given under section 17 of the Landlord and Tenant (Covenants) Act 1995.

2.   It relates to

let under a lease dated   and made between

[of which you were formerly a tenant].

3.   We as landlord hereby give you notice that the fixed charges of which details are set out in the attached Schedule are now due and unpaid, and that we intend to recover from you the amounts specified in the Schedule [and interest from the date and calculated on the basis specified in the Schedule].

4.   There is a possibility that your liability in respect of the fixed charges detailed in the Schedule will subsequently be determined to be for a greater amount.

5.   All correspondence about this notice should be sent to the landlord's agent at the address given below.

Dated the   day of   200

Signature of landlord's agent   ....

Name and address of landlord:

[Name and address of landlord's agent :

NOTES

1.   The person giving you this notice alleges that you are still liable for the performance of the tenant's obligations under the tenancy to which this notice relates, either as a previous tenant bound by privity of contract or an authorised guarantee agreement, or because you are the guarantor of a previous tenant. By giving you this notice, the landlord (or other person entitled to enforce payment, such as a management company) is protecting his right to require you to pay the amount specified in the notice. There may be other sums not covered by the notice which the landlord can also recover because they are not fixed charges (for example, in respect of repairs or costs if legal proceedings have to be brought). If you pay the amount specified in this notice in full, you will have the right to call on the landlord to grant you an "overriding lease", which puts you in the position of landlord to the present tenant. There are both advantages and drawbacks to doing this, and you should take advice before coming to a decision.

Validity of notice

2.   The landlord is required to give this notice within six months of the date on which the charge or charges in question became due (or, if it became due before 1 January 1996, within six months of that date). If the notice has been given late, it is not valid and the amount in the notice cannot be recovered from you. The date of the giving of the notice may not be the date written on the notice or the date on which you actually saw it. It may, for instance, be the date on which the notice was delivered through the post to your last address known to the landlord. If you are in any doubt, you should seek advice immediately.

Interest

3.   If interest is payable on the amount due, the landlord does not have to state the precise amount of interest, but he must state the basis on which interest is calculated to enable you to work out the likely amount, or he will not be able to claim interest at all. This does not include interest which may be payable under rules of court if legal proceedings are brought.

Change in amount due

4.   Apart from interest, the landlord is not entitled to recover an amount which is more than he has specified in the notice with one exception. This is where the amount cannot be finally determined within six months after it is due (for example, if there is a dispute concerning an outstanding rent review or if the charge is a service charge collected on account and adjusted following final determination). In such a case, if the amount due is eventually determined to be more than originally notified, the landlord may claim the larger amount if and only if he completes the paragraph giving notice of the possibility that the amount may change, and gives a further notice specifying the larger amount within three months of the final determination.

Appendix 3 EXTRACTS FROM LEGISLATION

The amendments made by the Commonhold and Leasehold Reform Act 2002, which were not yet in force at the publication of this book, are shown. Words in *italics* (other than headings) are to be repealed and words in square brackets are to be inserted. The sources of these amendments are listed at the end of this Appendix.

LANDLORD AND TENANT ACT 1985

Information to be given to tenant

1 Disclosure of landlord's identity

(1) If the tenant of premises occupied as a dwelling makes a written request for the landlord's name and address to—

  (a) any person who demands, or the last person who received, rent payable under the tenancy, or

  (b) any other person for the time being acting as agent for the landlord, in relation to the tenancy,

that person shall supply the tenant with a written statement of the landlord's name and address within the period of 21 days beginning with the day on which he receives the request.

(2) A person who, without reasonable excuse, fails to comply with subsection (1) commits a summary offence and is liable on conviction to a fine not exceeding level 4 on the standard scale.

(3) In this section and section 2—

  (a) 'tenant' includes a statutory tenant; and

  (b) 'landlord' means the immediate landlord.

2 Disclosure of directors, etc of corporate landlord

(1) Where a tenant is supplied under section 1 with the name and address of his landlord and the landlord is a body corporate, he may make a further written request to the landlord for the name and address of every director and of the secretary of the landlord.

(2) The landlord shall supply the tenant with a written statement of the information requested within the period of 21 days beginning with the day on which he receives the request.

(3) A request under this section is duly made to the landlord if it is made to—

  (a) an agent of the landlord, or

  (b) a person who demands the rent of the premises concerned;

and any such agent or person to whom such a request is made shall forward it to the landlord as soon as may be.

(4) A landlord who, without reasonable excuse, fails to comply with a request under this section, and a person who, without reasonable excuse, fails to comply with a requirement imposed on him by subsection (3), commits a summary offence and is liable on conviction to a fine not exceeding level 4 on the standard scale.

3   Duty to inform tenant of assignment of landlord's interest

(1) If the interest of the landlord under a tenancy of premises which consist of or include a dwelling is assigned, the new landlord shall give notice in writing of the assignment, and of his name and address, to the tenant not later than the next day on which rent is payable under the tenancy or, if that is within two months of the assignment, the end of that period of two months.

(2) If trustees constitute the new landlord, a collective description of the trustees as the trustees of the trust in question may be given as the name of the landlord, and where such a collective description is given—

   (a)   the address of the new landlord may be given as the address from which the affairs of the trust are conducted, and
   (b)   a change in the persons who are for the time being the trustees of the trust shall not be treated as an assignment of the interest of the landlord.

(3) A person who is the new landlord under a tenancy falling within subsection (1) and who fails, without reasonable excuse, to give the notice required by that subsection, commits a summary offence and is liable on conviction to a fine not exceeding level 4 on the standard scale.

(3A) The person who was the landlord under the tenancy immediately before the assignment ('the old landlord') shall be liable to the tenant in respect of any breach of any covenant, condition or agreement under the tenancy occurring before the end of the relevant period in like manner as if the interest assigned were still vested in him; and where the new landlord is also liable to the tenant in respect of any such breach occurring within that period, he and the old landlord shall be jointly and severally liable in respect of it.

(3B) In subsection (3A) 'the relevant period' means the period beginning with the date of the assignment and ending with the date when—

   (a)   notice in writing of the assignment, and of the new landlord's name and address is given to tenant by the new landlord (whether in accordance with subsection (1) or not),
   (b)   notice in writing of the assignment, and of the new landlord's name and last-known address, is given to the tenant by the old landlord,

whichever happens first.

(4) In this section—

   (a)   'tenancy' includes a statutory tenancy, and
   (b)   references to the assignment of the landlord's interest include any conveyance or mortgage or charge.

3A Duty to inform tenant of possible right to acquire landlord's interest

(1) Where a new landlord is required by section 3(1) to give notice to a tenant of an assignment to him, then if—

(a) the tenant is a qualifying tenant within the meaning of Part 1 of the Landlord and Tenant Act 1987 (tenants' rights of first refusal), and

(b) the assignment was a relevant disposal within the meaning of that Part affecting premises to which at the time of the disposal that Part applied,

the landlord shall give also notice in writing to the tenant to the following effect.

(2) The notice shall state—

(a) that the disposal to the landlord was one to which Part 1 of the Landlord and Tenant Act 1987 applied;

(b) that the tenant (together with other qualifying tenants) may have the right under that Part—

(i)   to obtain information about the disposal, and

(ii)   to acquire the landlord's interest in the whole or part of the premises in which the tenant's flat is situated; and

(c) the time within which any such right must be exercised, and the fact that the time would run from the date of receipt of notice under this section by the requisite majority of qualifying tenants (within the meaning of that Part).

(3) A person who is required to give notice under this section and who fails, without reasonable excuse, to do so within the time allowed for giving notice under section 3(1) commits a summary offence and is liable on conviction to a fine not exceeding level 4 on the standard scale.

...

8 Implied terms as to fitness for human habitation

(1) In a contract to which this section applies for the letting of a house for human habitation there is implied, notwithstanding any stipulation to the contrary—

(a) a condition that the house is fit for human habitation at the commencement of the tenancy, and

(b) an undertaking that the house will be kept by the landlord fit for human habitation during the tenancy.

(2) The landlord, or a person authorised by him in writing, may at reasonable times of the day, on giving 24 hours' notice in writing, to the tenant or occupier, enter premises to which this section applies for the purpose of viewing their state and condition.

(3) This section applies to a contract if—

(a) the rent does not exceed the figure applicable in accordance with subsection (4), and

(b) the letting is not on such terms as to the tenant's responsibility as are mentioned in subsection (5).

(4) The rent limit for the application of this section is shown by the following Table, by reference to the date of making of the contract and the situation of the premises;

TABLE

Date of making of contract	Rent limit
Before 31st July 1923.	In London: £40.
	Elsewhere: £26 or £16 (see Note 1).
On or after 31st July 1923 and before 6th July 1957.	In London: £40.
	Elsewhere: £26.
On or after 6th July 1957.	In London: £80.
	Elsewhere: £52.

Notes

1. The applicable figure for contracts made before 31st July 1923 is £26 in the case of premises situated in a borough or urban district which at the date of the contract had according to the last published census a population of 50,000 or more. In the case of a house situated elsewhere, the figure is £16.

2. The references to 'London' are, in relation to contracts made before 1st April 1965, to the administrative county of London and, in relation to contracts made on or after that date, to Greater London exclusive of the outer London boroughs.

(5) This section does not apply where a house is let for a term of three years or more (the lease not being determinable at the option of either party before the expiration of three years) upon terms that the tenant puts the premises into a condition reasonably fit for human habitation.

(6) In this section 'house' includes—

    (a) a part of a house, and

    (b) any yard, garden, outhouses and appurtenances belonging to the house or usually enjoyed with it.

9 Application of s 8 to certain houses occupied by agricultural workers

(1) Where under the contract of employment of a worker employed in agriculture the provision of a house for his occupation forms part of his remuneration and the provisions of section 8 (implied terms as to fitness for human habitation) are inapplicable by reason only of the house not being let to him—

    (a) there are implied as part of the contract of employment, notwithstanding any stipulation to the contrary, the like condition and undertaking as would be implied under that section if the house were so let, and

    (b) the provisions of that section apply accordingly, with the substitution of 'employer' for 'landlord' and such other modifications as may be necessary.

(2) This section does not affect any obligation of a person other than the employer to repair a house to which this section applies, or any remedy for enforcing such an obligation.

(3) In this section 'house' includes—

    (a) a part of a house, and

    (b) any yard, garden, outhouses and appurtenances belonging to the house or usually enjoyed with it.

10 Fitness for human habitation

In determining for the purposes of this Act whether a house is unfit for human habitation, regard shall be had to its condition in respect of the following matters—

repair,
stability,
freedom from damp,
internal arrangement,
natural lighting,
ventilation,
water supply,
drainage and sanitary conveniences,
facilities for preparation and cooking of food and for the disposal of waste water;

and the house shall be regarded as unfit for human habitation if, and only if, it is so far defective in one or more of those matters that it is not reasonably suitable for occupation in that condition.

Repairing obligations

11 Repairing obligations in short leases

(1) In a lease to which this section applies (as to which, see sections 13 and 14) there is implied a covenant by the lessor—

   (a) to keep in repair the structure and exterior of the dwelling-house (including drains, gutters and external pipes),

   (b) to keep in repair and proper working order the installations in the dwelling-house for the supply of water, gas and electricity and for sanitation (including basins, sinks, baths and sanitary conveniences, but not other fixtures, fittings and appliances for making use of the supply of water, gas or electricity), and

   (c) to keep in repair and proper working order the installations in the dwelling-house for space heating and heating water.

(1A) If a lease to which this section applies is a lease of a dwelling-house which forms part only of a building, then, subject to subsection (1B), the covenant implied by subsection (1) shall have effect as if—

   (a) the reference in paragraph (a) of that subsection to the dwelling-house included a reference to any part of the building in which the lessor has an estate or interest; and

   (b) any reference in paragraphs (b) and (c) of that subsection to an installation in the dwelling-house included a reference to an installation which, directly or indirectly, serves the dwelling-house and which either—

      (i) forms part of any part of a building in which the lessor has an estate or interest; or

      (ii) is owned by the lessor or under his control.

(1B) Nothing in subsection (1A) shall be construed as requiring the lessor to carry out any works or repairs unless the disrepair (or failure to maintain in working order) is such as to affect the lessee's enjoyment of the dwelling-house or of any common parts, as defined in section 60(1) of the Landlord and Tenant Act 1987, which the lessee, as such, is entitled to use.

(2) The covenant implied by subsection (1) ('the lessor's repairing covenant') shall not be construed as requiring the lessor—

    (a) to carry out works or repairs for which the lessee is liable by virtue of his duty to use the premises in a tenant-like manner, or would be so liable but for an express covenant on his part,

    (b) to rebuild or reinstate the premises in the case of destruction or damage by fire, or by tempest, flood or other inevitable accident, or

    (c) to keep in repair or maintain anything which the lessee is entitled to remove from the dwelling-house.

(3) In determining the standard of repair required by the lessor's repairing covenant, regard shall be had to the age, character and the dwelling-house and the locality in which it is situated.

(3A) In any case where—

    (a) the lessor's repairing covenant has effect as mentioned in subsection (1A), and

    (b) in order to comply with the covenant the lessor needs to carry out works or repairs otherwise than in, or to an installation in the dwelling-house, and

    (c) the lessor does not have a sufficient right in the part of the building or the installation concerned to enable him to carry out the required works or repairs,

then, in any proceedings relating to a failure to comply with the lessor's repairing covenant, so far as it requires the lessor to carry out the works or repairs in question, it shall be a defence for the lessor to prove that he used all reasonable endeavours to obtain, but was unable to obtain, such rights as would be adequate to enable him to carry out the works or repairs.

(4) A covenant by the lessee for the repair of the premises is of no effect so far as it relates to the matters mentioned in subsection (1)(a) to (c), except so far as it imposes on the lessee any of the requirements mentioned in subsection (2)(a) or (c).

(5) The reference in subsection (4) to a covenant by the lessee for the repair of the premises includes a covenant—

    (a) to put in repair or deliver up in repair,

    (b) to paint, point or render,

    (c) to pay money in lieu of repairs by the lessee, or

    (d) to pay money on account of repairs by the lessor.

(6) In a case in which the lessor's repairing covenant is implied there is also implied a covenant by the lessee that the lessor, or any person authorised by him in writing, may at reasonable times of the day and on giving 24 hours' notice in writing to the occupier, enter the premises comprised in the lease for the purpose of viewing their condition and state of repair.

12   Restriction on contracting out of s 11

(1) A covenant or agreement, whether contained in a lease to which section 11 applies or in an agreement collateral to such a lease, is void in so far as it purports—

    (a) to exclude or limit the obligations of the lessor or the immunities of the lessee under that section, or

(b) to authorise any forfeiture or impose on the lessee any penalty, disability or obligation in the event of his enforcing or relying upon those obligations or immunities,

unless the inclusion of the provision was authorised by the county court.

(2) The county court may, by order made with the consent of the parties, authorise the inclusion in a lease, or in an agreement collateral to a lease, of provisions excluding or modifying in relation to the lease, the provisions of section 11 with respect to the repairing obligations of the parties if it appears to the court that it is reasonable to do so, having regard to all the circumstances of the case, including the other terms and conditions of the lease.

13 Leases to which s 11 applies: general rule

(1) Section 11 (repairing obligations) applies to a lease of a dwelling-house granted on or after 24th October 1961 for a term of less than seven years.

(2) In determining whether a lease is one to which section 11 applies—

(a) any part of the term which falls before the grant shall be left out of account and the lease shall be treated as a lease for a term commencing with the grant,
(b) a lease which is determinable at the option of the lessor before the expiration of seven years from the commencement of the term shall be treated as a lease for a term of less than seven years, and
(c) a lease (other than a lease to which paragraph (b) applies) shall not be treated as a lease for a term of less than seven years if it confers on the lessee an option for renewal for a term which, together with the original term, amounts to seven years or more.

(3) This section has effect subject to—

(a) section 14 (leases to which section 11 applies: exceptions), and
(b) section 32(2) (provisions not applying to tenancies within Part II of the Landlord and Tenant Act 1954).

14 Leases to which s 11 applies: exceptions

(1) Section 11 (repairing obligations) does not apply to a new lease granted to an existing tenant, or to a former tenant still in possession, if the previous lease was not a lease to which section 11 applied (and, in the case of a lease granted before 24th October 1961, would not have been if it had been granted on or after that date).

(2) In subsection (1)—

'existing tenant' means a person who is when, or immediately before, the new lease is granted, the lessee under another lease of the dwelling-house;
'former tenant still in possession' means a person who—

(a) was the lessee under another lease of the dwelling-house which terminated at some time before the new lease was granted, and

(b) between the termination of that other lease and the grant of the new lease was continuously in possession of the dwelling-house or of the rents and profits of the dwelling-house; and 'the previous lease' means the other lease referred to in the above definitions.

(3) Section 11 does not apply to a lease of a dwelling-house which is a tenancy of an agricultural holding within the meaning of the Agricultural Holdings Act 1986 and in relation to which that Act applies or to a farm business tenancy within the meaning of the Agricultural Tenancies Act 1995.

(4) Section 11 does not apply to a lease granted on or after 3rd October 1980 to—

> a local authority,
> a National Park authority,
> a new town corporation,
> an urban development corporation,
> the Development Board for Rural Wales,
> a registered social landlord,
> a co-operative housing association,
> an educational institution or other body specified, or of a class specified, by regulations under section 8 of the Rent Act 1977 or paragraph 8 of Schedule 1 to the Housing Act 1988 (bodies making student lettings), or
> a housing action trust established under Part III of the Housing Act 1988.

(5) Section 11 does not apply to a lease granted on or after 3rd October 1980 to—

(a) Her Majesty in right of the Crown (unless the lease is under the management of the Crown Estate Commissioners), or

(b) a government department or a person holding in trust for Her Majesty for the purposes of a government department.

15 Jurisdiction of county court

The county court has jurisdiction to make a declaration that section 11 (repairing covenants) applies, or does not apply, to a lease—

(a) whatever the net annual value of the property in question, and

(b) notwithstanding that no other relief is sought than a declaration.

16 Meaning of 'lease' and related expressions

In sections 11 to 15 (repairing obligations in short leases)—

(a) 'lease' does not include a mortgage term;

(b) 'lease of a dwelling-house' means a lease by which a building or part of a building is let wholly or mainly as a private residence, and 'dwelling-house' means that building or part of a building;

(c) 'lessee' and 'lessor' mean, respectively, the person for the time being entitled to the term of a lease and to the reversion expectant on it.

17 Specific performance of landlord's repairing obligations

(1) In proceedings in which a tenant of a dwelling alleges a breach on the part of his landlord of a repairing covenant relating to any part of the premises in which the dwelling is comprised, the court may order specific performance of the covenant whether or not the breach relates to a part of the premises let to the tenant and notwithstanding any equitable rule restricting the scope of the remedy, whether on the basis of a lack of mutuality or otherwise.

(2) In this section—

(a) 'tenant' includes a statutory tenant,

(b) in relation to a statutory tenant the reference to the premises let to him is to the premises of which he is a statutory tenant,

(c) 'landlord', in relation to a tenant, includes any person against whom the tenant has a right to enforce a repairing covenant, and

(d) 'repairing covenant' means a covenant to repair, maintain, renew, construct or replace any property.

Service charges

18 Meaning of 'service charge' and 'relevant costs'

(1) In the following provisions of this Act 'service charge' means an amount payable by a tenant of a dwelling as part of or in addition to the rent—

(a) which is payable, directly or indirectly, for services, repairs, maintenance [, improvements] or insurance or the landlord's costs of management, and

(b) the whole or part of which varies or may vary according to the relevant costs.

(2) The relevant costs are the costs or estimated costs incurred or to be incurred by or on behalf of the landlord, or a superior landlord, in connection with the matters for which the service charge is payable.

(3) For this purpose—

(a) 'costs' includes overheads, and

(b) costs are relevant costs in relation to a service charge whether they are incurred, or to be incurred, in the period for which the service charge is payable or in an earlier or later period.

19 Limitation of service charges: reasonableness

(1) Relevant costs shall be taken into account in determining the amount of a service charge payable for a period—

(a) only to the extent that they are reasonably incurred, and

(b) where they are incurred on the provision of services or the carrying out of works, only if the services or works are of a reasonable standard;

and the amount payable shall be limited accordingly.

(2) Where a service charge is payable before the relevant costs are incurred, no greater amount than is reasonable is so payable, and after the relevant costs have been incurred any necessary adjustment shall be made by repayment, reduction or subsequent charges or otherwise.

(2A) A tenant by whom, or a landlord to whom, a service charge is alleged to be payable may apply to a leasehold valuation tribunal for a determination—

(a) whether costs incurred for services, repairs, maintenance, insurance or management were reasonably incurred,

(b) whether services or works for which costs were incurred are of a reasonable standard, or

(c) whether an amount payable before costs are incurred is reasonable.

(2B) An application may also be made to a leasehold valuation tribunal by a tenant by whom, or landlord to whom, a service charge may be payable for a determination—

(a)   *whether if costs were incurred for services, repairs, maintenance, insurance or management of any specified description they would be reasonable,*

(b)   *whether services provided or works carried out to a particular specification would be of a reasonable standard, or*

(c)   *what amount payable before costs are incurred would be reasonable.*

(2C) No application under subsection (2A) or (2B) may be made in respect of a matter which—

(a)   *has been agreed or admitted by the tenant,*

(b)   *under an arbitration agreement to which the tenant is a party is to be referred to arbitration, or*

(c)   *has been the subject of determination by a court or arbitral tribunal.*

(3) An agreement by the tenant of a dwelling (other than an arbitration agreement) is void in so far as it purports to provide for a determination in a particular manner, or on particular evidence, of any question—

(a)   *whether costs incurred for services, repairs, maintenance, insurance or management were reasonably incurred,*

(b)   *whether services or works for which costs were incurred are of a reasonable standard, or*

(c)   *whether an amount payable before costs are incurred is reasonable.*

(5) If a person takes any proceedings in the High Court in pursuance of any of the provisions of this Act relating to service charges and he could have taken those proceedings in the county court, he shall not be entitled to recover any costs.

20   Limitation of service charges: estimates and consultation

(1) Where relevant costs incurred on the carrying out of any qualifying works exceed the limit specified in subsection (3), the excess shall not be taken into account in determining the amount of a service charge unless the relevant requirements have been either—

(a)   *complied with, or*

(b)   *dispensed with by the court in accordance with subsection (9);*

and the amount payable shall be limited accordingly.

(2) In subsection (1) 'qualifying works', in relation to a service charge, means works (whether on a building or on any other premises) to the costs of which the tenant by whom the service charge is payable may be required under the terms of his lease to contribute by the payment of such a charge.

(3) The limit is whichever is the greater of—

(a)   *£25, or such other amount as may be prescribed by order of the Secretary of State, multiplied by the number of dwellings let to the tenants concerned; or*

(b)   *£500, or such other amount as may be so prescribed.*

(4) The relevant requirements in relation to such of the tenants concerned as are not represented by a recognised tenants' association are—

(a)   *At least two estimates for the works shall be obtained, one of them from a person wholly unconnected with the landlord.*

(b) A notice accompanied by a copy of the estimates shall be given to each of those tenants or shall be displayed in one or more places where it is likely to come to the notice of all those tenants.

(c) The notice shall describe the works to be carried out and invite observations on them and on the estimates and shall state the name and the address in the United Kingdom of the person to whom the observations may be sent and the date by which they are to be received.

(d) The date stated in the notice shall not be earlier than one month after the date on which the notice is given or displayed as required by paragraph (b).

(e) The landlord shall have regard to any observations received in pursuance of the notice; and unless the works are urgently required they shall not be begun earlier than the date specified in the notice.

(5) The relevant requirements in relation to such of the tenants concerned as are represented by a recognised tenants' association are—

(a) The landlord shall give to the secretary of the association a notice containing a detailed specification of the works in question and specifying a reasonable period within which the association may propose to the landlord the names of one or more persons from whom estimates for the works should in its view be obtained by the landlord.

(b) At least two estimates for the works shall be obtained, one of them from a person wholly unconnected with the landlord.

(c) A copy of each of the estimates shall be given to the secretary of the association.

(d) A notice shall be given to each of the tenants concerned represented by the association, which shall—

(i) describe briefly the works to be carried out,

(ii) summarise the estimates,

(iii) inform the tenant that he has a right to inspect and take copies of a detailed specification of the works to be carried out and of the estimates,

(iv) invite observations on those works and on the estimates, and

(v) specify the name and the address in the United Kingdom of the person to whom the observations may be sent and the date by which they are to be received.

(e) The date stated in the notice shall not be earlier than one month after the date on which the notice is given as required by paragraph (d).

(f) If any tenant to whom the notice is given so requests, the landlord shall afford him reasonable facilities for inspecting a detailed specification of the works to be carried out and the estimates, free of charge, and for taking copies of them on payment of such reasonable charge as the landlord may determine.

(g) The landlord shall have regard to any observations received in pursuance of the notice and, unless the works are urgently required, they shall not be begun earlier than the date specified in the notice.

(6) Paragraphs (d)(ii) and (iii) and (f) of subsection (5) shall not apply to any estimate of which a copy is enclosed with the notice given in pursuance of paragraph (d).

(7) The requirement imposed on the landlord by subsection (5)(f) to make any facilities available to a person free of charge shall not be construed as precluding the landlord from treating as part of his costs of management any costs incurred by him in connection with making those facilities so available.

(8) In this section 'the tenants concerned' means all the landlord's tenants who may be required under the terms of their leases to contribute to the costs of the works in question by the payment of service charges.

(9) In proceedings relating to a service charge the court may, if satisfied that the landlord acted reasonably, dispense with all or any of the relevant requirements.

(10) An order under this section—

    (a)   may make different provision with respect to different cases or descriptions of case, including different provision for different areas, and

    (b)   shall be made by statutory instrument which shall be subject to annulment in pursuance of a resolution of either House of Parliament.

[20   Limitation of service charges: consultation requirements

(1) Where this section applies to any qualifying works or qualifying long term agreement, the relevant contributions of tenants are limited in accordance with subsection (6) or (7) (or both) unless the consultation requirements have been either—

    (a)   complied with in relation to the works on agreement, or

    (b)   dispensed with in relation to the works or agreement by (or on appeal from) a leasehold valuation tribunal.

(2) In this section 'relevant contribution', in relation to a tenant and any works or agreement, is the amount which he may be required under the terms of his lease to contribute (by the payment of service charges) to relevant costs incurred on carrying out the works or under the agreement.

(3) This section applies to qualifying works if relevant costs incurred on carrying out the works exceed an appropriate amount.

(4) The Secretary of State may by regulations provide that this section applies to a qualifying long term agreement—

    (a)   if relevant costs incurred under the agreement exceed an appropriate amount, or

    (b)   if relevant costs incurred under the agreement during a period prescribed by the regulations exceed an appropriate amount.

(5) An appropriate amount is an amount set by regulations made by the Secretary of State; and the regulations may make provision for either or both of the following to be an appropriate amount—

    (a)   an amount prescribed by, or determined in accordance with, the regulations, and

    (b)   an amount which results in the relevant contribution of any one or more tenants being an amount prescribed by, or determined in accordance with, the regulations.

(6) Where an appropriate amount is set by virtue of paragraph (a) of subsection (5), the amount of the relevant costs incurred on carrying out the works or under the agreement which may be taken into account in determining the relevant contributions of tenants is limited to the appropriate amount.

(7) Where an appropriate amount is set by virtue of paragraph (b) of that subsection, the amount of the relevant contribution of the tenant, or each of the tenants, whose relevant contribution would otherwise exceed the amount prescribed by, or determined in accordance with, the regulations is limited to the amount so prescribed or determined.]

[20ZA   Consultation requirements: supplementary

(1) Where an application is made to a leasehold valuation tribunal for a determination to dispense with all or any of the consultation requirements in relation to any qualifying works or qualifying long term agreement, the tribunal may make the determination if satisfied that it is reasonable to dispense with the requirements.

(2) In section 20 and this section—

'qualifying works' means works on a building or any other premises, and
'qualifying long term agreement' means (subject to subsection (3)) an agreement entered into, by or on behalf of the landlord or a superior landlord, for a term of more than twelve months.

(3) The Secretary of State may by regulations provide that an agreement is not a qualifying long term agreement—

(a)   if it is an agreement of a description prescribed by the regulations, or
(b)   in any circumstances so prescribed.

(4) In section 20 and this section 'the consultation requirements' means requirements prescribed by regulations made by the Secretary of State.

(5) Regulations under subsection (4) may in particular include provision requiring the landlord—

(a)   to provide details of proposed works or agreements to tenants or the recognised tenants' association representing them,
(b)   to obtain estimates for proposed works or agreements,
(c)   to invite tenants or the recognised tenants' association to propose the names of persons from whom the landlord should try to obtain other estimates,
(d)   to have regard to observations made by tenants or the recognised tenants' association in relation to proposed works or agreements and estimates, and
(e)   to give reasons in prescribed circumstances for carrying out works or entering into agreements.

(6) Regulations under section 20 or this section—

(a)   may make provision generally or only in relation to specific cases, and
(b)   may make different provision for different purposes.

(7) Regulations under section 20 or this section shall be made by statutory instrument which shall be subject to annulment in pursuance of a resolution of either House of Parliament.]

20A   Limitation of service charges: grant-aided works

(1) Where relevant costs are incurred or to be incurred on the carrying out of works in respect of which a grant has been or is to be paid under section 523 of the Housing Act 1985 (assistance for provision of separate service pipe for water supply) or any provision of Part I of the Housing Grants, Construction and Regeneration Act 1996 (grants, etc for renewal of private sector housing) or any corresponding earlier enactment, the amount of the grant shall be deducted from the costs and the amount of the service charge payable shall be reduced accordingly.

(2) In any case where—

(a)   relevant costs are incurred or to be incurred on the carrying out of works which are included in the external works specified in a group repair scheme, within the meaning of Part I of the Housing Grants, Construction and Regeneration Act 1996, and
(b)   the landlord participated or is participating in that scheme as an assisted participant,

the amount which, in relation to the landlord, is the balance of the cost determined in accordance with section 69(3) of the Housing Grants, Construction and Regeneration Act 1996 shall be deducted from the costs, and the amount of the service charge payable shall be reduced accordingly.

20B Limitation of service charges: time limit on making demands

(1) If any of the relevant costs taken into account in determining the amount of any service charge were incurred more than 18 months before a demand for payment of the service charge is served on the tenant, then (subject to subsection (2)), the tenant shall not be liable to pay so much of the service charge as reflects the costs so incurred.

(2) Subsection (1) shall not apply if, within the period of 18 months beginning with the date when the relevant costs in question were incurred, the tenant was notified in writing that those costs had been incurred and that he would subsequently be required under the terms of his lease to contribute to them by the payment of a service charge.

20C Limitation of service charges: costs of proceedings

(1) A tenant may make an application for an order that all or any of the costs incurred, or to be incurred, by the landlord in connection with proceedings before a court or leasehold valuation tribunal, or the Lands Tribunal, or in connection with arbitration proceedings, are not to be regarded as relevant costs to be taken into account in determining the amount of any service charge payable by the tenant or any other person or persons specified in the application.

(2) The application shall be made—

   (a) in the case of court proceedings, to the court before which the proceedings are taking place or, if the application is made after the proceedings are concluded, to a county court;
   (b) in the case of proceedings before a leasehold valuation tribunal, to the tribunal before which the proceedings are taking place or, if the application is made after the proceedings are concluded, to any leasehold valuation tribunal;
   (c) in the case of proceedings before the Lands Tribunal, to the tribunal;
   (d) in the case of arbitration proceedings, to the arbitral tribunal or, if the application is made after the proceedings are concluded, to a county court.

(3) The court or tribunal to which the application is made may make such order on the application as it considers just and equitable in the circumstances.

21 *Request for summary of relevant costs*

(1) A tenant may require the landlord in writing to supply him with a written summary of the costs incurred—

   (a) if the relevant accounts are made up for periods of twelve months, in the last such period ending not later than the date of the request, or
   (b) if the accounts are not so made up, in the period of twelve months ending with the date of the request,

and which are relevant costs in relation to the service charges payable or demanded as payable in that or any other period.

(2) If the tenant is represented by a recognised tenants' association and he consents, the request may be made by the secretary of the association instead of by the tenant and may then be for the supply of the summary to the secretary.

(3) A request is duly served on the landlord if it is served on—

(a)   *an agent of the landlord named as such in the rent book or similar document, or*
(b)   *the person who receives the rent on behalf of the landlord;*

and a person on whom a request is so served shall forward it as soon as may be to the landlord.

(4) The landlord shall comply with the request within one month of the request or within six months of the end of the period referred to in subsection (1)(a) or (b) whichever is the later.

(5) The summary shall state whether any of the costs relate to works in respect of which a grant has been or is to be paid under section 523 of the Housing Act 1985 (assistance for provision of separate service pipe for water supply) or any provision of Part I of the Housing Grants, Construction and Regeneration Act 1996 (grants, etc for renewal of private sector housing) or any corresponding earlier enactment and set out the costs in a way showing how they have been or will be reflected in demands for service charges and, in addition, shall summarise each of the following items, namely—

(a)   *any of the costs in respect of which no demand for payment was received by the landlord within the period referred to in subsection (1)(a) or (b),*
(b)   *any of the costs in respect of which—*
   (i)   *a demand for payment was so received, but*
   (ii)   *no payment was made by the landlord within that period, and*
(c)   *any of the costs in respect of which—*
   (i)   *a demand for payment was so received, and*
   (ii)   *payment was made by the landlord within that period,*

and specify the aggregate of any amounts received by the landlord down to the end of that period on account of service charges in respect of relevant dwellings and still standing to the credit of the tenants of those dwellings at the end of that period.

(5A) In subsection (5) 'relevant dwelling' means a dwelling whose tenant is either—

(a)   *the person by or with the consent of whom the request was made, or*
(b)   *a person whose obligations under the terms of his lease as regards contributing to relevant costs relate to the same costs as the corresponding obligations of the person mentioned in paragraph (a) above relate to.*

(5B) The summary shall state whether any of the costs relate to works which are included in the external works specified in a group repair scheme, within the meaning of Chapter II of Part I of the Housing Grants, Construction and Regeneration Act 1996 or any corresponding earlier enactment, in which the landlord participated or is participating as an assisted participant.

(6) If the service charges in relation to which the costs are relevant costs as mentioned in subsection (1) are payable by the tenants of more than four dwellings, the summary shall be certified by a qualified accountant as—

(a)   *in his opinion a fair summary complying with the requirements of subsection (5), and*
(b)   *being sufficiently supported by accounts, receipts and other documents which have been produced to him.*

[21   Regular statements of account

(1) The landlord must supply to each tenant by whom services charges are payable, in relation to each accounting period, a written statement of account dealing with—

    (a)   service charges of the tenant and the tenants of dwellings associated with his dwelling,

    (b)   relevant costs relating to those service charges,

    (c)   the aggregate amount standing to the credit of the tenant and the tenants of those dwellings—

        (i)   at the beginning of the accounting period, and

        (ii)   at the end of the accounting period, and

    (d)   related matters.

(2) The statement of account in relation to an accounting period must be supplied to each such tenant not later than six months after the end of the accounting period.

(3) Where the landlord supplies a statement of account to a tenant he must also supply to him—

    (a)   a certificate of a qualified accountant that, in the accountant's opinion, the statement of account deals fairly with the matters with which it is required to deal and is sufficiently supported by accounts, receipts and other documents which have been produced to him, and

    (b)   a summary of the rights and obligations of tenants of dwellings in relation to service charges.

(4) The Secretary of State may make regulations prescribing requirements as to the form and content of—

    (a)   statements of account,

    (b)   accountants' certificates, and

    (c)   summaries of rights and obligations

required to be supplied under this section.

(5) The Secretary of State may make regulations prescribing exceptions from the requirement to supply an accountant's certificate.

(6) If the landlord has been notified by a tenant of an address in England and Wales at which he wishes to have supplied to him documents required to be so supplied under this section, the landlord must supply them to him at that address.

(7) And the landlord is to be taken to have been so notified if notification has been given to—

    (a)   an agent of the landlord named as such in the rent book or similar document, or

    (b)   the person who receives the rent on behalf of the landlord;

and where notification is given to such an agent or person he must forward it as soon as may be to the landlord.

(8) For the purposes of this section a dwelling is associated with another dwelling if the obligations of the tenants of the dwellings under the terms of their leases as regards contributing to relevant costs relate to the same costs.

(9) In this section 'accounting period' means such period—

    (a)   beginning with the relevant date, and

(b)   ending with such date, not later than twelve months after the relevant date,

as the landlord determines.

(10) In the case of the first accounting period in relation to any dwellings, the relevant date is the later of—

(a)   the date on which services charges are first payable under a lease of any of them, and

(b)   the date on which section 152 of the Commonhold and Leasehold Reform Act 2002 comes into force,

and, in the case of subsequent accounting periods, it is the date immediately following the end of the previous accounting period.

(11) Regulations under subsection (4) may make different provision for different purposes.

(12) Regulations under this section shall be made by statutory instrument which shall be subject to annulment in pursuance of a resolution of either House of Parliament.]

[21A   Withholding of service charges

(1) A tenant may withhold payment of a service charge if—

(a)   the landlord has not supplied a document to him by the time by which he is required to supply it under section 21, or

(b)   the form or content of a document which the landlord has supplied to him under that section (at any time) does not conform exactly or substantially with the requirements prescribed by regulations under subsection (4) of that section.

(2) The maximum amount which the tenant may withhold is an amount equal to the aggregate of—

(a)   the service charges paid by him in the accounting period to which the document concerned would or does relate, and

(b)   so much of the aggregate amount required to be dealt with in the statement of account for that accounting period by section 21(1)(c)(i) as stood to his credit.

(3) An amount may not be withheld under this section—

(a)   in a case within paragraph (a) of subsection (1), after the document concerned has been supplied to the tenant by the landlord, or

(b)   in a case within paragraph (b) of that subsection, after a document conforming exactly or substantially with the requirements prescribed by regulations under section 21(4) has been supplied to the tenant by the landlord by way of replacement of the one previously supplied.

(4) If, on an application made by the landlord to a leasehold valuation tribunal, the tribunal determines that the landlord has a reasonable excuse for a failure giving rise to the right of a tenant to withhold an amount under this section, the tenant may not withhold the amount after the determination is made.

(5) Where a tenant withholds a service charge under this section, any provisions of the tenancy relating to non-payment or late payment of service charges do not have effect in relation to the period for which he so withholds it.]

[21B   Notice to accompany demands for service charges

(1) A demand for the payment of a service charge must be accompanied by a summary of the rights and obligations of tenants of dwellings in relation to service charges.

(2) The Secretary of State may make regulations prescribing requirements as to the form and content of such summaries of rights and obligations.

(3) A tenant may withhold payment of a service charge which has been demanded from him if subsection (1) is not complied with in relation to the demand.

(4) Where a tenant withholds a service charge under this section, any provisions of the lease relating to non-payment or late payment of service charges do not have effect in relation to the period for which he so withholds it.

(5) Regulations under subsection (2) may make different provision for different purposes.

(6) Regulations under subsection (2) shall be made by statutory instrument which shall be subject to annulment in pursuance of a resolution of either House of Parliament.]

22   *Request to inspect supporting accounts, etc*

(1) This section applies where a tenant, or the secretary of a recognised tenants' association, has obtained such a summary as is referred to in section 21(1) (summary of relevant costs), whether in pursuance of that section or otherwise.

(2) The tenant, or the secretary with the consent of the tenant, may within six months of obtaining the summary require the landlord in writing to afford him reasonable facilities—

    (a)   for inspecting the accounts, receipts and other documents supporting the summary, and
    (b)   for taking copies or extracts from them.

(3) A request under this section is duly served on the landlord if it is served on—

    (a)   an agent of the landlord named as such in the rent book or similar document, or
    (b)   the person who receives the rent on behalf of the landlord;

and a person on whom a request is so served shall forward it as soon as may be to the landlord.

(4) The landlord shall make such facilities available to the tenant or secretary for a period of two months beginning not later than one month after the request is made.

(5) The landlord shall—

    (a)   where such facilities are for the inspection of any documents, make them so available free of charge;
    (b)   where such facilities are for the taking of copies or extracts, be entitled to make them so available on payment of such reasonable charge as he may determine.

(6) The requirement imposed on the landlord by subsection (5)(a) to make any facilities available to a person free of charge shall not be construed as precluding the landlord from treating as part of his costs of management any costs incurred by him in connection with making those facilities so available.

[22 Inspection, etc of documents

(1) A tenant may by notice in writing require the landlord—

    (a) to afford him reasonable facilities for inspecting accounts, receipts or other documents relevant to the matters which must be dealt with in a statement of account required to be supplied to him under section 21 and for taking copies of or extracts from them, or

    (b) to take copies of or extracts from any such accounts, receipts or other documents and either send them to him or afford him reasonable facilities for collecting them (as he specifies).

(2) If the tenant is represented by a recognised tenants' association and he consents, the notice may be served by the secretary of the association instead of by the tenant (and in that case any requirement imposed by it is to afford reasonable facilities, or to send copies or extracts, to the secretary).

(3) A notice under this section may not be served after the end of the period of six months beginning with the date by which the tenant is required to be supplied with the statement of account under section 21.

(4) But if—

    (a) the statement of account is not supplied to the tenant on or before that date, or

    (b) the statement of account so supplied does not conform exactly or substantially with the requirements prescribed by regulations under section 21(4),

the six month period mentioned in subsection (3) does not begin until any later date on which the statement of account (conforming exactly or substantially with those requirements) is supplied to him.

(5) A notice under this section is duly served on the landlord if it is served on—

    (a) an agent of the landlord named as such in the rent book or similar document, or

    (b) the person who receives the rent on behalf of the landlord;

and a person on whom such a notice is so served must forward it as soon as may be to the landlord.

(6) The landlord must comply with a requirement imposed by a notice under this section within the period of twenty-one days beginning with the day on which he receives the notice.

(7) To the extent that a notice under this section requires the landlord to afford facilities for inspecting documents—

    (a) he must do so free of charge, but

    (b) he may treat as part of his costs of management any costs incurred by him in doing so.

(8) The landlord may make a reasonable charge for doing anything else in compliance with a requirement imposed by a notice under this section.]

23 Request relating to information held by superior landlord

(1) If a request under section 21 (request for summary of relevant costs) relates in whole or in part to relevant costs incurred by or on behalf of a superior landlord, and the landlord to whom the request is made is not in possession of the relevant information—

(a)   *he shall in turn make a written request for the relevant information to the person who is his landlord (and so on, if that person is not himself the superior landlord),*

(b)   *the superior landlord shall comply with that request within a reasonable time, and*

(c)   *the immediate landlord shall then comply with the tenant's or secretary's request, or that part of it which relates to the relevant costs incurred by or on behalf of the superior landlord, within the time allowed by section 21 or such further time, if any, as is reasonable in the circumstances.*

(2) If a request under section 22 (request for facilities to inspect supporting accounts, etc) relates to a summary of costs incurred by or on behalf of a superior landlord—

(a)   *the landlord to whom the request is made shall forthwith inform the tenant or secretary of that fact and of the name and address of the superior landlord, and*

(b)   *section 22 shall then apply to the superior landlord as it applies to the immediate landlord.*

[23 Information held by superior landlord

(1) If a statement of account which the landlord is required to supply under section 21 relates to matters concerning a superior landlord and the landlord is not in possession of the relevant information—

(a)   he may by notice in writing require the person who is his landlord to give him the relevant information (and so on, if that person is not himself the superior landlord), and

(b)   the superior landlord must comply with the requirement within a reasonable time.

(2) If a notice under section 22 imposes a requirement in relation to documents held by a superior landlord—

(a)   the landlord shall immediately inform the tenant or secretary of that fact and of the name and address of the superior landlord, and

(b)   section 22 then applies in relation to the superior landlord (as in relation to the landlord).]

[23A Effect of change of landlord

(1) This section applies where, at a time when a duty imposed on the landlord or a superior landlord by or by virtue of any of sections 21 to 23 remains to be discharged by him, he disposes of the whole or part of his interest as landlord or superior landlord to another person.

(2) If the landlord or superior landlord is, despite the disposal, still in a position to discharge the duty to any extent, he remains responsible for discharging it to that extent.

(3) If the other person is in a position to discharge the duty to any extent, he is responsible for discharging it to that extent.

(4) Where the other person is responsible for discharging the duty to any extent (whether or not the landlord or superior landlord is also responsible for discharging it to that or any other extent)—

    (a) references to the landlord or superior landlord in sections 21 to 23 are to, or include, the other person so far as is appropriate to reflect his responsibility for discharging the duty to that extent, but

    (b) in connection with its discharge by the other person, section 22(6) applies as if the reference to the day on which the landlord receives the notice were to the date of the disposal referred to in subsection (1).]

24 *Effect of assignment on request*

The assignment of a tenancy does not affect the validity of a request made under section 21, 22 or 23 before the assignment; but a person is not obliged to provide a summary or make facilities available more than once for the same dwelling and for the same period.

[24 Effect of assignment

The assignment of a tenancy does not affect any duty imposed by or by virtue of any of sections 21 to 23A; but a person is not required to comply with more than a reasonable number of requirements imposed by any one person.]

25 Failure to comply with ss 21, 22 or 23 an offence

(1) It is a summary offence for a person to fail, without reasonable excuse, to perform a duty imposed on him *by section 21, 22 or 23* [by or by virtue of any of sections 21 to 23A].

(2) A person committing such an offence is liable on conviction to a fine not exceeding level 4 on the standard scale.

26 Exception: tenants of certain public authorities

(1) Sections 18 to 25 (limitation on service charges *and requests for information about costs* [, statements of account and inspection etc of documents]) do not apply to a service charge payable by a tenant of—

    a local authority,
    a National Park authority, or
    a new town corporation,

unless the tenancy is a long tenancy, in which case sections 18 to 24 apply but section 25 (offence of failure to comply) does not.

(2) The following are long tenancies for the purposes of subsection (1), subject to subsection (3)—

    (a) a tenancy granted for a term certain exceeding 21 years, whether or not it is (or may become) terminable before the end of that term by notice given by the tenant or by re-entry or forfeiture;

    (b) a tenancy for a term fixed by law under a grant with a covenant or obligation for perpetual renewal, other than a tenancy by sub-demise from one which is not a long tenancy;

(c) any tenancy granted in pursuance of Part V of the Housing Act 1985 (the right to buy), including any tenancy granted in pursuance of that Part as it has effect by virtue of section 17 of the Housing Act 1996 (the right to acquire).

(3) A tenancy granted so as to become terminable by notice after a death is not a long tenancy for the purposes of subsection (1), unless—

(a) it is granted by a housing association which at the time of the grant is a registered social landlord,

(b) it is granted at a premium calculated by reference to a percentage of the value of the dwelling-house or the cost of providing it, and

(c) at the time it is granted it complies with the requirements of the regulations then in force under section 140(4)(b) of the Housing Act 1980 or paragraph 4(2)(b) of Schedule 4A to the Leasehold Reform Act 1967 (conditions for exclusion of shared ownership leases from Part I of the Leasehold Reform Act 1967) or, in the case of a tenancy granted before any such regulations were brought into force, with the first such regulations to be in force.

27 Exception: rent registered and not entered as variable

Sections 18 and 25 (limitation on service charges *and requests for information about costs* [, statements of account and inspection etc of documents]) do not apply to a service charge payable by the tenant of a dwelling the rent of which is registered under Part IV of the Rent Act 1977, unless the amount registered is, in pursuance of section 71(4) of that Act, entered as a variable amount.

[27A Liability to pay service charges: jurisdiction

(1) Where an amount is alleged to be payable by way of service charge, an application may be made to a leasehold valuation tribunal for a determination whether or not any amount is so payable and, if it is, as to—

(a) the person by whom it is payable,

(b) the person to whom it is payable,

(c) the amount which is payable,

(d) the date at or by which it is payable, and

(e) the manner in which it is payable.

(2) Subsection (1) applies whether or not any payment has been made.

(3) An application may also be made to a leasehold valuation tribunal for a determination whether, if costs were incurred for services, repairs, maintenance, improvements, insurance or management of any specified description, a service charge would be payable for the costs and, if it would, as to—

(a) the person by whom it would be payable,

(b) the person to whom it would be payable,

(c) the amount which would be payable,

(d) the date at or by which it would be payable, and

(e) the manner in which it would be payable.

(4) No application under subsection (1) or (3) may be made in respect of a matter which—

(a) has been agreed or admitted by the tenant,

(b) has been, or is to be, referred to arbitration pursuant to a post-dispute arbitration agreement to which the tenant is a party,

(c) has been the subject of determination by a court, or

(d) has been the subject of determination by an arbitral tribunal pursuant to a post-dispute arbitration agreement.

(5) But the tenant is not to be taken to have agreed or admitted any matter by reason only of having paid the whole or any part of an amount alleged to be payable by way of service charge.

(6) An agreement by the tenant of a dwelling (other than a post-dispute arbitration agreement) is void in so far as it purports to provide for a determination—

(a) in a particular manner, or

(b) on particular evidence,

of any question which may be the subject of an application under subsection (1) or (3).

(7) The jurisdiction conferred on a leasehold valuation tribunal in respect of any matter by virtue of this section is in addition to any jurisdiction of a court in respect of the matter.]

28 Meaning of 'qualified accountant'

(1) The reference to a 'qualified accountant' in *section 21(6) (certification of summary of information about relevant costs)* [section 21(3)(a) (certification of statements of account)] is to a person who, in accordance with the following provisions, has the necessary qualification and is not disqualified from acting.

(2) A person has the necessary qualification if he is eligible for appointment as a company auditor under section 25 of the Companies Act 1989.

(4) The following are disqualified from acting—

(b) an officer, employee or partner of the landlord or, where the landlord is a company, of an associated company;

(c) a person who is a partner or employee of any such officer or employee;

(d) an agent of the landlord who is a managing agent for any premises to which *any of the costs covered by the summary in question relate* [the statement of account in question relates];

(e) an employee or partner of any such agent.

(5) For the purposes of subsection (4)(b) a company is associated with a landlord company if it is (within the meaning of section 736 of the Companies Act 1985) the landlord's holding company, a subsidiary of the landlord or another subsidiary of the landlord's holding company.

(5A) For the purposes of subsection (4)(d) a person is a managing agent for any premises to which *any costs relate* [any statement of account relates] if he has been appointed to discharge any of the landlord's obligations relating to the management by him of the premises and owed to the tenants who may be required under the terms of their leases to contribute to *those costs* [costs covered by the statement of account] by the payment of service charges.

(6) Where the landlord is [an emanation of the Crown,] a local authority, National Park authority or a new town corporation—

   (a)   the persons who have the necessary qualification include members of the Chartered Institute of Public Finance and Accountancy, and

   (b)   subsection (4)(b) (disqualification of officers and employees of landlord) does not apply.

29   Meaning of 'recognised tenants' association'

(1) A recognised tenants' association is an association of qualifying tenants (whether with or without other tenants) which is recognised for the purposes of the provisions of this Act relating to service charges either—

   (a)   by notice in writing given by the landlord to the secretary of the association, or

   (b)   by a certificate of a member of the local rent assessment committee panel.

(2) A notice given under subsection (1)(a) may be withdrawn by the landlord by notice in writing given to the secretary of the association not less than six months before the date on which it is to be withdrawn.

(3) A certificate given under subsection (1)(b) may be cancelled by any member of the local rent assessment committee panel.

(4) In this section the 'local rent assessment committee panel' means the persons appointed by the Lord Chancellor under the Rent Act 1977 to the panel of persons to act as members of a rent assessment committee for the registration area in which the dwellings let to the qualifying tenants are situated, and for the purposes of this section a number of tenants are qualifying tenants if each of them may be required under the terms of his lease to contribute to the same costs by the payment of a service charge.

(5) The Secretary of State may by regulations specify—

   (a)   the procedure which is to be followed in connection with an application for, or for the cancellation of, a certificate under subsection (1)(b);

   (b)   the matters to which regard is to be had in giving or cancelling such a certificate;

   (c)   the duration of such a certificate; and

   (d)   any circumstances in which a certificate is not to be given under subsection (1)(b).

(6) Regulations under subsection (5)—

   (a)   may make different provisions with respect to different cases or descriptions of case, including different provision for different areas, and

   (b)   shall be made by statutory instrument which shall be subject to annulment in pursuance of a resolution of either House of Parliament.

30   Meaning of 'flat', 'landlord' and 'tenant'

In the provisions of this Act relating to service charges—

   'landlord' includes any person who has a right to enforce payment of a service charge;
   'tenant' includes:

      (a)   a statutory tenant, and

(b) where the dwelling or part of it is sub-let, the sub-tenant.

Insurance

30A   Rights of tenants with respect to insurance

The Schedule to this Act (which confers on tenants certain rights with respect to the insurance of their dwellings) shall have effect.

Managing agents

30B   Recognised tenants' associations to be consulted about managing agents

(1) A recognised tenants' association may at any time serve a notice on the landlord requesting him to consult the association in accordance with this section on matters relating to the appointment or employment by him of a managing agent for any relevant premises.

(2) Where, at the time when any such notice is served by a recognised tenants' association, the landlord does not employ any managing agent for any relevant premises, the landlord shall, before appointing such a managing agent, serve on the association a notice specifying—

    (a) the name of the proposed managing agent;

    (b) the landlord's obligations to the tenants represented by the association which it is proposed that the managing agent should be required to discharge on his behalf; and

    (c) a period of not less than one month beginning with the date of service of the notice within which the association may make observations on the proposed appointment.

(3) Where, at the time when a notice is served under subsection (1) by a recognised tenants' association, the landlord employs a managing agent for any relevant premises, the landlord shall, within the period of one month beginning with the date of service of that notice serve on the association a notice specifying—

    (a) the landlord's obligations to the tenants represented by the association which the managing agent is required to discharge on his behalf; and

    (b) a reasonable period within which the association may make observations on the manner in which the managing agent has been discharging those obligations, and on the desirability of his continuing to discharge them.

(4) Subject to subsection (5), a landlord who has been served with a notice by an association under subsection (1) shall, so long as he employs a managing agent for any relevant premises—

    (a) serve on that association at least once in every five years a notice specifying—

        (i) any change occurring since the date of the last notice served by him on the association under this section in the obligations which the managing agent has been required to discharge on his behalf; and

        (ii) a reasonable period within which the association may make observations on the manner in which the managing agent has discharged those obligations since that date, and on the desirability of his continuing to discharge them;

   (b)   serve on that association, whenever he proposes to appoint a new managing agent for any relevant premises, a notice specifying the matters mentioned in paragraphs (a) to (c) of subsection (2).

(5) A landlord shall not, by virtue of a notice served by an association under subsection (1), be required to serve on the association a notice under subsection (4)(a) or (b) if the association subsequently serves on the landlord a notice withdrawing its request under subsection (1) to be consulted by him.

(6) Where—

   (a)   a recognised tenants' association has served a notice under subsection (1) with respect to any relevant premises, and
   (b)   the interest of the landlord in those premises becomes vested in a new landlord,

that notice shall cease to have effect with respect to those premises (without prejudice to the service by the association on the new landlord of a fresh notice under that subsection with respect to those premises).

(7) Any notice served by a landlord under this section shall specify the name and the address in the United Kingdom of the person to whom any observations made in pursuance of the notice are to be sent; and the landlord shall have regard to any such observations that are received by that person within the period specified in the notice.

(8) In this section—

     'landlord', in relation to a recognised tenants' association, means the immediate landlord of the tenants represented by the association or a person who has a right to enforce payment of service charges payable by any of those tenants;
     'managing agent', in relation to any relevant premises, means an agent of the landlord appointed to discharge any of the landlord's obligations to the tenants represented by the recognised tenants' association in question which relate to the management by him of those premises; and
     'tenant' includes a statutory tenant;

and for the purposes of this section any premises (whether a building or not) are relevant premises in relation to a recognised tenants' association if any of the tenants represented by the association may be required under the terms of their leases to contribute by the payment of service charges to costs relating to those premises.

31   Reserve power to limit rents

(1) The Secretary of State may by order provide for—

   (a)   restricting or preventing increases of rent for dwellings which would otherwise take place, or
   (b)   restricting the amount of rent which would otherwise be payable on new lettings of dwellings;

and may so provide either generally or in relation to any specified description of dwelling.

(2) An order may contain supplementary or incidental provisions, including provisions excluding, adapting or modifying any provision made by or under an enactment (whenever passed) relating to rent or the recovery of overpaid rent.

(3) In this section—

'new letting' includes any grant of a tenancy, whether or not the premises were previously let, and any grant of a licence;

'rent' includes a sum payable under a licence, but does not include a sum attributable to rates or council tax or, in the case of dwellings of local authorities, National Park authorities or new town corporations, to the use of furniture, or the provision of services;

and for the purposes of this section an increase in rent takes place at the beginning of the rental period for which the increased rent is payable.

(4) An order under this section shall be made by statutory instrument which shall be subject to annulment in pursuance of a resolution of either House of Parliament.

Supplementary provisions

31A   *Jurisdiction of leasehold valuation tribunal*

(1) The jurisdiction conferred by this Act on a leasehold valuation tribunal is exercisable by a rent assessment committee constituted in accordance with Schedule 10 to the Rent Act 1977 which when so constituted for the purposes of exercising any such jurisdiction shall be known as a leasehold valuation tribunal.

(2) The power to make regulations under section 74(1)(b) of the Rent Act 1977 (procedure of rent assessment committees) extends to prescribing the procedure to be followed in connection with any proceedings before a leasehold valuation tribunal under this Act.

(3) Such regulations may, in particular, make provision—

(a)   *for securing consistency where numerous applications under this Act are or may be brought in respect of the same or substantially the same matters; and*

(b)   *empowering a leasehold valuation tribunal to dismiss an application, in whole or in part, on the ground that it is frivolous or vexatious or otherwise an abuse of the process of the tribunal.*

(4) No costs incurred by a party in connection with proceedings under this Act before a leasehold valuation tribunal shall be recoverable by order of any court.

(5) Paragraphs 2, 3 and 7 of Schedule 22 to the Housing Act 1980 (supplementary provisions relating to leasehold valuation tribunals: appeals and provision of information) apply to a leasehold valuation tribunal constituted for the purposes of this section.

(6) No appeal shall lie to the Lands Tribunal from a decision of a leasehold valuation tribunal under this Act without the leave of the leasehold valuation tribunal concerned or the Lands Tribunal.

(7) On any such appeal—

(a)   *the Lands Tribunal may exercise any power available to the leasehold valuation tribunal in relation to the original matter, and*

(b)   *an order of the Lands Tribunal may be enforced in the same way as an order of the leasehold valuation tribunal.*

31B   *Leasehold valuation tribunal: applications and fees*

(1) The Secretary of State may make provision by order as to the form of, or the particulars to be contained in, an application made to a leasehold valuation tribunal under this Act.

(2) The Secretary of State may make provision by order—

  (a)   *requiring the payment of fees in respect of any such application, or in respect of any proceedings before, a leasehold valuation tribunal under this Act; and*

  (b)   *empowering a leasehold valuation tribunal to require a party to proceedings before it to reimburse any other party the whole or part of any fees paid by him.*

(3) The fees payable shall be such as may be specified in or determined in accordance with the order subject to this limit, that the fees payable in respect of any one application or reference by the court together with any proceedings before the tribunal arising out of that application or reference shall not exceed £500 or such other amount as may be specified by order of the Secretary of State.

(4) An order under this section may make different provision for different cases or classes of case or for different areas.

(5) An order may in particular—

  (a)   *make different provision in relation to proceedings transferred to the tribunal from that applicable where an application was made to the tribunal, and*

  (b)   *provide for the reduction or waiver of fees by reference to the financial resources of the party by whom they are to be paid or met.*

(6) In the latter case the order may apply, subject to such modifications as may be specified in the order, any other statutory means-testing regime as it has effect from time to time.

(7) An order under this section shall be made by statutory instrument.

(8) No order altering the limit under subsection (3) shall be made unless a draft of the order has been laid before and approved by a resolution of each House of Parliament.

(9) Any other order under this section, unless it contains only such provision as is mentioned in subsection (1), shall be subject to annulment in pursuance of a resolution of either House of Parliament.

31C   Transfer of cases from county court

(1) Where in any proceedings before a court there falls for determination a question falling within the jurisdiction of a leasehold valuation tribunal under this Act, the court—

  (a)   *may by order transfer to such a tribunal so much of the proceedings as relate to the determination of that question, and*

  (b)   *may then dispose of all or any remaining proceedings, or adjourn the disposal of all or any of such proceedings, pending the determination of that question by the tribunal, as it thinks fit.*

(2) When the tribunal has determined the question, the court may give effect to the determination in an order of the court.

(3) Any such order shall be treated as a determination by the court for the purposes of section 81 of the Housing Act 1996 (restriction on termination of tenancy for failure to pay service charge).

(4) Rules of court may prescribe the procedure to be followed in the court in connection with or in consequence of a transfer under this section.

32   Provisions not applying to tenancies within Part II of the Landlord and Tenant Act 1954

(1)   The following provisions do not apply to a tenancy to which Part II of the Landlord and Tenant Act 1954 (business tenancies) applies—

> sections 1 to 3A (information to be given to tenant),
> section 17 (specific performance of landlord's repairing obligations).

(2)   Section 11 (repairing obligations) does not apply to a new lease granted to an existing tenant, or to a former tenant still in possession, if the new lease is a tenancy to which Part II of the Landlord and Tenant Act 1954 applies and the previous lease either is such a tenancy or would be but for section 28 of that Act (tenancy not within Part II if renewal agreed between the parties).

In this subsection 'existing tenant', 'former tenant still in possession' and 'previous lease' have the same meaning as in section 14(2).

(3)   Section 31 (reserve power to limit rents) does not apply to a dwelling forming part of a property subject to a tenancy to which Part II of the Landlord and Tenant Act 1954 applies; but without prejudice to the application of that section in relation to a sub-tenancy of a part of the premises comprised in such a tenancy.

33   Liability of directors, etc for offences by body corporate

(1)   Where an offence under this Act which has been committed by a body corporate is proved—

  (a)   to have been committed with the consent or connivance of a director, manager, secretary or other similar officer of the body corporate, or a person purporting to act in any such capacity, or
  (b)   to be attributable to any neglect on the part of such an officer or person,

he, as well as the body corporate, is guilty of an offence and liable to be proceeded against and punished accordingly.

(2)   Where the affairs of a body corporate are managed by its members, subsection (1) applies in relation to the acts and defaults of a member in connection with his functions of management as if he were a director of the body corporate.

. . .

36   Meaning of 'lease' and 'tenancy' and related expressions

(1)   In this Act 'lease' and 'tenancy' have the same meaning.

(2)   Both expressions include—

  (a)   a sub-lease or sub-tenancy, and
  (b)   an agreement for a lease or tenancy (or sub-lease or sub-tenancy).

(3)   The expressions 'lessor' and 'lessee' and 'landlord' and 'tenant', and references to letting, to the grant of a lease or to covenants or terms, shall be construed accordingly.

37   Meaning of 'statutory tenant' and related expressions

In this Act—

(a) 'statutory tenancy' and 'statutory tenant' mean a statutory tenancy or statutory tenant within the meaning of the Rent Act 1977 or the Rent (Agriculture) Act 1976; and

(b) 'landlord', in relation to a statutory tenant, means the person who, apart from the statutory tenancy, would be entitled to possession of the premises.

38   Minor definitions

In this Act—

'address' means a person's place of abode or place of business or, in the case of a company, its registered office;

'arbitration agreement', 'arbitration proceedings' and 'arbitral tribunal' have the same meaning as in Part I of the Arbitration Act 1996 [and 'post-dispute arbitration agreement', in relation to any matter, means an arbitration agreement made after a dispute about the matter has arisen];

'co-operative housing association' has the same meaning as in the Housing Associations Act 1985;

'dwelling' means a building or part of a building occupied or intended to be occupied as a separate dwelling, together with any yard, garden, outhouses and appurtenances belonging to it or usually enjoyed with it;

'housing association' has the same meaning as in the Housing Associations Act 1985;

'local authority' means a district, county, county borough or London borough council, the Common Council of the City of London or the Council of the Isles of Scilly and in sections 14(4), 26(1) and 28(6) includes ... the Broads Authority, a police authority established under section 3 of the Police Act 1996, the Metropolitan Police Authority, a joint authority established by Part IV of the Local Government Act 1985 and the London Fire and Emergency Planning Authority;

'local housing authority' has the meaning given by section 1 of the Housing Act 1985;

'new town corporation' means—

(a) a development corporation established by an order made, or treated as made, under the New Towns Act 1981, or

(b) the Commission for the New Towns;

'protected tenancy' has the same meaning as in the Rent Act 1977;

'registered social landlord' has the same meaning as in the Housing Act 1985 (see section 5(4) and (5) of that Act);

'restricted contract' has the same meanng as in the Rent Act 1977;

'urban development corporation' has the same meaning as in Part XVI of the Local Government, Planning and Land Act 1980.

39   Index of defined expressions

The following Table shows provisions defining or otherwise explaining expressions used in this Act (other than provisions defining or explaining an expression in the same section):

address	section 38
arbitration agreement, arbitration proceedings *and arbitral tribunal* [, arbitral tribunal and post-dispute arbitration agreement]	section 38
co-operative housing association	section 38
dwelling	section 38
dwelling-house (in the provisions relating to repairing obligations)	section 16
fit for human habitation	section 10
flat (in the provisions relating to service charges)	*section 30*
housing association	section 38
landlord—	
(generally)	section 36(3)
(in sections 1 and 2)	section 1(3)
(in the provisions relating to rent books)	section 4(3)
(in the provisions relating to service charges)	section 30
(in relation to a statutory tenancy)	section 37(b)
lease, lessee and lessor—	
(generally)	section 36
(in the provisions relating to repairing obligations)	section 16
local authority	section 38
local housing authority	section 38
new town corporation	section 38
protected tenancy	section 38
qualified accountant (for the purposes of section *21(6)* [21(3)(a)]	section 28
registered social landlord	section 38
recognised tenants' association	section 29
relevant costs (in relation to a service charge)	section 18(2)
restricted contract	section 38
service charge	section 18(1)
statutory tenant	section 37(a)
tenancy and tenant—	
(generally)	section 36
(in sections 1 and 2)	section 1(3)
(in the provisions relating to rent books)	section 4(3)
(in the provisions relating to service charges)	section 30
urban development corporation	section 38

40 Short title, commencement and extent

(1) This Act may be cited as the Landlord and Tenant Act 1985.

(2) This Act comes into force on 1st April 1986.

(3) This Act extends to England and Wales.

SCHEDULE

Rights of tenants with respect to insurance   **Section 30A**

Construction

1 In this Schedule—

'landlord', in relation to a tenant by whom a service charge is payable which includes an amount payable directly or indirectly for insurance, includes any person who has a right to enforce payment of that service charge;

'relevant policy', in relation to a dwelling, means any policy of insurance under which the dwelling is insured (being, in the case of a flat, a policy covering the building containing it); and

'tenant' includes a statutory tenant.

Request for summary of insurance cover

2(1) Where a service charge is payable by the tenant of a dwelling which consists of or includes an amount payable directly or indirectly for insurance, the tenant may *require the landlord in writing* [by notice in writing require the landlord] to supply by him with a written summary of the insurance for the time being effected in relation to the dwelling.

(2) If the tenant is represented by a recognised tenants' association and he consents, the *request may be made* [notice may be served] by the secretary of the association instead of by the tenant and may then be for the supply of the summary to the secretary.

(3) A *request is duly* [notice under this paragraph is duly] served on the landlord if it is served on—

   (a)   an agent of the landlord named as such in the rent book or similar document, or
   (b)   the person who receives the rent on behalf of the landlord;

and a person on *whom a request* [whom such a notice] is so served shall forward it as soon as may be to the landlord.

(4) The landlord shall, within *one month of the request* [the period of twenty-one days beginning with the day on which he receives the notice], comply with it by supplying to the tenant or the secretary of the recognised tenants' association (as the case may require) such a summary as is mentioned in sub-paragraph (1), which shall include—

   (a)   the insured amount or amounts under any relevant policy, and
   (b)   the name of the insurer under any such policy, and
   (c)   the risks in respect of which the dwelling or (as the case may be) the building containing it is insured under any such policy.

(5) In sub-paragraph (4)(a) 'the insured amount or amounts', in relation to a relevant policy, means—

   (a)   in the case of a dwelling other than a flat, the amount for which the dwelling is insured under the policy; and
   (b)   in the case of a flat, the amount for which the building containing it is insured under the policy and, if specified in the policy, the amount for which the flat is insured under it.

(6) The landlord shall be taken to have complied with the *request* [notice] if, within the period mentioned in sub-paragraph (4), he instead supplies to the tenant or the secretary (as the case may require) a copy of every relevant policy.

(7) In a case where two or more buildings are insured under any relevant policy, the summary or copy supplied under sub-paragraph (4) or (6) so far as relating to that policy need only be of such parts of the policy as relate—

   (a)   to the dwelling, and

(b)   if the dwelling is a flat, to the building containing it.

Request to inspect insurance policy, etc

3(1) This paragraph applies where a tenant, or the secretary of a recognised tenants' association, has obtained either—

(a)   *such a summary as is referred to in paragraph 2(1), or*
(b)   *a copy of any relevant policy or of any such parts of any relevant policy as relate to the premises referred to in paragraph 2(7)(a) or (b),*

whether in pursuance of paragraph 2 or otherwise.

(2) The tenant, or the secretary with the consent of the tenant, may within six months of obtaining any such summary or copy as is mentioned in sub-paragraph (1)(a) or (b) require the landlord in writing to afford him reasonable facilities—

(a)   *for inspecting any relevant policy,*
(b)   *for inspecting any accounts, receipts or other documents which provide evidence of payment of any premiums due under any such policy in respect of the period of insurance which is current when the request is made and the period of insurance immediately preceding that period, and*
(c)   *for taking copies of or extracts from any of the documents referred to in paragraphs (a) and (b).*

(3) Any reference in this paragraph to a relevant policy includes a reference to a policy of insurance under which the dwelling in question was insured for the period of insurance immediately preceding that current when the request is made under this paragraph (being, in the case of a flat, a policy covering the building containing it).

(4) Subsections (3) to (6) of section 22 shall have effect in relation to a request made under this paragraph as they have effect in relation to a request made under that section.

[Inspection of insurance policy, etc

3(1) Where a service charge is payable by the tenant of a dwelling which consists of or includes an amount payable directly or indirectly for insurance, the tenant may by notice in writing require the landlord—

(a)   to afford him reasonable facilities for inspecting any relevant policy or associated documents and for taking copies of or extracts from them, or
(b)   to take copies of or extracts from any such policy or documents and either send them to him or afford him reasonable facilities for collecting them (as he specifies).

(2) If the tenant is represented by a recognised tenants' association and he consents, the notice may be served by the secretary of the association instead of by the tenant (and in that case any requirement imposed by it is to afford reasonable facilities, or to send copies or extracts, to the secretary).

(3) A notice under this paragraph is duly served on the landlord if it is served on—

(a)   an agent of the landlord named as such in the rent book or similar document, or
(b)   the person who receives the rent on behalf of the landlord;

and a person on whom such a notice is so served shall forward it as soon as may be to the landlord.

(4) The landlord shall comply with a requirement imposed by a notice under this paragraph within the period of twenty-one days beginning with the day on which he receives the notice.

(5) To the extent that a notice under this paragraph requires the landlord to afford facilities for inspecting documents—

(a) he shall do so free of charge, but
(b) he may treat as part of his costs of management any costs incurred by him in doing so.

(6) The landlord may make a reasonable charge for doing anything else in compliance with a requirement imposed by a notice under this paragraph.

(7) In this paragraph—

'relevant policy' includes a policy of insurance under which the dwelling was insured for the period of insurance immediately preceding that current when the notice is served (being, in the case of a flat, a policy covering the building containing it), and
'associated documents' means accounts, receipts or other documents which provide evidence of payment of any premiums due under a relevant policy in respect of the period of insurance which is current when the notice is served or the period of insurance immediately preceding that period.]

Request relating to insurance effected by superior landlord

4(1) If *a request is made* [a notice is served] under paragraph 2 in a case where a superior landlord has effected, in whole or in part, the insurance of the dwelling in question and the landlord *to whom the request is made* [on whom the notice is served] is not in possession of the relevant information—

(a) he shall in turn *make a written request for the relevant information to the person who is his landlord* [by notice in writing require the person who is his landlord to give him the relevant information] (and so on, if that person is not himself the superior landlord),
(b) the superior landlord shall comply with *that request* [the notice] within a reasonable time, and
(c) the immediate landlord shall then comply with the tenant's or secretary's *request* [notice] in the manner provided by sub-paragraphs (4) to (7) of paragraph 2 within the time allowed by that paragraph or such further time, if any, as is reasonable in the circumstances.

(2) If, in a case where a superior landlord has effected, in whole or in part, the insurance of the dwelling in question, a *request under paragraph 3 relates* [notice under paragraph 3 imposes a requirement relating] to any policy of insurance effected by the superior landlord—

(a) the landlord *to whom the request is made* [on whom the notice is served] shall forthwith inform the tenant or secretary of that fact and of the name and address of the superior landlord, and
(b) that paragraph shall then apply to the superior landlord in relation to that policy as it applies to the immediate landlord.

[Effect of change of landlord

4A(1) This paragraph applies where, at a time when a duty imposed on the landlord or a superior landlord by virtue of any of paragraphs 2 to 4 remains to be discharged by him, he disposes of the whole or part of his interest as landlord or superior landlord).

(2) If the landlord or superior landlord is, despite the disposal, still in a position to discharge the duty to any extent, he remains responsible for discharging it to that extent.

(3) If the other person is in a position to discharge the duty to any extent, he is responsible for discharging it to that extent.

(4) Where the other person is responsible for discharging the duty to any extent (whether or not the landlord or superior landlord is also responsible for discharging it to that or any other extent)—

    (a) references to the landlord or superior landlord in paragraphs 2 to 4 are to, or include, the other person so far as is appropriate to reflect his responsibility for discharging the duty to that extent, but

    (b) in connection with its discharge by that person, paragraphs 2(4) and 3(4) apply as if the reference to the day on which the landlord receives the notice were to the date of the disposal referred to in sub-paragraph (1).]

Effect of assignment *on request*

5 The assignment of a tenancy does not affect *the validity of a request made under paragraph 2, 3 or 4 before the assignment; but a person is not obliged to provide a summary or make facilities available more than once for the same dwelling and for the same period* [any duty imposed by virtue of any of paragraphs 2 to 4A; but a person is not required to comply with more than a reasonable number of requirements imposed by any one person].

Failure to comply with paragraph 2, 3 or 4 an offence [Offence of failure to comply]

6(1) It is a summary offence for a person to fail, without reasonable excuse, to perform a duty imposed on him by or by virtue of *paragraph 2, 3 or 4* [any of paragraphs 2 to 4A].

(2) A person committing such an offence is liable on conviction to a fine not exceeding level 4 on the standard scale.

Tenant's right to notify insurers of possible claim

7(1) This paragraph applies to any dwelling in respect of which the tenant pays to the landlord a service charge consisting of or including an amount payable directly or indirectly for insurance.

(2) Where—

    (a) it appears to the tenant of any such dwelling that damage has been caused—
        (i)   to the dwelling, or
        (ii) if the dwelling is a flat, to the dwelling or to any other part of the building containing it,
    in respect of which a claim could be made under the terms of a policy of insurance, and

    (b) it is a term of that policy that the person insured under the policy should give notice of any claim under it to the insurer within a specified period, the tenant may, within that specified period, serve on the insurer a notice in writing stating that it appears to him that damage has been caused as mentioned in paragraph (a) and describing briefly the nature of the damage.

(3) Where—

(a) any such notice is served on an insurer by a tenant in relation to any such damage, and

(b) the specified period referred to in sub-paragraph (2)(b) would expire earlier than the period of six months beginning with the date on which the notice is served,

the policy in question shall have effect as regards any claim subsequently made in respect of that damage by the person insured under the policy as if for the specified period there were substituted that period of six months.

(4) Where the tenancy of a dwelling to which this paragraph applies is held by joint tenants, a single notice under this paragraph may be given by any one or more of those tenants.

(5) The Secretary of State may by regulations prescribe the form of notices under this paragraph and the particulars which such notices must contain.

(6) Any such regulations—

(a) may make different provision with respect to different cases of descriptions of case, including different provision for different areas, and

(b) shall be made by statutory instrument.

Right to challenge landlord's choice of insurers

8(1) This paragraph applies where a tenancy of a dwelling requires the tenant to insure the dwelling with an insurer nominated [or approved] by the landlord.

(2) The tenant or landlord may apply to a county court or leasehold valuation tribunal for a determination whether—

(a) the insurance which is available from the nominated [or approved] insurer for insuring the tenant's dwelling is unsatisfactory in any respect, or

(b) the premiums payable in respect of any such insurance are excessive.

(3) No such application may be made in respect of a matter which—

(a) has been agreed or admitted by the tenant,

(b) under an arbitration agreement to which the tenant is a party is to be referred to arbitration, or

(c) has been the subject of determination by a court or arbitral tribunal.

(4) On an application under this paragraph the court or tribunal may make—

(a) an order requiring the landlord to nominate [or approve] such other insurer as is specified in the order, or

(b) an order requiring him to nominate [or approve] another insurer who satisfies such requirements in relation to the insurance of the dwelling as are specified in the order.

(5) Any such order of a leasehold valuation tribunal may, with the leave of the court, be enforced in the same way as an order of a county court to the same effect.

(6) An agreement by the tenant of a dwelling (other than an arbitration agreement) is void in so far as it purports to provide for a determination in a particular manner, or on particular evidence, of any question which may be the subject of an application under this paragraph.

Exception for tenants of certain public authorities

9(1) Paragraphs 2 to 8 do not apply to a tenant of—
a local authority,
a National Park authority, or
a new town corporation;

unless the tenancy is a long tenancy, in which case paragraphs 2 to 5 and 7 and 8 apply but paragraph 6 does not.

(2) Subsections (2) and (3) of section 26 shall apply for the purposes of sub-paragraph (1) as they apply for the purposes of subsection (1) of that section.

LANDLORD AND TENANT ACT 1987

PART IV – VARIATION OF LEASE

Applications relating to flats

35   Application by party to lease for variation of lease

(1) Any party to a long lease of a flat may make an application to *the court* [a leasehold valuation tribunal] for an order varying the lease in such manner as is specified in the application.

(2) The grounds on which any such application may be made are that the lease fails to make satisfactory provision with respect to one or more of the following matters, namely—

   (a)   the repair or maintenance of—
      (i)   the flat in question, or
      (ii)   the building containing the flat, or
      (iii) any land or building which is let to the tenant under the lease or in respect of which rights are conferred on him under it;
   (b)   the insurance of the flat or of any such building or land as is mentioned in paragraph (a)(ii) or (iii);
   [(b)   the insurance of the building containing the flat or of any such land or building as is mentioned in paragraph (a)(iii);]
   (c)   the repair or maintenance of any installations (whether they are in the same building as the flat or not) which are reasonably necessary to ensure that occupiers of the flat enjoy a reasonable standard of accommodation;
   (d)   the provision or maintenance of any services which are reasonably necessary to ensure that occupiers of the flat enjoy a reasonable standard of accommodation (whether they are services connected with any such installations or not, and whether they are services provided for the benefit of those occupiers or services provided for the benefit of the occupiers of a number of flats including that flat);
   (e)   the recovery by one party to the lease from another party to it of expenditure incurred or to be incurred by him, or on his behalf, for the benefit of that other party or of a number of persons who include that other party;
   (f)   the computation of a service charge payable under the lease.
   [(g)   such other matters as may be prescribed by regulations made by the Secretary of State].

(3) For the purposes of subsection (2)(c) and (d) the factors for determining, in relation to the occupiers of a flat, what is a reasonable standard of accommodation may include—

   (a)   factors relating to the safety and security of the flat and its occupiers and of any common parts of the building containing the flat; and
   (b)   other factors relating to the condition of any such common parts.

[(3A) For the purposes of subsection (2)(e) the factors for determining, in relation to a service charge payable under a lease, whether the lease makes satisfactory provision include whether it makes provision for an amount to be payable (by way of interest or otherwise) in respect of a failure to pay the service charge by the due date.]

(4) For the purposes of subsection (2)(f) a lease fails to make satisfactory provision with respect to the computation of a service charge payable under it if—

(a) it provides for any such charge to be a proportion of expenditure incurred, or to be incurred, by or on behalf of the landlord or a superior landlord; and

(b) other tenants of the landlord are also liable under their leases to pay by way of service charges proportions of any such expenditure; and

(c) the aggregate of the amounts that would, in any particular case, be payable by reference to the proportions referred to in paragraphs (a) and (b) would either exceed or be less than the whole of any such expenditure.

(5) *Rules of court* [Procedure regulations under Schedule 12 to the Commonhold and Leasehold Reform Act 2002] shall make provision—

(a) for requiring notice of any application under this Part to be served by the person making the application, and by any respondent to the application, on any person who the applicant, or (as the case may be) the respondent, knows or has reason to believe is likely to be affected by any variation specified in the application, and

(b) for enabling persons served with any such notice to be joined as parties to the proceedings.

(6) For the purposes of this Part a long lease shall not be regarded as a long lease of a flat if—

(a) the demised premises consist of or include three or more flats contained in the same building; or

(b) the lease constitutes a tenancy to which Part II of the Landlord and Tenant Act 1954 applies.

(8) In this section 'service charge' has the meaning given by section 18(1) of the 1985 Act.

36 Application by respondent for variation of other leases

(1) Where an application ('the original application') is made under section 35 by any party to a lease, any other party to the lease may make an application to the *court* [tribunal] asking it, in the event of its deciding to make an order effecting any variation of the lease in pursuance of the original application, to make an order which effects a corresponding variation of each of such one or more other leases as are specified in the application.

(2) Any lease so specified—

(a) must be a long lease of a flat under which the landlord is the same person as the landlord under the lease specified in the original application; but

(b) need not be a lease of a flat which is in the same building as the flat let under that lease, nor a lease drafted in terms identical to those of that lease.

(3) The grounds on which an application may be made under this section are—

(a) that each of the leases specified in the application fails to make satisfactory provision with respect to the matter or matters specified in the original application; and

(b) that, if any variation is effected in pursuance of the original application, it would be in the interests of the person making the application under this section, or in the interests of the other persons who are parties to the leases specified in that application, to have all of the leases in question (that is to say, the ones specified in that application together with the one specified in the original application) varied to the same effect.

37 Application by majority of parties for variation of leases

(1) Subject to the following provisions of this section, an application may be made to *the court* [a leasehold valuation tribunal] in respect of two or more leases for an order varying each of those leases in such manner as is specified in the application.

(2) Those leases must be long leases of flats under which the landlord is the same person, but they need not be leases of flats which are in the same building, nor leases which are drafted in identical terms.

(3) The grounds on which an application may be made under this section are that the object to be achieved by the variation cannot be satisfactorily achieved unless all the leases are varied to the same effect.

(4) An application under this section in respect of any leases may be made by the landlord or any of the tenants under the leases.

(5) Any such application shall only be made if—

(a) in a case where the application is in respect of less than nine leases, or all but one, of the parties concerned consent to it; or
(b) in a case where the application is in respect of more than eight leases, it is not opposed for any reason by more than 10 per cent of the total number of the parties concerned and at least 75 per cent of that number consent to it.

(6) For the purposes of subsection (5)—

(a) in the case of each lease in respect of which the application is made, the tenant under the lease shall constitute one of the parties concerned (so that in determining the total number of the parties concerned a person who is the tenant under a number of such leases shall be regarded as constituting a corresponding number of the parties concerned); and
(b) the landlord shall also constitute one of the parties concerned.

Orders varying leases

38 Orders *by the court* varying leases

(1) If, on an application under section 35, the grounds on which the application was made are established to the satisfaction of the *court* [tribunal], the *court* [tribunal] may (subject to subsections (6) and (7)) make an order varying the lease specified in the application in such manner as is specified in the order.

(2) If—

(a) an application under section 36 was made in connection with that application, and
(b) the grounds set out in subsection (3) of that section are established to the satisfaction of the *court* [tribunal] with respect to the leases specified in the application under section 36,

the *court* [tribunal] may (subject to subsections (6) and (7)) also make an order varying each of those leases in such manner as is specified in the order.

(3) If, on an application under section 37, the grounds set out in subsection (3) of that section are established to the satisfaction of the *court* [tribunal] with respect to the leases specified in the application, the *court* [tribunal] may (subject to subsections (6) and (7)) make an order varying each of those leases in such manner as is specified in the order.

(4) The variation specified in an order under subsection (1) or (2) may be either the variation specified in the relevant application under section 35 or 36 or such other variation as the *court* [tribunal] thinks fit.

(5) If the grounds referred to in subsection (2) or (3) (as the case may be) are established to the satisfaction of the *court* [tribunal] with respect to some but not all the leases specified in the application, the power to make an order under that subsection shall extend to those leases only.

(6) *The court* [A tribunal] shall not make an order under this section effecting any variation of a lease if it appears to the *court* [tribunal]—

    (a) that the variation would be likely substantially to prejudice—
        (i)   any respondent to the application, or
        (ii)   any person who is not a party to the application,
        and that an award under subsection (10) would not afford him adequate compensation, or
    (b) that for any other reason it would not be reasonable in the circumstances for the variation to be effected.

(7) *The court* [A tribunal] shall not, on an application relating to the provision to be made by a lease with respect to insurance, make an order under this section effecting any variation of the lease—

    (a) which terminates any existing right of the landlord under its terms to nominate an insurer for insurance purposes; or
    (b) which requires the landlord to nominate a number of insurers from which the tenant would be entitled to select an insurer for those purposes; or
    (c) which, in a case where the lease requires the tenant to effect insurance with a specified insurer, requires the tenant to effect insurance otherwise than with another specified insurer.

(8) *The court* [A tribunal] may, instead of making an order varying a lease in such manner as is specified in the order, make an order directing the parties to the lease to vary it in such manner as is so specified; and accordingly any reference in this Part (however expressed) to an order which effects any variation of a lease or to any variation effected by an order shall include a reference to an order which directs the parties to a lease to effect a variation of it or (as the case may be) a reference to any variation effected in pursuance of such an order.

(9) *The court* [A tribunal] may by order direct that a memorandum of any variation of a lease effected by an order under this section shall be endorsed on such documents as are specified in the order.

(10) Where *the court* [a tribunal] makes an order under this section varying a lease the *court* [tribunal] may, if it thinks fit, make an order providing for any party to the lease to pay, to any other party to the lease or to any other person, compensation in respect of any loss or disadvantage that the *court* [tribunal] considers he is likely to suffer as a result of the variation.

39   Effect of orders varying leases: applications by third parties

(1) Any variation effected by an order under section 38 shall be binding not only on the parties to the lease for the time being but also on other persons (including any predecessors in title of those parties), whether or not they were parties to the proceedings in which the order was made or were served with a notice by virtue of section 35(5).

(2) Without prejudice to the generality of subsection (1), any variation effected by any such order shall be binding on any surety who has guaranteed the performance of any obligation varied by the order; and the surety shall accordingly be taken to have guaranteed the performance of that obligation as so varied.

(3) Where any such order has been made and a person was, by virtue of section 35(5), required to be served with a notice relating to the proceedings in which it was made, but he was not so served, he may—

(a)   bring an action for damages for breach of statutory duty against the person by whom any such notice was so required to be served in respect of that person's failure to serve it;

(b)   apply to *the court* [a leasehold valuation tribunal] for the cancellation or modification of the variation in question.

(4) *The court* [A tribunal] may on an application under subsection (3)(b) with respect to any variation of a lease—

(a)   by order cancel that variation or modify it in such manner as is specified in the order, or

(b)   make such an order as is mentioned in section 38(10) in favour of the person making the application,

as it thinks fit.

(5) Where a variation is cancelled or modified under paragraph (a) of subsection (4)—

(a)   the cancellation of modification shall take effect as from the date of the making of the order under that paragraph or as from such later date as may be specified in the order, and

(b)   the *court* [tribunal] may by order direct that a memorandum of the cancellation or modification shall be endorsed on such documents as are specified in the order;

and, in a case where a variation is so modified, subsections (1) and (2) above shall, as from the date when the modification takes effect, apply to the variation as modified.

Applications relating to dwellings other than flats

40   Application for variation of insurance provisions of lease of dwelling other than a flat

(1) Any party to a long lease of a dwelling may make an application to *the court* [a leasehold valuation tribunal] for an order varying the lease, in such manner as is specified in the application, on the grounds that the lease fails to make satisfactory provision with respect to any matter relating to the insurance of the dwelling, including the recovery of the costs of such insurance.

(2) Sections 36 and 38 shall apply to an application under subsection (1) subject to the modifications specified in subsection (3).

(3) Those modifications are as follows—

  (a) in section 36—
     (i) in subsection (1), the reference to section 35 shall be read as a reference to subsection (1) above, and
     (ii) in subsection (2), any reference to a flat shall be read as a reference to a dwelling; and
  (b) in section 38—
     (i) any reference to an application under section 35 shall be read as a reference to an application under subsection (1) above, and
     (ii) any reference to an application under section 36 shall be read as a reference to an application under section 36 as applied by subsection (2) above.

(4) For the purposes of this section, a long lease shall not be regarded as a long lease of a dwelling if—

  (a) the demised premises consist of three or more dwellings; or
  (b) the lease constitutes a tenancy to which Part II of the Landlord and Tenant Act 1954 applies.

(4A) Without prejudice to subsection (4), an application under subsection (1) may not be made by a person who is a tenant under a long lease of a dwelling if, by virtue of that lease and one or more other long leases of dwellings, he is also a tenant from the same landlord of at least two other dwellings.

(4B) For the purposes of subsection (4A), any tenant of a dwelling who is a body corporate shall be treated as a tenant of any other dwelling held from the same landlord which is let under a long lease to an associated company, as defined in section 20(1).

(5) In this section, 'dwelling' means a dwelling other than a flat.

PART V – MANAGEMENT OF LEASEHOLD PROPERTY

Service charges

. . .

42 Service charge contributions to be held in trust

(1) This section applies where the tenants of two or more dwellings may be required under the terms of their leases to contribute to the same costs [or the tenant of a dwelling may be required under the terms of his lease to contribute to costs to which no other tenant of a dwelling may be required to contribute,] by the payment of service charges; and in this section—

  'the contributing tenants' means those tenants [and 'the sole contributing tenant' means that tenant];
  'the payee' means the landlord or other person to whom any such charges are payable by those tenants *under the terms of their leases* [, or that tenant, under the terms of their leases, or his lease];
  'relevant service charges' means any such charges;

'service charge' has the meaning given by section 18(1) of the 1985 Act, except that it does not include a service charge payable by the tenant of a dwelling the rent of which is registered under Part IV of the Rent Act 1977, unless the amount registered is, in pursuance of section 71(4) of that Act, entered as a variable amount;

'tenant' does not include a tenant of an exempt landlord; and

'trust fund' means the fund, or (as the case may be) any of the funds, mentioned in subsection (2) below.

(2) Any sums paid to the payee by the contributing tenants [, or the sole contributing tenant] by way of relevant service charges, *and any investments representing those sums*, shall (together with any income accruing thereon) be held by the payee either as a single fund or, if he thinks fit, in two or more separate funds.

(3) The payee shall hold any trust fund—

(a) on trust to defray costs incurred in connection with the matters for which the relevant service charges were payable (whether incurred by himself or by any other person), and

(b) subject to that, on trust for the persons who are the contributing tenants for the time being [, or the person who is the sole contributing tenant for the time being].

(4) Subject to subsections (6) to (8), the contributing tenants shall be treated as entitled by virtue of subsection (3)(b) to such shares in the residue of any such fund as are proportionate to their respective liabilities to pay relevant service charges [or the sole contributing tenant shall be treated as so entitled to the residue of any such fund].

(5) *If the Secretary of State by order so provides, any sums standing to the credit of any trust fund may, instead of being invested in any other manner authorised by law, be invested in such manner as may be specified in the order; and any such order may contain such incidental, supplemental or transitional provisions as the Secretary of State considers appropriate in connection with the order.*

(6) On the termination of the lease of *a contributing tenant* [any of the contributing tenants] the tenant shall not be entitled to any part of any trust fund, and (except where subsection (7) applies) any part of any such fund which is attributable to relevant service charges paid under the lease shall accordingly continue to be held on the trusts referred to in subsection (3).

(7) *If after the termination of any such lease there are no longer any contributing tenants* [On the termination of the lease of the last of the contributing tenants, or of the lease of the sole contributing tenant], any trust fund shall be dissolved as at the date of the termination of the lease, and any assets comprised in the fund immediately before its dissolution shall—

(a) if the payee is the landlord, be retained by him for his own use and benefit, and

(b) in any other case, be transferred to the landlord by the payee.

(8) Subsections (4), (6) and (7) shall have effect in relation to *a contributing tenant* [any of the contributing tenants, or the sole contributing tenant,] subject to any express terms of his lease [(whenever it was granted)] which relate to the distribution, either before or (as the case may be) at the termination of the lease, of amounts attributable to relevant service charges paid under its terms *(whether the lease was granted before or after the commencement of this section).*

(9) Subject to subsection (8), the provisions of this section shall prevail over the terms of any express or implied trust created by a lease so far as inconsistent with those provisions,

other than an express trust so created [, in the case of a lease of any of the contributing tenants,] before the commencement of this section [or, in the case of the lease of a sole contributing tenant, before the commencement of paragraph 15 of Schedule 10 to the Commonhold and Leasehold Reform Act 2002].

[42A Service charge contributions to be held in designated account

(1) The payee must hold any sums standing to the credit of any trust fund in a designated account at a relevant financial institution.

(2) An account is a designated account in relation to sums standing to the credit of a trust fund if—

(a) the relevant financial institution has been notified in writing that sums standing to the credit of the trust fund are to be (or are) held in it, and
(b) no other funds are held in the account,

and the account is an account of a description specified in regulations made by the Secretary of State.

(3) Any of the contributing tenants, or the sole contributing tenant, may by notice in writing require the payee—

(a) to afford him reasonable facilities for inspecting documents evidencing that subsection (1) is complied with and for taking copies of or extracts from them, or
(b) to take copies of or extracts from any such documents and either send them to him or afford him reasonable facilities for collecting them (as he specifies).

(4) If the tenant is represented by a recognised tenants' association and he consents, the notice may be served by the secretary of the association instead of by the tenant (and in that case any requirement imposed by it is to afford reasonable facilities, or to send copies or extracts, to the secretary).

(5) A notice under this section is duly served on the payee if it is served on—

(a) an agent of the payee named as such in the rent book or similar document, or
(b) the person who receives the rent on behalf of the payee;

and a person on whom such a notice is so served must forward it as soon as may be to the payee.

(6) The payee must comply with a requirement imposed by a notice under this section within the period of twenty-one days beginning with the day on which he receives the notice.

(7) To the extent that a notice under this section requires the payee to afford facilities for inspecting documents—

(a) he must do so free of charge, but
(b) he may treat as part of his costs of management any costs incurred by him in doing so.

(8) The payee may make a reasonable charge for doing anything else in compliance with a requirement imposed by a notice under this section.

(9) Any of the contributing tenants, or the sole contributing tenant, may withhold payment of a service charge if he has reasonable grounds for believing that the payee has failed to comply with the duty imposed on him by subsection (1); and any provisions of his tenancy relating to non-payment or late payment of service charges do not have effect in relation to the period for which he so withholds it.

(10) Nothing in this section applies to the payee if the circumstances are such as are specified in regulations made by the Secretary of State.

(11) In this section—

'recognised tenants' association' has the same meaning as in the 1985 Act, and 'relevant financial institution' has the meaning given by regulations made by the Secretary of State;

and expressions used both in section 42 and this section have the same meaning as in that section.]

[42B Failure to comply with section 42A

(1) If a person fails, without reasonable excuse, to comply with a duty imposed on him by or by virtue of section 42A he commits an offence.

(2) A person guilty of an offence under this section is liable on summary conviction to a fine not exceeding level 4 on the standard scale.

(3) Where an offence under this section committed by a body corporate is proved—

(a) to have been committed with the consent or connivance of a director, manager, secretary or other similar officer of the body corporate, or a person purporting to act in such a capacity, or

(b) to be due to any neglect on the part of such an officer or person,

he, as well as the body corporate, is guilty of the offence and liable to be proceeded against and punished accordingly.

(4) Where the affairs of a body corporate are managed by its members, subsection (3) applies in relation to the acts and defaults of a member in connection with his functions of management as if he were a director of the body corporate.

(5) Proceedings for an offence under this section may be brought by a local housing authority (within the meaning of section 1 of the Housing Act 1985).]

. . .

PART VI – INFORMATION TO BE FURNISHED TO TENANTS

46 Application of Part VI, etc

(1) This Part applies to premises which consist of or include a dwelling and are not held under a tenancy to which Part II of the Landlord and Tenant Act 1954 applies.

(2) In this Part 'service charge' has the meaning given by section 18(1) of the 1985 Act.

[(3) In this Part 'administration charge' has the meaning given by paragraph 1 of Schedule 11 to the Commonhold and Leasehold Reform Act 2002.]

47 Landlord's name and address to be contained in demands for rent, etc

(1) Where any written demand is given to a tenant of premises to which this Part applies, the demand must contain the following information, namely—

(a) the name and address of the Landlord, and
(b) if that address is not in England and Wales, an address in England and Wales at which notices (including notices in proceedings) may be served on the landlord by the tenant.

(2) Where—

(a) a tenant of any such premises is given such a demand, but
(b) it does not contain any information required to be contained in it by virtue of subsection (1),

then (subject to subsection (3)) any part of the amount demanded which consists of a service charge [or an administration charge] ('the relevant amount') shall be treated for all purposes as not being due from the tenant to the landlord at any time before that information is furnished by the landlord by notice given to the tenant.

(3) The relevant amount shall not be so treated in relation to any time when, by virtue of an order of any court [or tribunal], there is in force an appointment of a receiver or manager whose functions include the receiving of service charges [or (as the case may be) administration charges] from the tenant.

(4) In this section 'demand' means a demand for rent or other sums payable to the landlord under the terms of the tenancy.

48 Notification by landlord of address for service of notices

(1) A landlord of premises to which this Part applies shall by notice furnish the tenant with an address in England and Wales at which notices (including notices in proceedings) may be served on him by the tenant.

(2) Where a landlord of any such premises fails to comply with subsection (1), any rent *or service charge* [, service charge or administration charge] otherwise due from the tenant to the landlord shall (subject to subsection (3)) be treated for all purposes as not being due from the tenant to the landlord at any time before the landlord does comply with that subsection.

(3) Any such rent *or service charge* [, service charge or administration charge] shall not be so treated in relation to any time when, by virtue of an order of any court [or tribunal], there is in force an appointment of a receiver or manager whose functions include the receiving of rent *or (as the case may be) service charges* [, service charges or (as the case may be) administration charges] from the tenant.

. . .

53 Regulations and orders

(1) Any power of the Secretary of State to make an order or regulations under this Act shall be exercisable by statutory instrument and may be exercised so as to make different provision for different cases, including different provision for different areas.

(2) A statutory instrument containing—

(a) an order made under section 1(5), 25(6), *42(5)* or 55, or

(b) any regulations made under *section 52A(3)* or under section 20(4) [or 35(2)(g) or 42A],

shall be subject to annulment in pursuance of a resolution of either House of Parliament.

54 Notices

(1) Any notice required or authorised to be served under this Act—

(a) shall be in writing; and

(b) may be sent by post.

(2) Any notice purporting to be a notice served under any provision of Part I or III by the requisite majority of any qualifying tenants (as defined for the purposes of that provision) shall specify the names of all of the persons by whom it is served and the addresses of the flats of which they are qualifying tenants.

(3) The Secretary of State may by regulations prescribe—

(a) the form of any notices required or authorised to be served under or in pursuance of any provision of Parts I to III, and

(b) the particulars which any such notices must contain (whether in addition to, or in substitution for, any particulars required by virtue of the provision in question).

(4) Subsection (3)(b) shall not be construed as authorising the Secretary of State to make regulations under subsection (3) varying any of the periods specified in section 5A(4) or (5), 5B(5) or (6), 5C(4) or (5), 5D(4) or (5) or 5E(3) (which accordingly can only be varied by regulations under section 20(4)).

55 Application to Isles of Scilly

This Act shall apply to the Isles of Scilly subject to such exceptions, adaptations and modifications as the Secretary of State may by order direct.

56 Crown land

(1) *This Act* [Parts 1 and 3 and sections 42 to 42B (and so much of this Part as relates to those provisions)] shall apply to a tenancy from the Crown if there has ceased to be a Crown interest in the land subject to it.

(2) *A variation of any such tenancy effected by or in pursuance of an order under section 38 shall not, however, be treated as binding on the Crown, as a predecessor in title under the tenancy, by virtue of section 39(1).*

(3) Where there exists a Crown interest in any land subject to a tenancy from the Crown and the person holding that tenancy is himself the landlord under any other tenancy whose subject-matter comprises the whole or part of that land, *this Act* [the provisions mentioned in subsection (1)] shall apply to that other tenancy, and to any derivative sub-tenancy, notwithstanding the existence of that interest.

(4) For the purposes of this section 'tenancy from the Crown' means a tenancy of land in which there is, or has during the subsistence of the tenancy been, a Crown interest superior to the tenancy, and 'Crown interest' means—

(a) an interest comprised in the Crown Estate;

(b)   an interest belonging to Her Majesty in right of the Duchy of Lancaster;

(c)   an interest belonging to the Duchy of Cornwall;

(d)   any other interest belonging to a government department or held on behalf of Her Majesty for the purposes of a government department.

57   Financial provision

There shall be paid out of money provided by Parliament any increase attributable to this Act in the sums payable out of money so provided under any other Act.

58   Exempt landlords and resident landlords

(1) In this Act 'exempt landlord' means a landlord who is one of the following bodies, namely—

(a)   a district, county, county borough or London borough council, the Common Council of the City of London, the London Fire and Emergency Planning Authority, the Council of the Isles of Scilly, a police authority established under section 3 of the Police Act 1996, or a joint authority established by Part IV of the Local Government Act 1985;

(b)   the Commission for the New Towns or a development corporation established by an order made (or having effect as if made) under the New Towns Act 1981;

(c)   an urban development corporation within the meaning of Part XVI of the Local Government, Planning and Land Act 1980;

(ca) a housing action trust established under Part III of the Housing Act 1988;

(dd) the Broads Authority;

(de) a National Park authority;

(e)   the Housing Corporation;

(f)   a housing trust (as defined in section 6 of the Housing Act 1985) which is a charity;

(g)   a registered social landlord, or a fully mutual housing association which is not a registered social landlord; or

(h)   an authority established under section 10 of the Local Government Act 1985 (joint arrangements for waste disposal functions).

(1A) In subsection (1)(g)—

'fully mutual housing association' has the same meaning as in the Housing Associations Act 1985 (see section 1(1) and (2) of that Act); and

'registered social landlord' has the same meaning as in the Housing Act 1985 (see section 5(4) and (5) of that Act).

(2) For the purposes of this Act the landlord of any premises consisting of the whole or part of a building is a resident landlord of those premises at any time if—

(a)   the premises are not, and do not form part of, a purpose-built block of flats; and

(b)   at that time the landlord occupies a flat contained in the premises as his only or principal residence; and

(c)   he has so occupied such a flat throughout a period of not less than 12 months ending with that time.

(3) In subsection (2) 'purpose-built block of flats' means a building which contained as constructed, and contains, two or more flats.

59 Meaning of 'lease', 'long lease' and related expressions

(1) In this Act 'lease' and 'tenancy' have the same meaning; and both expressions include—

  (a) a sub-lease or sub-tenancy, and
  (b) an agreement for a lease or tenancy (or for a sub-lease or sub-tenancy).

(2) The expressions 'landlord' and 'tenant', and references to letting, to the grant of a lease or to covenants or the terms of a lease shall be construed accordingly.

(3) In this Act 'long lease' means—

  (a) a lease granted for a term certain exceeding 21 years, whether or not it is (or may become) terminable before the end of that by notice given by the tenant or by re-entry or forfeiture;
  (b) a lease for a term fixed by law under a grant with a covenant or obligation for perpetual renewal, other than a lease by sub-demise from one which is not a long lease; or
  (c) a lease granted in pursuance of Part V of the Housing Act 1985 (the right to buy), including a lease granted in pursuance of that Part as it has effect by virtue of section 17 of the Housing Act 1996 (the right to acquire).

60 General interpretation

(1) In this Act—

  'the 1985 Act' means the Landlord and Tenant Act 1985;
  'charity' means a charity within the meaning of the Charities Act 1993, and 'charitable purposes', in relation to a charity, means charitable purposes whether of that charity or of that charity and other charities;
  'common parts', in relation to any building or part of a building, includes the structure and exterior of that building or part and any common facilities within it;
  'the court' means the High Court or a county court;
  'dwelling' means a building or part of a building occupied or intended to be occupied as a separate dwelling, together with any yard, garden, outhouses and appurtenances belonging to it or usually enjoyed with it;
  'exempt landlord' has the meaning given by section 58(1);
  'flat' means a separate set of premises, whether or not on the same floor, which—

    (a) forms part of a building, and
    (b) is divided horizontally from some other part of that building, and
    (c) is constructed or adapted for use for the purposes of a dwelling;

  'functional land', in relation to a charity, means land occupied by the charity, or by trustees for it, and wholly or mainly used for charitable purposes;
  'landlord' (except for the purposes of Part I) means the immediate landlord or, in relation to a statutory tenant, the person who, apart from the statutory tenancy, would be entitled to possession of the premises subject to the tenancy;
  'lease' and related expressions shall be construed in accordance with section 59(1) and (2);
  'long lease' has the meaning given by section 59(3);
  'mortgage' includes any charge or lien, and references to a mortgagee shall be construed accordingly;

'notices in proceedings' means notices or other documents served in, or in connection with, any legal proceedings;

'resident landlord' shall be construed in accordance with section 58(2);

'statutory tenancy' and 'statutory tenant' mean a statutory tenancy or statutory tenant within the meaning of the Rent Act 1977 or the Rent (Agriculture) Act 1976;

'tenancy' includes a statutory tenancy.

LEASEHOLD REFORM, HOUSING AND URBAN DEVELOPMENT ACT 1993

CHAPTER V – TENANTS' RIGHT TO MANAGEMENT AUDIT

76   Right to audit management by landlord

(1) This Chapter has effect to confer on two or more qualifying tenants of dwellings held on leases from the same landlord the right, exercisable subject to and in accordance with this Chapter, to have an audit carried out on their behalf which relates to the management of the relevant premises and any appurtenant property by or on behalf of the landlord.

(2) That right shall be exercisable—

  (a)   where the relevant premises consist of or include two dwellings let to qualifying tenants of the same landlord, by either or both of those tenants; and
  (b)   where the relevant premises consist of or include three or more dwellings let to qualifying tenants of the same landlord, by not less than two-thirds of those tenants;

and in this Chapter the dwellings let to those qualifying tenants are referred to as 'the constituent dwellings'.

(3) In relation to an audit on behalf of two or more qualifying tenants—

  (a)   'the relevant premises' means so much of—
    (i)   the building or buildings containing the dwellings let to those tenants, and
    (ii) any other building or buildings,
    as constitutes premises in relation to which management functions are discharged in respect of the costs of which common service charge contributions are payable under the leases of those qualifying tenants; and
  (b)   'appurtenant property' means so much of any property not contained in the relevant premises as constitutes property in relation to which any such management functions are discharged.

(4) This Chapter also has effect to confer on a single qualifying tenant of a dwelling the right, exercisable subject to and in accordance with this Chapter, to have an audit carried out on his behalf which relates to the management of the relevant premises and any appurtenant property by or on behalf of the landlord.

(5) That right shall be exercisable by a single qualifying tenant of a dwelling where the relevant premises contain no other dwelling let to a qualifying tenant apart from that let to him.

(6) In relation to an audit on behalf of a single qualifying tenant—

  (a)   'the relevant premises' means so much of—
    (i)   the building containing the dwelling let to him, and
    (ii) any other building or buildings,
    as constitutes premises in relation to which management functions are discharged in respect of the costs of which a service charge is payable under his lease (whether as a common service charge contribution or otherwise); and
  (b)   'appurtenant property' means so much of any property not contained in the relevant premises as constitutes property in relation to which any such management functions are discharged.

(7) The provisions of sections 78 to 83 shall, with any necessary modifications, have effect in relation to an audit on behalf of a single qualifying tenant as they have effect in relation to an audit on behalf of two or more qualifying tenants.

(8) For the purposes of this section common service charge contributions are payable by two or more persons under their leases if they may be required under the terms of those leases to contribute to the same costs by the payment of service charges.

77 Qualifying tenants

(1) Subject to the following provisions of this section, a tenant is a qualifying tenant of a dwelling for the purposes of this Chapter if—

    (a) he is a tenant of the dwelling under a long lease other than a business lease; and

    (b) any service charge is payable under the lease.

(2) For the purposes of subsection (1) a lease is a long lease if—

    (a) it is a lease falling within any of paragraphs (a) to (c) of subsection (1) of section 7; or

    (b) it is a shared ownership lease (within the meaning of that section), whether granted in pursuance of Part V of the Housing Act 1985 or otherwise and whatever the share of the tenant under it.

(3) No dwelling shall have more than one qualifying tenant at any one time.

(4) Accordingly—

    (a) where a dwelling is for the time being let under two or more leases falling within subsection (1), any tenant under any of those leases which is superior to that held by any other such tenant shall not be a qualifying tenant of the dwelling for the purposes of this Chapter, and

    (b) where a dwelling is for the time being let to joint tenants under a lease falling within subsection (1), the joint tenants shall (subject to paragraph (a)) be regarded for the purposes of this Chapter as jointly constituting the qualifying tenant of the dwelling.

(5) A person can, however, be (or be among those constituting) the qualifying tenant of each of two or more dwellings at the same time, whether he is tenant of those dwellings under one lease or under two or more separate leases.

(6) Where two or more persons constitute the qualifying tenant of a dwelling in accordance with subsection (4)(b), any one or more of those persons may sign a notice under section 80 on behalf of both or all of them.

78 Management audits

(1) The audit referred to in section 76(1) is an audit carried out for the purpose of ascertaining—

    (a) the extent to which the obligations of the landlord which—

        (i)   are owed to the qualifying tenants of the constituent dwellings, and

        (ii) involve the discharge of management functions in relation to the relevant premises or any appurtenant property,

    are being discharged in an efficient and effective manner; and

(b) the extent to which sums payable by those tenants by way of service charges are being applied in an efficient and effective manner;

and in this Chapter any such audit is referred to as a 'management audit'.

(2) In determining whether any such obligations as are mentioned in subsection (1)(a) are being discharged in an efficient and effective manner, regard shall be had to any applicable provisions of any code of practice for the time being approved by the Secretary of State under section 87.

(3) A management audit shall be carried out by a person who—

(a) is qualified for appointment by virtue of subsection (4); and
(b) is appointed—
    (i) in the circumstances mentioned in section 76(2)(a), by either or both of the qualifying tenants of the constituent dwellings, or
    (ii) in the circumstances mentioned in section 76(2)(b), by not less than two-thirds of the qualifying tenants of the constituent dwellings;

and in this Chapter any such person is referred to as 'the auditor'.

(4) A person is qualified for appointment for the purposes of subsection (3) above if—

(a) he has the necessary qualification (within the meaning of subsection (1) of section 28 of the 1985 Act (meaning of 'qualified accountant')) or is a qualified surveyor;
(b) he is not disqualified from acting (within the meaning of that subsection); and
(c) he is not a tenant of any premises contained in the relevant premises.

(5) For the purposes of subsection (4)(a) above a person is a qualified surveyor if he is a fellow or professional associate of the Royal Institution of Chartered Surveyors or of the Incorporated Society of Valuers and Auctioneers or satisfies such other requirement or requirements as may be prescribed by regulations made by the Secretary of State.

(6) The auditor may appoint such persons to assist him in carrying out the audit as he thinks fit.

79   Rights exercisable in connection with management audits

(1) Where the qualifying tenants of any dwellings exercise under section 80 their right to have a management audit carried out on their behalf, the rights conferred on the auditor by *subsection (2)* [subsections (2) and (2A)] below shall be exercisable by him in connection with the audit.

(2) The rights conferred on the auditor by this subsection are—

(a) a right to require the landlord—
    (i) to supply him with such a summary as is referred to in section 21(1) of the 1985 Act (request for summary of relevant costs) in connection with any service charges payable by the qualifying tenants of the constituent dwellings, and
    (ii) to afford him reasonable facilities for inspecting, or taking copies of, or extracts from, the accounts, receipts and other documents supporting any such summary;
(b) a right to require the landlord or any relevant person to afford him reasonable facilities for inspecting any other documents sight of which is reasonably required by him for the purpose of carrying out the audit; and
(c) a right to require the landlord or any relevant person to afford him reasonable facilities for taking copies of or extracts from any documents falling within paragraph (b).

[(2) The right conferred on the auditor by this subsection is a right to require the landlord—

    (a)   to afford him reasonable facilities for inspecting accounts, receipts or other documents relevant to the matters which must be shown in any statement of account required to be supplied to the qualifying tenants of the constituent dwellings under section 21 of the 1985 Act and for taking copies of or extracts from them, or

    (b)   to take copies of or extracts from any such accounts, receipts or other documents and either send them to him or afford him reasonable facilities for collecting them (as he specifies).

(2A) The right conferred on the auditor by this subsection is a right to require the landlord or any relevant person—

    (a)   to afford him reasonable facilities for inspecting any other documents sight of which is reasonably required by him for the purpose of carrying out the audit and for taking copies of or extracts from them, or

    (b)   to take copies of or extracts from any such documents and either send them to him or afford him reasonable facilities for collecting them (as the auditor specifies).]

(3) The rights conferred on the auditor by *subsection (2)* [subsections (2) and (2A)] shall be exercisable by him—

    (a)   in relation to the landlord, by means of a notice under section 80; and

    (b)   in relation to any relevant person, by means of a notice given to that person at (so far as is reasonably practicable) the same time as a notice under section 80 is given to the landlord;

and, where a notice is given to any relevant person in accordance with paragraph (b) above, a copy of that notice shall be given to the landlord by the auditor.

(4) The auditor shall also be entitled, on giving notice in accordance with section 80, to carry out an inspection of any common parts comprised in the relevant premises or any appurtenant property.

(5) The landlord or (as the case may be) any relevant person shall—

    (a)   *where facilities for the inspection of any documents are required under subsection (2)(a)(ii) or (b), make those facilities available free of charge;*

    (b)   *where any documents are required to be supplied under subsection (2)(a)(i) or facilities for the taking of copies or extracts are required under subsection (2)(a)(ii) or (c), be entitled to supply those documents or (as the case may be) make those facilities available on payment of such reasonable charge as he may determine.*

(6) The requirement imposed on the landlord by subsection (5)(a) to make any facilities available free of charge shall not be construed as precluding the landlord from treating as part of his costs of management any costs incurred by him in connection with making those facilities so available.

[(5) To the extent that a requirement imposed under this section on the landlord or any relevant person requires him to afford facilities for inspecting documents, he shall do so free of charge; but the landlord may treat as part of his costs of management any costs incurred by him in doing so.

(6) The landlord or a relevant person may make a reasonable charge for doing anything else in compliance with such a requirement.]

(7) In this Chapter 'relevant person' means a person (other than the landlord) who—

    (a) is charged with responsibility—

        (i)   for the discharge of any such obligations as are mentioned in section 78(1)(a), or

        (ii)   for the application of any such service charges as are mentioned in section 78(1)(b); or

    (b) has a right to enforce payment of any such service charges.

(8) In this Chapter references to the auditor in the context of—

    (a) *being afforded any such facilities as are mentioned in subsection (2)* [a requirement imposed under subsection (2) or (2A)], or

    (b) the carrying out of any inspection under subsection (4)

shall be read as including a person appointed by the auditor under section 78(6).

80 Exercise of right to have a management audit

(1) The right of any qualifying tenants to have a management audit carried out on their behalf shall be exercisable by the giving of a notice under this section.

(2) A notice given under this section—

    (a) must be given to the landlord by the auditor, and

    (b) must be signed by each of the tenants on whose behalf it is given.

(3) Any such notice must—

    (a) state the full name of each of those tenants and the address of the dwelling of which he is a qualifying tenant;

    (b) state the name and address of the auditor;

    (c) specify any documents or description of documents—

        (i)   which the landlord is required to supply to the auditor under section 79(2)(a)(i), or

        (ii)   in respect of which he is required to afford the auditor facilities for inspection or for taking copies or extracts under any other provision of section 79(2); and

    [(c) specify any documents or description of documents in respect of which a requirement is imposed on him under section 79(2) or (2A); and]

    (d) if the auditor proposes to carry out an inspection under section 79(4), state the date on which he proposes to carry out the inspection.

(4) The date specified under subsection (3)(d) must be a date falling not less than one month nor more than two months after the date of the giving of the notice.

(5) A notice is duly given under this section to the landlord of any qualifying tenants if it is given to a person who receives on behalf of the landlord the rent payable by any such tenants; and a person to whom such a notice is so given shall forward it as soon as may be to the landlord.

81 Procedure following giving of notice under s 80

(1) Where the landlord is given a notice under section 80, then within the period of one month beginning with the date of the giving of the notice, he shall—

    (a) supply the auditor with any document specified under subsection (3)(c)(i) of that section, and afford him, in respect of any document falling within section 79(2)(a)(ii), any facilities specified in relation to it under subsection (3)(c)(ii) of section 80;

(b)   in the case of every other document or description of documents specified in the notice under subsection (3)(c)(ii) of that section, either—

    (i)   afford the auditor facilities for inspection or (as the case may be) taking copies or extracts in respect of that document or those documents, or

    (ii)   give the auditor a notice stating that he objects to doing so for such reasons as are specified in the notice; and

[(a) comply with it so far as it relates to documents within section 79(2);

(b) either—

    (i)   comply with it, or

    (ii)   give the auditor a notice stating that he objects to doing so for such reasons as are specified in the notice,

    so far as it relates to documents within section 79(2A); and]

(c) if a date is specified in the notice under subsection (3)(d) of that section, either approve the date or propose another date for the carrying out of an inspection under section 79(4).

(2) Any date proposed by the landlord under subsection (1)(c) must be a date falling not later than the end of the period of two months beginning with the date of the giving of the notice under section 80.

(3) Where a relevant person is given a notice under section 79 *requiring him to afford the auditor facilities for inspection or taking copies or extracts in respect of any documents or description of documents specified in the notice, then within the period of one month beginning with the date of the giving of the notice, he shall, in the case of every such document or description of documents, either—*

(a)   afford the auditor the facilities required by him; or

(b)   give the auditor a notice stating that he objects to doing so for such reasons as are specified in the notice.

[, then within the period of one month beginning with the date of the giving of the notice, he shall either—

(a) comply with it, or

(b) give the auditor a notice stating that he objects to doing so for such reasons as are specified in the notice,

in the case of every document or description or document specified in the notice.]

(4) If by the end of the period of two months beginning with—

(a) the date of the giving of the notice under section 80, or

(b) the date of the giving of such a notice under section 79 as is mentioned in subsection (3) above,

the landlord or (as the case may be) a relevant person has failed to comply with any requirement of the notice, the court may, on the application of the auditor, make an order requiring the landlord or (as the case may be) the relevant person to comply with that requirement within such period as is specified in the order.

(5) The court shall not make an order under subsection (4) in respect of any document or documents unless it is satisfied that the document or documents falls or fall within *paragraph (a) or (b) of section 79(2)* [section 79(2) or (2A)].

(6) If by the end of the period of two months specified in subsection (2) no inspection under section 79(4) has been carried out by the auditor, the court may, on the application of the auditor, make an order providing for such an inspection to be carried out on such date as is specified in the order.

(7) Any application for an order under subsection (4) or (6) must be made before the end of the period of four months beginning with—

(a) in the case of an application made in connection with a notice given under section 80, the date of the giving of that notice; or

(b) in the case of an application made in connection with such a notice under section 79 as is mentioned in subsection (3) above, the date of the giving of that notice.

82 Requirement relating to information etc held by superior landlord

(1) Where the landlord is required by a notice under section 80 to supply any summary falling within section 79(2)(a), and any information necessary for complying with the notice so far as relating to any such summary is in the possession of a superior landlord—

(a) the landlord shall make a written request for the relevant information to the person who is his landlord (and so on, if that person is himself not the superior landlord);

(b) the superior landlord shall comply with that request within the period of one month beginning with the date of the making of the request; and

(c) the landlord who received the notice shall then comply with it so far as relating to any such summary within the time allowed by section 81(1) or such further time, if any, as is reasonable.

(2) Where—

(a) the landlord is required by a notice under section 80 to afford the auditor facilities for inspection or taking copies or extracts in respect of any documents or description of documents specified in the notice, and

(b) any of the documents in question is in the custody or under the control of a superior landlord,

the landlord shall on receiving the notice inform the auditor as soon as may be of that fact and of the name and address of the superior landlord, and the auditor may then give the superior landlord a notice requiring him to afford the facilities in question in respect of the document.

[(1) Where the landlord is given a notice under section 80 imposing on him a requirement relating to any documents which are held by a superior landlord, he shall inform the auditor as soon as may be of that fact and of the name and address of the superior landlord.

(2) The auditor may then give the superior landlord a notice requiring him to comply with the requirement.]

(3) Subsections (3) to (5) and (7) of section 81 shall, with any necessary modifications, have effect in relation to a notice given to a superior landlord under subsection (2) above as they have effect in relation to any such notice given to a relevant person as is mentioned in subsection (3) of that section.

83 Supplementary provisions

(1) Where—

(a) a notice has been given to a landlord under section 80, and

   (b)   at a time when any obligations arising out of the notice remain to be discharged by him—

      (i)   he disposes of the whole or part of his interest as landlord of the qualifying tenants of the constituent dwellings, and

      (ii)   the person acquiring any such interest of the landlord is in a position to discharge any of those obligations to any extent,

that person shall be responsible for discharging those obligations to that extent, as if he had been given the notice under that section.

(2) If the landlord is, despite any such disposal, still in a position to discharge those obligations to the extent referred to in subsection (1), he shall remain responsible for so discharging them; but otherwise the person referred to in that subsection shall be responsible for so discharging them to the exclusion of the landlord.

(3) Where a person is so responsible for discharging any such obligations (whether with the landlord or otherwise):

   (a)   references to the landlord in section 81 shall be read as including, or as, references to that person to such extent as is appropriate to reflect his responsibility for discharging those obligations; but

   (b)   in connection with the discharge of any such obligations by that person, that section shall apply as if any reference to the date of the giving of the notice under section 80 were a reference to the date of the disposal referred to in subsection (1).

(4) Where—

   (a)   a notice has been given to a relevant person under section 79, and

   (b)   at a time when any obligations arising out of the notice remain to be discharged by him, he ceases to be a relevant person, but

   (c)   he is, despite ceasing to be a relevant person, still in a position to discharge those obligations to any extent,

he shall nevertheless remain responsible for discharging those obligations to that extent; and section 81 shall accordingly continue to apply to him as if he were still a relevant person.

(5) Where—

   (a)   a notice has been given to a landlord under section 80, or

   (b)   a notice has been given to a relevant person under section 79,

then during the period of twelve months beginning with the date of that notice, no subsequent such notice may be given to the landlord or (as the case may be) that person on behalf of any persons who, in relation to the earlier notice, were qualifying tenants of the constituent dwellings.

84 Interpretation of Chapter V

In this Chapter—

    'the 1985 Act' means the Landlord and Tenant Act 1985;
    'appurtenant property' shall be construed in accordance with section 76(3) or (6);
    'the auditor', in relation to a management audit, means such a person as is mentioned in section 78(3);

'the constituent dwellings' means the dwellings referred to in section 76(2)(a) or (b) (as the case may be);

'landlord' means immediate landlord;

'management audit' means such an audit as is mentioned in section 78(1);

'management functions' includes functions with respect to the provision of services or the repair, maintenance, [improvement] or insurance of property;

'relevant person' has the meaning given by section 79(7);

'the relevant premises' shall be construed in accordance with section 76(3) or (6);

'service charge' has the meaning given by section 18(1) of the 1985 Act.

CHAPTER VI – MISCELLANEOUS

. . .

Codes of practice

87   Approval by Secretary of State of codes of management practice

(1) The Secretary of State may, if he considers it appropriate to do so, by order—

  (a)   approve any code of practice—

    (i)   which appears to him to be designed to promote desirable practices in relation to any matter or matters directly or indirectly concerned with the management of residential property by relevant persons; and

    (ii)   which has been submitted to him for his approval;

  (b)   approve any modifications of any such code which have been so submitted; or

  (c)   withdraw his approval for any such code or modifications.

(2) The Secretary of State shall not approve any such code or any modifications of any such code unless he is satisfied that arrangements have been made for the text of the code or the modifications to be published in such manner as he considers appropriate for bringing the provisions of the code or the modifications to the notice of those likely to be affected by them (which, in the case of modifications of a code, may include publication of a text of the code incorporating the modifications).

(3) The power of the Secretary of State under this section to approve a code of practice which has been submitted to him for his approval includes power to approve a part of any such code; and references in this section to a code of practice may accordingly be read as including a reference to a part of a code of practice.

(4) At any one time there may be two or more codes of practice for the time being approved under this section.

(5) A code of practice approved under this section may make different provision with respect to different cases or descriptions of cases, including different provision for different areas.

(6) Without prejudice to the generality of subsections (1) and (5)—

  (a)   a code of practice approved under this section may, in relation to any such matter as is referred to in subsection (1), make provision in respect of relevant persons who are under an obligation to discharge any function in connection with that matter as well as in respect of relevant persons who are not under such an obligation; and

  (b)   any such code may make provision with respect to—

    (i)   the resolution of disputes with respect to residential property between relevant persons and the tenants of such property;

(ii) competitive tendering for works in connection with such property; and

(iii) the administration of trusts in respect of amounts paid by tenants by way of service charges.

(7) A failure on the part of any person to comply with any provision of a code of practice for the time being approved under this section shall not of itself render him liable to any proceedings; but in any proceedings before a court or tribunal—

(a) any code of practice approved under this section shall be admissible in evidence; and

(b) any provision of any such code which appears to the court or tribunal to be relevant to any question arising in the proceedings shall be taken into account in determining that question.

(8) For the purposes of this section—

(a) 'relevant person' means any landlord of residential property or any person who discharges management functions in respect of such property, and for this purpose 'management functions' includes functions with respect to the provision of services or the repair, maintenance [, improvement] or insurance of such property;

(b) 'residential property' means any building or part of a building which consists of one or more dwellings let on leases, but references to residential property include—

(i) any garage, outhouse, garden, yard and appurtenances belonging to or usually enjoyed with such dwellings,

(ii) any common parts of any such building or part, and

(iii) any common facilities which are not within any such building or part; and

(c) 'service charge' means an amount payable by a tenant of a dwelling as part of or in addition to the rent—

(i) which is payable, directly or indirectly, for services, repairs, maintenance [, improvements] or insurance or any relevant person's costs of management, and

(ii) the whole or part of which varies or may vary according to the costs or estimated costs incurred or to be incurred by any relevant person in connection with the matters mentioned in sub-paragraph (i).

(9) This section applies in relation to dwellings let on licences to occupy as it applies in relation to dwellings let on leases, and references in this section to landlords and tenants of residential property accordingly include references to licensors and licensees of such property.

HOUSING ACT 1996

PART III – LANDLORD AND TENANT

CHAPTER I – TENANTS' RIGHTS

Forfeiture

81   Restriction on termination of tenancy for failure to pay service charge

(1) A landlord may not, in relation to premises let as a dwelling, exercise a right of re-entry or forfeiture for failure to pay a service charge unless the amount of the service charge—

(a)   *is agreed or admitted by the tenant, or*

(b)   *has been the subject of determination by a court or by an arbitral tribunal in proceedings pursuant to an arbitration agreement (within the meaning of Part I of the Arbitration Act 1996).*

[(1) A landlord may not, in relation to premises let as a dwelling, exercise a right of re-entry or forfeiture for failure by a tenant to pay a service charge or administration charge unless—

(a)   it is finally determined by (or on appeal from) a leasehold valuation tribunal or by a court, or by an arbitral tribunal in proceedings pursuant to a post-dispute arbitration agreement, that the amount of the service charge or administration charge is payable by him, or

(b)   the tenant has admitted that it is so payable.]

(2) Where the amount is the subject of determination, the landlord may not exercise any such right of re-entry or forfeiture until after the end of the period of 14 days beginning with the day after that on which the decision of the court or arbitral tribunal is given.

[(2) The landlord may not exercise a right of re-entry or forfeiture by virtue of subsection (1)(a) until after the end of the period of 14 days beginning with the day after that on which the final determination is made.]

(3) For the purposes of this section the amount of a service charge shall be taken to be determined when the decision of the court or arbitral tribunal is given, notwithstanding the possibility of an appeal or other legal challenge to the decision.

[(3) For the purposes of this section it is finally determined that the amount of a service charge or administration charge is payable—

(a)   if a decision that it is payable is not appealed against or otherwise challenged, at the end of the time for bringing an appeal or other challenge, or

(b)   if such a decision is appealed against or otherwise challenged and not set aside in consequence of the appeal or other challenge, at the time specified in subsection (3A).

(3A) The time referred to in subsection (3)(b) is the time when the appeal or other challenge is disposed of–

(a)   by the determination of the appeal or other challenge and the expiry of the time for bringing a subsequent appeal (if any), or

(b)   by its being abandoned or otherwise ceasing to have effect.]

(4) The reference in subsection (1) to premises let as a dwelling does not include premises let on—

    (a) a tenancy to which Part II of the Landlord and Tenant Act 1954 applies (business tenancies),

    (b) a tenancy of an agricultural holding within the meaning of the Agricultural Holdings Act 1986 in relation to which that Act applies, or

    (c) a farm business tenancy within the meaning of the Agricultural Tenancies Act 1995.

[(4A) References in this section to the exercise of a right of re-entry or forfeiture include the service of a notice under section 146(1) of the Law of Property Act 1925 (restriction on re-entry or forfeiture).]

(5) In this section –

    [(a) 'administration charge' has the meaning given by Part 1 of Schedule 11 to the Commonhold and Leasehold Reform Act 2002,

    (b) 'arbitration agreement' and 'arbitral tribunal' have the same meaning as in Part 1 of the Arbitration Act 1996 and 'post-dispute arbitration agreement', in relation to any matter, means an arbitration agreement made after a dispute about the matter has arisen,

    (c) 'dwelling' has the same meaning as in the Landlord and Tenant Act 1985, and

    (d)] 'service charge' means a service charge within the meaning of section 18(1) of the Landlord and Tenant Act 1985, other than one excluded from that section by section 27 of that Act (rent of dwelling registered and not entered as variable).

[(5A) Any order of a court to give effect to a determination of a leasehold valuation tribunal shall be treated as a determination by the court for the purposes of this section.]

(6) Nothing in this section affects the exercise of a right of re-entry or forfeiture on other grounds.

82   *Notice under s 146 of the Law of Property Act 1925*

(1) Nothing in section 81 (restriction on termination of tenancy for failure to pay a service charge) affects the power of a landlord to serve a notice under section 146(1) of the Law of Property Act 1925 (restrictions on and relief against forfeiture: notice of breach of covenant or condition).

(2) But such a notice in respect of premises let as a dwelling and failure to pay a service charge is ineffective unless it complies with the following requirements.

(3) It must state that section 81 applies and set out the effect of subsection (1) of that section.

The Secretary of State may by regulations prescribe a form of words to be used for that purpose.

(4) The information or words required must be in characters not less conspicuous than those used in the notice—

    (a) to indicate that the tenancy may be forfeited, or

    (b) to specify the breach complained of,

whichever is the more conspicuous.

(5) In this section 'premises let as a dwelling' and 'service charge' have the same meaning as in section 81.

(6) Regulations under this section—

  (a)   shall be made by statutory instrument, and
  (b)   may make different provision for different cases or classes of case including different areas.

. . .

84   Right to appoint surveyor to advise on matters relating to service charges

(1) A recognised tenants' association may appoint a surveyor for the purposes of this section to advise on any matters relating to, or which may give rise to, service charges payable to a landlord by one or more members of the association.

The provisions of Schedule 4 have effect for conferring on a surveyor so appointed rights of access to documents and premises.

(2) A person shall not be so appointed unless he is a qualified surveyor. For this purpose 'qualified surveyor' has the same meaning as in section 78(4)(a) of the Leasehold Reform, Housing and Urban Development Act 1993 (persons qualified for appointment to carry out management audit).

(3) The appointment shall take effect for the purposes of this section upon notice in writing being given to the landlord by the association stating the name and address of the surveyor, the duration of his appointment and the matters in respect of which he is appointed.

(4) An appointment shall cease to have effect for the purposes of this section if the association gives notice in writing to the landlord to that effect or if the association ceases to exist.

(5) A notice is duly given under this section to a landlord of any tenants if it is given to a person who receives on behalf of the landlord the rent payable by those tenants; and a person to whom such a notice is so given shall forward it as soon as may be to the landlord.

(6) In this section—

  'recognised tenants' association' has the same meaning as in the provisions of the Landlord and Tenant Act 1985 relating to service charges (see section 29 of that Act); and
  'service charge' means a service charge within the meaning of section 18(1) of that Act other than one excluded from that section by section 27 of that Act (rent of dwelling registered and not entered as variable).

. . .

SCHEDULE 4

Rights exercisable by surveyor appointed by tenants' association

Section 84

Introductory

1(1) A surveyor appointed for the purposes of section 84 has the rights conferred by this Schedule.

(2) In this Schedule—

(a) 'the tenants' association' means the association by whom the surveyor was appointed, and

(b) the surveyor's 'functions' are his functions in connection with the matters in respect of which he was appointed.

Appointment of assistants

2(1) The surveyor may appoint such persons as he thinks fit to assist him in carrying out his functions.

(2) References in this Schedule to the surveyor in the context of—

(a) being afforded any such facilities as are mentioned in paragraph 3, or

(b) carrying out an inspection under paragraph 4,

include a person so appointed.

Right to inspect documents, etc

3(1) The surveyor has a right to require the landlord or any other relevant person—

(a) to afford him reasonable facilities for inspecting any document sight of which is reasonably required by him for the purposes of his functions, and

(b) to afford him reasonable facilities for taking copies of or extracts from any such documents.

(2) In sub-paragraph (1) 'other relevant person' means a person other than the landlord who is or, in relation to a future service charge, will be—

(a) responsible for applying the proceeds of the service charge, or

(b) under an obligation to a tenant who pays the service charge in respect of any matter to which the charge relates.

(3) The rights conferred on the surveyor by this paragraph are extricable by him by notice in writing given by him to the landlord or other person concerned.

Where a notice is given to a person other than the landlord, the surveyor shall give a copy of the notice to the landlord.

(4) The landlord or other person to whom notice is given shall, within the period of one week beginning with the date of the giving of the notice or as soon as reasonably practicable thereafter, either—

(a) afford the surveyor the facilities required by him for inspecting and taking copies or extracts of the documents to which the notice relates, or

(b) give the surveyor a notice stating that he objects to doing so for reasons specified in the notice.

(5) Facilities for the inspection of any documents required under sub-paragraph (1)(a) shall be made available free of charge.

This does not mean that the landlord cannot treat as part of his costs of management any costs incurred by him in connection with making the facilities available.

(6) A reasonable charge may be made for facilities for the taking of copies or extracts required under sub-paragraph (1)(b).

(7) A notice is duly given under this paragraph to the landlord of a tenant if it is given to a person who receives on behalf of the landlord the rent payable by that tenant.

A person to whom such a notice is so given shall forward it as soon as may be to the landlord.

Right to inspect premises

4(1) The surveyor also has the right to inspect any common parts comprised in relevant premises or any appurtenant property.

(2) In sub-paragraph (1)—

'common parts', in relation to a building or part of a building, includes the structure and exterior of the building or part and any common facilities within it;
'relevant premises' means so much of—

(i) the building or buildings containing the dwellings let to members of the tenants' association, and
(ii) any other building or buildings,

as constitute premises in relation to which management functions are discharged in respect of the costs of which service charges are payable by members of the association; and
'appurtenant property' means so much of any property not contained in relevant premises as constitutes property in relation to which any such management functions are discharged.

For the purposes of the above definitions 'management functions' includes functions with respect to the provision of services, or the repair, maintenance [, improvement] or insurance of property.

(3) On being requested to do so, the landlord shall afford the surveyor reasonable access for the purposes of carrying out an inspection under this paragraph.

(4) Such reasonable access shall be afforded to the surveyor free of charge. This does not mean that the landlord cannot treat as part of his costs of management any costs incurred by him in connection with affording reasonable access to the surveyor.

(5) A request is duly made under this paragraph to the landlord of a tenant if it is made to a person appointed by the landlord to deal with such requests or, if no such person has been appointed, to a person who receives on behalf of the landlord the rent payable by that tenant. A person to whom such a request is made shall notify the landlord of the request as soon as may be.

Enforcement of rights by the court

5(1) If the landlord or other person to whom notice was given under paragraph 3 has not, by the end of the period of one month beginning with the date on which notice was given, complied with the notice, the court may, on the application of the surveyor, make an order requiring him to do so within such period as is specified in the order.

(2) If the landlord does not, within a reasonable period after the making of a request under paragraph 4, afford the surveyor reasonable access for the purposes of carrying out an inspection under that paragraph, the court may, on the application of the surveyor, make an order requiring the landlord to do so on such date as is specified in the order.

(3) An application for an order under this paragraph must be made before the end of the period of four months beginning with the date on which notice was given under paragraph 3 or the request was made under paragraph 4.

(4) An order under this paragraph may be made in general terms or may require the landlord or other person to do specific things, as the court thinks fit.

Documents held by superior landlord

6(1) Where a landlord is required by a notice under paragraph 3 to afford the surveyor facilities for inspection or taking copies or extracts in respect of any document which is in the custody or under the control of a superior landlord—

  (a) the landlord shall on receiving the notice inform the surveyor as soon as may be of the name and address of the superior landlord, and
  (b) the surveyor may then give the superior landlord notice in writing requiring him facilities in question in respect of the document.

(2) Paragraphs 3 and 5(1) and (3) have effect, with any necessary modifications, in relation to a notice given to a superior landlord under this paragraph.

Effect of disposal by landlord

7(1) Where a notice under paragraph 3 has been given or a request under paragraph 4 has been made to a landlord, and at a time when any obligations arising out of the notice or request remain to be discharged by him—

  (a) he disposes of the whole or part of his interest as landlord of any member of the association, and
  (b) the person acquiring that interest ('the transferee') is in a position to discharge obligations to any extent,

that person shall be responsible for discharging those obligations to that extent, as if he had been given the notice under paragraph 3 or had received the request under paragraph 4.

(2) If the landlord is, despite the disposal, still in a position to discharge those obligations, he remains responsible for doing so. Otherwise, the transferee is responsible for discharging them to the exclusion of the landlord.

(3) In connection with the discharge of such obligations by the transferee, paragraphs 3 to 6 apply with the substitution for any reference to the date on which notice was given under paragraph 3 or the request was made under paragraph 4 of a reference to the date of the disposal.

(4) In this paragraph 'disposal' means a disposal whether by the creation or transfer of an estate or interest, and includes the surrender of a tenancy; and references to the transferee shall be construed accordingly.

Effect of person ceasing to be a relevant person

8 Where a notice under paragraph 3 has been given to a person other than the landlord and, at a time when any obligations arising out of the notice remain to be discharged by him, he ceases to be such a person as is mentioned in paragraph 3(2), then, if he is still in a position to discharge those obligations to any extent he remains responsible for discharging those obligations, and the provisions of this Schedule continue to apply to him, to that extent.

COMMONHOLD AND LEASEHOLD REFORM ACT 2002 *(not in force at date of publication)*

159   Charges under estate management schemes

(1) This section applies where a scheme under—

   (a)   section 19 of the 1967 Act (estate management schemes in connection with enfranchisement under that Act),

   (b)   Chapter 4 of Part 1 of the 1993 Act (estate management schemes in connection with enfranchisement under the 1967 Act or Chapter 1 of Part 1 of the 1993 Act), or

   (c)   section 94(6) of the 1993 Act (corresponding schemes in relation to areas occupied under leases from Crown),

includes provision imposing on persons occupying or interested in property an obligation to make payments ('estate charges').

(2) A variable estate charge is payable only to the extent that the amount of the charge is reasonable; and 'variable estate charge' means an estate charge which is neither—

   (a)   specified in the scheme, nor

   (b)   calculated in accordance with a formula specified in the scheme.

(3) Any person on whom an obligation to pay an estate charge is imposed by the scheme may apply to a leasehold valuation tribunal for an order varying the scheme in such manner as is specified in the application on the grounds that—

   (a)   any estate charge specified in the scheme is unreasonable, or

   (b)   any formula specified in the scheme in accordance with which any estate charge is calculated is unreasonable.

(4) If the grounds on which the application was made are established to the satisfaction of the tribunal, it may make an order varying the scheme in such manner as is specified in the order.

(5) The variation specified in the order may be—

   (a)   the variation specified in the application, or

   (b)   such other variation as the tribunal thinks fit.

(6) An application may be made to a leasehold valuation tribunal for a determination whether an estate charge is payable by a person and, if it is, as to—

   (a)   the person by whom it is payable,

   (b)   the person to whom it is payable,

   (c)   the amount which is payable,

   (d)   the date at or by which it is payable, and

   (e)   the manner in which it is payable.

(7) Subsection (6) applies whether or not any payment has been made.

(8) The jurisdiction conferred on a leasehold valuation tribunal in respect of any matter by virtue of subsection (6) is in addition to any jurisdiction of a court in respect of the matter.

(9) No application under subsection (6) may be made in respect of a matter which—

    (a)   has been agreed or admitted by the person concerned,

    (b)   has been, or is to be, referred to arbitration pursuant to a post-dispute arbitration agreement to which that person is a party,

    (c)   has been the subject of determination by a court, or

    (d)   has been the subject of determination by an arbitral tribunal pursuant to a post-dispute arbitration agreement.

(10) But the person is not to be taken to have agreed or admitted any matter by reason only of having made any payment.

(11) An agreement (other than a post-dispute arbitration agreement) is void in so far as it purports to provide for a determination—

    (a)   in a particular manner, or

    (b)   on particular evidence,

of any question which may be the subject matter of an application under subsection (6).

(12) In this section—

> 'post-dispute arbitration agreement' in relation to any matter, means an arbitration agreement made after a dispute about the matter has arisen, and
> 'arbitration agreement' and 'arbitral tribunal' have the same meanings as in Part 1 of the Arbitration Act 1996 (c. 23).

    . . .

164   Insurance otherwise than with landlord's insurer

(1) This section applies where a long lease of a house requires the tenant to insure the house with an insurer nominated or approved by the landlord ('the landlord's insurer').

(2) The tenant is not required to effect the insurance with the landlord's insurer if—

    (a)   the house is insured under a policy of insurance issued by an authorised insurer,

    (b)   the policy covers the interests of both the landlord and the tenant,

    (c)   the policy covers all the risks which the lease requires be covered by insurance provided by the landlord's insurer,

    (d)   the amount of the cover is not less than that which the lease requires to be provided by such insurance, and

    (e)   the tenant satisfies subsection (3).

(3) To satisfy this subsection the tenant—

    (a)   must have given a notice of cover to the landlord before the end of the period of fourteen days beginning with the relevant date, and

    (b)   if (after that date) he has been requested to do so by a new landlord, must have given a notice of cover to him within the period of fourteen days beginning with the day on which the request was given.

(4) For the purposes of subsection (3)—

    (a)   if the policy has not been renewed the relevant date is the day on which it took effect and if it has been renewed it is the day from which it was last renewed, and

(b) a person is a new landlord on any day if he acquired the interest of the previous landlord under the lease on a disposal made by him during the period of one month ending with that day.

(5) A notice of cover is a notice specifying—

(a) the name of the insurer,
(b) the risks covered by the policy,
(c) the amount and period of the cover, and
(d) such further information as may be prescribed.

(6) A notice of cover—

(a) must be in the prescribed form, and
(b) may be sent by post.

(7) If a notice of cover is sent by post, it may be addressed to the landlord at the address specified in subsection (8).

(8) That address is—

(a) the address last furnished to the tenant as the landlord's address for service in accordance with section 48 of the 1987 Act (notification of address for service of notices on landlord), or
(b) if no such address has been so furnished, the address last furnished to the tenant as the landlord's address in accordance with section 47 of the 1987 Act (landlord's name and address to be contained in demands for rent).

(9) But the tenant may not give a notice of cover to the landlord at the address specified in subsection (8) if he has been notified by the landlord of a different address in England and Wales at which he wishes to be given any such notice.

(10) In this section—

'authorised insurer', in relation to a policy of insurance, means a person who may carry on in the United Kingdom the business of effecting or carrying out contracts of insurance of the sort provided under the policy without contravening the prohibition imposed by section 19 of the Financial Services and Markets Act 2000 (c. 8),
'house' has the same meaning as for the purposes of Part 1 of the 1967 Act,
'landlord' and 'tenant' have the same meanings as in Chapter 1 of this Part,
'long lease' has the meaning given by sections 74 and 75 of this Act, and
'prescribed' means prescribed by regulations made by the appropriate national authority.

. . .

167 Failure to pay small amount for short period

(1) A landlord under a long lease of a dwelling may not exercise a right of re-entry or forfeiture for failure by a tenant to pay an amount consisting of rent, service charges or administration charges (or a combination of them) ('the unpaid amount') unless the unpaid amount—

(a) exceeds the prescribed sum, or

(b)   consists of or includes an amount which has been payable for more than a prescribed period.

(2)   The sum prescribed under subsection (1)(a) must not exceed £500.

(3)   If the unpaid amount includes a default charge, it is to be treated for the purposes of subsection (1)(a) as reduced by the amount of the charge; and for this purpose 'default charge' means an administration charge payable in respect of the tenant's failure to pay any part of the unpaid amount.

(4)   In this section 'long lease of a dwelling' does not include—

(a)   a tenancy to which Part 2 of the Landlord and Tenant Act 1954 (c. 56) (business tenancies) applies,

(c)   a tenancy of an agricultural holding within the meaning of the Agricultural Holdings Act 1986 (c. 5) in relation to which that Act applies, or

(d)   a farm business tenancy within the meaning of the Agricultural Tenancies Act 1995 (c. 8).

(5)   In this section—

'administration charge' has the same meaning as in Part 1 of Schedule 11,
'dwelling' has the same meaning as in the 1985 Act,
'landlord' and 'tenant' have the same meaning as in Chapter 1 of this Part,
'long lease' has the same meaning given by sections 74 and 75 of this Act, except that a shared ownership lease is a long lease whatever the tenant's total share,
'prescribed' means prescribed by regulations made by the appropriate national authority, and
'service charge' has the meaning given by section 18(1) of the 1985 Act.

. . .

Crown application

172   Application to Crown

(1)   The following provisions apply in relation to Crown land (as in relation to other land)—

(a)   sections 18 to 30B of (and the Schedule to) the 1985 Act (service charges, insurance and managing agents),

(b)   Part 2 of the 1987 Act (appointment of manager by leasehold valuation tribunal),

(c)   Part 4 of the 1987 Act (variation of leases),

(d)   sections 46 to 49 of the 1987 Act (information to be furnished to tenants),

(e)   Chapter 5 of Part 1 of the 1993 Act (management audit),

(f)   section 81 of the Housing Act 1996 (c. 52) (restriction on termination of tenancy for failure to pay service charge etc),

(g)   section 84 of (and Schedule 4 to) that Act (right to appoint surveyor), and

(h)   in this Chapter, the provisions relating to any of the provisions within paragraphs (a) to (g), Part 1 of Schedule 11 and sections 162 to 165 and sections 167 and 171.

(2)   Land is Crown land if there is or has at any time been an interest or estate in the land—

(a)   comprised in the Crown Estate,

(b)   belonging to Her Majesty in right of the Duchy of Lancaster,

(c) belonging to the Duchy of Cornwall, or

(d) belonging to a government department or held on behalf of Her Majesty for the purposes of a government department.

(3) No failure by the Crown to perform a duty imposed by or by virtue of any of sections 21 to 23A of, or any of paragraphs 2 to 4A of the Schedule to, the 1985 Act makes the Crown criminally liable; but the High Court may declare any such failure without reasonable excuse to be unlawful.

(4) Any sum payable under any of the provisions mentioned in subsection (1) by the Chancellor of the Duchy of Lancaster may be raised and paid under section 25 of the Duchy of Lancaster Act 1817 (c. 97) as an expense incurred in improvement of land belonging to Her Majesty in right of the Duchy.

(5) Any sum payable under such provision by the Duke of Cornwall (or any other possessor for the time being of the Duchy of Cornwall) may be raised and paid under section 8 of the Duchy of Cornwall Management Act 1863 (c. 49) as an expense incurred in permanently improving the possessions of the Duchy.

(6) In section 56 of the 1987 Act (Crown land)—

(a) in subsection (1), for 'This Act' substitute 'Parts 1 and 3 and sections 42 to 42B (and so much of this Part as relates to those provisions)', and

(b) in subsection (3), for 'this Act' substitute 'the provisions mentioned in subsection (1)'.

Leasehold Valuation Tribunals

173   Leasehold valuation tribunals

(1) Any jurisdiction conferred on a leasehold valuation tribunal by or under any enactment is exercisable by a rent assessment committee constituted in accordance with Schedule 10 to the Rent Act 1977 (c. 42).

(2) When so constituted for exercising any such jurisdiction a rent assessment committee is known as a leasehold valuation tribunal.

174   Procedure

Schedule 12 (leasehold valuation tribunals: procedure) has effect.

175   Appeals

(1) A party to proceedings before a leasehold valuation tribunal may appeal to the Lands Tribunal from a decision of the leasehold valuation tribunal.

(2) But the appeal may be made only with the permission of—

(a) the leasehold valuation tribunal, or

(b) the Lands Tribunal.

(3) And it must be made within the time specified by rules under section 3(6) of the Lands Tribunal Act 1949 (c. 42).

(4) On the appeal the Lands Tribunal may exercise any power which was available to the leasehold valuation tribunal.

(5) And a decision of the Lands Tribunal on the appeal may be enforced in the same way as a decision of the leasehold valuation tribunal.

(6) The Lands Tribunal may not order a party to the appeal to pay costs incurred by another party in connection with the appeal unless he has, in the opinion of the Lands Tribunal, acted frivolously, vexatiously, abusively, disruptively or otherwise unreasonably in connection with the appeal.

(7) In such a case the amount he may be ordered to pay shall not exceed the maximum amount which a party to proceedings before a leasehold valuation tribunal may be ordered to pay in the proceedings under or by virtue of paragraph 10(3) of Schedule 12.

(8) No appeal lies from a decision of a leasehold valuation tribunal to the High Court by virtue of section 11(1) of the Tribunals and Inquiries Act 1992 (c. 53).

(9) And no case may be stated for the opinion of the High Court in respect of such a decision by virtue of that provision.

(10) For the purposes of section 3(4) of the Lands Tribunal Act 1949 (which enables a person aggrieved by a decision of the Lands Tribunal to appeal to the Court of Appeal) a leasehold valuation tribunal is not a person aggrieved.

SCHEDULE 11
Administration charges
Section 158

Part 1 – Reasonableness of administration charges

Meaning of 'administration charge'

1(1) In this Part of this Schedule 'administration charge' means an amount payable by a tenant of a dwelling as part of or in addition to the rent which is payable, directly or indirectly—

(a) for or in connection with the grant of approvals under his lease, or applications for such approvals,

(b) for or in connection with the provision of information or documents by or on behalf of the landlord or a person who is party to his lease otherwise than as landlord or tenant,

(c) in respect of a failure by the tenant to make a payment by the due date to the landlord or a person who is party to his lease otherwise than as landlord or tenant, or

(d) in connection with a breach (or alleged breach) of a covenant or condition in his lease.

(2) But an amount payable by the tenant of a dwelling the rent of which is registered under Part 4 of the Rent Act 1977 (c. 42) is not an administration charge, unless the amount registered is entered as a variable amount in pursuance of section 71(4) of that Act.

(3) In this Part of this Schedule 'variable administration charge' means an administration charge payable by a tenant which is neither—

(a) specified in his lease, nor

(b) calculated in accordance with a formula specified in his lease.

(4) An order amending sub-paragraph (1) may be made by the appropriate national authority.

Reasonableness of administration charges

2 A variable administration charge is payable only to the extent that the amount of the charge is reasonable.

3(1) Any party to a lease of a dwelling may apply to a leasehold valuation tribunal for an order varying the lease in such manner as is specified in the application on the grounds that—

(a) any administration charge specified in the lease is unreasonable, or
(b) any formula specified in the lease in accordance with which any administration charge is calculated is unreasonable.

(2) If the grounds on which the application was made are established to the satisfaction of the tribunal, it may make an order varying the lease in such manner as is specified in the order.

(3) The variation specified in the order may be—

(a) the variation specified in the application, or
(b) such other variation as the tribunal thinks fit.

(4) The tribunal may, instead of making an order varying the lease in such manner as is specified in the order, make an order directing the parties to the lease to vary it in such manner as is so specified.

(5) The tribunal may by order direct that a memorandum of any variation of a lease effected by virtue of this paragraph be endorsed on such documents as are specified in the order.

(6) Any such variation of a lease shall be binding not only on the parties to the lease for the time being but also on other persons (including any predecessors in title), whether or not they were parties to the proceedings in which the order was made.

Notice in connection with demands for administration charges

4(1) A demand for the payment of an administration charge must be accompanied by a summary of the rights and obligations of tenants in dwellings in relation to administration charges.

(2) The appropriate national authority may make regulations prescribing requirements as to the form and content of such summaries of rights and obligations.

(3) A tenant may withhold payment of an administration charge which has been demanded from him if sub-paragraph (1) is not complied with in relation to the demand.

(4) Where a tenant withholds an administration charge under this paragraph, any provisions of the lease relating to non-payment or late payment of administration charges do not have effect in relation to the period for which he so withholds it.

Liability to pay administration charges

5(1) An application may be made to a leasehold valuation tribunal for a determination whether an administration charge is payable and, if it is, as to—

(a) the person by whom it is payable,

(b)   the person to whom it is payable,
(c)   the amount which is payable,
(d)   the date at or by which it is payable, and
(e)   the manner in which it is payable.

(2) Sub-paragraph (1) applies whether or not any payment has been made.

(3) The jurisdiction conferred on a leasehold valuation tribunal in respect of any matter by virtue of sub-paragraph (1) is in addition to any jurisdiction of a court in respect of the matter.

(4) No application under sub-paragraph (1) may be made in respect of a matter which—

(a)   has been agreed or admitted by the tenant,
(b)   has been, or is to be, referred to arbitration pursuant to a post-dispute arbitration agreement to which the tenant is a party,
(c)   has been the subject of determination by a court, or
(d)   has been the subject of determination by an arbitral tribunal pursuant to a post-dispute arbitration agreement.

(5) But the tenant is not to be taken to have agreed or admitted any matter by reason only of having made any payment.

(6) An agreement by the tenant of a dwelling (other than a post-dispute arbitration agreement) is void in so far as it purports to provide for a determination—

(a)   in a particular manner, or
(b)   on particular evidence,

of any question which may be the subject matter of an application under sub-paragraph (1).

Interpretation

6(1) This paragraph applies for the purposes of this Part of this Schedule.

(2) 'Tenant' includes a statutory tenant.

(3) 'Dwelling' and 'statutory tenant' (and 'landlord' in relation to a statutory tenant) have the same meanings as in the 1985 Act.

(4) 'Post-dispute arbitration agreement', in relation to any matter, means an arbitration agreement made after a dispute about the matter has arisen.

(5) 'Arbitration agreement' and 'arbitral tribunal' have the same meanings as in Part 1 of the Arbitration Act 1996.

. . .

SCHEDULE 12

Leasehold valuation tribunals: procedure

Section 174

Procedure regulations

1 The appropriate national authority may make regulations about the procedure of leasehold valuation tribunals ('procedure regulations').

Applications

2 Procedure regulations may include provision—

- (a) about the form of applications to leasehold valuation tribunals,
- (b) about the particulars that must be contained in such applications,
- (c) requiring the service of notices of such applications, and
- (d) for securing consistency where numerous applications are or may be brought in respect of the same or substantially the same matters.

Transfers

3(1) Where in any proceedings before a court there falls for determination a question falling within the jurisdiction of a leasehold valuation tribunal, the court—

- (a) may by order transfer to a leasehold valuation tribunal so much of the proceedings as relate to the determination of that question, and
- (b) may then dispose of all or any remaining proceedings, or adjourn the disposal of all or any remaining proceedings pending the determination of that question by the leasehold valuation tribunal, as it thinks fit.

(2) When the leasehold valuation tribunal has determined the question, the court may give effect to the determination in an order of the court.

(3) Rules of court may prescribe the procedure to be followed in a court in connection with or in consequence of a transfer under this paragraph.

(4) Procedure regulations may prescribe the procedure to be followed in a leasehold valuation tribunal consequent on a transfer under this paragraph.

Information

4(1) A leasehold valuation tribunal may serve a notice requiring any party to proceedings before it to give to the leasehold valuation tribunal any information which the leasehold valuation tribunal may reasonable require.

(2) The information shall be given to the leasehold valuation tribunal within such period (not being less than 14 days) from the service of the notice as is specified in the notice.

Pre-trial reviews

5(1) Procedure regulations may include provision for the holding of a pre-trial review (on the application of a party to proceedings or on the motion of a leasehold valuation tribunal).

(2) Procedure regulations may provide for the exercise of the functions of a leasehold valuation tribunal in relation to, or at, a pre-trial review by a single member of the panel provided for in Schedule 10 to the Rent Act 1977 (c. 42) who is qualified to exercise them.

(3) A member is qualified to exercise the functions specified in sub-paragraph (2) if he was appointed to that panel by the Lord Chancellor.

Parties

6 Procedure regulations may include provision enabling persons to be joined as parties to proceedings.

Dismissal

7 Procedure regulations may include provision empowering leasehold valuation tribunals to dismiss applications or transferred proceedings, in whole or in part, on the ground that they are—

    (a)   frivolous or vexatious, or
    (b)   otherwise an abuse of process.

Determination without hearing

8(1) Procedure regulations may include provision for the determination of applications or transferred proceedings without an oral hearing.

(2) Procedure regulations may provide for the determinations without an oral hearing by a single member of the panel provided for in Schedule 10 to the Rent Act 1977.

Fees

9(1) Procedure regulations may include provision requiring the payment of fees in respect of an application or transfer of proceedings to, or oral hearing by, a leasehold valuation tribunal in a case under—

    (a)   the 1985 Act (service charges and choice of insurers),
    (b)   Part 2 of the 1987 Act (managers),
    (c)   Part 4 of the 1987 Act (variation of leases),
    (d)   section 160(4) of this Act, or
    (e)   Schedule 11 to this Act.

(2) Procedure regulations may empower a leasehold valuation tribunal to require a party to proceedings to reimburse any other party to the proceedings the whole or part of any fees paid by him.

(3) The fees payable shall be such as are specified in or determined in accordance with procedure regulations; but the fee (or, where fees are payable in respect of both an application or transfer and an oral hearing, the aggregate of the fees) payable by a person in respect of any proceedings shall not exceed—

    (a)   £500, or
    (b)   such other amount as may be specified in procedure regulations.

(4) Procedure regulations may provide for the reduction or waiver of fees by reference to the financial resources of the party by whom they are to be paid or met.

(5) If they do so they may apply, subject to such modifications as may be specified in the regulations, any other statutory means-testing regime as it has effect from time to time.

Costs

10(1) A leasehold valuation tribunal may determine that a party to proceedings shall pay the costs incurred by another party in connection with the proceedings in any circumstances falling within sub-paragraph (2).

(2) The circumstances are where—

(a) he has made an application to the leasehold valuation tribunal which is dismissed in accordance with regulations made by virtue of paragraph 7, or

(b) he has, in the opinion of the leasehold valuation tribunal, acted frivolously, vexatiously, abusively, disruptively or otherwise unreasonably in connection with the proceedings.

(3) The amount which a party to proceedings may be ordered to pay in the proceedings by a determination under this paragraph shall not exceed—

(a) £500, or

(b) such other amount as may be specified in procedure regulations.

(4) A person shall not be required to pay costs incurred by another person in connection with proceedings before a leasehold valuation tribunal except by a determination under this paragraph or in accordance with provision made by any enactment other than this paragraph.

Enforcement

11 Procedure regulations may provide for decisions of leasehold valuation tribunals to be enforceable, with the permission of a county court, in the same way as orders of such a court.

THE LEASEHOLD VALUATION TRIBUNALS (SERVICE CHARGES, INSURANCE OR APPOINTMENT OF MANAGERS APPLICATIONS) ORDER 1997 (SI 1997/1853)

The Secretary of State for the Environment, in respect of applications to a leasehold valuation tribunal in England, and the Secretary of State for Wales, in respect of applications to a leasehold valuation tribunal in Wales, in exercise of the powers conferred by section 31B of the Landlord and Tenant Act 1985 and section 24B of the Landlord and Tenant Act 1987, and of all other powers enabling them in that behalf, hereby make the following Order:

Citation, commencement and interpretation

1(1) This Order may be cited as the Leasehold Valuation Tribunals (Service Charges, Insurance or Appointment of Managers Applications) Order 1997 and shall come into force on 1st September 1997.

(2) Unless the context otherwise requires, any expression in this Order—

(a)　where used in connection with a provision of the Landlord and Tenant Act 1985 has the same meaning as in that Act, and

(b)　where used in connection with the Landlord and Tenant Act 1987 has the same meaning as in that Act.

(3) In this Order 'tribunal' means a leasehold valuation tribunal.

Content of applications

2(1) An application to a tribunal under section 19(2A) or (2B) of the Landlord and Tenant Act 1985 (determination of reasonableness of service charges) shall contain—

(a)　where the applicant is a tenant, the particulars specified in Part I of Schedule 1 to this Order; and

(b)　where the applicant is a landlord, the particulars specified in Part II of that Schedule.

(2) An application to a tribunal under section 20C of the Landlord and Tenant Act 1985 (limitation of service charges: costs of proceedings), where such application is not made at the hearing, shall contain the particulars specified in Part III of that Schedule.

(3) An application to a tribunal under paragraph 8 of the Schedule to the Landlord and Tenant Act 1985 (right to challenge landlord's choice of insurers) shall contain the particulars specified in Part IV of that Schedule.

(4) An application to a tribunal for an order under section 22(3) of the Landlord and Tenant Act 1987 (preliminary notice by tenant) shall contain the particulars specified in Part I of Schedule 2 to this Order.

(5) An application to a tribunal for an order under section 24(1) of the Landlord and Tenant Act 1987 (appointment of manager by the tribunal) shall contain the particulars specified in Part II of that Schedule.

(6) An application to a tribunal for an order under section 24(9) of the Landlord and Tenant Act 1987 (variation or discharge of an order appointing a manager) shall contain the particulars specified in Part III of that Schedule.

(7) An application to a tribunal for leave to appeal to the Lands Tribunal shall contain—

- (a) the name and address of the party seeking leave to appeal, and
- (b) where that party is represented, the name, address and occupation of his representative,
- (c) the names and addresses of the other parties to the application,
- (d) the date of the decision and any reference number, and
- (e) the grounds of appeal.

SCHEDULE 1

Contents of Applications under the Landlord and Tenant Act 1985

Article 2(1) to (3)

Part I – Content of Tenant's Application for Determination of Reasonableness of Service Charge (section 19(2A) and (2B) of the 1985 Act)

1 The particulars specified for the purposes of article 2(1)(a) are set out in paragraphs 2 to 12 below.

2 The address of the property to which the service charge which is the subject of the application relates.

3 A statement setting out whether the application is made under section 19(2A) or (2B), or both, and—

- (a) in respect of an application under section 19(2A)—
  - (i) the costs incurred for services, repairs, maintenance, insurance or management, whether the applicant considers such costs to be reasonable and, if not, the applicant's reasons,
  - (ii) the services or works for which costs were incurred, whether the applicant considers such services or works to be of a reasonable standard and, if not, the applicant's reasons, or
  - (iii) the amount payable before costs are incurred, whether the applicant considers the amount is reasonable and, if not, the applicant's reasons;
- (b) in respect of an application under section 19(2B)—
  - (i) the costs to be incurred for services, repairs, maintenance, insurance or management of any specified description, whether the applicant considers them to be reasonable and, if not, the applicant's reasons,
  - (ii) the services to be provided or works to be carried out to a particular specification, whether the applicant considers such services or works would be of a reasonable standard and, if not, the applicant's reasons, or
  - (iii) the amount payable before costs are incurred and, if the applicant considers the amount unreasonable, the applicant's reasons.

4 The name and address of the applicant and the name, address and occupation of the applicant's representative, if any.

5 The name and address of the landlord and, if that address is not in England and Wales, an address in England and Wales at which notices may be served (if known to the applicant).

6 The name and address of every person known to the applicant who is or may be liable by way of service charge for any part of the expenditure which is or may be included in the service charge and, where a recognised tenants' association exists in respect of the property to which the service charge which is the subject of the application relates, the name and address of the secretary of the association.

7 A copy of the lease or other document under which the service charge is payable.

8 Either a copy of the disputed demand for payment of the service charge and a statement of the period to which it is attributable; or, if no such demand has been made, a copy of any notification specifying services which are to be provided or works which are to be carried out and, if known, the likely cost of such works or services.

9 The matters upon which the applicant intends to rely in support of his application; and where he intends to rely on any document, a copy of that document.

10 Whether the applicant intends to apply at the hearing for an order under section 20C of the Landlord and Tenant Act 1985 (limitation of service charges: costs of proceedings).

11 Whether the applicant claims a reduction or waiver of fees and, if so, the basis of the claim.

12 The date of the application.

Part II – Content of Landlord's Application for Determination of Reasonableness of Service Charge (section 19(2A) and (2B) of the 1985 Act)

1 The particulars specified for the purposes of article 2(1)(b) are set out in paragraphs 2 to 10 below.

2 The address of the property to which the service charge which is the subject of the application relates.

3 A statement setting out whether the application is made under section 19(2A) or (2B), or both, and—

   (a)   in respect of an application under section 19(2A)—
      (i)   the costs incurred for services, repairs, maintenance, insurance or management and the applicant's reasons for considering such costs reasonable,
      (ii)   the services or works for which costs were incurred and the applicant's reasons for considering the services or works to be of a reasonable standard, or
      (iii) the amount payable before costs are incurred and the applicant's reasons for considering such amount reasonable;
   (b)   in respect of an application under section 19(2B)—
      (i)   the costs to be incurred for services, repairs, maintenance, insurance or management of any specified description and the applicant's reasons for considering such costs reasonable,
      (ii)   the services to be provided or works to be carried out to a particular specification and the applicant's reasons for considering that such services or works would be of a reasonable standard, or
      (iii) the amount payable before costs are incurred which the applicant considers would be reasonable and the applicant's reasons.

4 The name and address of the applicant and the name, address and occupation of the applicant's representative, if any.

5 The name and address (where known to the applicant) of each respondent and each other person who is or may be liable by way of service charge for any part of the expenditure charged for in a service charge and the total number of dwellings in respect of which the same or substantially the same service charge is payable and where a recognised tenants' association exists in respect of the property to which the service charge relates, the name and address of the secretary of the association.

6(1) Subject to sub-paragraph (2), a copy of the lease or leases, or other document under which the service charge is payable and any demand for payment of the disputed service charge showing—

 (a) in the case of an application where a demand for payment of a service charge has been made, the amount of the service charge, the individual items included in the charge and the date when payment is due;
 (b) in the case of an application where a service charge or a demand for payment of the service charge has not yet been made—
  (i) the amount, or likely amount, to be included in the service charge,
  (ii) the individual items or estimated individual items to be included in the charge, and
  (iii) the date when such amount will, or may, be due for payment.

(2) Where the application relates to more than one dwelling and the leases or other documents and the demands for payment of the service charge for each such dwelling are in the same or substantially the same terms, the applicant need not provide such documents for each dwelling providing that the applicant does provide a specimen lease or other document and demand for payment accompanied by a statement—

 (a) specifying those respects in which such documents differ from the corresponding documents for all the other dwellings concerned in the application, and
 (b) confirming that in all other respects such documents are the same.

7 A breakdown of the amount of such of the costs incurred or, as the case may be, to be incurred for services, repairs, maintenance, insurance or management as together comprise the service charge, so as to show how the service charge and each element of it is calculated.

8 The matters upon which the applicant intends to rely in support of his application; and where he intends to rely on any document, a copy of that document.

9 Whether the applicant claims a reduction or waiver of fees and, if so, the basis of the claim.

10 The date of the application.

Part III – Content of Tenant's Application for an Order under Section 20C of the 1985 Act (limitation of service charges: costs of court proceedings)

1 The particulars for the purpose of article 2(2) are set out in paragraphs 2 to 11 below.

2 The address of the property in respect of which the service charge is payable.

3 The name and address of the applicant and the name, address and occupation of the applicant's representative, if any.

4 The name and address of the respondent landlord and, if that address is not in England and Wales, an address in England and Wales at which notices may be served (if known to the applicant).

5 The name and address (where known to the applicant) of every other party to the proceedings in respect of which the tenant seeks an order that the landlord's costs incurred in proceedings before the tribunal are not to be regarded as relevant costs to be taken into account in determining the amount of any service charge payable by the tenant or any other person or persons specified in the application.

6 The name and address of every person known to the applicant who is or may be liable by way of service charge for any part of the costs and, where a recognised tenants' association exists in respect of the property to which the service charge which is the subject of the application relates, the name and address of the secretary of the association.

7 A copy of the service charge demand (including, if known, a statement of the amount of the costs incurred by the landlord in connection with proceedings before the tribunal) in respect of which the applicant seeks an order.

8 A copy of the lease or other document under which the service charge, including the landlord's costs incurred in proceedings before the leasehold valuation tribunal, is payable.

9 A copy of the decision of the tribunal in the proceedings in respect of which the costs incurred by the landlord are included or are to be included in the service charge and in respect of which the applicant seeks an order.

10 The matters upon which the applicant intends to rely in support of his application; and where he intends to rely on any document, a copy of that document.

11 The date of the application.

Part IV – Content of Application to Challenge Landlord's Choice of Insurers (paragraph 8 of the Schedule to the 1985 Act)

1 The particulars specified for the purposes of article 2(3) are set out in paragraphs 2 to 11 below.

2 The address of the dwelling of which insurance is the subject of the application and, where the dwelling is not a house and forms part of a building, the address of the building.

3 A statement setting out the dispute which is the subject of the application including—

    (a)   whether it is alleged by the applicant that the insurance which is available from the nominated insurer for insuring the tenant's dwelling is unsatisfactory in any respect and, if so, in what respect,

    (b)   whether it is alleged by the applicant that the premiums in respect of any such insurance are excessive and, if so, in what respect,

    (c)   the amount of the premiums payable in respect of the insurance available from the nominated insurer,

    (d)   the cover provided by the insurance policy, and

    (e)   the period to which the insurance is attributable.

4 The name and address of the applicant and the name, address and occupation of the applicant's representative, if any.

5 The name and address of the respondent landlord and, if that address is not in England and Wales, an address in England and Wales at which notices may be served (if known to the applicant).

6 Where the dwelling forms part of a building which contains other dwellings, the name and address of every tenant or other person within that building who is known to the applicant who is or may be required to pay for or contribute to the costs of the same or substantially the same insurance and, where a recognised tenants' association exists in respect of the building, the name and address of the secretary of the association.

7 A copy of the lease under which the tenant is required to insure the dwelling with an insurer nominated by the landlord.

8 A copy of the insurance policy if this is within the possession of the applicant or can reasonably be obtained by the applicant.

9 The matters upon which the applicant intends to rely in support of his application; and where he intends to rely on any document, a copy of that document.

10 Whether the applicant claims a reduction or waiver of fees and, if so, the basis of the claim.

11 The date of the application.

SCHEDULE 2

Contents of Applications under Part II of the Landlord and Tenant Act 1987

Article 2(4) to (6)

Part I – Content of Tenant's Application to Dispense with Service of Preliminary Notice (section 22(3) of the 1987 Act)

1 The particulars specified for the purposes of article 2(4) are set out in paragraphs 2 to 6 below.

2 The address of the property which is to be the subject of an application for an order under section 24 of the Landlord and Tenant Act 1987.

3 A statement setting out the grounds of the application to dispense with service of a preliminary notice, including in particular, details of the applicant's attempts to ascertain the name and address of the landlord or an address in England and Wales at which a notice might be served.

4 The name and address of the applicant and the name, address and occupation of the applicant's representative, if any.

5 The name and address of every person known to the applicant who is likely to be affected by the application, including but not limited to, the other tenants of flats contained in the property, any mortgagee or superior landlord of the landlord and, where a recognised tenants' association exists in respect of the property to which the application relates, the name and address of the secretary of the association.

6 The date of the application.

Part II – Content of Tenant's Application for Appointment of a Manager (section 24(1) of the 1987 Act)

1 The particulars specified for the purposes of article 2(5) are set out in paragraphs 2 to 12 below.

2 The address of the property which is the subject of the application.

3 A statement setting out—

    (a)   the grounds of the application for an order to appoint a manager,

    (b)   the name, address and qualifications of the person it is desired to be appointed manager of the premises, and

    (c)   the functions which it is desired that the manager should carry out.

4 The name and address of the applicant and the name, address and occupation of the applicant's representative, if any.

5 The name and address of the respondent landlord and, if that address is not in England and Wales, an address in England and Wales at which notices may be served (if known to the applicant).

6 The name and address of every person known to the applicant who is likely to be affected by the application, including, but not limited to, the other tenants of flats contained in the property, any mortgagee or superior landlord of the landlord and, where a recognised tenants' association exists in respect of the property to which the application relates, the name and address of the secretary of the association.

7 A copy of the applicant's lease of his dwelling.

8 Except in a case to which paragraph 9 applies—

    (a)   a copy of the notice under section 22 of the Landlord and Tenant Act 1987 (preliminary notice by tenant) served by the applicant on the landlord; and

    (b)   a copy of any document received by the applicant in response to that notice.

9 Where a tenant has made an application under section 22(3) of the Landlord and Tenant Act 1987 to dispense with the requirement to serve a notice under section 22 of that Act (preliminary notice by tenant) the application shall contain—

    (a)   if the application under section 22(3) has not yet been determined, a copy of that application, or

    (b)   if the application under section 22(3) has been determined the following information—

        (i)   where the tribunal has given directions as to the service of other notices or the taking of other steps, a statement of the notices served or the other steps taken by the applicant in accordance with the tribunal's direction; or

        (ii)   where the tribunal has dispensed with service, a statement to that effect.

10 A statement of the grounds on which the tribunal will be asked to make an order under section 24 of the Landlord and Tenant Act 1987 and the matters that will be relied on by the applicant for the purpose of establishing those grounds.

11 Whether the application claims a reduction or waiver of fees and, if so, the basis of the claim.

12 The date of the application.

Part III – Content of Application to Vary or Discharge Order Appointing a Manager (section 24(9) of the 1987 Act)

1 The particulars specified for the purposes of article 2(6) are set out in paragraphs 2 to 11 below.

2 The address of the property which is the subject of the application.

3 A statement that the purpose of the application is to seek to vary or discharge an order under section 24 of the Landlord and Tenant Act 1987 (appointment of manager).

4 A copy of the order which the applicant seeks to vary or discharge.

5 The name and address of the applicant and the name, address and occupation of the applicant's representative, if any.

6 Where the application is made by the landlord of the premises the name and address (where known to the landlord) of every respondent which shall include every tenant of the premises.

7 Where the application is by a tenant, the name and address of the respondent landlord or the office of the landlord and, if that address is not in England and Wales, an address in England and Wales at which notices may be served (if known to the tenant).

8 The name of every person known to the applicant who is likely to be affected by the application, including but not limited to, the tenants (or, in the case of a tenant's application, the other tenants) of flats contained in the property, any mortgagee or superior landlord of the landlord and, where a recognised tenants' association exists, the name and address of the secretary of the association.

9 A statement of the grounds on which the tribunal will be asked to vary or discharge the order and the matters which will be relied upon by the applicant in establishing those grounds; and where the applicant intends to rely on any document, a copy of that document.

10 Whether the applicant claims a reduction or waiver of fees and, if so, the basis of the claim.

11 The date of the application.

Sources of amendments to prior Acts made by the Commonhold and Leasehold Reform Act 2002

AMENDMENT/REPEAL	SOURCE IN 2002 ACT
Landlord and Tenant Act 1985	
s 18	s 150, Sch 9, para 7
s 19(2A)–(3)	s 180, Sch 14
s 20	s 151
s 20ZA	s 151
s 21	s 152
s 21A	s 152
s 21B	s 153
s 22	s 154
s 23	s 157, Sch 10, para 1
s 23A	s 157, Sch 10, para 2
s 24	s 157, Sch 10, para 3
s 25	s 157, Sch 10, para 4
s 26	s 157, Sch 10, para 5
s	s 157, Sch 10, para 5
s 27A	s 155(1)
s 28	s 157, Sch 10, para 6
ss 31A to 31C	s 180, Sch 14
s 38	s 155(2)
s 39	ss 155(3), 157, 180, Sch 10, para 7, Sch 14
Sch, para 2	ss 157, 180, Sch 10, para 8, Sch 14
Sch, para 3	s 157, Sch 10, para 9
Sch, para 4	ss 157, 180, Sch 10, para 10, Sch 14
Sch, para 4A	s 157, Sch 10, para 11
Sch, para 5	ss 157, 180, Sch 10, para 12, Sch 14
Sch, para 6	s 157, Sch 10, para 13
Sch, para 8(1)	s 165(1), (2)
Sch, para 8(2)	s 165(1), (2)
Sch, para 8(4)	s 165(1), (3)
Sch, para 8(5)	s 180, Sch 14
Landlord and Tenant Act 1987	
s 35(1)	s 163(1), (2)
s 35(2), (3A)	s 162
s 35(5)	s 163(1), (2)
s 36	s 163(1), (3)
s 37	s 163(1), (4)
s 38	s 163(1), (5)
s 39	s 163(1), (6)
s 40	s 163(1), (7)
s 42	ss 157, 180, Sch 10, para 15, Sch 14
ss 42A–B	s 156(1)
s 46	s 158, Sch 11, para 9
s 47	s 158, Sch 11, para 10
s 48	s 158, Sch 11, para 11
s 53(2)(a)	s 180, Sch 14

AMENDMENT/REPEAL	SOURCE IN 2002 ACT
s 53(2)(b)	ss 156(2), 162(5)
s 56	ss 172(6), 180, Sch 14

Leasehold Reform, Housing and Urban Development Act 1993

s 79	s 157, Sch 10, para 16
s 80	s 157, Sch 10, para 17
s 81	s 157, Sch 10, para 18
s 82	s 157, Sch 10, para 19
s 84	s 150, Sch 9, para 10
s 87	s 150, Sch 9, para 11

Housing Act 1996

s 81	s 170
Sch 4	s 150, Sch 9, para 12

Appendix 4   CODE OF PRACTICE RELATING TO SERVICE CHARGES

SERVICE CHARGES IN COMMERCIAL PROPERTY – A GUIDE TO GOOD PRACTICE

Reproduced with the kind permission of the Royal Institution of Chartered Surveyors.

FOREWORD

Accountability for service charges, budgetary control and certification of actual costs in respect of commercial properties are all matters that demand considerable attention.

As certain types of property have become more complex and both customer and occupier expectations have changed; the services provided by owners have increased in scope. A modern service charge may therefore include provision for the recovery of a multiplicity of services.

In providing the services the owner's objective will be to maintain the quality and value of his investment with 100% recovery of the costs incurred. The occupier will seek reasonable enjoyment and use of the premises, at a reasonable cost, excluding unnecessary or inappropriate costs.

These differing aims therefore have the potential to produce conflict within the landlord and tenant relationship.

Statutory Regulation in respect of service charges for residential accommodation was introduced in the Housing Finance Act 1972 and has since been replaced by successive legislation imposing greater safeguards for tenants against abuse.

However, despite the wealth of legislation, and case law, dedicated to residential service charges, there is little legislation or case law that affects service charges in commercial premises.

In 1996 the first industry wide Guide to Good Practice was produced. Since then, business practice and relationships between owners and occupiers have continued to develop and the new edition of the Guide reflects this and is based on current good practice.

INTRODUCTION

1   In multi-occupied buildings, the owner will often retain responsibility for such matters as the structure and common parts areas and items of plant and machinery such as lifts, air conditioning and heating installations provided for the benefit of a number of occupiers.

2   The service charge is the means by which an owner is able to recover from the occupiers the cost of providing the services for the benefit of those premises. How the service charge is structured and the nature of the services provided will vary with the type of premises eg office blocks, industrial/warehousing, shopping centres and mixed use properties.

3   Accountability for service charges, budgetary control and certification of actual costs incurred are all matters that demand considerable attention.

4   This Guide sets out overall principles for good practice designed to cover all types of properties. The extent to which they apply will depend upon the nature, type and complexity of the property. The principles are set in the overall context of managing property but specifically apply to the delivery of common services and their costs on multi-let properties.

5   The Guide recommends these good principles should be aspired to and recognises that many property leases were entered into prior to the publication of the Guide.

         It cannot override the provisions of the lease but the parties should in negotiations between them seek, where possible, to interpret and apply the lease in accordance with the principles of the Guide.

6   The Guide promotes good administrative and business practice between owners and occupiers in the management of services in commercial properties.

7   The Guide encourages good working relationships to secure co-operation between owners and occupiers through consultation and communication about what services are required, their quality and cost.

8   Excellent communications and transparency in the way services and their costs are managed and administered are key principles to achieving good practice and underpin the whole basis of the Guide.

9   Individual clauses within the Guide should not be interpreted in isolation but should be read in context with the Guide as a whole.

SERVICE PROVISION

10   Contractors and suppliers of services should be required to perform according to written performance standards.[1]

11   Performance standards for services should be established to provide a clear definition of the standards to be achieved. Performance should be regularly measured and reviewed against the defined standard levels.

12   The services provided should be beneficial and relevant to the needs of the property, the owner, the occupiers and their customers.

13   The aim is to achieve value for money rather than lowest costs.

14   The levels and standards of service provided for each property will be different depending on the nature, type and complexity of the property.

15   Sufficient staffing of the right type and calibre should be provided to operate the services efficiently and cost effectively.

16   Where contracts are reviewed it is not unreasonable for the parties to agree that costs associated with achieving beneficial change, such as termination of contracts, should be recovered under the service charge where such costs can be

---

1   See Appendix 1.

justified following the analysis of reasonable options and the proposal achieves greater value for money.

Service charge costs

17   Service charge costs should be restricted to charges and associated administrative costs properly incurred by the owner in the operational management of the property including the reasonable costs of maintenance, repair and replacement (where beyond economic repair) of the fabric, plant, equipment and materials necessary for the property.

18   Service charge costs should not include:

(a)   Any initial costs incurred in relation to the original design and construction of the fabric, plant or equipment.

(b)   Any setting up costs that are reasonably to be considered part of the original development cost of the property.

(c)   Improvement costs above the cost of normal maintenance, repair or replacement.[1]

(d)   Future redevelopment costs.

(e)   Such costs as are matters between the owner and an individual occupier for instance; enforcement of covenants for collection of rent, costs of letting units, consents for assignments, sub-letting, alterations, rent reviews etc.

19   Service Charge costs may include enhancement of the fabric, plant or equipment where such expenditure can be justified following the analysis of reasonable options and alternatives. Owners should provide the facts and figures to justify such a decision.

Value for money

20   Service quality should be appropriate to the location, use and character of the property.

21   The owner should procure quality service standards to ensure that value for money is achieved at all times.

22   Occupiers should be proactive in assisting owners with operating and using services on a value for money and quality standards basis.

23   The owner should keep costs under review and where appropriate regularly require contractors and suppliers either to submit competitive tenders or to provide competing quotations. Tendering and/or benchmarking should be undertaken at least once every 3 years.

24   Major service providers should be acting with owners to continually review methods and processes that drive for value and efficiencies.

25   The owner should be entitled to use a procurement specialist to obtain these services so long as the purpose is to achieve greater value for money and cost effectiveness.

---

1   See Appendix 2.

26   Contracts and remuneration packages should be performance related where appropriate, based on market rates and benchmarked, and should have regard to the local and national economy.

Transparency

27   Greater transparency can be achieved where service charge payments are kept in a separately identified account. For example, it enables any interest earned to be identified and, after any appropriate deductions made (bank charges, tax etc), credited back to the account.

GENERAL

Communications

28   Communication and consultation between owners and occupiers should be timely and regular in order to encourage and promote a good working relationship and understanding with regard to the provision, relevance, cost and quality of services.

29   Effective communications are key to good practice and the aim should be to provide transparency between owner and occupier in the way services are provided and managed.

30   Communication should be before rather than after an event.

31   Owners and occupiers should deal with each other's reasonable enquiries and reciprocal obligations in a prompt and efficient manner.

32   Feedback from occupiers on the performance management standards and service delivery should be sought and actioned.

33   The owners or their managing agents should hold regular meetings with occupiers. The occupiers should use best endeavours to encourage and participate in these meetings.

34   A clear communication structure should be established. The owner should identify:

   (a)   Names and points of contact ie Management Surveyor, Credit Controller, Accounts Clerk etc,
   (b)   Names of on site staff,
   (c)   Their roles and responsibilities.

35   The occupier should advise the owner of who deals with service charges and of the allocation of responsibility between site and head office.

36   Communication plans should contain standard information about how the property is managed and the aims of the management team.

37   When significant variances in actual costs against budget are likely, the owner should give prompt notification to occupiers within the current service charge year.

38   When substantial works are planned the process should be communicated to provide full information on the programme of works, costs and the process to be adopted for keeping occupiers informed.

39   Where appropriate, a relationship should be established with relevant local community organisations.[1]

Promotions[2]

40   The funding of promotional activities is recognised as a shared cost to be borne by both owners and occupiers and in such cases, consultation is considered essential.

41   Service charge budgets should state what the gross expenditure on promotions is and how much is contributed by the owner.

42   Promotional plans should be prepared and presented to occupiers in advance of the period to which they relate.

43   Promotions should be reviewed with occupiers to analyse their effectiveness.

Income[3, 4]

44   There should be a clear statement of policy on how costs and income generated from services and activities in the malls are allocated.

45   Income derived from the provision of a service or activity, the finance for which is included in the service charge, should be treated as a service charge credit eg income from public telephones, toilet vending machines, photocopy and fax reimbursements etc. Similarly, income derived from promotional activity should be credited to the promotional expenditure budget.

46   Where the owner retains income from common parts areas and the space is of a permanent or semi-permanent nature eg barrows or kiosks within shopping malls, the space should be included in the service charge apportionment matrix. Alternatively, a sum should be credited to the service charge to reflect a contribution towards the benefit of the services enjoyed.

47   Expenditure and income receipts should be shown separately in the service charge account and income should be credited to the service charge after calculation of the management fee.

ADMINISTRATION

Management

48   The owner has the duty to manage the property.

49   The owner should ensure that the standards of services provided are monitored, that the quality and cost of the services provided are regularly reviewed and, where possible, demonstrate that value for money is being obtained.

50   Owners should operate sound management procedures to ensure that the respective obligations of owner and occupier are discharged and the services are provided in an efficient and economic manner.

---

1   See Appendix 3.
2   Relates principally to shopping centres, retail and leisure parks.
3   Relates principally to shopping centres, retail and leisure parks.
4   See Appendix 4.

51   Management policies should be established that define the procurement, administration and management of services provided. These policies should be communicated to the occupiers.

52   The owner should inform occupiers of the plans for the property in so far as they have an implication on the service charge.

53   On-site management staff should have a sound knowledge of modern business practices and be adequately skilled to provide best/agreed performance standards.

54   Occupiers should amend their records when advised of changes by the owner or managing agent, ie revised budgets, new payee, new agents etc.

Management fees

55   The fee should be reasonable for the work properly done in relation to the operation and management of the services and have due regard to the principles of the Guide.

56   The management service should be regularly tendered or benchmarked against the market.

57   The provider of the service should have defined quality standard procedures.

Apportionment[1]

58   Apportionment of costs to each occupier should be on a fair and reasonable basis, in accordance with the principles of good estate management and applied fairly and consistently throughout the property having regard to the physical size, nature of use and the benefit to the occupier or occupiers.

59   An apportionment schedule should be available showing the total apportionment for each unit within the property/complex.[2]

60   The occupiers should not be charged through the service charge or otherwise collectively toward the costs attributable to unlet premises. Also, the owner should meet the cost of any special concession given by an owner to any one occupier. A properly constituted weighting formula is not regarded as a special concession.

61   The owner should bear a fair proportion of costs attributable to his use of the property eg where a centre management suite is used in part as the owner's regional office.

62   Where there is a separate cost/profit centre within a property complex that generates income for the owner, which is not credited to the service charge account, the costs associated with maintaining and running that cost centre should not be allocated to the service charge account (eg car parks).

63   Where services are provided for the benefit of specific occupiers only, these costs should be allocated to the specific occupiers that benefit from or need them.

---

1   See Appendix 5.
2   See Appendix 6.

64   If the property is fully let the owner should normally be able to recover all expenditure on services through the service charge.

65   The estimated budget of service charge expenditure and certified accounts should set out the method and calculation used to determine each occupier's share of the costs and how costs are apportioned.

Budgets/accounts[1]

66   The owner should provide an estimate of likely service charge expenditure to the occupiers at least one month prior to the commencement of the service charge year.

67   The owner should submit certified accounts to the occupiers in a timely manner and in any event within 6 months of the end of the service charge year.

68   This should give an adequately detailed and comprehensive summary of items of expenditure and in a reasonably consistent format year on year, which the occupiers can understand. There should be a clear correlation between a head of expenditure and its breakdown.

69   The budget should be issued in such a way that provides sufficient information to enable occupiers to compare it with the last issued certified accounts.

70   The budgets and accounts should be issued with a report that provides the following minimum information:

    (a)   A reasonably comprehensive level of detail to enable occupiers to compare expenditure against estimated budget.

    (b)   Explanations on significant individual costs and on variances from the previous year's budget/accounts.

    (c)   Comparison against the previous two years' actual costs.

    (d)   Information on core matters that are critical to that account (eg levels of apportionment, contracts, report on tendering, etc).

    (e)   The achieved and/or targeted measures of improved management performance (eg successes in delivering improved quality services and greater value for money).

    (f)   Separately identified on-site management team costs.

    (g)   Details and results of the last previous and forthcoming tendering exercise. Occupiers should be advised of the contractors who are providing the services.

    (h)   A statement detailing how income generated from operating the property, how shared services are dealt with, and how they impact on the service charge.

71   The owner should allow occupiers a reasonable period in which to raise enquiries in respect of the certified accounts.

72   Owners should deal with reasonable enquiries in a prompt and efficient manner and make relevant papers available for inspection.

---

1   See Appendices 8–12.

73   Where copies are requested and can be made available, an appropriate fee may be charged.

74   The account should be certified by an auditor and charged to the service charge account. If an occupier requests an independent audit, the owner should agree and the audit fee charged to the occupier.

75   Where the owner or managing agent was not responsible for the earlier years, they should convert the data into a consistent format for comparison.

76   As soon as practicable, but not later than six months, following the date of completion of a sale of a property, the Vendor should provide the Purchaser with full details of all service charge expenditure, accruals, pre-payments etc for all outstanding service charge years up to the date of sale.

Sinking funds[1]

77   Any monies accumulated in a sinking fund, replacement fund or reserve fund should be held in an interest bearing trust account, separate from the owner's own monies.

78   The annual budget and reconciliation accounts should clearly state contributions to and expenditure from the sinking fund account.

79   Upon completion of the sale of a property, the Vendor should pass all sinking fund monies held, together with all accrued interest, to the Purchaser.

APPENDICES

The Appendices provide examples of what is considered to be good practice and illustrates how some of the principles outlined in the Guide can be achieved.

Guidance notes and examples provided are:

1.   Performance contracts
2.   Improvement and refurbishment
3.   Local community organisations
4.   Treatment of miscellaneous income
5.   Common methods of apportionment
6.   Apportionment matrix example
7.   Sinking/reserve funds
8.   Service charge reconciliation and expenditure report
9.   Landlord's surveyor's service charge certificate
10.   Expenditure report summary
11.   Detailed expenditure report
12.   Service charge variance report.

Appendix 1
Performance contracts

Traditionally, service contracts are based on a detailed specification detailing what services are required, how these services are to be performed and at what frequency.

---

1   See Appendix 7.

For example, a cleaning specification may detail what surfaces are to be cleaned, how the cleaning is to be carried out, how often and at what times. However, this may not always result in value for money being achieved.

The contractor may adhere rigidly to the detailed specification but this may result in a higher or lower standard of cleaning than required. The higher standard of cleaning may carry with it an unnecessarily high cost, whilst the lower standard may be achieved at a lower cost but will not meet the customer's requirements and expectations.

Performance contracts are a contracting methodology designed to meet the specific needs set down by the user, and where achievement against set performance standards can be measured and reflected in the cost incurred for the level of service actually provided.

By specifying the standards to be achieved, rather than the process, the onus is upon the contractor, particularly in a competitive tendering situation, to ensure the most cost-effective processes and procedures are employed in order to achieve the specific needs of the customer. In this way, value for money can be achieved by ensuring that the optimum price is obtained to meet the specific standard of service required.

Setting performance standards

There are various methods of setting performance standards, which will be dependent upon the asset type, the service provided, the needs of the customer, and the facilities to record and monitor the standards to be achieved such as:

- Establishing the periods during which an item of equipment must be in full operational order.

- A minimum specified standard of service is to be provided and maintained.

- Limiting the number of faults allowed in a period.

- Setting specific response targets for attending to repairs etc.

Once established and agreed the level of performance achieved must be measured and reviewed on a regular basis.

Remuneration for the delivery of the service would then be linked to the performance achieved against the target performance standards set. If performance falls below the agreed standard there would be a reduction in cost. Similarly, the remuneration might be increased in the event that target performance standards are exceeded.

Performance Management focuses on the needs of the business, individual and customer. Performance contracts will clearly vary in style and content but where implemented successfully should drive continual improvement in the delivery of services.

Appendix 2
Improvement and refurbishment

Improvement to existing equipment

Example: *A new piece of equipment is added to an existing boiler to better control fuel consumption. This will result in a saving on fuel bills and a reduction in maintenance costs.*

The occupiers will benefit from the 'improvement' through reduced energy bills and maintenance costs. It is not therefore unreasonable to expect the cost of the 'improvement' to be recovered through the service charge providing a reasonable payback period on the investment can be justified.

However, this would strictly be an improvement under the terms of the lease and the lease would therefore need to specifically provide for these costs to be recoverable – it is unlikely a sound argument could be put forward that such work would constitute a repair.

If the owner is unable to recover the costs of this 'improvement' to the heating system he may choose not to proceed with the works in which case the occupiers would continue to pay higher fuel bills and maintenance costs than they need to.

This is an example where it is hoped common sense would prevail and, through proper communication and dialogue, the owner and occupiers can agree to expenditure being incurred, and recovered through the service charge, that would not otherwise be permitted under the terms of the lease.

Replacement with enhancement

Example: *A heating system that has reached the end of its life requires replacement. However, an identical replacement heating system is no longer available due to the impact of technological change since the original equipment was installed and therefore the replacement system is an 'improvement' upon the old.*

In order to consider whether the costs are recoverable through the service charge, the intention when undertaking the work will need to be considered. Is it the intention to improve or simply to repair the existing equipment, albeit by way of replacement?

There is therefore a common sense argument to justify inclusion of the cost of minor 'improvements' within the service charge when replacing components of a building even though the lease may only provide for the cost of repair. Lord Denning supported this view in *Morcom v Campbell-Johnson* in which he stated:

> '*If the work which is done is the provision of something new for the benefit of the occupier, that is, properly speaking an improvement; but if it is only the replacement of something already there, which has become dilapidated or worn out, then albeit that it is a replacement by its modern equivalent, it comes within the category of repairs and not improvements.*'

If the replacement works go beyond the minimum specification necessary to effect a repair, and this additional cost can be justified in terms of reduced maintenance costs etc (as above) it would not be unreasonable for these additional costs to be recovered through the service charge. Again communication and dialogue with occupiers should achieve a practical solution.

The provision of new equipment

Example: *A new CCTV system is installed in a property that, at the time of its original construction, pre-dated the advent of CCTV. For the purposes of the example it is assumed that the introduction of CCTV will result in a decrease in manned security costs, an increase in the level of service provided to occupiers, and improved value for money in terms of the overall service charge costs.*

If a brand new piece of equipment were installed, where no equivalent previously existed, this would undoubtedly constitute an improvement.

In order to recover the costs of this new equipment the lease would need to be considered and would need to specifically allow for the costs of provision of new equipment to be included.

Many leases will not necessarily preclude the provision of further services that were not originally in contemplation when the lease was granted and the cost of the provision of new equipment may be a recoverable cost under the terms of the lease.

However, as above, if the additional expenditure cost of carrying out the improvement can be justified on the basis of a cost benefit analysis eg a reduction in the cost of manned security, reduced insurance premiums etc then communication and dialogue should achieve a common sense result.

Refurbishment

Refurbishment is a different concept to improvement and within the scope of the refurbishment works proposed there may be elements of catching up on accumulated disrepair and elements of improvement.

The extent to which occupiers will be obliged to contribute towards the cost of refurbishment would depend on the extent and nature of the works proposed and the precise wording of the lease.

Market forces might often dictate the timing of a refurbishment. The owner will seek to protect the value of his investment and to maximise rental levels. A refurbishment will often be timed to coincide with a number of rent reviews or lease expiries and in such circumstances, occupiers will object to contributing towards the cost of refurbishment on the basis that they are dealt a 'double whammy'. Not only will they pay for the cost of the refurbishment through the service charge but also through increased rents as a result of the improvements made to the property. It is generally accepted that, when a refurbishment would result in higher rental values, the cost would usually be the owner's responsibility.

However, the need to carry out extensive repairs or replacement of services will also be a considering factor in the decision to refurbish. In the period prior to a refurbishment, which might take some years to plan and programme, major repairs or replacements may be deferred in order to benefit from economies of scale through the placing of one major works contract and to avoid unnecessary expenditure or disruption. Furthermore, the improved efficiency of the new environment and improved services may produce cost savings in the day to day management of the services with the result that the annual service charge may be reduced both in the short and long term.

In these circumstances, occupiers may still be liable for the cost of repair or replacement carried out as part of a larger refurbishment contract as if the works had been instigated separately from the refurbishment.

Communication

In all instances where it is proposed to include the cost of improvements within the service charge it is essential that this be communicated to occupiers in advance of the expenditure being committed in order to ensure proper dialogue and agreement.

In the case of a refurbishment, the owner's proposals should be fully communicated to all occupiers during the lead up to the refurbishment to clearly explain which costs included in the package of works are considered to be the responsibility of the occupiers through the service charge. It is also considered as best practice to establish regular communication between the owner and occupiers to monitor the refurbishment and the extent of works to be considered as service charge costs. This would help to avoid possibly acrimonious debate post completion of the works and the risk of unexpected costs falling to the owner or occupiers.

Appendix 3
Local community organisations

Examples of local community organisations:

• Town Centre Managers

• Chambers of Commerce

• Police Authorities

• Local Authorities

• Local Community Groups

• Fire Authorities

• Environmental Health Officers

The type and location of the property will generally dictate what relationships should be established. An edge of town industrial park for example, should benefit from establishing good relationships with the Police Authority and Environmental Health Officers whilst an in-town shopping centre should benefit from good relationships with them all.

Appendix 4
Treatment of miscellaneous income

In addition to rents collected in respect of occupational leases, many properties also receive income from a number of other sources. Many properties may receive income from public telephones, sale of cardboard and other recyclable waste etc, whilst shopping centres may also benefit from income from promotional space and various licences granted in respect of other mall activities (eg kiddie rides, photo machines etc). In addition, occupiers may have the use of photocopiers and fax facilities located in the management offices and for which a charge is made for their use. The treatment of this income is a subject of considerable variance from property to property, owner to owner.

The owner will usually seek to optimise the income from his investment. However occupiers object to income generated from common areas being retained by the owner when it is the occupiers who pay for the cleaning, lighting and other costs associated with these areas.

It is important to maintain records of income receipts from different sources and activities as the nature of the activity would generally indicate whether the owner or the occupiers should receive the benefit of the income.

Owners should clearly state their policy with regard to how costs and income generated from services and activities are allocated.

Any income derived from the provision of a service or activity, the cost of which is included in the service charge, should be treated as a service charge credit eg income from public telephones, toilet vending machines, photocopy and fax reimbursements etc. Similarly, for shopping centres, income derived from any promotional activity would normally be credited to the promotional expenditure budget.

If the use of the space is of a permanent or semi-permanent nature eg barrows or kiosks located within shopping malls, it is common practice for the owner to retain the income as rent. In these circumstances, the letting would be regarded in the same way as any letting of a standard shop unit and should bear a proportion of the service charge. Alternatively, a sum should be credited to the service charge to reflect a contribution towards the benefit of the services enjoyed.

Examples of miscellaneous income receipts:

- Car park receipts

- Concessionary parking fees

- Wheel clamping fees

- Public telephones/phonecards

- Toilet/vending receipts

- Waste paper and cardboard recycling receipts

- Conference room hire

- Use of photocopier/fax

- Licence fees (ie barrows/kiosks)

- Exhibitions/promotions

- Children's rides

- Photo-booths/weighing machines

- Sale of postcards/souvenirs/postage stamps

- Commission from information bureau (eg sale of theatre ticket)

The list would only be used for calculating apportionments for future years. This may mean that apportionments change each year but avoids continual retrospective adjustment as individual rateable values are appealed. Many occupiers have accepted this as a common sense approach and this is generally considered to be in accordance with best practice.

There are other problems associated with this method of apportionment, which is now usually only found in old leases, as other methods of apportionment are easier to apply and may more accurately reflect the fair apportionment of costs to be borne by each tenant.

Floor Area

This is the most common method of apportionment used and is in most circumstances, the fairest. The standard floor area apportionment is simply the ratio that the demise bears to the total lettable parts of the building.

The RICS Code of Measuring Practice sets out definitions relating to the measurement of buildings and their recommended applications. With regard to the calculation of service charges, the main definitions are as follows:

- Gross Internal Area (GIA)
  Applied to Industrial and Warehouses (including ancillary offices)

- Net Internal Area (NIA)
  Applied to Offices and Shops

Weighted Floor Area

In many larger shopping centres a 'Weighted floor area' formula is common to reflect the different costs involved in servicing different sized units. Thus, a 5,000 sq m unit will not cost 5 times that of a 1,000 sq m unit, but a 500 sq m unit may cost twice that of a 250 sq m unit.

A 'weighted floor area' apportionment will discount the percentage the occupier will pay over a certain size in an effort to reflect the benefit of the services provided. The floor area is divided into bands with a progressive discount and, conceptually, is a similar idea to the zoning of shops for rental purposes.

For Example:

The first 500 sq metres	@ 100%
The next 500 sq metres	@ 80%
The next 1,000 sq metres	@ 60%
The next 1,000 sq metres	@ 50%
The next 1,000 sq metres	@ 40%
Excess over 4,000 sq metres	@ 30%

In the example above a 1,000 sq metre unit will have a weighted floor area of 900 sq metres [ie £500 × 100%) + (500 × 80%)] whereas a 10,000 sq metre unit will have a weighted area of 4,200 sq metres. Therefore although ten times larger in floor area terms, the 10,000 sq metre unit will pay approximately four and a half times the service charge of the smaller unit.

In a similar way, basement and upper floors accommodation, used possibly for storage or staff rooms, can be 'weighted', say by dividing the floor area by a factor of 2, to reflect the benefit derived from the services as distinct from the ground floor retail space.

Weighted floor areas are also commonly used to provide a discount to an anchor tenant to reflect the benefit the anchor tenant brings to the shopping centre. Such weightings must be approached with a degree of caution as in some cases the weighting is in fact calculated to provide the anchor store with a 'concession', with the purpose being to spread the cost of the concession amongst the remaining occupiers. The owner should meet the cost of any special concession given by an owner to any one occupier.

A reasonable and fairly administered weighting formula for apportionment of the service charge cannot usually be considered a concession.

A Fair and Reasonable Proportion

The lease will usually incorporate a provision for the proportion to be determined by the owner's surveyor.

This has the benefit of providing flexibility and, for the owner, full recovery. Unless coupled with a statement as to how the occupier's apportionment is to be calculated, uncertainty and disputes can often arise, although 'fair and reasonable' places an onus on the owner to ensure that no one occupier is disadvantaged against the others.

Apportionment Schedules

In many cases, particularly in mixed-use buildings (such as offices with retail shops located on the ground floor) not all occupiers in the building will enjoy the benefit of the owner's services to the same extent. For example, office tenants may benefit from a full range of services including a lift and an independent central heating system whilst the retail shops may only benefit from general repairs and maintenance to the exterior of the property and maintenance of a comprehensive fire protection system. For these reasons it may be necessary to divide the service charge into separate parts, (or Schedules) with the costs being apportioned between occupiers according to usage.

Unit Description	Floor Area (sq ft)	Schedule 1 (All Tenants)	Schedule 2 (Offices only)
Shop 1	1,000	5.0%	
Shop 2	1,000	5.0%	
Shop 3	2,000	10.0%	
First Floor	4,000	20.0%	25.0%
Part Second Floor	1,600	8.0%	10.0%
Part Second Floor	2,400	12.0%	15.0%
Third Floor	4,000	20.0%	25.0%
Fourth Floor	4,000	20.0%	25.0%
Total	20,000	100%	100%

Appendix 6
Apportionment matrix – Example

Unit	Ground Floor Area (sq ft)	First Floor Area (sq ft)	Total Area	Total Weighted Floor Area	Schedule 1 All Tenants	Schedule 2 Waste Removal
1	940	585	1,525	1,232.50	2.1489	3.3085
2	830	500	1,330	1,080.00	1.8830	2.8991
3	900	495	1,395	1,147.50	2.0007	3.0803
4–6	6,355	3,290	9,645	8,000.00	13.9482	21.4751
7	2,550	2,110	4,660	3,605.00	6.2854	9.6772
Supermarket	16,255	7,695	23,950	20,102.50	35.0493	0.0000
9	1,170	620	1,790	1,480.00	2.5804	3.9729
10–11	2,500	1,155	3,655	3,077.50	5.3657	8.2612
12	1,295	775	2,070	1,682.50	2.9335	4.5165
13	2,195	655	2,850	2,522.50	4.3980	6.7714
14	945	1,820	2,765	1,855.00	3.2342	4.9795
15	1,590	850	2,440	2,015.00	3.5132	5.4090
16	780	435	1,215	997.50	1.7392	2.6777
17	720	340	1,060	890.00	1.5517	2.3891
18	690	515	1,205	947.50	1.6520	2.5435
19	625	550	1,175	900.00	1.5692	2.4159
20	485	240	725	605.00	1.0548	1.6241
21	1,175	550	1,725	1,450.00	2.5281	3.8924
22	1,670	1,190	2,860	2,265.00	3.9491	6.0801
23	1,265	470	1,735	1,500.00	2.6153	4.0266
Totals	44,935	24,840	69,775	57,355.00	100.0000	100.0000

Basis of Calculation

Service charge apportionments are calculated on a weighted floor area basis.

The weighted floor area is calculated by reference to the net area of ground floor space added to the internal area of the upper floors multiplied by 0.5.

All costs of refuse disposal are recovered under schedule 2 excluding the Supermarket which has its own dedicated facilities.

Appendix 7
Sinking/Reserve funds

Sinking funds are often confused with reserve funds.

A sinking fund is a replacement fund by which the owner aims to build up, over time, a fund to pay for repair and replacement of major items of plant and equipment.

A reserve fund is a fund built up to equalise expenditure in respect of regularly recurring service items so as to avoid fluctuations in the amount of service charge payable each year. Some leases make provision for the inclusion in the service charge of a fund to be accumulated to cover the cost of major items of repair and replacement in the future.

In theory, sinking funds are a very good idea. They have distinct advantages in that the occupier is not faced with a disproportionately heavy bill (which minimises the risk of tenant insolvency) and the owner has funds available to meet heavy expenditure when necessary.

However, the occupier may not see the benefit of his contributions to a sinking fund if he assigns his lease or vacates the premises at the expiration of the term, and the need for major expenditure has not occurred. Sinking funds are also expensive to administer and the occupier is at risk of becoming an unsecured creditor if the owner becomes insolvent where the sinking fund is not held on trust.

Occasionally leases provide for a depreciation fund to be accumulated. These are based on the initial cost of an installation, rather than the future cost of replacement or repair. Depreciation Funds would not usually be regarded as funds jointly held in trust between the owner and the occupiers. The owner will regard the money as his own to do with what he will. However, as and when major plant or equipment requires replacement the owner would be solely responsible for the costs. It would therefore be prudent for the owner to retain any moneys collected from occupiers by way of the depreciation fund to ensure he has funds available at the appropriate time. Occupiers are however wary of such funds as the owner is not obliged to hold the money as a provision against future large expenditure. In some instances, the owner may not have sufficient funds available when major expenditure is necessary and would therefore be in breach of his contractual obligations in failing to replace equipment when required.

Understandably occupiers, especially major contributors to service costs, show much interest in the way in which funds accumulated to provide for plant or other replacement are dealt with by the owner. Many major tenants prefer to pay for large items of expenditure as they occur rather than see their own funds locked away in a trustee investment over which they have little or no control.

Whilst having distinct advantages, and where the disadvantages can largely be managed, sinking, reserve and depreciation funds are rare in practice due chiefly to associated tax and administrative problems.

Appendix 8
Service charge reconciliation and expenditure report

This, and the further appendices that follow, sets out an example of a reconciliation and expenditure report in respect of a large complex property.

Service charge reconciliation reports may vary in detail between different asset types eg a large complex shopping centre, where a multiplicity of services are supplied, compared with a small industrial estate, where the services supplied may be limited to lighting and maintenance of the estate roads.

It is also recognised that the format of the service charge report may vary within the industry and that the detail to which the service charge account will be further broken down is a matter for individual owners and their agents.

However, the guide strongly supports a move towards transparency of information provided to occupiers and standardisation and consistency of main account headings, as detailed in the examples given, to enable comparison year on year and property to property.

An example of a budget report is **not** included but this should generally be in a similar format, using the same account headings etc as for the actual expenditure report. Rather than providing a detailed commentary upon the variances between the budget and actual expenditure incurred, the budget report should provide tenants with concise notes of assumptions made etc in arriving at the budgeted figures.

SERVICE CHARGE RECONCILIATION AND EXPENDITURE REPORT
[PROPERTY ADDRESS]

[Date From] TO [Date To]

Executive summary

Overall   Budget: £   Actual: £

Add notes to explain what happened and why in overall terms.

Introduction

[Managing Agent/Landlord Name] are committed to the delivery of high quality management services in the [Centre/Building] you occupy. Our aim is to provide services that are value for money, that are regularly tendered, benchmarked against comparable properties and we seek to adopt best industry practice.

This report has been produced having regard to the best practice guidelines for service charges in commercial property that have been published through the collaboration of a number of professional bodies representing a diversity of interests throughout the property industry.

The reconciled service charge is for the period [Date From] to [Date To] details of this are set out in the report. In order to allow you to understand what services are provided in return for the service charge comprehensive explanatory notes have been prepared.

Rate per square metre comparison

The total expenditure, including the Management Fee and net of Miscellaneous Income, of £[amount] equates to £[amount] per sq m (£[amount] per sq ft) calculated on the total lettable area of the [Centre/Building] of [figure] sq m ([figure] sq ft).

This compares with the budgeted expenditure of £[amount] equating to £[amount] per sq m (£[amount] per sq ft) and the actual expenditure for the previous service charge year of £[amount] equating to £[amount] per sq m (£[amount] per sq ft).

This represents a broad comparison for the building but may vary from the actual rate per sq m from tenancy to tenancy according to the benefit of services received and basis of calculation of apportionment.

Apportionment

Expenditure is apportioned to numbered schedules that have been set up to reflect the physical layout of the building and the areas to which services are supplied.

The schedules for this property are detailed as follows:

Schedule 1 – [Schedule Name]

Schedule 2 – [Schedule Name]

Schedule 3 – [Schedule Name]

Schedule 4 – [Schedule Name]

Basis of calculation

The apportionment of the service charge payable by tenants is calculated by reference to the proportion that the net lettable area of the demised premises bears to the total aggregate net lettable area of the [Centre/Building] excluding management accommodation.

Your percentage contribution is set out on the attached schedule.

Empty units and concessions granted to tenants

The Landlord pays the service charge for any void or empty units. Likewise if any tenant has any form of concession, whereby their contribution towards the service charge is capped, or is lower than the apportionment due, then the Landlord pays the difference.

Income

Income derived from the provision of any service or activity, the costs of which are paid out of the service charge, will be credited in full to the service charge after allowing for the management fee. It will remain solely at the owner's discretion whether any other income, the costs of which are not paid for out of the service charge, is similarly credited to the service charge.

Notional rent

State if notional rent included is a service charge cost.

State the accommodation to which it relates.

Confirm basis of calculation and compare it to the budget and last year's expenditure.

VAT

[As a consequence of the landlord having elected to waive the exemption from Value Added Tax, the service charge expenditure is shown exclusive of VAT. VAT will be charged at the appropriate rate on all service charge payments invoiced by the landlord and shown as a separate item on a VAT invoice.]

[The landlord has decided **not** to exercise the right to elect to waive the exemption from VAT. Consequently, all expenditure and costs are shown inclusive of VAT. Charges invoiced by the landlord will be inclusive of VAT; the VAT element will not be shown as a separate amount on the invoice produced.]

Management contacts

Your property is looked after by a team from [Managing Agent/Landlord name]. You can contact any one of the team if you have a problem, but they look after the following areas:

[Name] [Title]	Overall responsibility for the management of the Landlord portfolio [Tel No]
[Name] Property Manager	Overall responsibility for the management of the property [Tel No]
[Name] Client liaison	If you do not understand your bill, in the first place please call [Tel No]
[Name] [Centre/Building Manager]	Responsible for the day to day running of the [Centre/Building] [Tel No]

EXPLANATORY NOTES

<u>Security</u>

All Schedules   **Budget: £**   **Actual: £**

State the total cost and compare it to the budget and last year's expenditure.

Explain the variances.

List costs over £1,000.

Who provides the service?

How long is the contract?

When was it last re-tendered or market tested?

When will it next be re-tendered or market tested?

How is performance measured?

Were the performance objectives met?

Are written standards available?

Cleaning and Environmental

All Schedules   **Budget: £**   **Actual: £**

State the total cost and compare it to the budget and last year's expenditure.

Explain the variances.

List costs over £1,000.

Who provides the service?

How long is the contract?

When was it last re-tendered or market tested?

When will it next be re-tendered or market tested?

How is performance measured?

Were the performance objectives met?

Are written standards available?

Energy

All Schedules   **Budget: £**   **Actual: £**

State the total cost and compare it to the budget and last year's expenditure.

Explain the variances.

Who provides the energy?

If it is bulk purchased, state this.

State the savings associated with bulk purchasing.

Who is procuring energy? How much do they charge?

Mechanical & Electrical (M&E)

All Schedules   **Budget: £**   **Actual: £**

State the total cost and compare it to the budget and last year's expenditure.

Explain the variances.

List costs over £1,000, compare to budget and previous years.

Break costs down between contract and repairs.

Is there an overall contractor appointed to manage the services?

For each supplier identify:

> *Who provides the service?*
> *How long is the contract?*
> *When was it last re-tendered or market tested?*

Fabric Repairs & Maintenance

All Schedules   **Budget: £**   **Actual: £**

State the total cost and compare it to the budget and last year's expenditure.

Explain the variances.

List costs over £1,000, compare to budget and previous years.

Who provides the service?

How long is the contract?

When was it last re-tendered or market tested?

Are any handymen employed?

Promotions

All Schedules   **Budget: £**   **Actual: £**

State the total cost and compare it to the budget and last year's expenditure.

Explain the variances.

List major costs and contracts.

Refer to marketing plan. Were the objectives met? How are these monitored?

Have tenants been made aware of the impact of the plan?

Insurance

All Schedules   **Budget: £**   **Actual: £**

State what Insurance covers.

Who provides the cover?

Was it tendered?

Rates

All Schedules   **Budget: £**   **Actual: £**

State the total cost and compare it to the budget and last year's expenditure.

Explain the variances.

Break costs down between general rates and water/sewerage rates.

State premises to which general rates relate (eg management accommodation), Rateable Value, when last re-valued and whether re-valuation is subject to appeal.

Premises Management

All Schedules   **Budget: £**   **Actual: £**

State the total cost and compare it to the budget and last year's expenditure.

Explain the variances.

Set out details of staff employed at the building with brief details of their roles and responsibilities.

List major costs and contracts (eg photocopier maintenance etc).

Management fees

All Schedules   **Budget: £**   **Actual: £**

What is the basis of the management fee?

Compare this year's fee with the budget and last years.

Explain the variances.

How long is the management contract?

Income

All Schedules   **Budget: £**   **Actual: £**

State what income covers.

Identify and explain variances to budgets and last year's income.

Appendix 9
Landlord's surveyor's service charge certificate

Property: ....

I hereby certify that, according to the information available to me, the attached statement of the service charge expenditure records the true cost to the landlord of providing the services to the premises for the period [Date From] to [Date To], in accordance with the terms of the lease.

Signed: .... Date: ....

For and on behalf of: ....

As agents for: ....

Appendix 10
Expenditure report summary

Expenditure Summary Report for the Period [Date From] to [Date To]

Property Address:

Description	Expense	Schedule 1 Total (£)	Schedule 2
Security	58,456	58,456	0
Cleaning and Environmental	43,241	37,301	5,940
Energy	3,578	3,578	0
Mechanical & Electrical	4,209	4,209	0
Fabric Repairs & Maintenance	6,850	6,850	0
Marketing & Promotions	26,436	26,436	0
Insurance	229	229	0
Rates	3,645	3,645	0
Premises Management	17,474	17,474	0
Expense Total	**164,118**	**158,178**	**5,940**
Management Fee	16,412	15,818	594
Income	−9,960	−9,960	0
GRAND TOTAL	**170,570**	**164,036**	**6,534**

Appendix 11
Detailed expenditure report

Detailed Expenditure Report for the Period [Date From] to [Date To]

Property Address:

Description	Expense	Schedule 1 Total (£)	Schedule 2
Security			
Security Clothing	491	491	0
Security Contract Supply	56,000	56,000	0
CCTV Maintenance/Repair	1,480	1,480	0
Security Radios Maintenance/ Repair	485	485	0
Account Total	58,456	58,456	0

Detailed expenditure report *cont*
Cleaning and
Environmental

General Cleaning Clothing	245	245	0
General Cleaning Contract Supply	18,315	18,315	0
Other Periodic Cleaning	1,980	1,980	0
Snow Clearance	1,485	1,485	0
Cleaning Equipment Maintenance	4,158	4,158	0
Hygiene Services/Toiletries	200	200	0
Waste Removal	3,465	0	3,465
Waste Management Equipment Repair	2,475	0	2,475
Pest Control	990	990	0
External Landscaping Maintenance	9,928	9,928	0
Account Total	43,241	37,301	5,940

Energy

Electricity Lighting and Power	2,988	2,988	0
Electricity Management Accommodation	590	590	0
Account Total	3,578	3,578	0

Mechanical & Electrical

Microbiological Testing/ Treatment	264	264	
Electrical Installation Mtce/Re-lamping	2,625	2,625	0
Electrical Installation Repairs	1,320	1,320	0
Account Total	4,209	4,209	0

Fabric Repairs &
Maintenance

Plumbing Mtce/Repair	440	440	0
Door & Window Mtce/Repair	264	264	0
Drain & Gutter Mtce/Repair	880	880	0
Ground Surface Mtce/Repair	816	816	0
Gates & Fences Mtce/Repair	897	897	0
Signage Mtce/Repair	435	435	0
External Non-Structural Repairs	892	892	0
Health & Safety	1,760	1,760	0
Fire Precautions Mtce/Repair	466	466	0
Account Total	6,850	6,850	0

Detailed expenditure report *cont*

Marketing & Promotions

Advertising	13,500	13,500	0
Promotions	4,609	4,609	0
Seasonal Decorations	8,327	8,327	0
Account Total	26,436	26,436	0

Insurance

Engineering Insurance	229	229	0
Account Total	229	229	0

Rates

General Rates – Management Accommodation	2,200	2,200	0
Metered Water	1,445	1,445	0
Account Total	3,645	3,645	0

Premises Management

Management Salaries and On-costs	11,385	11,385	0
Management Vehicles	1,116	1,116	0
Management Expenses	698	698	0
Management Accommodation Telephone	945	945	0
Management Accommodation Stationery	915	915	0
Management Accommodation Equipment	715	715	0
Licence: Communication	150	150	0
Audit Fees and Expenses	1,162	1,162	
Health & Safety Assessments	388	388	
Account Total	17,474	17,474	0

Expense Total	**164,118**	**158,178**	**5,940**
Management Fee	16,412	15,818	594

Miscellaneous Income

Landlord's contribution to promotions	−9,960	−9,960	0
Account Total	−9,960	−9,960	0
GRAND TOTAL	**170,570**	**164,036**	**6,534**

Appendix 12
Service charge variance report

Service Charge Variance Report for the Period [Date From] to [Date To]

Property Address: _____

Description	Actual for the Period 1998 (£)	Budget for the Period 1999 (£)	Actual for the Period 1999 (£)	Budget for the Period 2000 (£)	Variances Actual 1999 against Budget 1999	Actual 1998 against Actual 1999
Security	53,692	59,500	58,456	59,500	-1.75	8.87
Cleaning and Environmental	37,152	43,650	43,241	47,550	-0.94	16.39
Energy	4,262	6,000	3,578	4,750	-40.37	-16.05
Mechanical & Electrical	1,966	4,800	4,209	3,000	-12.31	114.09
Fabric Repairs & Maintenance	3,803	7,800	6,850	8,750	-12.18	80.12
Marketing & Promotions	26,520	26,500	26,436	26,500	-0.24	-0.32
Insurance	170	300	229	250	-23.67	34.71
Rates	4,553	5,000	3,645	4,300	-27.10	-19.94
Premises Management	16,625	18,850	17,474	18,290	-7.30	5.11
Expense Total	**148,743**	**172,400**	**164,118**	**172,890**	**-4.80**	**10.34**
Management Fee	14,874	17,240	16,412	17,289	-4.80	10.34
Income	-10,718	-10,000	-9,960	-10,000	-0.40	-7.07
GRAND TOTAL	**152,899**	**179,640**	**170,570**	**180,179**	**-5.05**	**11.56**

Acknowledgements

Service Charge in Commercial Property: Guide to Good Practice Working Party:

Christopher Edwards	Phoenix Beard
Peter Forrester	Prudential Property Investment Managers Ltd
Graham Hewitt	WH Smith Group PLC
Andrew Martin	Boots The Chemist Limited
William McKee	British Property Federation
Michael Smedley	Jones Lang LaSalle
Alf Strange	Land Securities Properties Limited

The industry organisations represented on the Working Party, and who support and endorse the Guide are:

British Council of Shopping Centres

British Council for Offices

British Property Federation

British Retail Consortium

Property Managers Association

Shopping Centre Management Group

The Royal Institution of Chartered Surveyors

The members of the Working Party would also like to thank Manches and DJ Freeman solicitors for their help and advice.

INDEX

References in the right-hand column are to paragraph or Appendix numbers.